Please remember that this is a library book,
and that it belongs only temporarily to each
person who uses it. Be considerate. Do
not write in this, or any, library book.

Developmental Theories of Crime and Delinquency

Advances in Criminological Theory,
Volume Seven

Developmental Theories of Crime and Delinquency

Terence P. Thornberry,
editor

TRANSACTION PUBLISHERS
New Brunswick (U.S.A.) and London (U.K.)

ISSN: 0894-2366
ISBN: 1-56000-199-2
Printed in the United States of America

Editor's Note

The contributions to the first six volumes of *Advances in Criminological Theory* have generated lively discussion and comment. These comments themselves are contributing to the advance of criminological theory. There is one comment in this volume. The editors invite others to contribute to this series. Comments need not be in article form. Brief notes are equally welcome.

Contents

Comment

Introduction:
Some Advantages of Developmental and Life-Course Perspectives for the Study of Crime and Delinquency

Terence P. Thornberry

> *"A developmental perspective implies that changes in social behavior are related to age in an orderly way."*
> —Gerald Patterson (1993)

One of the most stable empirical findings to emerge from decades of criminological research is the relationship between age and crime. Criminal behavior is relatively uncommon during childhood, even though many youngsters exhibit precursor behaviors during this developmental stage. The onset of actual delinquent and criminal behavior increases rapidly during late childhood and early adolescence, roughly from the ages of ten through fourteen. The prevalence of criminal involvement reaches a peak during middle to late adolescence, at about ages sixteen and seventeen. Following that peak, there is a rapid decline in offending, with criminal behavior tapering off by the early twenties for most offenders. Although there are some historical variations in this pattern (e.g., Greenberg 1985), an impressive number of studies have observed an age-crime curve that generally fits the pattern just described (e.g., Blumstein et al. 1986; Elliott et al. 1983; Farrington 1986; Wolfgang et al. 1987).

These data strongly suggest the utility of adopting a developmental perspective in the study of the causes of criminal behavior. That is, criminological research routinely observes changes in a social behavior—delinquency and crime—that are related to age in an orderly way. De-

1

spite the uniformity and strength of this observation, traditional criminological theory has been remarkably nondevelopmental in orientation. Most theories, especially those that derive from sociological perspectives, pay relatively little attention to developmental or life-course issues and present rather static explanations for criminal behavior. This state of affairs is unfortunate for several reasons.

First, nondevelopmental perspectives fail to identify and offer explanations for a number of interesting and important dimensions of criminal behavior. These dimensions include prevalence, age of onset of offending, duration of careers, escalation and de-escalation of criminal behavior in terms of both frequency and seriousness, and desistance from criminal involvement. Explaining each of these dimensions is an important theoretical issue in its own right and there is no a priori reason to expect that an explanation for one of these attributes provides an explanation for any of the other attributes, let alone for all of them, that is, for "delinquency." Theoretical explanations for prevalence—the separation of delinquents from nondelinquents—may be quite different from explanations for escalation— why one offender changes from less serious to more serious offending patterns while another offender fails to do so. The difference relates, among other things, to the reduction in variability within offender populations as compared to the variability between offenders and nonoffenders (Blumstein et al. 1986). Similarly, the factors that account for desistance may be quite different from the ones that explain onset or maintenance and we cannot assume that the causes of desistance from delinquency are simply the mirror images of the causes of the initiation of delinquency.

Second, while nondevelopmental perspectives examine different causal structures for certain types of offenders—for example, violent versus nonviolent offenders—they fail to identify types of offenders based on developmental considerations. Recently, several researchers (Patterson et al. 1991; Moffitt 1993; Simons et al. 1994) have argued that the overall delinquent population contains two fundamentally different types of offenders. One type, alternately called early starters or life-course-persistent offenders, begins offending early and exhibits great stability in offending patterns over long portions of the life-course. The other type, alternately called late starters or adolescent-limited offenders, has both a late onset and an early termination of their delinquent careers. These researchers argue that there are different causal explanations for the behaviors of these different types of offenders. If this is true, and it is by no means certain that it is, then failure to distinguish between these types has serious deleterious consequences for theory construction and testing. Theoretical models would presumably contain a mushy combination of two somewhat different causal processes, one for early starters and one for late starters. Results of empirical studies would run the risk of under-estimating true causal effects because relationships would be estimated for a combination of early and late starters, even though the theoretical proposition may only apply to one type or the other.

The distinction between early and late starters also forces criminological theory to attend to the almost paradoxical relationship between stability and change evident in criminal careers. As Robins has noted, even though "adult antisocial behavior virtually *requires* childhood anti-social behavior...most antisocial children do *not* become antisocial adults" (1978: 61). Thus, on the one hand, criminological theory needs to account for the substantial stability in criminal behavior exhibited by some people; that is, it needs to explain why some offenders are involved in antisocial and criminal behavior over long portions of the life-course. On the other hand, criminological theory needs to account for the substantial degree of change that criminal behavior represents for other people; that is, once initiated why do some people end their involvement in crime after relatively short stints? Simultaneously accounting for these behavioral patterns is an important challenge to all criminological theories and one that is highlighted by developmental perspectives.

Third, nondevelopmental explanations do not focus attention on either the precursors or consequences of criminal behavior. While it is true that criminal behavior is initiated mainly during early adolescence and is overwhelmingly an adolescent/early adult phenomenon, that does not mean that either the behavioral or life-course pathways that eventually lead to these adolescent outcomes also began during adolescence. Indeed, adolescent involvement in serious delinquency and crime appears to have deep developmental roots marked by heavy involvement in precursor behaviors such as conduct disorder and general antisocial behavior (e.g., Farrington 1991; Loeber 1991; Loeber and LeBlanc 1990; Patterson et al. 1992; Robins 1978; White et al. 1990). Understanding the causal forces that lead to these precursor behaviors, and that lead only some of the youngsters exhibiting these behaviors to continue into full-blown delinquent careers, has great potential for enhancing our understanding of the etiology of delinquency.

Also, involvement in delinquency and crime has consequences for other aspects of a person's development. Serious and prolonged involvement in delinquent behavior is likely to adversely influence social relations with family and peers, belief systems, and the success and timing of transitions to adult roles and life course (e.g., Newcomb and Bentler 1988; Patterson et al. 1992; Sampson and Laub 1993; Thornberry 1987; Thornberry et al. 1994). Understanding these and other consequences of delinquent behavior provides for a fuller and more accurate explanation for delinquent and criminal behavior.

Finally, and perhaps most importantly, nondevelopmental perspectives fail to use systematically our understanding of the developmental changes that occur over the life-course to explain changing patterns of delinquent behavior. Elder and his colleagues have defined the life course as the "sequence of culturally defined agegraded roles and social transitions that are enacted over time" (Caspi et al. 1990: 15). These sequences are described in terms of trajectories and transitions. Trajectories are long-term, age-graded patterns of development in major social institutions such as family, education, occupation, and crime. Transitions refer to events or short-term changes within these trajectories that can deflect the trajectory's arc or growth curve. Marriage and divorce are transitions, as are changes in employment status, dropping out of school, and being incarcerated.

Trajectories have a number of characteristics or dimensions, each of which has consequences for the individual's overall pattern of development. Only three dimensions will be mentioned here: entrance, success, and timing.

First, not all individuals enter into all developmental trajectories. For example, not everyone marries and, therefore, not everyone has a life-course trajectory with respect to marriage. Similarly, not everyone becomes a parent and, therefore, not everyone has a trajectory with respect to parenthood. Thus, people can be described in terms of the trajectories they enter—or the careers they have—and patterns of entrances can be related to a variety of outcomes.

Second, people are varyingly successful in accomplishing the developmental tasks that are embedded in the trajectories they do enter. Some people are high school dropouts and ill-prepared for adult roles; others graduate and move smoothly on to the roles and statuses of adulthood. Some people have stable employment careers; others bounce from job to job or are chronically unemployed.

Finally, the core of developmental and life-course perspectives is that progress along trajectories is age-graded. Because of that, some transitions are age-appropriate while others are "off-age," occurring either too early or too late. Off-age transitions, for example, prematurely leaving one's parental home or becoming a teenaged parent, decrease the chances of success in the trajectory and often have adverse consequences for other behavioral trajectories. Moreover, as Rindfuss et al. (1987) have shown, off-age transitions—"disorder" in the life-course—are quite common.

Thus, an individual's development can be described in terms of the trajectories the person enters, the successful accomplishment of developmental tasks in those trajectories, and the timing of transitions along those trajectories. In turn, all of these attributes, in multiple trajectories, can be used to enhance our understanding of delinquent and criminal behavior. Developmental perspectives do not simply emphasize a person's static attributes or level on explanatory variables; rather, they emphasize dynamic changes in those attributes throughout a person's course of development and use variations in those changes to explain outcomes.

In sum, therefore, nondevelopmental theories of crime suffer from a number of limitations. They fail to identify and explain different dimensions of delinquent careers, to define and explain subtypes of offenders based on developmental considerations, to study systematically the precursors and consequences of delinquency, and to utilize changes in development over the life-course to help explain changing patterns of crime and delinquency. A developmental approach argues that each of these limitations, and their combination, retards the construction of a fuller and more complete explanation for criminal behavior.

I Even though traditional theories of delinquency and crime generally adopt a nondevelopmental perspective, they are, interestingly enough, not antithetical to developmental approaches. Indeed, one of the basic arguments of the articles in this volume is the underlying consistency between traditional criminological theories and developmental perspectives. This can be seen, for example, in the chapters by Agnew on strain theory, Conger and Simons on social learning theory, Le Blanc on social control theory, Matsueda and Heimer on symbolic interactionism theory, and Sampson and Laub on control and labelling theories. The leitmotif — connecting all of the chapters in this volume is the argument that the explanatory power of many, if not all, traditional theories of crime and delinquency can be enhanced by explicitly considering developmental and life-course concepts and perspectives. Thus, in many ways these chapters do not offer novel explanations for crime and delinquency; rather, they greatly expand the scope and make evident the dynamic qualities of traditional theories. In doing so, they attempt to provide new and better models for understanding the onset, continuation, and termination of criminal careers.

While a complete developmental theory of criminal behavior would include a consideration of all stages of the life-course, from prenatal influences through the effects of old age, current theories tend to emphasize the causal influence of some stages more than others. The articles in this volume are themselves organized along a developmental continuum. Those that emphasize childhood and early adolescent influences come first, followed by those that highlight adolescent factors, followed by those that more explicitly focus on late adolescent and adult issues.

Terrie Moffitt's article, "Adolescence-Limited and Life-Course-Persistent Offending: A Complementary Pair of Developmental Theories," is heavily influenced by psychological and neuropsychological concepts. In this paper Moffitt argues that offenders who exhibit persistent, stable involvement in crime and offenders who exhibit more temporary, episodic involvement in crime are qualitatively different types of people, with distinct etiological structures. The causes of life-course persistent offending are to be found in childhood and in faulty interactions between difficult infants and ineffective parents. Neuropsychological deficits are viewed as potentially serious risk factors for the onset of antisocial behavior and its continuation is produced by interactions between the individual's makeup and the social environment. The causes of adolescent-limited offending are found more in the social world of adolescent development, social mimicry, and the reinforcements and models provided by peers.

In their article, "Life-course Contingencies in the Development of Adolescent Antisocial Behavior: A Matching Law Approach," Conger and Simons present a social learning theory explanation for the development of antisocial behavior. They concentrate on childhood and early adolescent stages of development and pay particular attention to the role of family processes in the genesis and perpetuation of delinquent careers. Their article astutely uses the principle of the Matching Law from operant theory to show how the relative, rather than absolute, value of reinforcements and punishments generated by multiple environmental contingencies shape human behavior. Their model predicts both the relative frequency of antisocial behaviors and the relative amount of time spent in more or less antisocial environments. The issue of time allocation is not often studied but it has important implications for developmental theories of delinquency and crime as Conger and Simons demonstrate.

— Strain theory has enjoyed a considerable resurgence in the past ten years or so, in large part because of the work of Robert Agnew and the development of his general strain theory (1992; see also the essays in Adler and Laufer, 1995). Despite recent work in this theoretical tradition, relatively little attention has been devoted to the developmental aspects of strain theory. Indeed, as Agnew notes, recent advances in developmental criminology have been dominated by psychological, learning, and control theories while strain theory has, by and large, sat on the sidelines. Agnew's article, "Stability and Change in Crime Over the Life Course: A Strain Theory" fundamentally changes this. Agnew argues forcefully that developmental and strain theory concepts are quite consistent with one another and that strain theory has a great deal to offer developmental perspectives. In particular, his description of adolescent development from a strain theory perspective represents a significant contribution to our understanding of stability and change in offending over the life-course.

— Sampson and Laub's article, "A Life-Course Theory of Cumulative Disadvantage and the Stability of Delinquency," builds a general developmental theory of crime across the life-course by emphasizing the more dynamic aspects of social control theory and labelling theory. While their general model is designed to account for both the stability and change that is characteristic of criminal careers, the present paper focuses more centrally on issues related to stability. They use the concept of cumulative disadvantage to help explain the pronounced level of continuity in criminal behavior observed for many offenders. In their view, early antisocial and delinquent behavior, as well as society's reactions to that behavior, have direct and indirect causal effects on the continuity of criminal behavior. While individual differences may well account for some portion of the behavioral stability observed in criminal careers, Sampson and Laub highlight the causal significance of social interactions in producing stability.

— Most sociological theories of crime that adopt a life-course approach are rooted in the structural functionalism perspective of sociological theory. In their paper "A Symbolic Interactionist Theory of Role-Transitions, Role Commitments, and Delinquency" Matsueda and Heimer offer a complementary life-course approach that is rooted in the symbolic interactionist perspective of sociological theory. As noted by the authors, symbolic interactionism has a great deal to offer a general developmental perspective on delinquency and crime. For example, symbolic interactionism assumes a biosocial view of development in which behavior is brought about by the interaction between the biological organism and ongoing processes of interactionism in the social world. It also highlights the importance of symbolic meanings attached to the unfolding of role transitions across the life-course, rather than focusing solely on the role transitions themselves. Finally, symbolic interactionism reminds us of the importance of subcultural variations in accounting for the development of criminal careers across the life-course.

In his article "A Generic Theory of the Criminal Phenomenon: The Structural and Dynamic Statements of an Integrative Multilayered Control Theory," Marc Le Blanc offers the most comprehensive developmental theory yet proposed. His model builds directly on the principles of social control theory and offers an explanation for what he refers to as the three levels of the "criminal phenomenon." These levels are: criminality—the study of the total number of infractions at a given time and place; criminal—the study of the characteristics and causes of individual transgressors; and crime—the study of the interactions surrounding the criminal event. For each of these levels, LeBlanc constructs both static and dynamic explanations and shows how they are interrelated. He also draws out the developmental implications of his multilayered control theory, attending to such issues as behavioral continuity and change, and developmental processes.

Hagan, in his essay "Crime and Capitalization: Toward a Developmental Theory of Street Crime in America," places developmental and life-course theories into a broader, structural framework. His theory emphasizes the impact that recent social and economic changes, especially those associated with the process of capital disinvestment, have had on the volume and quality of criminal behavior in American cities. Capital disinvestment impairs the development of human, social, and cultural capital and that, in turn, leads to efforts at recapitalization through ethnic vice industries and deviance service centers. The consequences of these structural processes for the developmental and life-course tasks that confront adolescents and early adults are explored in the concluding sections of Hagan's essay.

⌐ Most criminological theories focus on offending during adolescence and very few deal specifically with adult crime. Relatedly, traditional theories are more concerned with the initiation of offending and deal with termination in passing, if at all. Kenneth Adams, in his chapter "Developmental Aspects of Adult Crime," rectifies this situation by dealing explicitly with adult criminality. He uses developmental theories both to address the observed continuity of behavior from adolescence to adulthood and to address the high rate of desistance that is observed during the early adult years. His approach is broad-based and shows how a variety of theories from developmental psychology can be useful in explaining patterns of adult crime. These theories include life-span changes in biological development, cognitive and moral development, intellect and personality, and changing patterns of social roles.

Finally, in keeping with *Advances in Criminological Theory's* policy to foster intellectual debate and dialogue, this volume closes with a comment by Gary Jensen entitled, "'Setting the Record Straight': A Response to Hagan, Gillis and Simpson." In this comment, Jensen responds to Hagan et al.'s discussion of his article on power control theory versus social control theory, which appeared in volume 4 of this series.

References

Adler, F., and W. S. Laufer. 1995. *The Legacy of Anomie Theory*. New Brunswick, NJ: Transaction Publishers.

Agnew, R. 1992. "Foundation for a General Strain Theory of Crime and Delinquency." *Criminology* 30: 47–87.

Blumstein, A., J. Cohen, J. A. Roth, and C. A. Visher (eds.). 1986. *Criminal Careers and "Career Criminals"* (Volume 1). Washington, DC: National Academy Press.

Caspi, A., and G. H. Elder, Jr. and E. S. Herbener. 1990. "Childhood Personality and the Prediction of Life-course Patterns." In *Straight and Devious Pathways from Childhood to Adulthood.*, eds. L. Robins and M. Rutter. Cambridge: Cambridge University Press.

Elliott, D. S., S. S. Ageton, D. H. Huizinga, B. A. Knowles and R. J. Canter. 1983. The Prevalence and Incidence of Delinquent Behavior 1976–1980. National Youth Survey Report No. 26. Boulder, CO: Behavioral Research Institute.

Farrington, D. P. 1986. Age and crime. In *Crime and Justice: An Annual Review of Research.*, eds. M. Tonry and N. Morris. Chicago: University of Chicago Press.

Farrington, D. P. 1991. "Antisocial Personality from Childhood to Adulthood." *The Psychologist* 4: 389–94.

Greenberg, D. F. 1985. "Age, Crime and Social Explanation." *American Journal of Sociology* 91: 1–21.

Loeber, R. 1991. "Antisocial Behavior: More Enduring than Changeable?" *Journal of the American Academy of Child and Adolescent Psychiatry* 30: 393–96.

Loeber, R. and M. Le Blanc. 1990. "Toward a Developmental Criminology." In *Crime and Justice, An Annual Review*, Vol. 7, eds. M. Tonry and N. Morris, 375–473. Chicago: University of Chicago Press.

Moffitt, T. E. 1993. "Adolescence-limited and Life-course-persistent Antisocial Behaviour: A Developmental Taxonomy." *Psychological Review* 100: 674–701.

Newcomb, M. D. and P. M. Bentler. 1988. *Consequences of Adolescent Drug Use: Impact on the Lives of Young Adults*. Newbury Park: Sage.

Patterson, G. R., D. Capaldi and L. Bank. 1991. An Early Starter Model for Predicting Delinquency. In *The Development and Treatment of Childhood Aggression.*, eds. D.J. Pepler and K.H. Rubin. Hillsdale, NJ: Erlbaum.

Patterson, G. R., J. B. Reid and T. J. Dishion. 1992. *Antisocial Boys*. Eugene, OR: Castalia Publishing Co.

Rindfuss, R. R., C. Gray Swicegood and R. A. Rosenfeld. 1987. "Disorder in the Life Course: How Common and Does it Matter?" *American Sociological Review* 52: 785–801.

Robins, L.N. 1978. "Sturdy Childhood Predictors of Adult Antisocial Behaviour: Replications from Longitudinal Studies." *Psychological Medicine* 8: 611–22.

Sampson, R. J. and J. H. Laub. 1993. *Crime in the Making: Pathways and Turning Points through Life*. Cambridge, MA: Harvard University Press.

Simons, R. L. C. Wu, R. D. Conger and F. O. Lorenz. 1994. "Two Routes to Delinquency: Differences between Early and Late Starters in the Impact of Parenting and Deviant Peers." *Criminology* 32: 247–76.

Thornberry, T. P. 1987. "Toward an Interactional Theory of Delinquency." *Criminology* 25: 863–91.

Thornberry, T. P., A. J. Lizotte, M. D. Krohn, M. Farnworth, and S. J. Jang. 1994. "Delinquent Peers, Beliefs, and Delinquent Behavior: A Longitudinal Test of Interactional Theory." *Criminology* 32: 601–37.

White, J., T. E. Moffitt, F. Earls, L. N. Robins, and P. A. Silva. 1990. "How Early Can We Tell? Preschool Predictors of Boys' Conduct Disorder and Delinquency." *Criminology* 28: 507–33.

Wolfgang, M. E., T. P. Thornberry and R. M. Figlio. 1987. *From Boy to Man, From Delinquency to Crime*. Chicago: University of Chicago Press.

1

Adolescence-Limited and Life-Course-Persistent Offending: A Complementary Pair of Developmental Theories

Terrie E. Moffitt

Introduction

There are marked individual differences in the stability of antisocial behavior. Many people behave antisocially, but their antisocial behavior is temporary and situational. By contrast, the antisocial behavior of some people is very stable and persistent. Temporary, situational antisocial behavior is quite common in the population, especially among male and female adolescents. Persistent, stable antisocial behavior is found among a relatively small number of mostly males. The central tenet of this essay is that temporary versus persistent antisocial persons constitute two qualitatively distinct types of persons. In particular, I suggest that juvenile delinquency conceals two qualitatively distinct categories of individuals, each in need of its own distinct theoretical explanation.

A Typology that Addresses the Shape of the Curve of Crime Over Age

When official rates of crime are plotted against age, the rates for both prevalence and incidence of offending appear highest during adolescence; they peak sharply at about age seventeen and drop precipitously in young

11

adulthood. With the advent of alternate measurement strategies—most notably self-reports of deviant behavior—we have learned that arrest statistics merely reflect the tip of the deviance iceberg (Hood and Sparks 1970). Actual rates of illegal behavior soar so high during adolescence that participation in delinquency appears to be a normal part of teen life (Elliott, Ageton, Huizinga, Knowles, and Canter 1983). The majority of criminal offenders are teenagers; by the early twenties, the number of active offenders decreases by over 50 percent; by age twenty-eight, almost 85 percent of former delinquents desist from offending (Blumstein and Cohen 1987; Farrington 1986). With slight variations, this general relation between age and crime obtains among males and females, for most types of crimes, during recent historical periods, and in numerous Western nations (Hirschi and Gottfredson 1983).

Until recently, research on age and crime has relied on official data, primarily arrest and conviction records. As a result, the left-hand side of the age-crime curve has been censored. Indeed, in many empirical comparisons between early onset and late onset antisocial behavior, "early" has been artifactually defined as mid-adolescence on the basis of first police arrest or court conviction (Farrington et al. 1990). However, research on childhood conduct disorder has now documented that antisocial behavior begins long before the age when it is first encoded in police data banks. Indeed, we now know that the steep decline in antisocial behavior between ages seventeen and thirty is mirrored by a steep incline in antisocial behavior between ages seven and seventeen (Loeber, Stouthamer-Loeber, Van Kammen, and Farrington 1989; Wolfgang, Figlio, and Sellin 1972). Further, we may extend the left-hand tail of the age-crime curve by adding developmental psychologists' reports of childhood aggression (Pepler and Rubin 1991), and mental health researchers' reports of conduct disorder (Kazdin 1987), to criminologists' studies of self-reported delinquency and official crime. So doing, it becomes obvious that manifestations of antisocial behavior emerge very early in the life course, and remain present thereafter.

Although there is widespread agreement about the curve of crime over age, there are few convincing explanations for the shape of the curve. The typology presented here addresses this issue by drawing attention to two trajectories concealed within the curve of crime over age. Timing and duration of the course of antisocial involvement are the defining features of the two proposed types of offenders.

Evidence for a Life-Course-Persistent Type

In this typology, a small group of persons engages in antisocial behavior of one sort or another at every stage of life; they make up the childhood and adulthood tails of the age-crime curve, and participate during adolescence too. I have labelled these persons *life-course-persistent*, to reflect the continuous course of their antisocial behavior.

Is there any evidence that a small number of persons in the general population show antisocial behavior that is life-course-persistent? To begin, epidemiological research has shown that there is remarkable uniformity in the prevalence rates of different manifestations of severe antisocial behavior: Regardless of their age, fewer than 10 percent of males warrant an official antisocial designation. For example, about 5 percent of preschool boys are considered by their parents or caretakers to be "very difficult to manage" (McGee, Partridge, Williams, and Silva 1991). The prevalence of Conduct Disorder among elementary-school-aged boys has been found to be between 4 percent and 9 percent in several countries (Costello 1989). About 6 percent of boys are first arrested by police as preteens (Moffitt and Silva 1988a; Wolfgang et al. 1972); such early arrest is important because it is the best predictor of long-term recidivistic offending. The rate of conviction for a violent offense in young adult males is between 3 percent and 6 percent (Moffitt, Mednick, and Gabrielli 1989), and about 4 percent of male adolescents self-report sustained careers of serious violence (three or more violent offenses per year for five years; Elliott, Huizinga, and Morse 1986). Finally, the prevalence of adult men with antisocial personality disorder is estimated at about 4 percent to 5 percent (Robins 1985).

It is possible, of course, that the persons who constitute these epidemiological statistics at different ages are all different individuals. But the longitudinal data suggest otherwise: it is more likely that the remarkable constancy of prevalence rates reflects the reoccurrence of the same life-course-persistent individuals in different antisocial categories at different ages. Robins (1966, 1978) has shown that there are virtually no cases of adult antisocial personality disorder that did not also have conduct disorder as children. White, Moffitt, Earls, Robins, and Silva (1990) found notable continuity from disobedient and aggressive behavior at age three to later childhood conduct disorder, and then to arrest by police in the early teen years. Loeber (1982) reviewed research that pinpoints a first arrest between ages seven and eleven as particularly important for predicting long-term adult offending. Hare and McPherson (1984) have reported that a conviction for violence in the early twenties is characteristic of almost all men who later become diagnosed with antisocial (psychopathic) personality disorder.

In his analysis of a sample of third-grade boys, Patterson (1982) found that the most aggressive 5 percent of the boys constituted the most persistent group as well; 39 percent of them ranked above the ninety-fifth percentile on aggression ten years later, and 100 percent of them were still above the median. Similarly, Loeber (1982) has reviewed research showing that stability of youngsters' antisocial behavior across time is linked with stability across situations, and that both forms of stability are characteristic of a relatively small group of persons with extremely antisocial behavior. This point is illustrated in a longitudinal investigation of a representative cohort of 1037 New Zealand children born in 1972–73. In this sample, I identified a group of boys whose antisocial behavior was rated above average at each of seven biennial assessments (ages three, five, seven, nine, eleven, thirteen, and fifteen). The boys were also rated as very antisocial by three different reporting agents (parents, teachers, and self). Five percent of the boys in the sample met these selection criteria. As a group, their mean antisocial ratings were more than a standard deviation above the norm for boys at every age. A disproportionate amount of the measured stability in the New Zealand sample could be attributed to these few boys; when they were excluded from calculations, the 8-year stability coefficient for teacher ratings was reduced from .28 (R^2 = .078) to .16 (R^2 = .025), indicating that 5 percent of the sample accounted for 68 percent of the sample's stability. (If antisocial behavior had been a stable characteristic throughout the sample, with most boys retaining their relative standing in the group across time, then excluding the top 5 percent of the sample should not have affected the stability coefficient.)

In a test of this taxonomy conducted recently by Nagin and colleagues (Nagin and Land 1993; Nagin, Farrington, and Moffitt, 1995) a group of males whose history of criminal conviction resembles the life-course-persistent pattern was identified among the 411 members of the sample studied by Farrington and West (1990). The group, which contained 12 percent of this working-class London sample and was labelled "high-rate chronic offenders" by Nagin and Land, showed a distinctive pattern of the lambda index of individual offending rate that remained high and stable from age ten to thirty-two, with only a small peak near age eighteen.

There are still gaps in the epidemiological data base; each of the above-cited studies connected only two or three points in the life course. Nonetheless, the consistency is impressive: A substantial body of longitudinal research consistently points to a very small group of males who display high rates of antisocial behavior across time and in diverse situations. The professional nomenclature may change, but the faces remain the same as they drift through successive systems aimed at curbing their deviance; schools, juvenile-justice programs, psychiatric-treatment centers, and prisons. The topography of their behavior may change with changing opportunities, but the disposition to act antisocially persists throughout the life course.

Evidence for an Adolescence-Limited Type

In contrast to the small group of life-course-persistent antisocials, a larger group of persons fills out the adolescent peak of the age-crime curve with crime careers of shorter duration. Consistent with this notion, English and American studies have shown that the adolescent peak reflects a temporary increase in the number of people involved in antisocial behavior, not a temporary acceleration in the offense rates of individuals (Farrington 1983; Wolfgang, Thornberry and Figlio 1987). I have labelled these persons *adolescence-limited*, to reflect their more temporary involvement in antisocial behavior. The brief tenure of their delinquent participation should not obscure their prevalence in the population, or the gravity of their crimes.

By contrast with the rare life-course-persistent type, adolescence-limited delinquency is ubiquitous. Several studies have shown that about one-third of males are arrested during their lifetime for a serious criminal offense, while fully four-fifths of males have police contact for some minor infringement (Farrington, Ohlin and Wilson 1986). Most of these police contacts are made during the adolescent years. Indeed, numerous rigorous self-report studies of representative samples have now documented that it is statistically aberrant to refrain from crime during adolescence (Elliott et al. 1983; Hirschi 1969; Moffitt, Lynam and Silva 1994). This tidal wave of adolescent onset has been studied in the aforementioned representative sample of New Zealand boys (Moffitt 1991).

Between ages eleven and fifteen, about one third of the sample joined the delinquent lifestyles of the 5 percent of boys who had shown stable and pervasive antisocial behavior since preschool. As a group, these adolescent newcomers to antisocial ways had not formerly exceeded the normative levels of antisocial behavior for boys at ages three, five, seven, nine, or eleven. Despite their lack of prior experience, by age fifteen, the newcomers equalled their preschool-onset antisocial peers in the variety of laws they had broken, the frequency with which they broke them, and the number of times they appeared in juvenile court (Moffitt 1991). When interviewed at age eighteen, only 7 percent of the New Zealand boys denied all delinquent activities during the past year. By their mid-twenties, at least three-quarters of these new offenders are expected to cease all offending (Farrington 1986).

As implied by the proffered label, discontinuity is the hallmark of teen-aged delinquents who have no notable history of antisocial behavior in childhood and little future for such behavior in adulthood. Compared to the life-course-persistent type, adolescence-limited delinquents show relatively little continuity in their antisocial behavior. *Across age*, change in delinquent involvement is often abrupt, especially during the periods of onset and desistence (Moffitt 1990a). Adolescence-limited delinquents may also have sporadic, crime-free periods in the midst of their brief crime careers. And, in contrast to the life-course-persistent type, they lack consistency in their antisocial behavior *across situations*. For example, they may shoplift in stores and use drugs with friends, but continue to obey the rules at school. Because of the chimeric nature of their delinquency, different reporters (such as self, parent, and teacher) are less likely to agree about their behavior problems when asked to complete rating scales or clinical interviews (Loeber and Schmaling 1985; Loeber, Green, Lahey, and Stouthamer-Loeber 1990).

In the aforementioned test of this taxonomy by Nagin and Land (1993) a group of males whose history of criminal conviction resembles the adolescence-limited pattern was identified among the 411 members of the London sample. The group, which contained 33 percent of this working-class London sample, showed a distinctive pattern of the lambda index of individual offending rate. Lambda began low at age ten, rose to a peak during mid-adolescence, and then fell precipitously. By age twenty-two and thereafter, lambda for this group was effectively zero. Although conviction data do not provide the closest index to actual offending behavior, and although the study generated a third group of offenders with a chronically low level of lambda that was not anticipated by this taxonomy, the Nagin and Land study is the first to confirm the existence of distinctive individual trajectories concealed within the population-level curve of crime over age.

Implications

If correct, this simple typology can serve a powerful organizing function, with important implications for theory and research on the causes of crime. For delinquents whose criminal activity is confined to the adolescent years, the causal factors may be proximal—specific to the period of adolescent development—and theory must account for the *dis*continuity in their lives. By contrast, for persons whose adolescent delinquency is merely one inflection in a continuous lifelong antisocial course, a theory of antisocial behavior must locate its causal factors early in their childhoods, and must explain the continuity in their troubled lives. If the causal theories are correct, and the causes and correlates of delinquency differ for the two groups, then research that fails to analyze them separately is predestined to generate attenuated findings about both groups. Next, I turn to the causal theories.

An Etiological Theory for Life-Course-Persistent Antisocial Behavior

If some individuals' antisocial behavior is stable from preschool to adulthood as the data imply, then we are compelled to look for its roots early in life, in factors that are present before or soon after birth. I believe that the juxtaposition of a vulnerable and difficult infant with an adverse rearing context initiates risk for the life-course-persistent pattern of antisocial behavior. The ensuing process is a transactional one in which the challenge of coping with a difficult child evokes a chain of failed parent/child encounters (Sameroff and Chandler 1975). This chain promotes the persistence and unfolding of antisocial behavior problems from infancy to adolescence. It is possible that the etiological chain begins with some factor capable of producing individual differences in the neuropsychological functions of the infant nervous system (see Moffitt, 1993a, 1993b, or 1994, for a fuller explication of the theory of life-course-persistent development).

Life-Course-Persistent Behavior Begins with Social Interactions
Between Problem Children and Problem Parents

Before describing how neuropsychological variation might constitute risk for antisocial behavior, it is useful to define what is meant here by neuropsychological. By combining "neuro" with "psychological" I refer broadly to the extent to which anatomical structures and physiological processes within the nervous system engender differences between children in activity level, emotional reactivity, or self-regulation (temperament), speech, motor coordination, or impulse control (behavioral development), and attention, language, learning, memory, or reasoning (cognitive abilities). Toddlers with subtle neuropsychological deficits may be clumsy and awkward, overactive, inattentive, irritable, impulsive, hard to keep on schedule, delayed in reaching developmental milestones, poor at verbal comprehension, deficient at expressing themselves, or slow at learning new things (Hertzig 1983; Rutter 1983; Wender 1971). Irritable newborns elicit more negative and less positive parenting behavior from their mothers (van den Boom and Hoeksma 1994).

Parent/child interactions should be most likely to produce lasting antisocial behavior problems if caretaker reactions are more likely to exacerbate than ameliorate children's problem behavior (Sameroff and Chandler 1975). Children with neuropsychological problems evoke a challenge to even the most resourceful, loving, and patient families. Unfortunately, such children are unlikely to find themselves in resourceful, loving and patient families. Vulnerable infants are disproportionately found in environments that will not be ameliorative because many sources of neural maldevelopment co-occur with family disadvantage or parental deviance. Indeed, because some characteristics of parents and children tend to be correlated, parents of children who are at risk for antisocial behavior often inadvertently provide their children with criminogenic environments (Sameroff and Chandler 1975).

Problem children are likely to have problem parents. The inter-generational transmission of severe antisocial behavior has been carefully documented in a study of three generations (Huesmann, Eron, Lefkowitz, and Walder 1984). In that study of 600 subjects, the stability of individuals' aggressive behavior from age eight to age thirty was exceeded by the stability of aggression across the generations: from grandparent to parent to child.

Because intergenerational transmission is so common, parents of children who are difficult to manage often lack the necessary psychological and physical resources to cope constructively with a difficult child (Snyder and Patterson 1987). For example, parents and children are similar to each other on temperament and personality (Plomin, Chipuer, and Loehlin 1990). This suggests that children whose hyperactivity and angry outbursts might be curbed by firm discipline will tend to have parents who are inconsistent disciplinarians; the parents are impatient and irritable too. Parents and children also resemble each other on cognitive ability (Bouchard and McGue 1981). This implies that children who are most in need of remedial schooling and professional therapy will have parents who may be least able to provide it because the parents' low cognitive abilities set limits on their own educational and occupational success (Barrett and Depinet 1991). This perverse compounding of children's vulnerabilities with their families' imperfections sets the stage for the development of life-course-persistent antisocial behavior. If both poor parenting and child risk characteristics combine to lay the foundation for persistent antisocial behavior, then we would expect to find that interaction effects between parent and child measures significantly predict later serious antisocial outcomes. Such effects have been reported for the New Zealand sample: child cognitive ability interacts with family adversity to predict adolescent aggression (Moffitt 1990a) and preschool temperament interacts with parenting to predict convictions for violence (Henry, Moffitt, Caspi and Silva 1994).

There is good evidence that children who ultimately become persistently antisocial do suffer from deficits in neuropsychological abilities. I have elsewhere reviewed the available empirical and theoretical literatures; the link between neuropsychological intellectual impairment and antisocial outcomes is one of the most robust effects in the study of antisocial behavior (Moffitt 1990b; 1993b; see also Hirschi and Hindelang 1977). Two sorts of neuropsychological deficits are empirically associated with antisocial behavior: verbal and "executive" functions. The verbal deficits of antisocial children are pervasive, affecting receptive listening and reading, problem solving, expressive speech and writing, and memory. In addition, brain dysfunction can produce what is sometimes referred to as a "executive deficits" or a "comportmental learning disability" (Price, Daffner, Stowe, and Mesulam 1990), including symptoms such as inattention, impulsivity, aggression, and poor judgement. These cognitive deficits and antisocial behavior share variance that is independent of social class, race, test motivation, and academic attainment (Moffitt, 1990b; Lynam, Moffitt, and Stouthamer-Loeber 1993). In addition, the relation is not an artifact of slow-witted delinquents' greater susceptibility to detection by police; undetected delinquents have weak cognitive skills, too (Moffitt and Silva 1988b).

The evidence is strong that neuropsychological deficits are linked to the kind of antisocial behavior that begins in childhood and is sustained for lengthy periods. In a series of articles (Moffitt 1990a; Moffitt and Henry 1989; Moffitt and Silva 1988c; Moffitt, Lynam and Silva 1994), I have shown that poor verbal and executive functions are associated with antisocial behavior, *if* the behavior is extreme and persistent. In these studies, adolescent New Zealand boys who exhibited both conduct problems and attention-deficit disorder (ADD) scored very poorly on neuropsychological tests of verbal and executive functions, and had histories of extreme antisocial behavior that persisted from age three to age fifteen. Apparently, their neuropsychological deficits were as longstanding as their antisocial behavior; at ages three and five these boys had scored more than a standard deviation below the age norm for boys on the Bayley and McCarthy tests of motor coordination, and on the Stanford Binet test of cognitive performance. Later, when the New Zealand sample was followed to age eighteen, prospective neuropsychological scores predicted the early onset of arrest by police and conviction in criminal court, as well as the stability of self-reports of serious delinquency across ages thirteen, fifteen, and eighteen (Moffitt et al. 1994).

In a study designed to improve on measurement of executive functions (White, Moffitt, Caspi, Jeglum, Needles and Stouthamer-Loeber 1994), we gathered data on self-control and impulsivity for 430 Pittsburgh youths. Twelve measures were taken from multiple sources (mother, teacher, self, observer) via multiple methods (rating scales, performance tests, computer games, Q-sorts, and videotaped observations). A linear composite of the impulsivity measures was strongly related to the three-year longevity of antisocial behavior, even after controlling for IQ, race, and social class. Boys who were very delinquent from ages ten to thirteen scored significantly higher on impulsivity than both their nondelinquent and temporarily delinquent age mates. Taken together, the New Zealand and Pittsburgh longitudinal studies suggest that neuropsychological dysfunctions that manifest themselves as poor scores on tests of language and self-control, and as the inattentive, overactive and impulsive symptoms of attention deficit disorder, are linked with the early, childhood emergence of aggressive antisocial behavior, and with its subsequent persistence.

Why the Antisocial Youngsters' Style Persists into Adulthood

If the child who steps off on the wrong foot remains on his ill-starred path, subsequent stepping-stone experiences may culminate in life-course-persistent antisocial behavior. For life-course-persistent antisocial individuals, deviant behavior patterns later in life may thus reflect early individual differences that are perpetuated or exacerbated by interactions with the social environment; first at home, and later at school. Quay (1987: 121) summarizes: "This youth is likely to be at odds with everyone in the environment, and most particularly with those who must interact with him on a daily basis to raise, educate, or otherwise control him...this pattern is the most troublesome to society, seems least amenable to change, and has the most pessimistic prognosis for adult adjustment." But inauspicious beginnings do not complete the story. The theory must explain why life-course-persistent people continue their antisocial style into adulthood. Transactions between the person and environment can produce two kinds of consequences for the adult life course: *contemporary consequences* and *cumulative consequences* (Caspi and Bem 1990).

Contemporary continuity arises if the life-course-persistent person continues to carry into adulthood the same underlying constellation of traits that got him into trouble as a child, such as high activity level, irritability, poor self-control, and low cognitive ability. The evidence that these particular traits remain stable well into mid-life is strong (see Conley 1984, for a review). Because such individual differences themselves persist into adulthood, they may continue to increase the probability of adult antisocial behavior in a proximal contemporary fashion. Pennington and Bennetto (1993) present evidence for contemporary effects of neuropsychological deficit on antisocial behavior in adulthood. In another report of contemporary continuity, Caspi, Bem, and Elder (1989; Caspi et al. 1987), using data from the longitudinal Berkeley Guidance Study, identified men who had a history of temper tantrums during late childhood (when tantrums are *not* developmentally normative). Then, they traced the consequences of this personality style across the subsequent thirty years of the subjects' lives. Contemporary consequences were implied by the strong direct link between hot temper and occupational stability.

Men with childhood tantrums continued to be hot-tempered in adulthood, where it got them into trouble. They had more erratic work and home lives, changing jobs more frequently, experiencing more unemployment between ages eighteen and forty, and being twice as likely as other men to get divorced.

Cumulative consequences for crime ensue if early individual differences set in motion a downhill snowball of cumulative problems that increase the probability of offending. In the aforementioned study by Caspi et al. (1987, 1989), cumulative consequences were implied by the indirect effect of childhood temper on occupational status at mid-life: Tantrums predicted lower educational attainment, and educational attainment, in turn, predicted lower occupational status. Two sources of cumulative continuity deserve emphasis here because they have special implications for the questions of why life-course-persistent individuals fail to desist from delinquency as young adults, and why they are so impervious to intervention. They limit the options for change. These processes are (1) failing to learn conventional prosocial alternatives to antisocial behavior, and (2) becoming ensnared in a deviant lifestyle by crime's consequences.

Life-course-persistents have a restricted behavioral repertoire. This theory of life-course-persistent antisocial behavior asserts that the causal sequence begins very early and the formative years are dominated by chains of cumulative and contemporary continuity. As a consequence, little opportunity is afforded for the life-course-persistent antisocial individual to learn a behavioral repertoire of prosocial alternatives. Thus, one overlooked and pernicious source of continuity in antisocial behavior is simply a lack of recourse to any other options. In keeping with this prediction, Vitaro, Gagnon, and Tremblay (1990) have shown that aggressive children whose behavioral repertoires consist almost solely of antisocial behaviors are less likely to change over years than are aggressive children whose repertoires comprise some prosocial behaviors as well.

Life-course-persistent persons miss out on opportunities to acquire and practice prosocial alternatives at each stage of development. Children with poor self-control and aggressive behavior are often rejected by peers and adults (Coie, Belding, and Underwood 1988). In turn, children who have learned to expect rejection are likely in later settings to withdraw or strike out preemptively, precluding opportunities to affiliate with prosocial peers (Dodge and Frame 1982; Nasby, Hayden, and dePaulo 1979). Such children are robbed of chances to practice conventional social skills. Or consider this sequence of narrowing options: Behavior problems at school and failure to attain basic math and reading skills place a limit on the variety of job skills that can be acquired, and thereby cut off options to pursue legitimate employment alternatives to the underground economy (Farrington, Gallagher, Morley, Ledger, and West 1986; Maughan, Gray, and Rutter 1985). Simply put, if social and academic skills are not learned in childhood, it is very difficult to later recover lost opportunities.

Life-course-persistents become ensnared by the consequences of their antisocial behavior. Personal characteristics such as poor self-control, impulsivity and inability to delay gratification increase the risk that antisocial youngsters will make irrevocable decisions that close the doors of opportunity. Teenaged parenthood, addiction to drugs or alcohol, school drop-out, disabling or disfiguring injuries, patchy work histories, and time spent incarcerated, are *snares* that diminish the probabilities of later success by eliminating opportunities for breaking the chain of cumulative continuity (Wilson and Herrnstein 1985). Similarly, labels accrued early in life can foreclose later opportunities; an early arrest record or a "bad" reputation may rule out lucrative jobs, higher education, or an advantageous marriage (Farrington 1977; Klein 1986). In short, the behavior of life-course-persistent antisocial persons is increasingly maintained and supported by narrowing options for any sort of conventional behavior. I have described how developmental processes of contemporary and cumulative continuity can conspire to construct an antisocial personality and criminal lifestyle. This analysis suggests the hypothesis that opportunities for change will often be actively transformed by life-course-persistents into opportunities for continuity: residential corrections programs provide a chance to learn from criminal peers, a new job furnishes a new opportunity to steal, and new romantic partner provides a new victim for assault. This analysis of life-course-persistent antisocial behavior anticipates disappointing outcomes when such antisocial persons are thrust into new situations that purportedly offer the chance to turn over a new leaf.

Life-Course-Persistent Antisocial Behavior is a Form of Individual Psychopathology

The life-course-persistent antisocial pattern, as described here, has many characteristics that, taken together, suggest psychopathology (for a detailed explication, see Raine 1993). First, the pattern is *statistically unusual*; much research converges to suggest that it is characteristic of about 5 percent of males. Its rarity is thus consistent with a simple statistical definition of abnormality. Second, the pattern is *maladaptive*, in the sense that it fails to change in response to changing circumstances. Life-course-persistent antisocial behavior is tenacious across time and in diverse circumstances, implying that this high-probability response style is relied upon even in situations where it is clearly inappropriate or disadvantageous, especially if there is a very limited repertoire of alternative conventional behaviors. Third, the pattern of life-course-persistent antisocial behavior has a theoretical *biological basis* in subtle dysfunctions of the nervous system. Fourth, the pattern is *associated with other mental disorders*. An impressive body of research documents an overlap between persistent trajectories of antisocial behavior and other conditions of childhood such as learning disabilities and hyperactivity (Moffitt 1990a). Three studies (Elliott, Huizinga, and Menard 1989; Farrington, Loeber, and Van Kammen 1990; Moffitt 1990a) have now shown that the presence of multiple behavioral disorders predicts persistence of illegal behavior over the course of years. This proliferation of mental disorders is common among life-course-persistent antisocial persons. For example, in the Epidemiological Catchment Area (ECA) study of mental disorders among 19,000 adults, over 90 percent of the cases with persistent antisocial personality disorder had at least one additional psychiatric diagnosis (Robins and Regier 1991).

Of course, no one or two of these parameters is enough to warrant the classification of life-course-persistent antisocial behavior as psychopathology. Nonetheless, when taken together they form a more persuasive argument that persons whose antisocial behavior is stable and pervasive over the life course may constitute a category that is qualitatively distinct from persons whose antisocial behavior is short-term and situational.

An Etiological Theory for Adolescence-Limited Antisocial Behavior

A theory of adolescence-limited delinquency must account for several empirical observations: modal onset in early adolescence, widespread prevalence, lack of continuity, and recovery by young adulthood. Why do youngsters who have little or no history of behavior problems in childhood suddenly become antisocial in adolescence? Why do they develop antisocial problems rather than other difficulties? Why is delinquency so common among teens? How are they able to spontaneously recover from an antisocial lifestyle within a few short years? Just as the childhood onset of life-course-persistent persons compelled us to look for causal factors early in their lives, the coincidence of puberty with the rise in the prevalence of delinquent behavior compels us to look for clues in adolescent development. Critical features of this developmental period are variability in biological age, the increasing importance of peer relationships, and the budding of teenagers' self-conscious values, attitudes, and aspirations. These developmental tasks form the building blocks for a theory of adolescence-limited delinquency.

Adolescence-Limited Delinquency is Motivated, Mimicked, and Reinforced

Why do adolescence-limited delinquents begin delinquency? The answer advanced here is that their delinquency is *social mimicry* of the antisocial style of life-course-persistent youths. The concept of social mimicry is borrowed from ethology. Social mimicry occurs when two animal species share a single niche and one of the species has cornered the market on a resource that is needed to promote fitness (Moynihan 1968). In such circumstances, the "mimic" species adopts the social behavior of the more successful species in order to obtain access to the valuable resource. Social mimicry may also allow some species to safely pass among a more successful group and thus share access to desired resources. For example, some monkey species have learned to mimic bird calls. One such species of monkeys, rufous-naped tamarins, is able to share the delights of ripe fruit after a tree has been located by tyrannid flycatchers, whose superior avian capacities in flight and distance vision better equip them to discover bearing trees. If social mimicry is to explain why adolescence-limited delinquents begin to mimic the antisocial behavior of their life-course-persistent peers, then logically, delinquency must be a social behavior that allows access to some desirable resource. I suggest that the "resource" is mature status, with its consequent power and privilege.

Before modernization, biological maturity came at a later age, social adult-status arrived at an earlier age, and rites of passage more clearly

delineated the point at which youths assumed new roles and responsibilities. In the past century, improved nutrition and health care have decreased the age of biological maturity at the rate of three-tenths of a year
per decade (Tanner 1978; Wyshak and Frisch 1982). Simultaneously,
modernization of work has delayed the age of labor-force participation
to ever later points in development (Horan and Hargis 1991; Panel on
Youth 1974). Thus, secular changes in health and work have lengthened
the duration of adolescence. The ensuing gap leaves modern teenagers in
a five-to-ten-year role vacuum (Erikson 1960). They are biologically
capable and compelled to be sexual beings, yet they are asked to delay
most of the positive aspects of adult life. In most American states, teens
are not allowed to work or get a driver's license before sixteen, marry or
vote before eighteen, or buy alcohol before twenty-one, and they are
admonished to delay having children and establishing their own private
dwellings until their education is completed at twenty-two, sometimes
more than ten years after they attain sexual maturity. They remain finan-
cially and socially dependent on their families of origin, and are allowed
few decisions of any real import. Yet they want desperately to establish
intimate bonds with the opposite sex, to accrue material belongings, to
make their own decisions, and to be regarded as consequential by adults
(Csikszentmihalyi and Larson 1984; Marwell 1966; see Buchanan, Eccles
and Becker 1992 for a review of studies of the compelling influence of
pubertal hormones on teens' behavior). Contemporary adolescents are
thus trapped in a *maturity gap*, chronological hostages of a time warp
between biological age and social age.

This emergent phenomenology begins to color the world for most teens
in the first years of adolescence. Steinberg has shown that, between ages
ten and fifteen, a dramatic increase in youngster's self-perceptions of
autonomy and self-reliance takes place. Moreover, the timing of the shift
for individuals is connected with their pubertal maturation (Steinberg
1987, Steinberg and Silverberg 1986; Udry 1988). At the time of biological maturity, salient pubertal changes make the remoteness of as-
cribed social maturity painfully apparent to teens. This new awareness
coincides with their promotion into a teenaged society where they become aware of the delinquent behavior of older teens, especially life-
course-persistent ones. Thus, just as teens begin to feel the discomfort of
the maturity gap, they are exposed to a social reference group that has
already perfected delinquent ways. Indeed, several researchers have dem-

onstrated that exposure to delinquent peer models, when coupled with puberty, is an important determinant of adolescence-onset cases of delinquency (Caspi, Lynam, Moffitt and Silva 1993; Magnusson 1988; Simmons and Blyth 1987).

Healthy adolescents are capable of noticing that the few life-course-persistent youths in their midst do not seem to suffer much from the maturity gap. At a prevalence rate of about 5 percent, we might expect a handful of such very experienced delinquents in every junior high school. Life-course-persistent boys appear relatively free of the apron strings of their families of origin; they seem to go their own way, making their own rules. As evidence that they make their own decisions, they take risks and do dangerous things that parents could not possibly endorse. As evidence that they have social consequence in the adult world, they have personal attorneys, social workers and probation officers; they operate small businesses in the underground economy; they have fathered children (Weiher, Huizinga, Lizotte, and Van Kammen 1991). Already adept at deviance, life-course-persistent youths are able to obtain possessions by theft or vice that are otherwise inaccessible to teens who have no independent incomes (cars, clothes, drugs, entry to "adults-only" leisure settings). Life-course-persistent boys are more sexually experienced and have already initiated relations with the opposite sex. Consistent with my contention that life-course-persistent members of a young adolescent population corner the market on sexual resources, several longitudinal studies have shown that a history of antisocial behavior predicts early sexual experience for males relative to their age peers (Elliott and Morse 1987; Jessor, Costa, Jessor and Donovan 1983; Weiher et al. 1991). Specifically, almost all of the sexual experience of an early-adolescent cohort is concentrated among the most seriously delinquent 5 percent of its boys (Elliott and Morse 1987). As advertising agencies know, a behavior that is linked with the implied availability of sex is extremely likely to be mimicked, especially by postpubertal males. Rumored or real, the life-course-persistents' success in the sexual arena may be a powerful inducement to other adolescents to mimic their behavioral style.

Viewed from within contemporary adolescent culture, the antisocial precocity of life-course-persistent youths becomes a coveted social asset (Finnegan 1990a and 1990b; Jessor and Jessor 1977; Silbereisen and Noack 1988). Like the aforementioned bird calls that were mimicked by hungry tamarin monkeys, antisocial behavior becomes a valuable technique that is demonstrated by life-course-persistents and imitated carefully by adolescence-limiteds. The effect of peer-delinquency on the onset of delinquency is among the most robust facts in criminology research (Elliott and Menard in press; Reiss 1986; Sarnecki 1986). Indeed, Warr (1993) has shown that shifts in peer relations during the adolescent period can account for the increase in delinquent offending during that period. But is there evidence consistent with a social mimicry interpretation of the effect?

Social Mimicry and the Relations Between Life-Course-Persistent and Adolescence-Limited Delinquents

One hypothesized by-product of the maturity gap is a shift during early adolescence by life-course-persistent antisocial youth from peripheral to more influential positions in the peer social structure. This shift should occur as aspects of their antisocial style become more interesting to other teens. Consider that the behavior problems of the few pioneering antisocial children in an age cohort must develop on an individual basis; such early childhood pioneers lack the influence of delinquent peers (excepting family members). But near adolescence, a few boys join the life-course-persistent ones, then a few more, until a critical mass is reached when almost all adolescents are involved in some delinquency with age-peers. Elliott and Menard (in press) have analyzed change in peer group membership from age eleven to twenty-four in a national probability sample. Their data show a gradual population drift from membership in nondelinquent peer groups to membership in delinquent peer groups up to age seventeen; the trend reverses thereafter. For example, 78 percent of eleven-year-olds reported no or minimal delinquency among the their friends. By contrast, 66 percent of seventeen-year-olds reported substantial delinquency on the part of the friends in their group.

The word "friends" in the previous sentence seems to imply a personal relationship between life-course-persistents and adolescence-limiteds that is implausible. Much evidence suggests that, before adolescence, life-course-persistent antisocial children are ignored and rejected by other children because of their unpredictable, aggressive behavior (Coie et al. 1988). After adolescence has passed, life-course-persistent adults are often described as incapable of loyalty or friendship, and lacking bonds to friends or family (Cleckley 1976; Robins 1985). At first, these observations may seem contrary to my assertion that life-course-persistents assume social influence over youths who admire and emulate their style during adolescence. However, it is important to recall that social mimicry required no exchange of affection, nor even any communication, between the successful birds and their monkey mimics. In this theory, adolescents who wish to prove their maturity need only notice that the style of life-course-persistents resembles adulthood more than it resembles childhood. Then, they need only observe antisocial behavior closely enough and long enough to imitate it successfully. What is contended is that adolescence-limited youths should regard life-course-persistent youths as *models*, and life-course-persistent teens should regard themselves as *magnets* for other teens. Neither perception need involve reciprocal liking between individuals.

A modelling role would imply that measures of exposure to delinquent peers (e.g., knowledge of their delinquent behavior or time spent in proximity to them) should be better predictors of self-delinquency than measures of relationship quality (e.g., shared attitudes or attachment to delinquent peers). Few studies have parsed peer-delinquency effects into separate components, but two findings consistent with this prediction have been reported from the National Youth Survey, a representative sample of over 1500 teens. Agnew (1991) examined relationship characteristics in interaction with levels of peer delinquency. He argued that attachment to peers should encourage deviance if peers are delinquent, but discourage it if they are not. Agnew's results showed that such interaction terms were good predictors. However, the results also showed that "time spent with delinquent peers" was a stronger unique predictor of self-delinquency than the interaction between peer attachment and peer crime. Warr and Stafford (1991) found that the knowledge of friends' delinquent behavior was 2.5 to five times more important for self-delinquency than friends' attitudes about delinquency. (This pattern has been replicated in another sample by Nagin and Paternoster 1991.) Moreover, the effect of peer delinquency was direct; it was not mediated via influencing the respondents' attitudes to be more like those of deviant peers. These findings are not consistent with the notion that teens take up delinquency after pro-delinquency attitudes are transferred in the context of intimate social relations. Rather, Warr and Stafford concluded that the data on peer effects are best interpreted in terms of imitation or vicarious reinforcement.

A magnet role would imply that children who were rejected and ignored by others should experience newfound "popularity" as teens, relative to their former rejected status. That is, life-course-persistent youth should encounter more contacts with peers during adolescence when other adolescents draw near so as to imitate their lifestyle. A longitudinal test of this hypothesis is needed; definitive sociometric research must follow up aggressive/rejected children into adolescence to test whether they develop relationships de novo that include late-onset delinquents. However, some research is consistent with the interpretation, if one assumes that very aggressive children exemplify Life-Course-Persistent cases. Aggressive seventh-graders in the Carolina Longitudinal Study were rated as popular as often as nonaggressive youths by both teachers and themselves, and were as likely as other youths to be nuclear members of peer groups (Cairns, Cairns, Neckerman, Gest, and Gariepy 1988). In their review of peer-relations studies, Coie, Dodge, and Kupersmidt (1990) noted that the relation between overt aggression and peer rejection is strong in child samples, but weaker, or absent, in adolescent samples. Findings such as these suggest that although life-course-persistents are rejected isolates in elementary school, in high school they do experience regular interactions with peers. Similarly, in the Oregon Youth Study, rejection by peers at age ten was prognostic of greater involvement with delinquent peers two years later (Dishion, Patterson, Stoolmiller and Skinner 1991). Although the Oregon researchers interpreted their results as suggesting that aggressive children seek delinquent friends, their data are equally consistent with my interpretation that experienced delinquents begin to serve as a magnet for novice delinquents during early adolescence.

Researchers from the Carolina Longitudinal Study have carefully documented that boys with an aggressive history do participate in peer networks in adolescence, but that the networks are not very stable (Cairns et al. 1988). Consistent with a social mimicry hypothesis, delinquent groups have frequent membership turnover. In addition, the interchanges between network members are characterized by much reciprocal antisocial behavior (Cairns et al. 1988). Reiss and Farrington (1991) have shown that the most experienced high-rate young offenders tend to recruit different co-offenders for each offense. Life-course-persistents serve as core members of revolving networks, by virtue of being role models or trainers for new recruits (Reiss, 1986). They exploit peers as drug customers, as fences, as lookouts, or as sexual partners. Such interactions among life-course-persistent and adolescence-limited delinquents may represent a symbiosis of mutual exploitation. Alternatively, life-course-persistent offenders need not even be aware of all of the adolescence-limited young-sters who imitate their style. Unlike adolescence-limited offenders, who appear to need peer support for crime, life-course-persistent offenders should theoretically be willing to offend alone (Knight and West 1975). The point is that the phenomena of "delinquent peer networks" and "co-offending" during the adolescent period do not necessarily connote sup-portive friendships based on intimacy, trust, and loyalty, as is sometimes assumed. Social mimicry of delinquency can take place if experienced offenders actively educate new recruits. However, it can also take place if motivated learners merely observe antisocial models from afar.

One empirical test of the social mimicry hypothesis would require that differential pathways via peers to offending be found for life-course-persistent (childhood-onset) versus adolescence-limited (teen-onset) de-linquents. Such a finding has been reported in two samples (Caspi et al. 1993; Simons, Wu, Conger, and Lorenz 1994). In these studies, early-onset cases showed a direct relation between early behavior problems and later delinquency that did not require mediation via peers. In con-trast, adolescent-onset cases' pathway to delinquency was a direct effect of peer delinquency.

Reinforcement of Delinquency by its Negative Consequences

For teens who become adolescence-limited delinquents, antisocial be-havior is an effective means of knifing-off childhood apron strings and of proving that they can act independently to conquer new challenges (Erikson 1960). I suggest that every curfew violated, car stolen, drug taken, and baby conceived is a statement that one has left childhood behind, and thus is a reinforcer for delinquent involvement. Delinquent acts hold sym-bolic value as evidence that teens have the ability to resist adult demands and the capacity to act without adult permission (Marwell 1966). Ethno-graphic interviews with delinquents reveal that proving maturity and autonomy are strong personal motives for offending (e.g. Goldstein, 1990). Compelling epidemiological studies have confirmed that adolescent ini-tiation of tobacco, alcohol, and drug abuse are reinforced because they symbolize independence and maturity to youth (Kandel 1980; Mausner and Platt 1971).

A longitudinal analysis by Agnew (1984) has documented a link between autonomy needs and delinquency. Using data for 1,886 representative American boys from the Youth in Transition survey, Agnew found that an autonomy scale endorsed by the boys in tenth grade significantly and positively predicted delinquency two years later. The scale was made up of items such as "One of my goals in life is to be free of the control of others." The link between the boys' wish for autonomy and their offending did not depend on low social class or weak social controls at home and at school (factors that should characterize life-course-persistents, but not necessarily adolescence-limiteds). Agnew's findings are important for two reasons: (a) The study locates the phenomenon at the precise point of development suggested by this theory; need for autonomy measured near the peak age for male puberty predicted boys' subsequent delinquent participation at the peak age for offending; and (b) Agnew's study suggests that the effect of autonomy on delinquency applies broadly to delinquents, which is essential if we are to infer that autonomy wishes motivate the widespread adolescence-limited offender type.

Why Doesn't Every Teenager Become Delinquent?

The proffered theory of adolescence-limited delinquency regards this sort of delinquency as a reasonable adaptation to untoward contextual circumstances. As a consequence, the theory seems to predict that every teen will engage in delinquency. Indeed, the theory does predict that total abstention from delinquency will be very unusual among contemporary adolescents. Data from epidemiological studies using the self-report method suggest that almost all adolescents do commit some illegal acts (Elliott et al. 1983, Moffitt et al. 1993). And even studies using official records of arrest by police find prevalence rates that seem surprisingly high (for a review see Farrington et al. 1986). Nevertheless, some youths commit less delinquency than others, and a small minority abstains completely. Unfortunately, very little research sheds light on the characteristics of teens who abstain from antisocial behavior altogether. Because most offenders evade detection, lack of an official record cannot be used to designate abstainers for research; self-report data are required. Speculations are thus ill-informed by empirical observations. However, some predictions may be derived from the present theory of adolescence-limited delinquency. The predictions center on two theoretical prerequisites for adolescent-onset delinquency: the motivating maturity gap and anti-social role models. Some youths may skip the maturity gap because of late puberty or early initiation into adult roles. Others may be excluded from opportunities for mimicking life-course-persistent delinquent models.

Some youths who refrain from antisocial behavior may, for some reason, not sense the maturity gap, and therefore lack the hypothesized motivation for experimenting with crime. Some abstainers experience very late puberty, so that the gap between biological and social adulthood is not signalled to them early in adolescence. For example, Caspi and Moffitt (1991) have shown that girls who do not menstruate by age fifteen tend not to become involved in delinquency; in fact they evidence fewer than normal behavior problems as teens. Other abstainers belong to cultural or religious subgroups in which adolescents are given legitimate access to adult privileges and accountability. In his vivid ethnographic account, Anderson (1990) described how "old heads" in a poor black neighborhood drew certain teens into their own work and social lives, deliberately and publicly initiating the boys into manhood and preventing delinquent involvement.

Some nondelinquent teens may lack structural opportunities for modelling antisocial peers. For instance, school structures may constrain or facilitate access to life-course-persistent models. Caspi et al. (1993) found that early puberty was associated with delinquency in girls, but *only* if they had access to boys via coed high schools. Girls who were enrolled in girls' schools did not engage in delinquency. In that study, the difference in delinquent involvement between coed and single-sex school settings could not be explained by any personal or family characteristics that may have influenced how the girls came to be enrolled in their schools; access to delinquent role models was clearly the best explanation for the girls' behavior problems.

The explanation most central to this theory is that abstainers are excluded from opportunities to mimic antisocial peers because of some personal characteristics that cause them to be excluded from the delinquent peer groups, which ascend to importance during adolescence. Shedler and Block (1990) found such an effect on the use of illegal drugs. They compared the personality styles of three adolescent groups; teens who abstained from trying any drug, teens who experimented with drugs, and teens who were frequent heavy drug users. Surprisingly, the abstainers were problem teens: they were "relatively tense, overcontrolled, emotionally constricted,…somewhat socially isolated and lacking in interpersonal skills" (pg. 618). This personality style was an enduring personality configuration. At age seven, these abstainers had been prospectively described by raters as "overcontrolled, timid, fearful and morose…, they were not warm and responsive, not curious and open to new experience, not active, not vital, and not cheerful" (pp. 619–620).

In the New Zealand birth cohort, we studied the personal styles of the males who said they had engaged in no delinquency between age seventeen and eighteen, an age when delinquent participation had become normative for the sample. On a personality inventory, these abstainers had described themselves as overconstrained, passive, submissive, not fond of leadership roles, lacking capacity to influence others, and preferring conventionality (Krueger, Schmutte, Caspi, Moffitt, Campbell, and Silva 1994). Similarly, Farrington and West (1990) reported that boys from criminogenic circumstances who did not become delinquent seemed nervous and withdrawn, and had few or no friends. These provocative findings remind us that "deviance" is defined in relation to its normative context. During adolescence, when delinquent behavior becomes the norm, nondelinquents warrant our scientific scrutiny. Research is beginning to suggest that abstaining from delinquency is not necessarily a sign of good adolescent adjustment.

Adolescence-Limiteds Desist from Crime Because They can Respond to Shifting Reinforcement Contingencies

By definition, adolescence-limited delinquents generally do not maintain their delinquent behavior into adulthood. The account of life-course-persistent persons made earlier in this essay required an analysis of maintenance factors. In contrast, this account of adolescence-limited delinquents demands an analysis of desistence: Why do adolescence-limited delinquents desist from delinquency? This theory's answer: Healthy youths respond to changing contingencies. If motivational and learning mechanisms initiate and maintain their delinquency, then, likewise, changing contingencies will extinguish it.

Preoccupied with explaining the origins of crime, most theories of delinquency have neglected to address the massive shift in the prevalence of criminal involvement between adolescence and adulthood. Gove (1985) reviewed six of the most influential theories of deviance: labelling theory, conflict theory, differential association theory, control theory, anomie theory, and functional theory. He concluded, "All of these theoretical perspectives either explicitly or implicitly suggest that deviant behavior is an amplifying process that leads to further and more serious deviance" (118). A general application of an amplifying process to all delinquency is inconsistent with the empirical observation that desistence from crime is the normative pattern.

In contrast to amplifying theories, the present maturity gap theory does anticipate desistance. With the inevitable progression of chronological age, more legitimate and tangible adult roles become available to teens. Adolescence-limited delinquents gradually experience a loss of motivation for delinquency as they exit the maturity gap. Moreover, when aging delinquents attain some of the privileges they coveted as teens, the consequences of illegal behavior shift from rewarding to punishing, *in their perception*. They realize that continued participation in crime could threaten their newfound and long-awaited autonomy. Important for this theory, research shows that "commitment costs" (defined as a person's judgement that past accomplishments will be jeopardized or that future goals will be foreclosed) are among the factors weighed by young adults when they decide to discontinue offending (Williams and Hawkins 1986). Criminal behavior incurs commitment costs if it risks informal sanctions (disapproval by family, community, or employer) as well as formal sanctions (arrest or conviction penalty). Unlike life-course-persistents, adolescence-limiteds have something to lose if they persist in crime beyond the teen years: they have family ties and career opportunities. Paternoster and colleagues have tested the proposed effects of commitment costs in a follow-up study of 300 young adults. They found that criminal offending one year later was best predicted by prospective indexes of commitment costs ($r = -.23$) and informal sanctions ($r = -.40$). Those variables outdid gender, perceived risk of arrest, grade point average, and peer attachment (Paternoster, Saltzman, Waldo and Chiricos 1983). The Paternoster et al. study is important for this theory because it locates the phenomenon at the developmental point specified by the theory, during the peak rate of the desistence process. It also shows that commitment costs influence participation among college students, who are more likely to be exemplars of the adolescence-limited pattern than the life-course-persistent pattern.

Adolescence-Limited Delinquents Have Good Options for Change

Consistent with this motivational analysis, the antisocial behavior of many delinquent teens has been found to decline after they leave high school (Elliott and Voss 1974), join the army (Elder 1986; Mattick 1960), marry a prosocial spouse (Sampson and Laub 1990), move away from the old neighborhood (West 1982), or get a full-time job (Sampson and Laub 1990). As these citations show, links between the assumption of adult roles and criminal desistance have been observed before. The issue left unaddressed by theory is: Why are some delinquents able to desist when others are not? What enables adolescence-limited delinquents to make these (often abrupt) transitions away from crime? Why do adolescence-limited delinquents come to realize that they have something to lose, while life-course-persistent delinquents remain undeterred? Here, two positions are advanced: unlike their life-course-persistent counterparts, adolescence-limited delinquents are relatively exempt from the forces of (a) contemporary and (b) cumulative continuity.

First, in stark contrast to the earlier account of life-course-persistent offenders, personality disorder and cognitive deficits play no part in the delinquency of adolescence-limited offenders. As a result, they are exempt from the sources of contemporary continuity that plague their life-course-persistent counterparts. In general, these young adults have adequate social skills; they have a record of average or better academic achievement; their mental health is sturdy; they still possess the capacity to forge close attachment relationships; they do well at self-control, and they retain the good intelligence they had when they entered adolescence. These characteristics make them eligible for postsecondary education, good marriages and desirable jobs. One study has illustrated that individual differences influence which adolescents are able to attain prosocial outcomes in young adulthood (Quinton and Rutter 1988; Quinton, Pickles, Maughan and Rutter 1993). In that study, some girls reared in institutions were able to escape adversity for advantage via marriage to a supportive husband, but a constellation of individual psychological gifts determined *which* girls were able to marry well.

Second, without a lifelong history of antisocial behavior, the forces of cumulative continuity have had fewer years in which to gather the momentum of a downhill snowball. Prior to taking up delinquency, adolescence-limited offenders had ample years to develop an accomplished repertoire of prosocial behaviors and basic academic skills, as well as good relationships with others. Delaying onset of deviance for the first ten to fifteen years of life precludes the accumulation of life problems that contribute to continuity.

Differential accumulation of the consequences of crime may explain why some adolescence-limited delinquents desist later than others. The desistence portion of the age-crime curve slopes more gradually than the abrupt criminal initiation portion, suggesting that some adolescence-limiteds desist a few years after the end of adolescence. Although the forces of cumulative continuity build up less momentum over the course of their relatively short crime careers, many adolescence-limited youths will fall prey to many of the same *snares* that maintain continuity among life-course-persistent persons. Those whose teen forays into delinquency inadvertently attracted damaging consequences may have more difficulty desisting. A drug habit, an incarceration, interrupted education, or a teen pregnancy are snares that require extra effort and time from which to escape. In the New Zealand sample, males who exemplified life-course-persistent and adolescence-limited trajectories from age three to eighteen showed elevated rates of snares at age 18 such as unemployment, sex with multiple partners without a condom, drunk driving without a seatbelt, and dependence on alcohol or drugs. However, relative to their life-course-persistent counterparts, adolescence-limited males had avoided snares such as early school-leaving and broken family bonds (Moffitt et al. 1996). This theory predicts that variability in age at desistence from crime should be accounted for by the cumulative number and type of ensnaring life events that entangle persons in a deviant lifestyle.

At the crossroads of young adulthood, adolescence-limited and life-course-persistent delinquents go different ways. This happens because the developmental histories and personal traits of adolescence-limiteds allow them the option of exploring new life pathways. The histories and traits of life-course-persistents have foreclosed their options, entrenching them in the antisocial path. To test this hypothesis, research must examine conditional effects of individual histories on opportunities for desistance from crime.

Adolescence-Limited Delinquency and Secular Change

I have suggested that adolescence-limited delinquency is a by-product of modernization, an adolescent adaptation to a maturity gap engendered by the opposing social forces of improved health and a smaller, better-educated work force. If this theory is correct, then secular changes should have rendered the age-crime curve relatively steeper with increasing modernization. The theory predicts that, in contemporary preindustrial nations and in earlier historical periods, the age-crime curve should have a flatter kurtosis; in other words, it will lack the characteristic sharp peak between the ages of fifteen–eighteen.

Empirical data support this prediction. Greenberg (1985) compared crime statistics from the mid-1800s to 1980s in the United States, France, Norway, and Holland. He also made cross-cultural comparisons between India and Uganda and more industrialized nations. The results show that the steepness of the age-crime curve is indeed greatest during recent times, and among modern nations. Farrington (1986) compared the relation between age and crime for English males using British Home Office statistics from 1938, 1961, and 1983. His results show that the rate of offending by adolescents increased considerably over this historical period.

Diverse factors may be influential in accounting for the changing nature of the age-crime curve (Wilson 1983). But I suggest that many of these factors are the very features of modernization and modernity invoked in this theory of adolescence-limited delinquency: the earlier age of puberty and the extension of the period of childhood.

Important for this theory, additional data suggest that secular changes may have influenced the age-pattern of some crimes, but not all. A comparison of the age-crime curve for data from the FBI's *Uniform Crime Reports* for 1940, 1960, and 1980 showed that the adolescent peakedness of the curves for most crimes increased in a linear fashion over the forty-year period (Steffensmeier, Allan, Harer, and Streifel 1989). However, the authors noted that "the shift toward more peaked distributions is greater for some types of offenses than for others. The shifts are comparatively small for the person crimes and for those property offenses primarily involving older offenders (e.g., fraud and forgery), while the shifts are moderate to substantial for the youth-oriented, low-yield property offenses (e.g., robbery and burglary), public order offenses, and the substance-abuse offenses" (823). Steffensmeier's finding of different curves for different offenses is consistent with the distinction I have made between two hypothetical types of offenders. Life-course-persistent offenders (with mild neuropsychological impairment, poor self-control, pathological interpersonal relationships, weak connections to other people, and a life-long antisocial personality configuration) should account for violence against persons as well as for crimes committed in late life. In contrast, adolescence-limited offenders should account primarily for crimes that serve to meet adolescents' lust for acknowledgement and privilege: theft, vandalism, public order, and substance abuse.

Adolescence-Limited Antisocial Behavior is not Pathological, and Will not be Predicted by Individual Characteristics

In an earlier section it was contended that life-course-persistent antisocial behavior represented an especially pernicious and tenacious form of individual psychopathology. My view of adolescence-limited delinquency is strikingly different: Its prevalence is so great that it is normative, rather than abnormal. It is flexible and adaptable rather than rigid and stable; most delinquent careers are of relatively short duration because the consequences of crime—while reinforcing for youths caught inside the maturity gap—become punishing to youths as soon as they age out of it. Instead of a biological basis in the nervous system, the origins of adolescence-limited delinquency lie in normal teens' best efforts to cope with the widening gap between biological and social maturity. Moreover, neither this theory nor the empirical evidence suggests that there are any links between mental disorders and short-term adolescent delinquency. In fact, studies of teens who abstain from delinquency are beginning to suggest that at least some participation may be a sign of a healthy personality.

According to this theory of adolescence-limited delinquency, the behavior of youths who make the transition to delinquent groups near adolescence is readily understood as a group social phenomenon, it does not represent individual-level deviance. Quay (1987: 131) concurs: "A second pattern...involves behavior of a less overtly aggressive and interpersonally alienated nature. In fact, good peer relations in the context of delinquency are at the core of this pattern...There is little, if any, reason to ascribe psychopathology to youths manifesting this pattern; it may well represent an adjustive response to environmental circumstances."

Strategies for Research

Epidemiological Predictions

According to the theory, natural histories of antisocial behavior should be found at predictable prevalence rates in samples followed from childhood until adolescence. Under ten percent of males should show extreme antisocial behavior that begins during early childhood and is thereafter sustained at a high level across time and across circumstances, throughout childhood and adolescence. A much larger number of males should show similar levels of antisocial behavior during the adolescent age period, but should fail to meet research criteria for a childhood history of stable and pervasive problem behavior. Teenaged males who abstain from any and all delinquency should be relatively rare. False-positive cases, who meet criteria for a stable and pervasive antisocial childhood history, yet recover (eschew delinquency) after puberty, should be extremely rare.

A specific research design is needed to evaluate whether these epidemiological parameters will be borne out. Samples should be representative, to tap the population range of natural histories. The same individuals should be studied longitudinally, to describe the trajectories of individuals, as opposed to population shifts. Reports of antisocial behavior should be gathered from multiple sources, to tap pervasiveness across circumstances. Antisocial behavior should be assessed repeatedly from childhood through adulthood, to capture stability and change across time. Measures of antisocial behavior should be sensitive to developmental heterogeneity, to tap individual differences while allowing for the emergence of new forms of antisocial behavior (e.g., automobile theft), or the forsaking of old forms (e.g., tantrums). If appropriate research designs fail to yield the predicted individual natural histories (or growth curves), at or near the predicted base rates, then the theory is wrong. But, if subjects are found who match the natural histories of this taxonomy, then the following hypotheses may be tested about differential predictors and outcomes.

Predictions About Types of Offenses

According to the theory, the two types will tend to engage in different patterns of offending. Adolescence-limited offenders should engage in proportionately more crimes that symbolize adult privilege or that demonstrate autonomy from parental control: vandalism, public order offenses, substance abuse, "status" crimes such as running away, and theft. Life-course-persistent offenders should spawn a wider variety of offenses, including types of crimes that are often committed by lone offenders. Thus, in addition to all of the aforementioned crime types, they should commit proportionately more of the victim-oriented offenses, such as violence and fraud. If groups of life-course-persistent and adolescence-limited delinquents, defined on the basis of their natural histories, do not show the predicted differential patterns of antisocial behaviors, then that part of the theory is wrong.

Predictions About Desistence from Crime

According to this theory, transition events in the life-course are *not* unconditional determinants of desistence from crime. Indeed, events such as marriage, employment, or military service can provide opportunities for desistance, but such events can also provide opportunities for continuity. According to this theory, individuals' reactions to life transition events will vary predictably, depending on their personal antisocial histories. Adolescence-limited delinquents can profit from opportunities for desistance because they retain the option of successfully resuming a conventional lifestyle. Life-course-persistent delinquents may make transitions into marriage or work, but their injurious childhoods make it less likely that they can leave their past behind; they should select jobs and spouses that support their antisocial style, and they should express antisocial behavior at home and at work. If life-course-persistent and adolescence-limited delinquents, defined on the basis of their natural histories, do not show the predicted differential responses to young-adulthood transitions, then that part of the theory is wrong.

Predictions About Teenagers Who Abstain from Delinquency

I have proposed that adolescence-limited delinquency does not constitute pathology. Rather, it is social activity that is normative as well as understandable from the perspective of contemporary teens. If this assertion is true, the existence of people (however few) who abstain from all delinquency during their adolescent years requires explanation. Earlier, I suggested that adolescents who commit no antisocial behavior have either (a) pathological characteristics that exclude them from peer networks; (b) structural barriers that prevent them from learning about delinquency; or (c) no experience of the maturity gap (because of late puberty, or early access to accountable, respected adult roles). If adolescence-limited delinquents and abstainers, defined on the basis of their natural histories, do not differ in these predicted ways, then that part of the theory is wrong.

Predictions About the Longitudinal Stability of Antisocial Behavior

I have proposed that most adults who behave in an antisocial fashion are the same individuals who began antisocial behavior in early childhood. During the peak participation period of adolescence, those persistent individuals will be masked by the noise of their more numerous mimics. Following from this observation, estimates of the individual stability of antisocial behavior are expected to violate the "longitudinal law," that relations between variables become weaker as the time interval between them grows longer (Clarke and Clarke 1984). One study has found evidence that the longitudinal law is violated in this way when antisocial behavior is studied in the same individuals over time. Stattin and Magnusson (1984) reported that adult crime was predicted more strongly by behavior at age ten than by behavior between ages fifteen and seventeen. This prediction awaits additional corroboration.

Predictions About Differential Correlates of Life-Course-Persistent and Adolescence-Limited Antisocial Behavior

According to the theory, the life-course-persistent type has its origins in neuropsychological problems that assume measurable influence when difficult children interact with criminogenic home environments. Beginning in childhood, discipline problems and academic failures accumulate increasing momentum, cutting off opportunities to practice prosocial behavior. As time passes, recovery is precluded by maladaptive individual dispositions and narrowing life options, and delinquents are channeled into antisocial adult lifestyles. Thus, the strongest prospective predictors of persistent antisocial behavior are anticipated to be measures of individual and family characteristics. These measures include health, gender, temperament, cognitive abilities, school achievement, personality traits, mental disorders (e.g., hyperactivity), family attachment bonds, child-rearing practices, parent and sibling deviance, and socioeconomic status, *but not age.*

According to the description of adolescence-limited delinquency, youths with little risk from personal or environmental disadvantage encounter motivation for crime for the first time when they enter adolescence. For them, an emerging appreciation of desirable adult privileges is met with an awareness that those privileges are yet forbidden. After observing their antisocial peers' effective solution to the modern dilemma of the maturity gap, youths mimic that delinquent solution. Perversely, the consequences of delinquency reinforce and sustain their efforts, but only until aging brings a subjective shift in the valence of the consequences of crime. Then, such youths readily desist from crime, substituting the prosocial skills they practiced before they entered adolescence. This narrative suggests a direct contrast to the predictions made for persistent antisocial behavior. Individual differences should play little or no role in the prediction of short-term adolescent offending careers. Instead, the strongest prospective predictors of short-term offending should be knowledge of peer delinquency, attitudes toward adulthood and autonomy, cultural and historical context, *and age*. If life-course-persistent and adolescence-limited delinquents, defined on the basis of their natural histories, do not show the predicted differential patterns of correlates, then that part of the theory is wrong.

Comparing This Taxonomy with General Theories:
Implications for Explanatory Power

Students of antisocial behavior have been blessed with a number of thoughtful theories. As a group, the theories have tended to be "general" theories of crime; each extends its causal explanation to all offenders. I find general theories unsatisfying because they do not account very well for the epidemiological facts about antisocial behavior.

General theories that summon sociological processes to explain crime and delinquency have provided valuable insights about the proximal mechanisms that promote juvenile delinquency (e.g., Becker 1968; Cloward and Ohlin 1960; Hagan 1987; Hirschi 1969; Lemert 1967; Sutherland and Cressey 1978). However, sociologists have trained their lenses on the adolescent age period, when the peak prevalence of criminal involvement occurs, and when antisocial behavior is most easily studied with survey methods (Hagan, Gillis, and Simpson 1985; Sampson and Laub 1990). Historically, reliance on legal definitions of antisocial behavior and record sources of data kept delinquency researchers focussed on the adolescent onset of illegal behavior. Consequently, many delinquency theories have failed to address the stability of antisocial behavior that begins *before* adolescence, during early childhood. And most sociological theories invoke amplifying causal mechanisms that seem to ignore the empirical facts about the enormous amount of desistance from crime that happens soon *after* adolescence (Gove 1985). Causal factors such as low social class, unemployment, cultural approval for violence, and deviant labels do not seem to wane contemporaneously with that undeniable downward shift in the prevalence of offenders during early adulthood.

General theories that invoke causal variables from personality psychology or psychobiology have taught us much about how individual differences predispose toward crime (e.g., Bowlby 1988; Cloninger 1987; Eysenck 1977; Gorenstein and Newman 1980; Gottfredson and Hirschi 1990; Mednick 1977). But these theories, too, fail to provide a satisfying account. Because such theorists have trained their lenses on early childhood and adulthood (often to the neglect of adolescence), they have failed to anticipate the enormous surge in the prevalence of antisocial involvement that occurs *during* adolescence. Such theories typically rely on the stability of individual differences in traits such as impulsivity, neuroticism, autonomic nervous system reactivity, or low intelligence. Psychological theories cannot explain the onset and desistance of adolescent delinquency, without positing compelling reasons for a sudden and dramatic population shift in criminogenic traits, followed by return to baseline a few years later.

Implications for the Explanatory Power of Correlates of Crime

If the taxonomy introduced here has merit then all past research that has failed to analyze the two groups separately has probably reported attenuated effect sizes. What is the rationale for this assertion? First, in samples of delinquent teens, adolescence-limited subjects will far outnumber their life-course-persistent peers. The New Zealand and London samples yield prevalence rates near 10 percent for life-course-persistents versus 33 percent for adolescence-limiteds.

Second, if the two complementary etiological theories are correct, then measures of personal characteristics and social background are related to delinquency primarily among life-course-persistents. Measures of autonomy needs, commitment costs, and biological age are related to delinquency primarily among adolescence-limiteds. Only measures of peer delinquency should apply to both types of offenders (which may explain why the peer delinquency effect is such a large one).

Third, commonly used measures of delinquency will yield similar scores for adolescence-limited and life-course-persistent members of adolescent samples. This assertion may surprise readers who incorrectly presume that the two patterns can be easily distinguished using a cross-sectional measure of the frequency or severity of their offending. Again, the New Zealand sample provides an example: At age fifteen, both the childhood-persistent and adolescent-onset groups had members who scored more than five standard deviations above the mean on self-report delinquency, and by age nineteen both groups had some members with more than fifty convictions for crimes in the New Zealand courts. Based on commonly used indices of adolescent delinquency, the two delinquent groups were practically indistinguishable. In the analysis of conviction trajectories conducted by Nagin and Land (1993) in the London longitudinal sample, the adolescence-limited group resembled the high-level chronics more closely than they resembled unconvicted males on several self-report measures of offending taken during adolescence (e.g., marijuana smoking, frequent gambling, and violence). Elliott and Huizinga (1984) report similarly poor classification in a representative sample of American teens. They attempted to discriminate, at the time of first arrest, individual future career offenders from adolescence-limited offenders. Discrimination could not be improved beyond chance by entering the kinds of information typically available to officials: type of current offense, age, sex, race, class, involvement with delinquent peers, and attitudes toward deviance. Addition of measures of the extremity of self-reported delinquency and emotional problems improved prediction only seven percent beyond chance. In three large samples from three nations, persistent and temporary offenders could not be discriminated using cross-sectional deviance data during the period of adolescence.

If scores on correlates differ between two groups while their delinquency scores are similar, but the two groups are treated as one for statistical analysis, then correlations between delinquency and correlate variables will be attenuated. As an example, in the New Zealand sample, comparison of delinquents with nondelinquents replicates the oft-reported eight-point IQ difference, and the cross-sectional correlation between age-fifteen self-report delinquency and IQ in the full sample of boys is .22.

Effects of this size are common in delinquency research, and are usually viewed as interesting but not very conclusive. However, when prospective longitudinal data were used to divide the New Zealand delinquents into life-course-persistent and adolescence-limited subgroups, the finding emerged that the overall IQ effect is the pooled result of a one-point mean deficit for adolescence-onset delinquents and a seventeen-point mean deficit for childhood-onset delinquents. The same pattern obtains for measures of reading achievement, impulsivity, and neuropsychological deficit (Moffitt 1990a; White et al. in press; Moffitt et al. 1993). Thus, research that fails to attend to the heterogeneity of delinquents obscures some potential causal factors from view, and produces underestimates of the strength of others. Such research particularly underestimates the strength of correlates and predictors of persistent criminal offending because the data for persistent cases are washed out by the larger number of adolescence-limited offenders.

More evidence that treating delinquents as homogeneous can obscure the correlates of persistent antisocial behavior comes from the phenomenon of effects that appear, disappear, and reappear as a function of the age of research subjects. Some correlates show strong relations to antisocial behavior measured in childhood and adulthood (when life-course-persistents predominate), but only weak relations to antisocial behavior measured during adolescence (when adolescence-limiteds predominate). Behavior-genetic studies have shown that childhood aggression and adult crime are heritable whereas juvenile delinquency is much less so (DiLalla and Gottesman 1989). Such age-related fluctuations in effect size have also been noticed for the associations between antisocial behavior and social class (Elliott and Huizinga 1983), gender (Smith and Visher 1980), and reading problems (Murray 1976).

I am suggesting the possibility that past research on the causes of delinquency may have been misguided by the assumption that the relation between delinquency and causal variables is linear. This linear assumption is inherent in general theories of crime. It ought not be accepted uncritically before research tests whether linear models fit the data better than categorical models.

Despite the imperfect fit of many existing theories of crime to the epidemiological facts, data in partial support of each theory abound. The resulting stalemate has engendered among students of crime a gentlemen's agreement to disagree. This agreement is all very cordial within academia, but it is not very helpful to policy makers who seek guidance for preventing crime. The dual taxonomy described in this essay argues that this compromise may be needless. The competing theories may all be correct, but the processes they describe may fit better for different types of delinquents, or may operate at different developmental stages in the natural history of antisocial behavior. Almost all of the many causal mechanisms invoked in this complementary pair of developmental theories is already under investigation by researchers. In our past efforts to uncover the causes of persistent predatory crime, we have been studying many of the right variables, but in the wrong subjects at the wrong point in the life course. If the taxonomy is shown to have useful application, crime researchers may be able to explain crime much better than anyone thought possible.

References

Agnew, R. 1984. "Autonomy and Delinquency." *Sociological Perspectives* 27: 219–40.

———. 1991. "The Interactive Effect of Peer Variables on Delinquency." *Criminology* 29: 47–72.

Anderson, E. 1990. *Streetwise*. Chicago, IL: University of Chicago Press.

Barrett, G. V., and R. L. Depinet. 1991. "A Reconsideration of Testing for Competence Rather Than for Intelligence." *American Psychologist* 46: 1012–24.

Becker, G. S. 1968. Crime and Punishment: An Economic Approach. *Journal of Political Economy* 76: 169–217.

Blumstein, A., and J. Cohen. 1987. "Characterizing Criminal Careers." *Science* 237: 985–91.

Bouchard, T., and M. McGue. 1981. "Familial Studies of Intelligence: A Review." *Science* 212: 1055–59.

Bowlby, J. 1988. "Developmental Psychiatry Comes of Age." *American Journal of Psychiatry* 145: 1–10.

Buchanan, C. M., J. S. Eccles, and J. B. Becker. 1992. "Are Adolescents the Victims of Raging Hormones: Evidence for Activational Effects of Hormones on Moods and Behavior at Adolescence." *Psychological Bulletin* 111: 62–107.

Cairns, R. B., B. D. Cairns, H. J. Neckerman, S. D. Gest, and J-L. Gariepy. 1988. "Social Networks and Aggressive Behavior: Peer Support or Peer Rejection?" *Developmental Psychology* 24 : 815–23.

Caspi, A., and D. J. Bem. 1990. "Personality Continuity and Change Across the Life Course." In *Handbook of Personality Theory and Research* , ed. L. Pervin, 549–75. New York, NY: Guilford.

Caspi, A., D. J. Bem, and G. H. Elder, Jr. 1989. "Continuities and Consequences of Interactional Styles across the Life Course." *Journal of Personality* 57: 375–406.

Caspi, A., G. H. Elder, and D. J. Bem. 1987. "Moving Against the World: Life-course Patterns of Explosive Children." *Developmental Psychology* 23: 308–13.

Caspi, A., D. Lynam, T. E. Moffitt, and P. A. Silva. 1993. "Unraveling Girls' Delinquency: Biological, Dispositional, and Contextual Contributions to Adolescent Misbehavior." *Developmental Psychology* 29: 19–30.

Caspi, A., and T. E. Moffitt. 1991. "Individual Differences are Accentuated during Periods of Social Change: The Sample Case of Girls at Puberty." *Journal of Personality and Social Psychology* 61: 157–68.

Clarke, A. D. B., and A. M. Clarke. 1984. "Constancy and Change in the Growth of Human Characteristics." *Journal of Child Psychology and Psychiatry* 25: 191–210.

Cleckley, H. 1976. *The Mask of Sanity* . 5th ed. St. Louis, MO: Mosby.

Cloninger, C. R. 1987. "A Systematic Method for Clinical Description and Classification of Personality Variants." *Archives of General Psychiatry* 44: 573–88.

Cloward, R. A., and L. E. Ohlin. 1960. *Delinquency and Opportunity*. New York, NY: Free Press.

Coie, J. D., M. Belding, and M. Underwood. 1988. "Aggression and Peer Rejection in Childhood." In *Advances in Cinical Child Psychology* , ed. B. Lahey and A. Kazdin, vol. 2, 125–58. New York, NY: Plenum Press.

Coie, J. D., K. Dodge, and J. Kupersmidt. 1990. "Peer Group Behavior and Social Status." In *Peer Rejection in Childhood* , ed. S. R. Asher and J. D. Coie, 17–59. New York: Cambridge University Press.

Conley, J. J. 1984. "The Hierarchy of Consistency: A Review and Model of Longitudinal Findings on Adult Individual Differences in Intelligence, Personality, and Self-Opinion." *Personality and Individual Differences* 5: 11–25.

Costello, E. J. 1989. "Developments in Child Psychiatric Epidemiology." *Journal of the American Academy of Child and Adolescent Psychiatry* 28: 836–41.

Csikszentmihalyi, M., and R. Larson. 1984. *Being Adolescent: Conflict and Growth in the Teenage Years*. New York, NY: Basic Books.

DiLalla, L. F., and I. I. Gottesman. 1989. "Heterogeneity of Causes for Delinquency and Criminality: Lifespan Perspectives." *Development and Psychopathology* 1: 339–49.

Dishion, T. J., G. R. Patterson, M. Stoolmiller, and M. L. Skinner. 1991. "Family, School, and Behavioral Antecedents to Early Adolescent Involvement with Antisocial Peers." *Developmental Psychology* 27: 172–80.

Dodge, K. A., and C. L. Frame. 1982. "Social Cognitive Biases and Deficits in Aggressive Boys." *Child Development* 53: 629–35.

Elder, G. H., Jr. 1986. "Military Times and Turning Points in Men's Lives." *Developmental Psychology* 22: 233–45.

Elliott, D. S., S. S. Ageton, D. Huizinga, B. A. Knowles, and R. J. Canter. 1983. *The Prevalence and Incidence of Delinquent Behavior: 1976–1980*. (The National Youth Survey Report No. 26). Boulder, CO: Behavioral Research Institute.

Elliott, D. S., and D. Huizinga. 1983. Social Class and Delinquent Behavior in a National Youth Panel: 1976–1980. *Criminology* 21: 149–77.

Elliott, D. S., and D. Huizinga. April 1984.*The Relationship Between Delinquent Behavior and ADM Problems*. Paper presented at the ADAMHA/OJJDP State-of-the-Art Research Conference on Juvenile Offenders with Serious Drug, Alcohol and Mental Health Problems, Rockville, MD.

Elliott, D. S., D. Huizinga, and S. Menard. 1989. *Multiple Problem Youth: Delinquency, Substance Use, and Mental Health Problems*. New York, NY: Springer-Verlag.

Elliott, D. S., D. Huizinga, and B. Morse. 1986. "Self-reported Violent Offending: A Descriptive Analysis of Juvenile Violent Offenders and Their Offending Careers." *Journal of Interpersonal Violence* 1: 472–514.

Elliott, D., and S. Menard. In press. "Delinquent Friends and Delinquent Behavior: Temporal and Developmental Patterns." In *Some Current Theories of Deviance and Crime*, ed. D. Hawkins, New York, NY: Springer-Verlag.

Elliott, D. S., and B. J. Morse. 1987. "Drug Use, Delinquency, and Sexual Activity." In *Drug Abuse and Adolescent Sexual Activity, Pregnancy, and Parenthood.*, eds. C. Jones and E. McAnarney, 32-60. NIDA, Washington, D.C.: U.S. Government Printing Office.

Elliott, D. S., and H. L. Voss. 1974. *Delinquency and Dropout.*. Lexington, MA: D.C. Heath and Company.

Erikson, E. H. 1960. "Youth and the Life Cycle." *Children Today* 7: 187–94.

Eysenck, H. J. 1977. *Crime and Personality*. London, England: Routledge and Kegan Paul.

Farrington, D. P. 1977. "The Effects of Public Labelling." *British Journal of Criminology* 17: 112–25.

———. 1983. "Offending from 10 to 25 Years of Age." In *Prospective Studies of Crime and Delinquency* , eds. K. Van Dusen and S.A. Mednick, 17–38. Boston, MA: Kluwer-Nijhoff Publishing.

———. 1986. "Age and Crime." In *Crime and Justice: An Annual Review of Research*, eds. M. Tonry and N. Morris, 7: 189–250.

Farrington, D. P., B. Gallagher, L. Morley, R. J. Ledger, and D. J. West. 1986. "Unemployment, School Leaving and Crime." *British Journal of Criminology* 26: 335–56.

Farrington, D. P., R. Loeber, and W. B. Van Kammen. 1990. "Long-term Criminal Outcomes of Hyperactivity-Impulsivity-Attention Deficit and Conduct Problems in Childhood." In *Straight and Devious Pathways from Childhood to Adulthood*, ed. L. N. Robins and M. R. Rutter, 62–81. New York, NY: Cambridge University Press.

Farrington, D., L. Ohlin, and J. Q. Wilson. 1986. *Understanding and Controlling Crime*. New York, NY: Springer-Verlag.

Farrington, D. P., and D. J. West. 1990. "The Cambridge Study of Delinquent Development: A Long-term Follow-up of 411 London Males." In *Kriminalitat*, eds. H. J. Kerner and G. Kaiser, 117–138. New York, NY: Springer-Verlag.

Farrington, D. P., R. Loeber, D. S. Elliott, D. J. Hawkins, D. B. Kandel, M. W. Klein, J. McCord, D. Rowe, and R. Tremblay. 1990. "Advancing Knowledge About the Onset of Delinquency and Crime." In *Advances in Clinical Child Psychology* , ed. B. Lahey and A. Kazdin, vol. 13, 283–342. New York, NY: Plenum Press.

Finnegan, W. 1990a. Out there, I. *The New Yorker, Sept.*, 51–86.

———. 1990b. Out there, II. *The New Yorker, Nov.*, 60–90.

Goldstein, A. P. 1990. *Delinquents on Delinquency*. Champaign, IL: Research Press.

Gorenstein, E. E. and J. P. Newman. 1980. Disinhibitory Psychopathology: A New Perspective and a Model for Research. *Psychological Review* 87: 301–15.

Gottfredson, M., and T. Hirschi. 1986. "The Value of Lambda Would Appear to be Zero: An Essay on Career Criminals, Criminal Careers, Selective Incapacitation, Cohort Studies, and Related Topics." *Criminology* 24: 213–34.

———. 1990. *A General Theory of Crime*. Stanford, CA: Stanford University Press.

Gove, W. R. 1985. "The Effect of Age and Gender on Deviant Behavior: A Biopsychosocial Perspective." In *Gender and the Life Course* , ed. A. Rossi, 115–44. New York, NY: Aldine.

Greenberg, D. F. 1985. "Age, Crime, and Social Explanation." *American Journal of Sociology* 90: 1–21.

Hagan, J. 1987. "Class in the Household: A Power-control Theory of Gender and Delinquency." *American Journal of Sociology* 92: 788–816.

Hagan, J., A. R. Gillis, and J. Simpson. 1985. "The Class Structure of Gender and Delinquency: Toward a Power-control Theory of Common Delinquent Behavior." *American Journal of Sociology* 90: 1151–79.

Hare, R. D., and L. M. McPherson. 1984. "Violent and Aggressive Behavior by Criminal Psychopaths." *International Journal of Law and Psychiatry* 7: 35–50.

Henry, B., A. Caspi, T. Moffitt, and P. Silva. 1994. Temperament and Family Predictors of Violent and Nonviolent Criminal Conviction: From Age 3 to Age 18. Manuscript submitted for publication.

Hertzig, M. 1983. "Temperament and Neurological Status." In *Developmental Neuropsychiatry* , ed. M. Rutter, 164–80. New York, NY: Guilford Press.

Hirschi, T. 1969. *Causes of delinquency.* Berkeley, CA: University of California Press.

Hirschi, T., and M. Gottfredson. 1983. "Age and the Explanation of Crime." *American Journal of Sociology* 89: 552–84.

Hirschi, T., and M. J. Hindelang . 1977. "Intelligence and Delinquency: A Revisionist Review." *American Sociological Review* 42: 571–87.

Hood, R., and R. Sparks. 1970. *Key Issues in Criminology.* Wallop, Hampshire: BAS Printers Limited.

Horan, P. M., and P. G. Hargis. 1991. "Children's Work and Schooling in the Late Nineteenth-century Family Economy." *American Sociological Review* 56: 583–96.

Huesmann, L. R., L. D. Eron, M. M. Lefkowitz, and L. O. Walder. 1984. "Stability of Aggression over Time and Generations." *Developmental Psychology* 20: 1120–34.

Jessor, R. F. Costa, L. Jessor, and J. E. Donovan. 1983. "Time of First Intercourse: A Prospective Study." *Journal of Personality and Social Psychology* 44: 608–26.

Jessor, R., and S. L. Jessor. 1977. *Problem Behavior and Psychosocial Development: A Longitudinal Study of Youth.* New York, NY: Academic Press.

Kandel, D. 1980. "Drug and Drinking Behavior Among Youth." *Annual Review of Sociology* 6: 235–85.

Kazdin, A. E. 1987. *Conduct dDsorders in Childhood and Adolescence.* Beverly Hills, CA: Sage Publications.

Klein, M. W. 1986. "Labelling Theory and Delinquency Policy." *Criminal Justice and Behavior* 13: 47–79.

Knight, B. J., and D. J. West. 1975. "Temporary and Continuing Delinquency." *British Journal of Criminology*15: 43–50.

Krueger, R., P. S. Schmutte, A. Caspi, T. Moffitt, K. Campbell, and P. A. Silva. 1994. "Personality Traits are Linked to Crime: Evidence from a Birth Cohort." *Journal of Abnormal Psychology* 103: 328–33.

Lemert, E. M. 1967. *Human Deviance, Social Problems, and Social Control.* Englewood Cliffs, NJ: Prentice-Hall.

Loeber, R. 1982. "The Stability of Antisocial and Delinquent Child Behavior: A Review." *Child Development* 53: 1431–46.

Loeber, R., S. Green, B. Lahey, and M. Stouthamer-Loeber. 1990. "Optimal Informants on Childhood Disruptive Behaviors." *Development and Psychopathology* 1: 317–37.

Loeber, R., and K. B. Schmaling. 1985. "Empirical Evidence for Overt and Covert Patterns of Antisocial Conduct Problems: A meta Analysis." *Journal of Abnormal Child Psychology* 13: 337–52.

Loeber, R., M. Stouthamer-Loeber, W. Van Kammen, and D. P. Farrington. 1989. "Development of a New Measure of Self-reported Antisocial Behavior for Young Children: Prevalence and Reliability." In *Cross-national Research in Self-reported Crime and Delinquency* , ed. M. Klein, 203-26. Boston, MA: Kluwer-Nijhoff.

Lynam, D., T. E. Moffitt, and M. Stouthamer-Loeber. 1993. "Explaining the Relation between IQ and Delinquency: Class, Race, Test Motivation, School Failure, or Self-control?" *Journal of Abnormal Psychology* 102: 187–96.

Magnusson, D. 1988. *Individual Developments from an Interactional Perspective: A Longitudinal Study*. Hillsdale, NJ: Lawrence.

Marwell, G. 1966. "Adolescent Powerlessness and Delinquent Behavior." *Social Problems* 14: 35–47.

Mattick, H. W. 1960. "Parolees in the Army during World War II." *Federal Probation* 24: 49–55.

Maughan, B., G. Gray, and M. Rutter. 1985. "Reading Retardation and Antisocial Behavior: A Follow-up into Employment." *Journal of Child Psychiatry and Psychology* 26: 741–58.

Mausner, B. and E. S. Platt. 1971. *Smoking: A Behavioral Analysis*. New York: Pergamon Press.

McGee, R., F. Partridge, S. M. Williams, and P. A. Silva. 1991. "A Twelve Year Follow Up of Preschool Hyperactive Children." *Journal of the American Academy of Child and Adolescent Psychiatry* 30: 224–32.

Mednick, S. A. 1977. "A Bio-social Theory of the Learning of Law-abiding Behavior." In *Biosocial Bases of Criminal Behavior*, ed. S. A. Mednick and K. O. Christiansen, 1–8. New York, NY: Gardner Press.

Moffitt, T. E. 1990a. "Juvenile Delinquency and Attention-deficit Disorder: Developmental Trajectories from Age 3 to 15." *Child Development* 61: 893–910.

———. 1990b. "The Neuropsychology of Delinquency: A Critical Review of Theory and Research." In *Crime and Justice*, eds. N. Morris and M. Tonry, Vol. 12, 99–169). Chicago, IL: University of Chicago Press.

———. 1991. *Juvenile Delinquency: Seed of a Career in Violent Crime, Just Sowing Wild Oats—or Both?* Paper presented at the Science and Public Policy Seminars of the Federation of Behavioral, Psychological and Cognitive Sciences, Washington, D.C.

———. 1993a. "Life-course-persistent" and "Adolescence-limited" Antisocial Behavior: A Developmental Taxonomy. *Psychological Review* 100: 674–701.

———. 1993b. The Neuropsychology of Conduct Disorder. *Development and Psychopathology* 5: 133–51.

———. 1994. "Natural Histories of Delinquency." In *Cross-national Longitudinal Research on Human Development and Criminal Behavior,* ed. H. J. Kerner and E. Weitekamp, 3–64. Dordrecht: Kluwer Academic Press.

Moffitt, T. E., and Silva, P. A. 1988a. "Self-reported Delinquency: Results from an Instrument for New Zealand." *Australian and New Zealand Journal of Criminology* 21: 227–40.

———. 1988b. "IQ and Delinquency: A Direct Test of the Differential Detection Hypothesis." *Journal of Abnormal Psychology* 97: 330–33.

————. 1988c. "Neuropsychological Deficit and Self-Reported Delinquency in an Unselected Birth Cohort." *Journal of the American Academy of Child and Adolescent Psychiatry* 27: 233–40.

Moffitt, T. E., and B. Henry. 1989. "Neuropsychological Assessment of Executive Functions in Self-reported Delinquents." *Development and Psychopathology* 1: 105–18.

Moffitt, T. E., S. A. Mednick, and W. F. Gabrielli. 1989. "Predicting Criminal Violence: Descriptive Data and Predispositional Factors." In *Current Approaches to the Prediction of Violence*, ed. D. Brizer and M. Crowner, 13–34. New York, NY: American Psychiatric Association Press.

Moffitt, T. E., D. R. Lynam, and P. A. Silva. 1994. "Neuropsychological Tests Predict Persistent Male Delinquency." *Criminology* 32: 101–24.

Moffitt, T. E., D. Begg, A. Caspi, N. Dickson, J. Langley, R. McGee, C. Paul, P. Silva, W. Stanton, and P. Stevenson. 1996. Childhood-onset Versus Adolescent-onset Antisocial Conduct in Males: Natural History from Age 3 to Age 18. *Development and Psychopathology, 32,* 1–9.

Moynihan, M. 1968. "Social Mimicry: Character Convergence Versus Character Displacement." *Evolution* 22: 315–31.

Murray, C. A. 1976. *The Link between Learning Disabilities and Juvenile Delinquency.* Washington, D.C.: U.S. Department of Justice.

Nagin, D., and R. Paternoster. 1991. "The Preventive Effects of the Perceived Risk of Arrest: Testing an Expanded Conception of Deterrence." *Criminology* 29: 561–88.

Nagin, D., and K. Land. 1993. "Age, Criminal Careers, and Population Heterogeneity: Specification and Estimation of a Nonparametric Mixed Poisson Model." *Criminology* 31: 327–62.

Nagin, D., D. Farrington, and T. E. Moffitt. 1995. "Life-course Trajectories of Different Types of Offenders." *Criminology* 33: 111–139.

Nasby, W., B. Hayden, and B. M. dePaulo. 1979. "Attributional Bias Among Aggressive Boys to Interpret Unambiguous Social Stimuli as Displays of Hostility." *Journal of Abnormal Psychology* 89: 459–68.

Panel on Youth of the President's Science Advisory Committee 1974. *Transition to Adulthood.* Chicago, IL: University of Chicago Press.

Paternoster, R., L. E. Saltzman, G. P. Waldo, and T. G. Chiricos. 1983. "Perceived Risk and Social Control: Do Sanctions Really Deter?" *Law and Society Review* 17: 457–79.

Patterson, G. R. 1982. *Coercive Family Process.* Eugene, OR: Castalia.

Pennington, B. F., and L. Bennetto. 1993. Main Effects or Transactions in the Neuropsychology of Conduct Disorder? *Development and Psychopathology* 5: 153–64.

Pepler, D. and K. Rubin, eds. 1991. *The Development and Teatment of Childhood Aggression.* Hillsdale, NJ: Erlbaum.

Plomin, R., H. M. Chipuer, and J. C. Loehlin. 1990. "Behavioral Genetics and Personality." In *Handbook of Personality Theory and Research*, ed. L.A. Pervin, 225–43. New York, NY: Guilford Press.

Price, B. H., K. R. Daffner, R. M. Stowe, and M. M. Mesulam. 1990. "The Comportmental Learning Disabilities of Early Frontal Lobe Damage." *Brain* 113: 1383–93.

Quay, H. C. 1987. "Patterns of Delinquent Behavior." In *Handbook of Juvenile Delinquency* , ed. H. C. Quay, 118–38. New York, NY: John Wiley and Sons.

Quinton, D., and M. Rutter. 1988. *Parenting Breakdown: The Making and Breaking of Intergenerational Links*. Aldershot, England: Avebury.

Quinton, D., A. Pickles, B. Maughan, and M. Rutter. 1993. "Partners, Peers, and Pathways: Assortative pairing and Continuities in Conduct Disorder." *Development and Psychopathology* 5: 763–83.

Raine, A. 1993. *The Psychopathology of Crime*. New York: Academic Press.

Reiss, A. J., Jr. 1986. "Co-offender Influences on Criminal Careers." In *Criminal Careers and Career Criminals,* ed. A. Blumstein, J. Cohen, J. A. Roth, and C. Visher, 121–60. Washington, D.C.: National Academy Press.

Reiss, A. J.. Jr. and D. P. Farrington. 1991. "Advancing Knowledge About Co-offending: Results from a Prospective Longitudinal Survey of London Males." *Journal of Criminal Law and Criminology* 82: 360–95.

Robins, L. N. 1966. *Deviant Children Grown Up*. Baltimore, MD: Williams and Wilkins.

———. 1978. "Sturdy Childhood Predictors of Adult Antisocial Behaviour: Replications from Longitudinal Studies." *Psychological Medicine* 8: 611–22.

———. 1985. "Epidemiology of Antisocial Personality." In *Psychiatry* , ed. J. O. Cavenar, vol. 3, 1–14. Philadelphia, PA: Lippincott.

Robins, L. N. and D. A. Regier. 1991. *Psychiatric Disorders in America*. New York, NY: The Free Press.

Rutter, M., ed..1983. *Developmental Neuropsychiatry*. New York, NY: Guilford.

Sameroff, A., and Chandler, M. 1975. "Reproductive Risk and the Continuum of Caretaking Casualty." In *Review of Child Development Research* , ed. F. Horowitz, M. Hetherington, S. Scarr-Salapatek, & G. Siegel, Vol. 4, 187–244. Chicago, IL: University of Chicago Press.

Sampson, R. J., and J. H. Laub. 1990. "Crime and Deviance over the Life Course: The Salience of Adult Social Bonds." *American Sociological Review* 55: 609–27.

Sarnecki, J. 1986. *Delinquent Networks*. Stockholm: National Council for Crime Prevention.

Shedler, J., and J. Block. 1990. Adolescent Drug Use and Psychological Health. *American Psychologist* 45: 612–30.

Silbereisen, R. K., and P. Noack. 1988. "On the Constructive Role of Problem Behavior in Adolescence." In *Persons in Context: Developmental Processes* , ed. N. Bolger, A. Caspi, G. Downey, and M. Moorehouse, 152–80. New York, NY: Cambridge University Press.

Simmons, R. G., and D. A. Blyth. 1987. *Moving into Adolescence: The Impact of Pubertal Change and School Context*. New York, NY: Aldine De Gruyter.

Simons, R. L., C. Wu, R. Conger, and F. Lorenz. 1994. "Two Routes to Delinquency: Differences between Early and Late Starters in the Impact of Parenting and Deviant Peers." *Criminology*, 32: 247–76.

Smith, D. A., and C. A. Visher. 1980. "Sex and Involvement in Deviance/Crime: A Quantitative Review of the Literature." *American Sociological Review* 45: 691–701.

Snyder, J., and G. Patterson. 1987. "Family Interaction and Delinquent Behavior." In *Handbook of Juvenile Delinquency* , ed. H. Quay, 216–43. New York, NY: John Wiley.

Stattin, H., and D. Magnusson. 1984. *The Role of Early Aggressive Behavior for the Frequency, the Seriousness, and the Types of Later Criminal Offenses* (Report). Stockholm: Department of Psychology, University of Stockholm.

Steffensmeier, D. J., E. A. Allan, M. D. Harer, and C. Streifel. 1989. "Age and the Distribution of Crime." *American Journal of Sociology* 94: 803–31.

Steinberg, L. 1987. "Impact of Puberty on Family Relations: Effects of Pubertal Status and Pubertal Timing." *Developmental Psychology* 23: 451–60.

Steinberg, L., and S. B. Silverberg. 1986. "The Vicissitudes of Autonomy in Early Adolescence." *Child Development* 57: 841–51.

Sutherland, E., and D. R. Cressey. 1978. *Criminology*, Philadelphia, PA: Lippincott.

Tanner, J. M. 1978. *Fetus into Man.* Cambridge, MA: Harvard University Press.

Udry, J. R. 1988. "Biological Predispositions and Social Control in Adolescent Sexual Behavior. "*American Sociological Review* 53: 709–22.

van den Boom, D., and J. Hoeksma. 1994. "The Effect of Infant Irritability on Mother-infant Interaction: A Growth-curve Analysis." *Developmental Psychology* 30: 581–90.

Vitaro, F., C. Gagnon, and R. E. Tremblay. 1990. "Predicting Stable Peer Rejection from Kindergarten to Grade One." *Journal of Clinical Child Psychology* 19: 257–64.

Warr, M. 1993. "Age, Peers and Delinquency." *Criminology* 31: 17–40.

Warr, M. and M. Stafford. 1991. The Influence of Delinquent Peers: What They Think or What They Do? *Criminology* 29: 851–66.

Weiher, A., D. Huizinga, A. J. Lizotte, and W. B. Van Kammen. 1991. "The Relationship between Sexual Activity, Pregnancy, Delinquency, and Drug Abuse. "Chapter 6. In *Urban Delinquency and Substance Abuse: A Technical Report.*, ed. D. Huizinga, R. Loeber, and T. Thornberry, Washington D.C.: Office of Juvenile Justice and Delinquency Prevention.

Wender, P. H. 1971. *Minimal Brain Dysfunction in Children.* New York, NY: Wiley.

West, D. J. 1982. *Delinquency.* Cambridge, MA: Harvard University Press.

White, J., T. E. Moffitt, A. Caspi, D. Jeglum-Bartusch, D. Needles, and M. Stouthamer-Loeber. 1994. "Measuring Impulsivity and Examining its Relation to Delinquency." *Journal of Abnormal Psychology* 103 192–205.

White, J., T. E. Moffitt, F. Earls, L. N. Robins, and P. A. Silva. 1990. "How Early Can We Tell? Preschool Predictors of Boys' Conduct Disorder and Delinquency." *Criminology* 28: 507–33.

Williams, K. R., and R. Hawkins. 1986. "Perceptual Research on General Deterrence: A Review." *Law and Society Review* 20: 545–72.

Wilson, J. Q. 1983. "Crime and American Culture." *The Public Interest* 70: 22–48.

Wilson, J. Q. and R. J. Herrnstein. 1985. *Crime and Human Nature.* New York, NY: Simon and Schuster.

Wolfgang, M. E., R. M. Figlio, and T. Sellin. 1972. *Delinquency in a Birth Cohort.* Chicago, IL: The University of Chicago Press.

Wolfgang, M. E., T. P. Thornberry, and R. M. Figlio. 1987. *From Boy to Man, From Delinquency to Crime.* Chicago, IL: The University of Chicago Press.

Wyshak, G. and R. E. Frisch. 1982. Evidence for a Secular Trend in Age of Menarche. *New England Journal of Medicine* 306: 1033–35.

2

Life-Course Contingencies in the Development of Adolescent Antisocial Behavior: A Matching Law Approach

Rand D. Conger and Ronald L. Simons

Almost twenty years ago, Conger (1976) proposed that delinquent behavior could be explained, at least in part, by the multiple contingencies of reinforcement and punishment that characterize the social environments of children and adolescents. This perspective involves the application of social learning principles to the operation of multiple environmental influences, a view that can be linked to the Matching Law in operant psychology (Conger and Killeen 1974; McDowell 1988). Conger (1980) also suggested that individual differences in temperament and in the ability to process social information should influence the ways in which these environmental contingencies affect specific individuals. Accumulating empirical evidence and theoretical developments during the past fifteen years are consistent with these earlier ideas. In the present chapter, we first review several elements of contemporary thought regarding social deviance during childhood and adolescence. Based on this review, we then propose a revised explanatory model derived from a Matching Law approach to understanding the development of antisocial behavior. The chapter concludes by considering the empirical evidence

This work was supported by grants from the National Institute of Mental Health (MH48165, MH51361, MH49217) and the National Institute on Drug Abuse (DA07029).

for this perspective as well as future research that is needed to assess predictions from the model.

Although much of the present discussion likely applies equally as well to adult criminality as to delinquent behavior, we confine this review to the early years of the life-course, from childhood to middle or late adolescence. This period encompasses a time during which young children, who commit essentially no criminal acts, become adolescents who exhibit the highest prevalence of illegal behavior of any age group in our society (Gottfredson and Hirschi 1990). Indeed, some researchers contend that the commission of some criminal or delinquent acts represents normative conduct during middle to late adolescence (Moffitt 1993) and others report that adolescent misbehavior is the single most important mechanism linking earlier life experiences to criminal behavior during adulthood (Sampson and Laub 1993). The central question guiding this review concerns the identification of processes that might account for this dramatic developmental change in such a relatively brief span of time. How does it happen that in less than two decades a given cohort of children moves from a time of relative innocence to become a major source of antisocial conduct in our society and what factors account for the extremely high number of criminal acts committed by a relatively small proportion of adolescents in a cohort?

Theories of crime and delinquency vary in their proposed explanatory constructs, which range from macrosociological structures to biological processes. Some theories have invoked unitary causes for criminality and others have utilized multivariate explanatory frameworks (Akers 1994). Moreover, some critics have suggested that attempts to explain crime and delinquency have followed as much from disciplinary priorities as from a careful evaluation of conceptual or empirical insights (Gottfredson and Hirschi 1990). Nevertheless, we believe that during the past decade or two there have been several important theoretical and empirical advances in the study of adolescent misbehavior, advances that are reflected in the following six major themes in the recent literature.

Contemporary Themes in Delinquency Theory

For our purposes, the most basic premise in the current understanding of delinquency is that adolescent crime involves a developmental progression from relatively minor to more serious antisocial behaviors (Elliott,

Huizinga, and Menard 1989; Loeber and Le Blanc 1990; Patterson 1993). In their longitudinal study of a national sample of children and adolescents, for example, Elliott and his colleagues (1989: 189) found that "Minor delinquency comes first, followed by alcohol use, serious delinquency, and serious drug use." Findings such as these illustrate the contemporary view that delinquent acts do not suddenly emerge as serious antisocial behaviors at age fifteen or sixteen with little or no prior experimentation with deviant activities. This understanding that crime and delinquency represent developmental processes suggests that general principles related to the full range of human developmental phenomena may apply equally well to the explanation of social deviance.

Placing the study of early crime and delinquency within a broader developmental context brings with it an elaboration of the domain of behaviors to be explained by theories of social deviance. More specifically, contemporary scholars suggest that criminological theories should account for a broad range of antisocial behaviors including multiple forms of interpersonal aggression, substance abuse, risky acts, and illegal conduct (Gottfredson and Hirschi 1990; Sampson and Laub 1993). Gottfredson and Hirschi (1990) propose that criminality derives from a general dispositional trait involving low self-control and that "...people who lack self-control will tend to be impulsive, insensitive, physical (as opposed to mental), risk-taking, short-sighted, and nonverbal, and they will tend therefore to engage in criminal and analogous acts" (90). The emphasis here is on "analogous" acts involving impulsive and irresponsible behaviors that may lead to failures in school, with peers, at work, and in the family. These oppositional or risky acts, which may or may not be illegal, increasingly have been added to the class of responses to be explained by a general developmental theory of criminal and delinquent behavior (Conger, Patterson, & Ge 1995; Sampson & Laub 1993). Developmental failures associated with a risk-taking or aggressive behavioral style, in turn, help to explain the progression to more serious deviant conduct.

A developmental approach involving a broader domain of behavior than illegal acts alone has also moved the study of crime and delinquency to an earlier point in the life course. Contemporary thought suggests that a comprehensive understanding of crime and delinquency requires the explanation of antisocial behaviors such as temper tantrums and noncompliance during early childhood, before the age when criminal acts are likely to occur (Gottfredson and Hirschi 1990; Moffitt 1993; Simons, Wu, Conger, and Lorenz 1994a). Current theory and empirical evidence suggest that delinquency cannot be understood only in terms of causal influences and criminal actions occurring during adolescence. Indeed, several theorists now postulate that different explanatory models are required to account for early and late onset delinquency and that the most powerful predictors of later chronic offending during the teenage years include noncriminal antisocial conduct during childhood (e.g., Moffitt 1993). From this perspective, an understanding of adolescent antisocial behavior requires an explanation of childhood misconduct that serves as a primary precursor to later delinquent acts (Moffitt 1993; Patterson 1993).

The realization that the early behavioral manifestations of later criminal conduct likely become apparent prior to adolescence has placed new emphasis on the role of the family in explanations of delinquency. Contemporary scholars representing diverse theoretical approaches now assign a central role to family processes in the early development of antisocial behavior and later criminal conduct (Akers 1994; Gottfredson and Hirschi 1990; Loeber and Stouthamer-Loeber 1986; Patterson, Reid, and Dishion 1992; Moffitt 1993; Thornberry 1987). Numerous studies have clearly demonstrated that parents increase the probability of having an antisocial child when they: (1) fail to adequately supervise their children; (2) do not provide appropriate discipline for misconduct; (3) treat their children in a neglecting or hostile fashion; and (4) fail to positively attend to or reinforce conventional activities or socially desirable behavior (Conger et al. 1992, 1993, 1994; Patterson et al. 1992; Simons et al. 1994a; Simons et al. 1994b). Particularly important, this renewed interest in family process brings with it a more sophisticated, contemporary view of family dynamics and deviant developmental trajectories.

The current perspective suggests that family interactions involve reciprocal influences in parent and child behaviors that affect both the probability of child misconduct and also disruptions in effective childrearing practices (Lytton 1990; Thornberry, Lizotte, Krohn, Farnworth, and Jang 1991; Vuchinich, Bank and Patterson 1992). Vuchinich et al. (1992), for example, demonstrated that antisocial behavior by eleven–twelve-year-old boys had an adverse influence on effective disciplinary practices of parents, controlling for the same parent behaviors assessed two years earlier. Thus, these boys' misconduct, which included generally oppositional behavior (e.g., noncompliance with parent requests) as well as potentially delinquent acts (e.g., stealing), was related to reduced parenting competence across time. Effective disciplinary practices, on the other hand, were associated with relatively fewer (compared to other boys in the sample) antisocial behaviors at the second wave of assessment. Thus, the parents and boys in this study apparently had reciprocal influences on changes in one another's behavior, consistent with the contemporary view of bidirectional effects (Thornberry 1987) but inconsistent with earlier models that postulated only an impact of parenting on deviance and delinquency (e.g., Hirschi 1969).

The theme just discussed emphasizes the importance of the family as a social institution that regulates, or fails to regulate, the development of child and adolescent antisocial behavior across time. It has long been recognized, of course, that the family represents only one of several interrelated social contexts that affects the developmental trajectories of youth. An important advance in the field has been the recent recognition that reciprocal influences exist not only within the family, but also between the behaviors of individual family members and the other social contexts important to the development or restraint of adolescent misconduct. Related to the school environment, Thornberry et al. (1991) have shown a reciprocal negative influence between delinquent behavior and school commitment across time. Their results demonstrate not only that commitment to academic pursuits decreases involvement in delinquency, but also that antisocial behavior decreases success in school.

Regarding peers, Melby, Conger, Conger, and Lorenz (1993) found that tobacco use by parents and siblings increased the likelihood that seventh graders would select friends who use tobacco, and Conger and Rueter (in press) showed these same influences for adolescent drinking problems. Association with deviant friends, of course, is usually the strongest correlate of delinquent behavior (Elliott et al. 1989). These findings suggest that family influences affect the selection of peers who, in turn, are likely to exacerbate problem behaviors that will have an adverse impact on the family. In addition, Sampson and Groves (1989) have shown that community participation and involvement in extensive friendship networks by adults, presumably including parents, reduces adolescent misconduct at the community level. Thus, parents' roles in the community can affect the degree of exposure by their children to criminogenic influences that, in turn, will increase the difficulty of successful childrearing (Richters and Martinez 1993).

From our perspective, a useful theory of adolescent conduct problems will need to address these six contemporary themes in the study of delinquent behavior: (1) its developmental nature; (2) its inclusion within a broader class of antisocial or problematic activities; (3) its link to oppositional or aversive acts in early childhood; (4) its foundations in family relationships; (5) its role in bidirectional influences within the family; and (6) its enmeshment in reciprocal effects among the behaviors of family members and the responses of other social contexts (peers, school, and community) important to the developing child or adolescent. In the next section we describe several strengths and some limitations in a Matching Law approach to understanding human behavior in general. Following that discussion, we apply the principles of behavioral matching in the development of a model for understanding the phenomena described by the themes just reviewed.

Social Learning and the Matching Law

At some very basic level, antisocial behavior involves a choice between conventional and unconventional lines of action. And yet the decision to engage in excessive levels of unacceptable behavior seemingly runs counter to the rational pursuit of one's long-term self-interest (Gottfredson and Hirschi 1990; Wilson and Herrnstein 1985). How do we account for such decision-making? We propose that a contemporary approach to social learning and conditioning, summarized mathematically by the Matching Law of behavior, provides important insights regarding the processes through which individual children and adolescents develop a propensity for conduct problems. From earliest childhood, we expect that variations in environmental contingencies related to reinforcement and punishment processes heavily influence choices regarding socially accepted versus antisocial behavior. Moreover, as the following discussion suggests, the operation of such contingencies in relation to choosing between deviant and conventional activities does not require higher level cognitive processing.

The Matching Law

Until the 1960s, the role of reinforcement and punishment in animal and human behavior typically was examined by investigating the connection between one type of behavior (e.g., pressing a lever) and one type of reinforcer (e.g., food) or punishment (e.g., electrical shock). In 1961, Herrnstein published a set of findings that changed the way that researchers investigated and thought about principles of learning. Basically, Herrnstein reasoned that individuals are naturally exposed to multiple environmental contingencies and that it is the relative, rather than the absolute reinforcement value of these different sources of punishment or reward that should determine differential rates of behavior.

Herrnstein's work led to a mathematical formulation that accurately predicts the behavior of animals and humans in experimental situations (McDowell 1988, 1989). The formula, called the Matching Law, proposes that the relative frequency of a particular behavior will be proportional to its relative rate of reinforcement in the environment, as shown in equation 1 for a simple situation in which two possible responses are available. For example, in a laboratory experiment a person might be given two buttons to press. If pressing button #1 (response #1 in the equation) produced, over time, an average of three nickels per minute (reinforcement #1 in the equation) and button # 2 (response #2 in the equation) an average of one nickel per minute (reinforcement #2 in the equation), the formula states that .75 of the subject's button presses will occur on button #1, .25 on button #2.

$$\frac{\text{Response 1}}{\text{Response 1 + Response 2}} = \frac{\text{Reinforcement 1}}{\text{Reinforcement 1 + Reinforcement 2}} \quad (1)$$

That is, responses on button 1 (reinforcement 1) will produce an average rate of reinforcement of up to three nickels per minute, button 2 (reinforcement 2) an average rate of one nickel per minute. Therefore, according to equation 1, the reinforcement side of the equation will equal $3 (3+1) = .75$. Because the proportion of responses is predicted to equal the proportion of reinforcement available for a particular behavior, three out of every four responses should be on button 1, which will equal .75 of all responses. Notice that the formula only tells us about the relative distribution of responses, not about the actual rate of response, which should be determined both by the activity level of the respondent and by the value or utility of a particular reinforcer (Hamblin 1977).

An interesting feature of the Matching Law is that it describes choice behavior without assuming a highly rational organism capable of weighing the long-term costs and benefits of a particular act. For instance, in the previous example the most rational course of action would be to spend most if not all of one's effort on the more reinforcing of the two available response alternatives. And yet previous research shows that the equation holds for human as well as nonhuman behavior, contrary to the notion of a highly rational hedonic calculus. Indeed, laboratory studies show that, under experimental conditions, the equation predicts as well to the behavior of rats and pigeons as to the behavior of humans and other primates (McDowell 1988). Cognizant of Gottfredson and Hirschi's (1990) concern that choices related to deviant behavior are unlikely to be highly rational, we need only assume that children and adolescents have the same cognitive capacity of rats or pigeons to apply the concept of behavioral matching in an explanatory model of conventional or antisocial behavior.

From our perspective, even more important than the relative response form of matching described in equation #1 is the time allocation version of the model. In the years since Herrnstein first proposed the Matching Law, several investigators have demonstrated that time spent in an environment will also be relative to the rate of reinforcement provided by that environment (Conger and Killeen 1974; McDowell 1988). Returning to our earlier example, if a person in a laboratory experiment received an average of three nickels per minute for sitting on one end of a sofa and an average of one nickel per minute for sitting at the other end, the Matching Law predicts that, over time, the individual will spend 75 percent of her time sitting in the three nickel environment, and 25 percent of her time at the other end of the sofa. This time allocation version of matching can be written as follows:

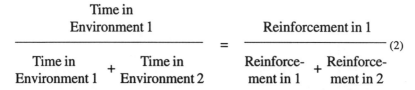

$$\frac{\text{Time in Environment 1}}{\text{Time in Environment 1} + \text{Time in Environment 2}} = \frac{\text{Reinforcement in 1}}{\text{Reinforcement in 1} + \text{Reinforcement in 2}} \quad (2)$$

Extensions of equations 1 and 2 have shown that behavioral matching applies to situations in which multiple rather than just two response alternatives are available. And, although these equations have been modified a bit to account for slight departures from matching (McDowell 1989), they convey enough of the basic sense of the paradigm for present purposes. As noted earlier, the predictive validity of the relative response and time allocation versions of the matching equation has been well-established in laboratory studies with a variety of species (e.g., pigeons, monkeys, and humans), responses (e.g., standing, talking, aggressive behavior, and lever-pressing), and reinforcers (e.g., shock avoidance, food, money, and the opportunity to listen to comedy records) (see McDowell 1988 for an extensive review of the available research).

Particularly important for our purposes is evidence that the Matching Law applies to human behavior in social situations. Conger and Killeen (1974) conducted the first experiment to demonstrate that naturally occurring social behaviors (talking with other people in a small group) adhered to the time allocation version of the Matching Law. They recruited naive subjects for a small group experiment in which participants were asked to discuss their views regarding an important social problem, substance abuse. Two colleagues of the experimenters systematically reinforced the opinions expressed by the participants. For example, when cued by the experimenters in a fashion not noticeable to the subjects, these colleagues would comment that the participant had made "a good point!" or they would express their agreement with the subject's perspective.

As predicted by equation #2, the subjects allocated the amount of time they spoke to each of the experimental confederates proportional to the amount of social reinforcement provided by these individuals. The analyses showed that, after the first few minutes of discussion, approximately 70 percent of each subject's verbal behavior was directed to the confederate providing 70 percent of the social reinforcers. When the confederates switched roles so that the individual initially providing 30 percent of the reinforcement shifted to providing 70 percent, the subjects' behaviors adjusted to these new reinforcement contingencies as predicted by equation #2. The matching equation accounted for 81 percent of the variance in the participants' behavior.

Hamblin (1977) later extended the analyses from the Conger and Killeen report and showed that they replicated with data from a variety of small group studies. In addition, McDowell (1988) reviewed evidence from several nonexperimental studies that demonstrated the utility of the Matching Law for predicting human behavior ranging from calm discussions to interpersonal assault in naturally occurring social environments. Thus, there appears to be good evidence that the principle of behavioral matching applies: (1) to human as well as infrahuman behavior; (2) to social as well as nonsocial behavior and reinforcers; (3) to time spent as well as to rate of response in a particular environment; and (4) to activities occurring in nonexperimental as well as in experimental settings. These points will have special import when we apply the Matching Law to explaining the occurrence of child and adolescent conduct problems. Before turning to that discussion, however, we review several additional issues concerning this theoretical approach.

Learning versus Performance

Patterson (1982) and others (e.g., Akers 1994; Bandura 1977) have noted that behaviors can be learned by simple observation as well as by the trial and error experiences involved in the environmental "shaping" of behavior, such as occurred in the experiment reported by Conger and Killeen (1974). Indeed Patterson et al. (1992: 6) suggest that:

> Almost all children in our culture have learned a variety of antisocial behaviors by the time they are 3 or 4 years old…Extensive exposure to television violence and aggression have undoubtedly enhanced the extent of this learning in modern times. In a sense, all children have *learned* about antisocial behavior. From a social interactional standpoint the question is, why do some children *perform* antisocial behaviors at higher rates than others?

The answer to this question, according to Patterson and his colleagues, involves the contingencies of reinforcement and punishment extant in the child's environment. This is basically our position as well. We believe that most children learn a good deal about antisocial behavior through simple observation. Importantly, however, most rarely engage in such actions.

From our perspective, the performance or maintenance of antisocial behavior is heavily influenced by environmental contingencies related to reinforcement or punishment for misconduct. As will become clearer in later discussion, a behavioral matching perspective predicts that juvenile misbehavior will be relatively more frequent when it is supported by reinforcement from one or more social environments important to the adolescent. The strength of the matching approach is that it also considers the reinforcing value of conventionality, as well as the effects of punitive outcomes associated with both socially approved and disapproved behavior. The Matching Law has important limitations, however, inasmuch as it focuses exclusively on phenomena that can be conceptualized in terms of environmental contingencies and related responses. It ignores several individual characteristics often linked to antisocial conduct; most prominently emotional functioning, cognitive processes, and biological substrates of behavior.

Limitations of the Matching Law

We recognize that a Matching Law approach to understanding child and adolescent misconduct relates only tangentially to several of the major issues in contemporary theories of human behavior. In this section, we consider some of these limitations in the proposed perspective, indicate how they might be systematically incorporated into future model building and empirical research, and provide the rationale for focusing on a relatively simple model as a first step in the creation of a theory of delinquency and antisocial behavior. We consider, in turn, possible relations between emotions, biological processes, and cognitions and a behavioral matching approach to the explanation of human behavior.

The role of emotions. An important finding in research on reinforcement and punishment contingencies is that humans and other animals demonstrate a range of negative emotional responses when positive outcomes are lost or denied and when painful stimuli are experienced (Berkowitz 1989; Bolger, DeLongis, Kessler, and Schilling 1989; Conger, Ge, Elder, Lorenz, and Simons 1994; Patterson et al. 1992). These emotional responses include antisocial behaviors such as aggression, anger, and irritability as well as internalizing symptoms such as depression and anxiety (Berkowitz 1989; Conger et al. 1994; Simons, Lorenz, Wu, and Conger 1993). Moreover, negative moods such as depressive symptoms are also associated with anger, irritability, and less socially competent behaviors, which again relate to a broad range of antisocial activities (Downey & Coyne 1990).

It appears, then, that environmental contingencies involving reinforcement and punishment that are important to a behavioral matching perspective have the capacity both to *elicit* as well as to *shape or maintain* problematic emotions or behaviors. The important point is that ongoing social constraints or contingencies may operate to exacerbate emotional characteristics that make an individual child or adolescent even more vulnerable to adjustment problems (Cairns 1991; Cairns and Cairns 1991). High levels of emotional distress may disrupt social interactional or academic skills, leaving the individual less capable of profiting from available reinforcement for conventional activities and increasing the salience of unconventional behaviors and environments.

Thus, we see emotional dispositions as an important corollary of environmental contingencies. These dispositions intensify an individual's tendency to behave in a hostile, aggressive, or irritable fashion and also disrupt competent, socially desirable activities. Although these emotional responses are affected by environmental events and conditions, they are also linked to basic biological processes. We next consider the evidence for such influences and their relation to a behavioral matching perspective.

The role of biological processes. Theoretical warfare regarding the role of biology in the occurrence of child and adolescent conduct problems has continued for decades (e.g., Akers 1994; Gottfredson and Hirschi 1990; Plomin, Chipuer, and Neiderhiser 1994). We enter the debate with some trepidation and with the observation that it would seem odd indeed for a biological organism not to be influenced by its basic biological structure and physiology. The possible mechanisms for such influence are far from well understood, however. Moreover, relations between variables interpreted as biological effects oftentimes represent environmental influences. For example, the type of physiological arousal known as the "flight or fight" response results from environmental threats that affect physiological functioning rather than the reverse.

At the most basic level, biological processes are involved in the way children and adolescents learn, remember, think, behave, and make choices about future activities (White and Milner 1992). Consideration of these fundamental, biological substrates of human behavior are beyond the scope of this review, but they certainly have significance for human behavior in general and, thus for problem behaviors as well. Most important for the elaboration of a behavioral matching model is work that has been conducted in the areas of *genetic influence* and what Moffitt (1993) has termed "*neuropsychological risk.*"

Perhaps no theoretical perspective has been more vigorously debated than the view that criminal or delinquent behavior is an inherited disposition (e.g., Gottfredson and Hirschi 1990). Present evidence suggests that there may well be a genetic vulnerability to antisocial conduct, but this vulnerability accounts for only some of the variance in delinquency (Plomin et al. 1994). In fact Plomin, a leading behavioral geneticist, argues that the study of behavioral genetics has bolstered the argument for the importance of environmental influences on behavior. He notes (Plomin and Rende 1991: 179), "The same data that point to significant genetic influence provide the best available evidence for the importance of nongenetic factors. Rarely do behavioral-genetic data yield heritability estimates that exceed 50 percent, which means that behavioral variability is due at least as much to environment as to heredity."

Interestingly enough, delinquent behavior, compared to other forms of developmental disorder, tends to show the least evidence of heritability and the greatest evidence of shared environmental influence for siblings living in the same family (Plomin et al. 1994). Current empirical findings suggest relatively strong environmental compared to genetic influences on delinquency, and these influences appear to operate similarly for children raised in the same social environment. The results regarding the heritability of delinquency, then, suggest important environmental influences, consistent with a behavioral matching approach, which predicts developmental trajectories from the social contingencies available to children and adolescents. We assume that genetic factors affect vulnerability to conduct problems, but their possible influence does not diminish at all the importance of understanding how different environmental circumstances intensify or diminish the expression of genetically related behavioral dispositions.

In addition to their genetic roots, Moffitt (1993) has carefully reviewed the environmental correlates of biological structure and process as well as the link between biology and developmental characteristics related to delinquency. She notes that several dimensions of social disadvantage, such as poverty and living in a high crime rate area, are also related to genetic and perinatal risks for biological insult. For example, parents living in the most disadvantaged circumstances are more likely to have an antisocial history themselves (see also Simons, Beaman, Conger, and Chao 1993), suggesting possible genetic as well as social risks for child behavior problems. They also are more likely to suffer poor nutrition and inadequate perinatal care, suggesting environmental risk for prenatal and postnatal biological development (Moffitt 1993).

Moffitt (1993) notes that a child with even minor biological anomalies, whether the result of inheritance or environmental factors, appears to be at risk for poorer emotional regulation, behavioral control, and cognitive functioning. The picture that emerges is one of biological influence on general competence for children who are thus less capable of acquiring appropriate social and academic skills. These deficits characterize youth at risk for delinquency, as has been noted in the general literature on crime and delinquency (Gottfredson and Hirschi 1990). It appears, then, that biology plays its strongest role in creating risk for delinquency by threatening the emotional, behavioral, and cognitive functioning of the individual child. A great deal of this biological risk appears to result from the same disadvantaged social environments that play a major role in a behavioral matching perspective on delinquency.

Thus, in a fashion similar to difficulties in emotional functioning, genetically or environmentally induced biological deficits may reduce overall competence or exacerbate behavioral problems. These individual characteristics likely influence responsiveness to environmental contingencies related to reinforcement or punishment. For example, the academically less able will be less likely to be restrained from misconduct by the payoffs associated with academic performance (Conger 1976; Gottfredson and Hirschi 1990). The less competent child also may be more difficult to raise, thus decreasing the probability that a reciprocally reinforcing bond will develop between parent and child (Moffitt 1993). The important point is that biological deficits may affect the way in which an individual child or adolescent relates to multiple environmental contingencies, but they do not diminish the importance of those contingencies.

The role of cognition. Cognitive variables play an important role in various approaches to understanding delinquent behavior. Sociologists often assert that beliefs or definitions regarding conventional or antisocial behavior are important factors in fostering or restraining conduct problems (Akers 1994; Hirschi 1969). More recent work on models of information processing or self-regulation also propose a central role for cognitive processes in child and adolescent adjustment problems (Crick and Dodge 1994; Feldman and Weinberger 1994). Even behavioral theories of delinquency include constructs related to beliefs, moral judgments, expectations, and definitions of the situation (Akers 1994).

A behavioral matching perspective is simply mute on the question of cognitive processes. The matching law proposes that the relative level of reinforcement for a specific behavior across all available sources of reinforcement or punishment will determine the relative rate of response for that behavior. Interestingly, such environmental contingencies also affect the way that people think about themselves and others. For example, Feldman and Weinberger (1994) showed that a sense of self-restraint reduces the likelihood of later delinquency. They also found, however, that a youth's sense-of-self was strongly predicted by the quality of family relationships. Similarly, Crick and Dodge (1994) suggest that cognitive processes that affect conduct problems may derive substantially from interactions with others.

Our thesis is that cognitive processes such as beliefs, values, attributions regarding self and others, etc., derive largely from social experience (see also Patterson et al. 1992). Although cognitions may play a mediating role between experience and action (e.g., Feldman and Weinberger 1994), we expect that contingencies of reinforcement and punishment play a major role in shaping cognitions as well as behavior. This is particularly apt to be the case during childhood. There is rather strong evidence, for example, that aggressive boys tend to perceive other people as having hostile intentions (Crick and Dodge 1994). Although this is often labeled an information processing bias, Patterson et al. (1992) note that the assumption of hostile intentions accurately reflects the interactional experiences of the antisocial boys in their longitudinal studies. This finding suggests that the propensity of aggressive boys to perceive hostile intentions is more a reflection of their reality than a perceptual bias. Similarly, it is likely that children's perceptions of self-efficacy or their causal attributions regarding themselves or others are significantly related to the contingencies of reinforcement and punishment operating in their family, school, and community. It may be, however, that over time these beliefs and assumptions crystallize with the result being a tendency to misconstrue the situations and events that exist in new and changing environments. Such cognitive biases might serve to foster antisocial and other maladjusted behavior during late adolescence and adulthood.

Our primary concern is identification of the factors that initiate and sustain a life-course trajectory of antisocial behavior. Hence, we concentrate on contingencies of reinforcement and punishment, which we view as the fundamental determinant of both behavior and cognitions. We limit our basic model to these central experiential factors with the understanding that, across time, the causal influence of experience may be substantially mediated by the cognitive processes it affects. From our view, construction of the basic behavioral matching model is central, with appropriate sensitivity to the emotional, biological, and cognitive factors just reviewed. They may make the basic model more complex, but they do not alter its underlying premises.

The Matching Law and Antisocial Behavior

Our approach to understanding antisocial conduct is based on the premise that people choose to engage in a particular behavior because of the benefits and costs associated with it versus alternative courses of action. Other theorists also identify this postulate as the starting point for their perspectives. Gottfredson and Hirschi (1990: 19) state, for example, that their theory of crime derives from "the classical theory of human behavior, which asserted that people pursue self-interest by avoiding pain and seeking pleasure." Similarly, Wilson and Herrnstein (1985: 42) note that their theory of law violation rests on the assumption that "a person will do that thing the consequences of which are perceived by him or her to be preferable to the consequences of doing something else." While we share these authors' assumption that human behavior is a function of choices related to contingencies of reinforcement and punishment, we differ in our use of this idea to explain antisocial behavior.

General Principles of Behavior

The difficulty with both Gottfredson and Hirschi's and Wilson and Herrnstein's approach is that they do not adhere to their central assumption in explaining both deviant and conventional behavior. They argue that the benefits of crime are relatively immediate whereas the advantages of conventional behavior tend to be delayed. Given this assumption, they are faced with the dilemma of explaining why antisocial persons discount long-term consequences more than conforming individuals. Gottfredson and Hirschi resolve this puzzle by positing that antisocial actors lack self-control, an idea that poses problems of tautology. Wilson and Herrnstein suggest that personal characteristics such as impulsivity or low intelligence account for the antisocial person's disregard for long-term consequences. Thus, their solution suggests that the antisocial individual suffers from a personal defect that alters the manner in which (s)he responds to environmental contingencies. We believe that such theorizing is based upon a largely erroneous notion regarding the consequences that motivate both conventional and antisocial behavior.

From a Matching Law perspective, we propose that both conventional and antisocial behaviors during childhood and adolescence are related to the pursuit of self-interest within the social contexts available to the developing individual. Contrary to the approach taken by Gottfredson and Hirschi, or Wilson and Herrnstein, we propose that conventional behaviors are promoted by short-term benefits just as is the case for misconduct. From our perspective, when children and adolescents receive continuing and relatively immediate benefits from conventional behaviors reinforced by family, friends, and community institutions such as schools, and when violations of conventional standards threaten the continuity of these benefits (e.g., when parents appropriately punish antisocial behavior), then relatively high rates of socially desirable behavior are likely to occur.

A behavioral matching perspective, then, agrees with the basic approach taken by Gottfredson and Hirschi and by Wilson and Herrnstein by suggesting that both deviant and conventional activities involve the pursuit of self-interest and that both types of acts derive from the same basic principles of human conduct. We disagree with their theories inasmuch as we assume that conventionality is also likely to be maintained by relatively immediate consequences provided by a youth's social environment. In that sense, we would argue that a behavioral matching perspective, compared to the notion of low self-control, is more consistent with Gottfredson and Hirschi's basic tenant that "people naturally pursue their own interests and unless socialized to the contrary, will use whatever means are available to them for such purposes" (1990: 117). From our perspective, "socialized to the contrary" involves social environments that (1) regularly provide benefits for conventionality; (2) assist in the acquisition of skills that increase the probability of access to those benefits throughout childhood, adolescence, and into adulthood; and (3) effectively punish antisocial behavior.

The important difference in our approach compared to one based on the concept of low self-control or impulsivity is that we assume that both conventionality and deviance are most likely to be maintained by relatively immediate and regular benefits. A simple example will help to illustrate the point. A child born into a relatively affluent, well-educated middle-class family is likely to win regular and fairly immediate approval from parents for the acquisition of socially valued cognitive and social skills. The parents are also likely to provide material and social rewards for success in school, and to monitor and appropriately punish antisocial conduct. This child is likely to have peers from similar homes whose parents are advocating conventional pursuits and long-term goals.

Thus, both peers and teachers are likely to frequently approve of this child's socially appropriate activities and to disapprove of antisocial conduct. The pursuit and endorsement of conventional goals likely derives from these reinforcement contingencies rather than from a sense of "high self-control." As noted earlier, cognitions as well as behaviors supportive of conventional activities should result from such strongly normative environments.

Contrast our middle-class child with one born into a family that suffers from severe financial disadvantage, residence in a high crime-rate area, low parent education, a family tradition of control through violence and physical punishment, and parents who are so stressed by their own financial and emotional needs that they have little time to monitor or respond to either the conventional or deviant activities of their child. For this youngster, payoffs in the home may result from aggressive behaviors that, at a minimum, blunt the painful intrusions of others (Patterson et al. 1992). A child from such a home likely will enter school with few skills to promote success in that environment or success with conventional peers. Indeed, in a high crime area association with groups of antisocial youngsters may be promoted (i.e., negatively reinforced) by reducing the probability of victimization. This very different environment provides multiple sources of benefit for antisocial conduct and little payoff for conventional activities. Those benefits that do exist involve no more immediate or frequent payoffs than the benefits for conventionality available to our middle-class child.

Although our basic proposition is that both conventional and antisocial behaviors by children are largely a function of the relatively immediate and continuing rewards available in their closest environments, it is often the case that individuals become more responsive to the long-term consequences of various lines of conduct during late adolescence. We expect, however, that adolescents learn to plan and focus on long-term goals as a result of the relatively immediate and continuing reinforcement for such behavior provided by parents, teachers, and peers. While the environments of some adolescents may reinforce thinking about more distant goals, such as plans for a college education, the daily experiences of others may discourage such a focus. Given the poverty of reinforcement available, many adolescents in seriously disadvantaged neighborhoods may learn to be opportunistic, to take advantage of any occasion for reinforcement that might present itself. For example, the relatively high risk of violent death or disabling injury for young males in certain urban neighborhoods should discourage long-term planning for what many reasonably perceive as a short-term future. Thus, we propose that both conventional and antisocial children and adolescents are primarily responsive to the relatively immediate contingencies of reinforcement and punishment in their proximate environment, and whether more long-term considerations become a part of the person's thinking during adolescence is a matter of the extent to which such behavior is reinforced by others with whom they regularly interact. With these ideas in mind, we turn to the elaboration of our matching model.

The Theoretical Model

Any explanatory framework that invokes constructs such as *self-interest or relative benefits* immediately faces the problem of defining such terms. It certainly is the case that not all people are equally influenced by all possible sources of pain or pleasure. Nevertheless, the weight of the evidence suggests that most of the time most children and adolescents will invest time and effort to: (1) maintain social contact with others; (2) produce material rewards such as money, toys, etc.; (3) avoid or terminate aversive intrusions from adults or peers (e.g., withdrawal of valued resources or activities or verbally or physically violent acts); (4) engage in activities approved by peers and adults (e.g., age-appropriate games and pursuits), and, with the transition into adolescence; (5) gain access to opportunities generally sanctioned only for adults such as sexual intimacy, substance use, and increased freedom of choice (McDowell 1988; Moffitt 1993; Patterson et al. 1992; Parker and Asher 1993). These possible benefits resulting from specific behaviors identify the sources of reinforcement and punishment central to our behavioral matching model. Their elaboration makes possible empirical tests of specific hypotheses related to the more general theoretical framework.

Two other important points need to be made regarding the operation of the model. First, unlike earlier social learning approaches (e.g., Akers 1994), the present model applies specifically to *time allocation* as well as to *differential response rates*. As noted earlier, research shows that people are likely to spend relatively more of their time in environments that are relatively more rewarding or relatively less punishing for them. This aspect of the model is especially important inasmuch as, even for chronic delinquents, seriously antisocial behavior quite likely occurs at a relatively low rate compared to other activities. We expect, however, that youth at high risk spend a great deal more time in settings that provide opportunities for deviance compared to more conventional peers. Thus, the way in which children and adolescents allocate their time to various environments should have a significant impact on the probability of antisocial behavior.

Second, a behavioral matching approach takes a life course perspective in that the nature of environmental contingencies is expected to change with chronological age and stage of life experience. With successive life stages from childhood to adolescence and then to the adult years, societal demands change for the developing individual (Elder 1992). Within a relatively short span of time, the largely dependent young child moves along a pathway of increasing expectations regarding cognitive, social, and instrumental competence. The behaviors that bring social approval and recognition at age ten will not be sufficient to maintain such reinforcing responses at age twenty. For example, in most instances to win approval from family and conventional peers, by late adolescence a youth must acquire the skills needed to achieve increasing independence in social, academic, and work-related activities; demands not placed on the young child. Moreover, attention-getting devices appropriate for a young child, such as crying or minor outbursts of temper, will bring strong disapproval for older children and adolescents. These shifting demands, in effect, represent altered contingencies of reinforcement and punishment that are directly linked to specific life stages from childhood to old age.

Moreover, these evolving behavioral contingencies are located within a set of significant social contexts for youth. As shown in figure 2.1, a behavioral matching approach is based on the identification of contingencies of reinforcement and punishment for antisocial and normative behavior within these interrelated social contexts. Figure 2.1 illustrates the expected relationship between child/adolescent behavior and contingencies of reinforcement and punishment for antisocial and conventional behavior provided by the family, peers, school, and community. As predicted by the matching perspective, figure 2.1 illustrates the relationship between a given youth's activities and concurrent schedules of reinforcement and punishment within and across significant developmental contexts.

Based on matching equation #1, the model in figure 2.1 indicates that a child or adolescent will engage in a relatively high proportion of anti-

FIGURE 2.1
Contextual Risks for Child and Adolescent Delinquent/Antisocial
Behavior from a Matching Perspective

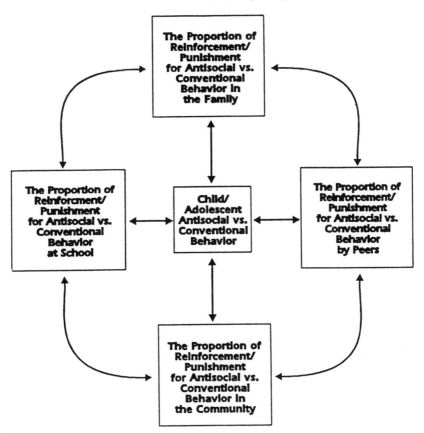

social compared to conventional behaviors within a specific context (family, peer group, school, or community) when (1) reinforcement for antisocial behavior is relatively high; (2) punishment for antisocial behavior is relatively low; (3) reinforcement for conventional behavior is relatively low; and (4) punishment for conventional behavior (e.g., school failure) is relatively high. Looking across contexts, equation #2 predicts that a youth will attempt to maximize time spent in those settings that are relatively more reinforcing and less punishing. For example, an adolescent who has many punitive experiences at school and home because (s)he is failing many classes and living in a violent family, but who concurrently receives approval for antisocial activities by a deviant peer group, would be expected to limit time at home and school and to maximize time with peers in unsupervised community settings.

The matching model (figure 2.1) also proposes that these developmental contexts are interrelated. Returning to our earlier examples, a child living in an upper-middle-class suburb is likely to live in a community characterized by (1) a high proportion of conventional age-mates; (2) relatively effective community control of crime (i.e., low crime rates); and (3) well-supported schools that can both maximize attention and support for academic effort as well as relatively effectively control antisocial behavior in school. In effect, the task of child socialization in such a place is considerably easier than for disadvantaged families that must struggle both with their own significant financial problems as well as with a community less able to promote conventional success or to minimize child and adolescent opportunities for misconduct.

Summarizing the discussion of our matching model of delinquent/antisocial behavior to this point, we have proposed that misconduct derives from the same general principles of behavior as conventional activities. According to the model, both domains of action are maintained by contingencies of reinforcement and punishment that exist in the daily lives of children and adolescents. We have identified several dimensions of social or material reinforcement/punishment that can be used in empirical tests of these general principles. Because societal expectations for appropriate behavior are related to chronological age and life stage, we noted that the matching model is consistent with a life-course perspective on individual development. Finally, the prior discussion locates the primary contingencies for child and adolescent behavior, and their relation to the matching equations, within four interrelated social contexts: family, peer group, school, and the general community. With this background information in mind, we now turn to the relationship between the behavioral matching model and the six contemporary themes in delinquency theory reviewed earlier.

Contemporary Themes and Behavioral Matching

Antisocial and Delinquent Behavior as a Developmental Progression

The first three contemporary themes in delinquency research reviewed earlier concern: (1) the empirically demonstrated developmental progression from minor to more serious delinquency; (2) the broadening of the theoretical focus in criminological theory from only illegal acts to a wider class of both criminal and analogous behaviors; and (3) the identification of early childhood behaviors that increase risk for later law violation. For present purposes, these three themes can be collapsed into the single observation that a useful theory of delinquency must account for developmental trajectories that appear to lead from oppositional behaviors and other conduct problems during early childhood to more serious, oftentimes criminal acts during adolescence and to social and instrumental failures that are associated with delinquency. How does a behavioral matching approach account for such phenomena across time?

Family processes and child oppositional behaviors. Returning to figure 2.1, and consistent with *our fourth general theme* in the current literature regarding delinquent acts, the primary social context for the development of antisocial behaviors such as temper tantrums and noncompliance during the preschool years will be the family. Although many theorists equate family influences only with parents' behaviors, a growing body of literature suggests that other family members, especially siblings and alternative caregivers such as grandparents (Conger and Rueter in press; Kellam 1990; Lauritsen 1993; Patterson 1988), may have a powerful influence on early conduct problems. Most important for our purposes is the fact that the family itself is a source of multiple environmental influences. Behavior by one family member that fails to restrain or that actually reinforces child misconduct constitutes only one part of the family system and such behavior may be at least partially negated by effective, prosocial behaviors from other family members (e.g., Egeland, Carlson, and Sroufe 1993; Elder and Caspi 1988; Werner 1993).

With multiple family members, the young child may be presented with multiple and differing contingencies regarding reinforcement, punishment, and modeling of antisocial behavior. For example, Elder and Caspi (1988) showed that arbitrary and irritable behavior by fathers exacerbated conduct problems of preschool children only when mother was aloof and unavailable. The presence of an effective mother, even with significant exposure to what we would label an antisocial father, created an alternative set of environmental contingencies that protected against the development of childhood problem behaviors. Conger, Rueter, and Conger (1994) identified a similar process during early adolescence. They found that older sibling alcohol abuse predicted drinking problems for an early adolescent in the family only when parents were hostile, coercive, and uninvolved in the focal child's life. Sibling drinking had no affect on a younger adolescent's substance use when parents were meeting their childrearing obligations.

How, specifically, do these observed family processes support a behavioral matching perspective? We noted earlier that there is a broad range of empirical support for the notion that children will be at risk for antisocial behavior if their parents (1) fail to adequately supervise their activities; (2) do not appropriately discipline them for misconduct; (3) treat children in a hostile or rejecting fashion; and (4) fail to provide approval or other forms of support for conventional or socially desirable behavior. Carefully considered, we can see that all of these parental behaviors involve contingencies of reinforcement or punishment for child activities, consistent with a matching perspective. The core of the model involves parental supervision. Parents who do not track, monitor, or otherwise supervise their child's behavior cannot respond contingently to either the child's antisocial or conventional activities (Conger et al. 1992; Hirschi and Gottfredson 1990; Patterson et al. 1992).

Nurturant and involved childrearing practices. On the positive side of the equation, parents who track the activities of the young child will be in a position to provide approval or other forms of material or social benefits when the youngster meets appropriate, conventional standards for conduct that take into account the cognitive, emotional, and motoric capacities available at a particular age. This scenario provides a classic example of positive reinforcement through which a particular activity is maintained or strengthened because of the valued outcomes it elicits from the environment. Following from the matching equations described earlier, these positively reinforcing behaviors of parents should not only influence differential rates of socially approved child behaviors, they should also affect allocation of time. A developmental history of living in a welcome and approving home environment should make wandering on the streets with potentially deviant companions less attractive as the child ages and has such opportunities.

Thus, warm and supportive behaviors by parents in general, according to a behavioral matching perspective, should increase time spent in the conventional surrounds of the home environment, similar to Simmon's and Blyth's (1987) conception of the well-functioning family as an "arena of comfort" for children. Moreover, both the positive reinforcement of socially appropriate behavior and the concomitant modeling of such activities by parents should strengthen conventional behaviors by children. A corollary of this process is the acquisition of social skills that will assist the child as (s)he becomes increasingly involved outside of the home in school, in the community and with peers (Conger et al. 1992, 1993; Patterson et al. 1992). These skills, in turn, should increase the probability that the child will elicit positively reinforcing outcomes such as acceptance and approval in other conventional environments such as the school. These valued outcomes, again, should increase time allocation to conventional activities and environments, thus reducing the time available for unsupervised wandering or associations with deviant companions.

Equally, and in some ways perhaps even more important than positive reinforcement contingencies, are family processes that directly punish misconduct or that lead to avoidance conditioning (see Patterson 1988). In the language of operant psychology, punishment occurs when an unpleasant outcome is contingent on a particular response, which, as a consequence of this contingency, is reduced in strength. The research shows that when misconduct leads to appropriate and consistent disciplinary action that is not overly harsh or violent (e.g., parent disapproval or withdrawal of valued benefits such as television viewing, etc.), the likelihood of child antisocial behavior is reduced (Patterson et al. 1992; Sampson & Laub 1993). Young children, of course, come with an extensive repertoire of behaviors such as yelling, kicking, crying, etc., that become increasingly unacceptable with age (Moffitt 1993; Patterson 1982). If these behaviors do not decline to acceptable levels as a result of effective disciplinary practices, the young child is at increased risk for failures in school and peer relations, difficulties that become part of an antisocial syndrome predictive of later delinquent activities (Conger et al. 1994; Moffitt 1993; Sampson & Laub 1993; Simons et al. 1994a).

From a matching perspective, we expect that consistency across family members (e.g., mother, father, older siblings, extended relations) in supervision, positive reinforcement for conventional behavior, and appropriate discipline will create an environment in which the varied family relationships available to the child provide contingencies most likely to reduce risk for antisocial conduct and to increase the probability of success in extrafamilial settings. More specifically, under such conditions the preschool child can maximize benefits and minimize costs across multiple family relationships by engaging in relatively more socially appropriate and relatively fewer antisocial activities. Moreover, children will be more likely to spend time in such a family setting. Failures in consistency across family members should increase risk for conduct problems, but the research tends to show that even one effective caregiver can have an important protective influence (e.g., Egeland et al. 1993).

Hostile, rejecting and coercive childrearing. In addition to supervision, positive parenting, and consistent discipline, we have identified hostile, rejecting or coercive parenting as a risk factor for child conduct problems. In terms of a matching or social learning perspective, we expect that parental behaviors of this type affect the young child in at least three ways by (1) providing a model for antisocial conduct; (2) promoting direct training for antisocial behavior; and (3) in some cases linking hostile social interactions within the family to a broader network of antisocial and even criminal activities. Hostile and rejecting behaviors by parents, both to a specific child and to other family members, model an approach to conducting social relationships that can be mimicked by the young child both within and outside the family. Highly antisocial families typically demonstrate significant levels of aversive interaction (Patterson 1982). Observational learning should lead to the acquisition of similar behavioral tendencies at an early age.

Our thesis, however, is that behaviors must produce some benefit in the environment for them to be maintained across time. A recent paper by Snyder and Patterson (in press) has demonstrated that such contingencies appear to exist in the families of young, aggressive boys. They showed that, for highly antisocial children, aggressive behaviors by these youngsters were likely to terminate the aversive intrusions of mothers. This finding suggests a negative reinforcement process, or avoidance conditioning, in which the child escapes a negative environmental situation (mother's aversive behavior) through aggressive behavior toward a parent. For nonaggressive boys, Snyder and Patterson found that prosocial verbal behavior was an effective means for reducing aversive actions by mothers. Overall, they showed that both level of mother's aversive behavior (suggesting an observational or modeling influence) and mother's contingent reduction of her aversiveness in response to son's aggression (a training effect), were positively and independently related to the frequency of the young child's aggression.

Very little research exists that can provide evidence for our third proposed route of influence for hostile and rejecting parental behavior, i.e., its link to a broader network of antisocial or even criminal conduct in the home. Perhaps most pertinent to this thesis is the recent report by Richters and Martinez (1993) who found that young children exposed to guns or drugs at home were at high risk for developing behavioral problems and for failing in the early years of elementary school. These results are consistent with other work linking antisocial and criminal conduct by parents to failures in child management skills (Patterson et al. 1992; Sampson & Laub 1993; Simons et al. 1993). We expect that actual criminal activities by parents or siblings are associated with a generally aversive home environment and that exposure by young children to this degree of antisocial behavior creates a learning situation conducive to experimenting with such behaviors outside the home (Conger, Rueter, and Conger 1994; Melby, Conger, Conger, and Lorenz 1993).

Biology, emotions, and cognition. We suggested earlier that there should be a connection between these early environmental influences and children's biological, cognitive, and emotional functioning. As noted, young children may be genetically or environmentally disposed to *a biological constitution* that either increases the probability of oppositional, noncompliant and aversive behaviors during the preschool years and/or leads to deficits in learning skills related to prosocial behaviors, such as failing to understand the connection between one's own actions and other's response. From our view, these individual differences may create greater or fewer difficulties for family members attempting to socialize the young child, but they do not negate the influence of the multiple family contingencies just described, except in extreme cases of severe biological dysfunction. More generally, we expect that the reinforcement and punishment processes we have just described will affect the behavior of most children, but their influence will be conditioned to some degree by a given child's unique biological development.

Also consistent with earlier discussion, we expect that these family processes will elicit different *emotional responses* from young children. In particular, a highly aversive family environment should elicit negative feelings that range from sadness to anger (Conger et al. 1994; Richters and Martinez 1993; Simons, Johnson, and Conger in press). Consistent with this thesis, in a recent public television special on inner-city life (Iowa Public Television 1994), several young African-American males who experienced violence both at home and in the community described themselves as feeling anxious, hopeless, and angry at themselves and others. Such negative emotions impair the development of social and instrumental competencies (Berkowitz 1989; Downey and Coyne 1990), placing the young child at risk for problems within and outside the family. Socialization practices that are clear, consistent, and supportive, on the other hand, should reduce these negative feelings and their possible adverse consequences (Conger, et al. 1992, 1993; Simons et al. in press). As with biologically related characteristics, environmentally linked emotions should condition, but not negate the impact of family contingencies on the behavior of the young child.

Finally, these early family experiences will influence the *cognitive development* of the child. They should make children more or less able to adapt to the early school years, and they may generate attributions about self and others that will affect their ability to socialize appropriately with peers and teachers (Crick and Dodge 1993). Research on the linkages between family experience, social cognitions, and later child and adolescent behavior is in its infancy. At this point, we cannot say whether these cognitions have a causal influence on social development or whether they are simply one more consequence of the multiple learning contingencies influencing a child's life. Future research will be needed to clarify these connections (Patterson 1993).

Research implications regarding family influences. Figure 2.2 summarizes the development of the matching model as it relates to family functioning. It shows that the family can be envisioned as several different social environments involving mother, father, siblings, and extended kin, each of which has the potential for providing contingent reinforcement or punishment for a young child's behavior. The figure shows that these family subsystems can be described as more or less antisocial. Just as the child who is angry, oppositional, and fails to engage in socially appropriate activities is labeled antisocial, family members who fail to provide adequate caregiving and/or serve as a source of training or modeling for aversive or criminal behaviors, as previously described, can also be considered antisocial. To the extent that family members are highly antisocial in these ways, figure 2.2 shows that the young child will be at increased risk for developing behavioral (e.g., aggressive, oppositional) or emotional (e.g., anxious, sad, hopeless) problems prior to or following entrance into the elementary school years.

The model also suggests that even one effective caregiver might compensate to some degree for several antisocial family members as sug-

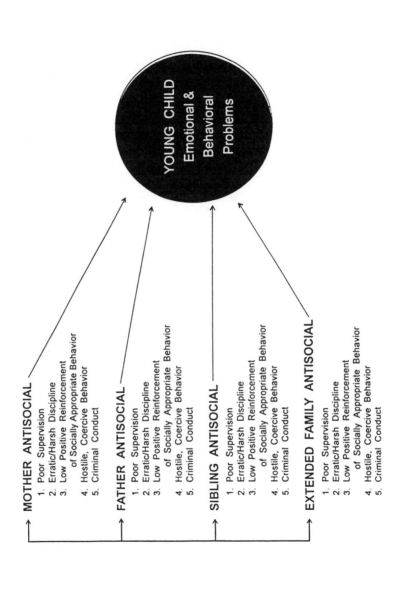

FIGURE 2.2

Multiple Family Environments Predicting to the Young Child's Behavioral and Emotional Problems

gested by the literature on children's resilience in the face of environmental risks. Moreover, the time allocation dimension of the matching equation would predict that the young child would attempt to spend time in the company of more supportive as opposed to more aggressive family members, although we know of no research that addresses this question.

The clear *research implication* of this early life portion of the matching model is that more extensive study is needed of the family system itself in relation to conduct problems expected to lead to later risk for delinquent behavior. Simply studying an available parent will not provide the richness of information required to generate a fuller understanding of multiple family influences on the early development of child maladjustment. For example, figure 2.1 indicates that a complete picture of family influences requires analyses of contingencies related to both prosocial and antisocial child behavior and figure 2.2 indicates that these contingencies must be studied for multiple family members. Also important, moving to an earlier point in the life span and to a broader view of the family context takes us well beyond two of the major contemporary perspectives on delinquency: social control theory and integrated control theories (see Thornberry, et al. 1991).

Classical control theory proposes that there is no motivation to delinquent behavior, and that only the failure of family and then school to constrain natural amoral tendencies leads to conduct problems. In the face of overwhelming evidence for motivational influences involving peers, integrated control theories combine social learning and control notions and suggest that families that fail to effectively socialize their young produce children who are at greater risk of being influenced by peers to become delinquent. From our behavioral matching perspective, we take this line of reasoning one step further to propose that training for antisocial behavior, and even criminal behavior, may also occur within the family. Consistent with Patterson and his colleagues (1992), we expect that aversive, aggressive, and oppositional behaviors used in the community are often learned at home from parents and siblings. In the most high-risk family environments, such as those studied by Richters & Martinez (1993), criminal behaviors may be learned at home as well. More extensive family studies with very high-risk populations that begin prior to adolescence will be needed to evaluate these hypotheses.

Reciprocal Influences in Deviant Trajectories

The last two contemporary themes discussed earlier involve reciprocal influences within the family as well as between family members and
the outside community. The young child surrounded by multiple antisocial influences within a dysfunctional family environment (figure 2.2)
likely has developed conduct and emotional problems that exacerbate
family tensions and that will make difficult the transition to school and
interactions with conventional peers. This youngster typically will lack
requisite social and academic skills, and thus will have few resources to
compensate for the difficulties created by his or her aversive behaviors
toward others (Patterson et al. 1992).

Reciprocity in the family. An important corollary of a behavioral matching approach to delinquency is that, just as parents, siblings and other kin
are social sources of reinforcement and punishment for the young child,
the child plays a similar role for other family members. Consider, for example, our antisocial parent who is hostile, coercive and rejecting toward
the child, as well as toward other family members, and who has few
childrearing skills. The parent does not carefully monitor or provide appropriate consequences for the child's behavior. The parent's prototypical
response to misbehavior will likely involve angry threats or harsh punishment meted out in an inconsistent fashion. In these circumstances, we would
predict that the child will emulate the parent's style by attempting to control the parent's behavior through aggressive actions. Consistent with this
thesis, Snyder and Patterson (in press) found that mothers and young aggressive children both negatively reinforced one another's aversive behaviors and also reciprocated one another's aggressivity.

In our truly antisocial family, with multiple relationships involving
similar dynamics, the young child rapidly develops an interactional style
that is unpleasant for other family members, but there is no realization
within the family about the basis for this outcome (Conger et al. 1994).
That is, through all the yelling and disagreement, parents do not realize
that the anger directed toward them by the child is, in large part, a function of their own hostile behaviors coupled with their failure to provide
appropriate and consistent contingencies for the prosocial and antisocial
behavior of their child.

According to a matching perspective, a child who is or becomes particularly difficult to socialize will be a source of punishment for a parent

or for other family members. Oftentimes, it is the disadvantaged and otherwise challenged parent who is likely to face the difficulty of a hard-to-control youngster (Moffitt 1993). The matching equation would predict that the response contingencies provided by a troubled child will, over time, lead to withdrawal of parental time, childrearing effort, and attention. If nothing the parent does copes effectively with the situation, and especially if the parent does not have the skills needed to deal with a difficult child, the Matching Law suggests that over the years the parent should elect to spend relatively more time and effort in more rewarding and less punishing relationships and activities.

In a dysfunctional family, then, a child's behavioral problems add to the ongoing tensions and conflicts, thus producing further deterioration in parental skills and childrearing activities (see Patterson et al. 1992). The child's own behavior exacerbates and adds to an antisocial family system. These processes are matters of degree, of course, and should escalate into disaster only in the most extreme situations. From a research perspective, we know very little about how these processes of animosity, rejection, and possible disengagement occur. Research is needed to determine how these contingent, reciprocal processes develop across time, and, in the worst situations, lead to abdication of the parental role or to high levels of violence or aggression in multiple family relationships. We also need additional research on the means by which these reciprocal influences within the family translate into specific types of interactions with the larger community.

From family to peer, school, and community relations. Turning again to the child from a highly antisocial family environment, this youngster will likely enter school and begin to interact with peers with a well-developed repertoire of oppositional behaviors and few prosocial skills. Once outside the home environment, the child has an increasingly broad selection of possible interactional contexts (see figure 2.1). The primary opportunities for social involvement will be with peers, at school, or on the street.

As noted earlier, the matching perspective proposes that the child will invest time and effort in those environments that provide the greatest benefits and generate the fewest costs. For a poorly skilled, conduct problem child from an antisocial family, school will likely be a punitive experience with little chance for academic success and a high probability of disapproval from teachers. School personnel, just like parents, are likely to find interactions with an antisocial child to be extremely aversive, and we would expect that they are more likely to invest time and effort in more rewarding children. Even in those situations where teachers make a determined effort to help a troubled youth, highly antisocial parents are unlikely to be cooperative partners in these activities, thus making success even more difficult to achieve.

Just as school success is likely to allude the young, antisocial child, so too does success with conventional peers (Parker and Asher 1993). The evidence also shows, however, that antisocial youngsters will find friends who have characteristics similar to their own, and that these friends will actively reinforce one another's antisocial behaviors (Dishion, Andrews, and Crosby in press; Dishion, Patterson, and Griesler 1994; Simons et al. 1994a). Contrary to the social control notion that youth with conduct problems do not have close social ties, there is now ample evidence that deviant youngsters form friendships that frequently involve approval for delinquent or antisocial behavior (Conger 1980; Dishion et al. in press; Warr and Stafford 1991). Most important and consistent with the Matching Law, peer reinforcement for delinquent acts leads to increases in such behavior across time (Thornberry, Lizotte, Krohn, Farnworth, and Jang 1994).

Again, a matching approach suggests that low levels of positive reinforcement for normative behaviors from home, school, and relations with conventional peers, as well as noxious experiences or failures in those environments, should lead to more time and energy being invested in environments in which social approval is available (see figure 2.1). The setting that appears to increase the probability of social reinforcement for the young antisocial child appears to be the environment provided by deviant peers. Importantly, the individual youth contributes to this environment by providing similar reinforcement to his or her deviant friends in a reciprocal process. Also important, these deviant peer relations appear to develop during childhood, prior to adolescence. Moreover, they foster behavior, such as wandering on the street, that minimizes contact with conventional environments and adult influence and maximizes adventures with similarly antisocial friends (Patterson 1993).

Thus, the matching law perspective suggests a developmental sequence, beginning in the family, whereby childhood oppositional behavior escalates to adolescent crime and delinquency. Children who grow up in a family characterized by hostile sibling interaction and inept parenting suffer serious social skill deficits. They are aggressive and defiant in their interactions with others, which causes them to be rejected by conventional peers. These socially rejected youth are attracted to each other and form a deviant peer group. This deviant peer group provides a training ground for learning to commit criminal acts (see Thornberry, Krohn, Lizotte, and Chard-Wierschem 1993). Ultimately, this developmental sequence influences rates of delinquent behavior at the community level. Thus, we propose that community context affects individual development, which, in a reciprocal process, influences the quality of community life. As noted in the introduction, however, some researchers have proposed that there are important qualitative distinctions between different types of delinquents and their related life-course trajectories. How does the matching model deal with these possible developmental differences and their proposed influence on family and community life?

Differences in Developmental Trajectories of Delinquency

The developmental sequence we have proposed describes the life-course trajectories of persons classified by Patterson and his colleagues (1992) as "early starters" and by Moffitt (1993) as "life-course-persistent." These individuals represent the small percentage of an age cohort who show early and continued involvement in antisocial behavior. They display conduct problems during childhood, chronic delinquency during adolescence, and unstable employment, relationship difficulties, and criminal behavior as young adults (Farrington and West 1990; Sampson and Laub 1993). This small group of individuals is responsible for over half of the crime and delinquency, and for the most serious delinquent acts, committed by their age cohort (Farrington, Ohlin, and Wilson 1986; Loeber and Le Blanc 1990).

Whereas a small percentage of a cohort demonstrates childhood conduct problems and persistent antisocial behavior, the majority of individuals who become antisocial do so during adolescence (Elliott et al. 1989; Moffitt 1993). Patterson et al. (1992) refer to these newcomers to deviant behavior as "late starters." Late starters experiment with delinquent acts during mid to late adolescence when such rebellious behavior is quite prevalent and tend to discontinue their delinquency within a short period of time. They are at low risk for adult crime. Indeed, Moffitt (1993) refers to such individuals as "adolescent-limited" delinquents.

Further, she maintains that life-course-persistent and adolescent-limited delinquents are "two qualitatively different categories of individuals, each in need of its own distinct theoretical explanation" (674). She goes on to posit that adolescent-limited delinquents are youths who use antisocial behavior as a means of demonstrating their independence and maturity, whereas life-course-persistent delinquents suffer from neuropsychological problems that interact with their criminogenic environment. Although she uses reinforcement contingencies to explain the behavior of adolescent-limited delinquents, Moffitt maintains that these principles have limited utility in understanding the actions of the psychologically troubled life-course- persistent delinquents.

In contrast, we take the view that differential reinforcement and punishment, as proposed by the matching law, largely accounts for the behavior of both groups. We expect that early starters (life-course-persistent deviants) have been exposed to a more disadvantaged family environment than late starters (adolescent-limited deviants). As a consequence, they suffer from the early onset of social skill deficiencies, school failures, and rejection by conventional peers. These aversive conditions result in these individuals being attracted to and spending much of their time with other antisocial youths. The number of such peers is apt to be plentiful in neighborhoods where there are many disadvantaged families. These antisocial youngsters will tend to reinforce and amplify each other's antisocial tendencies.

Compared to early starters, we propose that late starters are likely to come from more adequate families, possess more ample social skills, perform better in school, and form relationships with more conventional peers (Simons, Wu, Conger, and Lorenz 1994a). Their short-term involvement with delinquent behavior is initiated and maintained by its reinforcing consequences such as adventure, independence, access to the prerogatives of adulthood, and reinforcement from peers for these risky behaviors. With the transition to early adulthood, late starters have more of the personal skills and resources necessary to assume rewarding involvement in the world of work, marriage, and parenthood. Early starters, on the other hand, have difficulty assuming conventional adult roles. The cumulative disadvantage of growing up in a dysfunctional family, early and continuing academic failure, and extensive interaction with deviant peers leaves them with few of the skills necessary for rewarding participation in adult roles.

For these reasons, the behavioral matching perspective suggests that the behavior of both early and late starters is a function of the alternative rewards and costs associated with their social environment. Discrepancies in the life-course trajectories of the two groups is explained largely in terms of differences in the level of disadvantage experienced by the two sets of youngsters. We expect that the majority of early starters come from more troubled families and are more likely to live in neighborhoods with inadequate schools and a relatively high density of deviant peers. In sum, we propose that differences in the degree of social disadvantage, as opposed to differences in personal constitution, largely account for individual differences in the time of onset, chronicity, and severity of delinquent activities.

Families and Youth in Community Context

Figure 2.3 summarizes the hypothesized reciprocal processes among families, peers, school, community, and individual youth. As shown in the figure, an antisocial family, as we have defined it, increases risk for producing an antisocial child who further contributes to tensions and disruptions in the family. The child's troublesome behaviors create difficulties for teachers and other school personnel who, much like parents, will withdraw from investing time and effort in the child. Delinquent acts by this youth will also contribute to the aggregate rate for such problems in the community. The antisocial parent is unlikely to work cooperatively with school personnel, or to contribute to general community well-being, leading to reciprocal disengagement between these two socializing influences. Moreover, antisocial parents do not protect the child from association with deviant peers and those associations feed back to create even greater family disruption. The end result of this process is that antisocial peers and our troubled youth tend to come together as mutual sources of companionship and approval that reinforces both deviant behavior and the avoidance of conventional influences.

An especially important aspect of the model in figure 2.3 is the proposed reciprocal link between peers, antisocial youth, and their school/ community. In high-crime rate areas, which are usually economically disadvantaged, we would expect relatively low investment in education and large numbers of antisocial youth. School failures place youth in the community at even higher risk for involvement in deviant activities, and

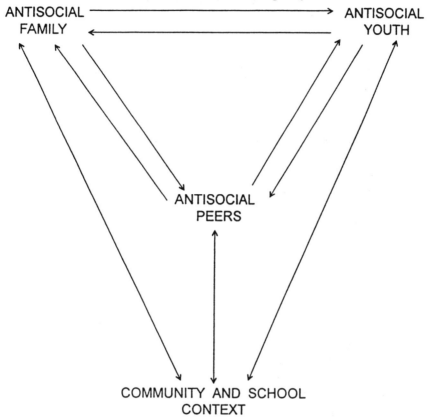

ANTISOCIAL   →   ANTISOCIAL
FAMILY   ←   YOUTH

ANTISOCIAL
PEERS

COMMUNITY AND SCHOOL
CONTEXT

troublesome behavior by children and teenagers makes even harder the task of providing an effective educational experience. In addition, community problems, such as the lack of coordinated social control efforts by adults (Sampson and Groves 1989), are associated with high-crime rates and, presumably, with the number of antisocial families in the community.

The reciprocal relations depicted in figure 2.3 bring us back to the notion of environmental contingencies provided by a variety of social settings or institutions. Just as in family relations, if the child or teenager is exposed to multiple social influences that fail to constrain antisocial behavior and that also fail to reinforce and help develop conventional skills and competencies, the youngster will be at high risk for becoming a serious delinquent. School, peers, and the broader community become part of this matrix of influences. But as figure 2.3 illustrates, other elements of the matrix are also reciprocally interrelated.

Family behaviors and priorities affect the quality of community and school functioning as well as the reverse. For example, communities that provide little support, employment opportunities, or safety for families place exceptional demands on parents as caregivers (Conger and Elder 1994; Sampson and Laub 1993; Sampson and Groves 1989). The emphasis in a matching perspective on multiple environmental influences leads to a research agenda aimed at understanding the effects of these different social settings on the developing individual as well as the individual's role in influencing the larger community context. These difficult research questions regarding individual and community reciprocity remain to be addressed (Patterson 1993), but we believe they are central both for the development of more adequate criminological theory and for the construction of programs that can actually reduce rates of antisocial and delinquent behavior.

Discussion

We have proposed that an adequate theory of antisocial and delinquent behavior must be consistent with six contemporary themes that have emerged from recent studies of juvenile and early adult misconduct. Such a theory must address the finding that serious criminal acts during the teenage years typically evolve from earlier, relatively minor infractions. Moreover, early crime and delinquency appear to be part of a broader spectrum of risky, impulsive behaviors many of which are not illegal.

These correlative acts likely begin as defiant, oppositional, or aggressive behaviors even during the preschool years. The early emergence of such activities, which have proven to be predictive of later conduct problems, has refocused attention on family processes that may help to account both for their initial occurrence and for their maintenance across time. The last two contemporary themes note that childhood problem behaviors reciprocally influence family functioning and that the behaviors of individual family members are reciprocally interrelated with events and conditions in the broader community.

The Matching Law and Environmental Contingencies

On several grounds, we have argued that the general principles of behavior represented by the Matching Law provide an heuristic theoretical frame for understanding the phenomena described by these six general themes. The matching equations state that people will allocate time and effort in proportion to the benefits and costs associated with specific environments and activities. Especially important, we believe, is the time allocation dimension of behavioral matching.

Several theorists (e.g., Gottfredson and Hirschi 1990; Sampson and Laub 1993) have noted that delinquent acts, in large part, appear to be a function of being in places or situations that maximize opportunity for deviant activities. As illustrated in figure 2.1, the Matching Law proposes that high levels of punishment or low levels of reinforcement in conventional settings, such as family or school, will increase the relative reinforcement value associated with time on the streets or with association with age-mates who may be as interested in thrills as in the pursuit of long-term conventional goals. Thus, a matching approach helps to account for the allocation of time to environments that provide significant opportunity for misbehavior outside the purview of adults.

Also important, predictions involving the Matching Law are testable. We have identified specific dimensions of reinforcement and punishment, such as social approval or violent acts, that can be used to operationalize the central concepts involving costs and benefits. These indices of reinforcement and punishment can be used to measure the behavioral contingencies present in the proximate social settings identified in figure 2.1 and hypothesized to encompass the primary sources of behavioral influence for children and adolescents.

Finally, the behavioral matching approach clearly links both conventional and antisocial behaviors to the same general principles of behavior. Unlike many previous theoretical perspectives, we have not resorted to special constitutional factors to explain why some people fail to respond as we think they should to principles of pain and pleasure. We note that conventional activities for relatively prosocial children and adolescents likely result in relatively immediate and continuing reinforcement, consistent with the maintenance of such behaviors as illustrated in figure 2.1. Especially important, when these generally conventional youths experiment with antisocial behaviors during their teenage years, their history of success in conventional environments gives them the skills needed to transition out of such activities and into a lifestyle consistent with the normative demands of early adulthood.

Individual Differences in Development

We have also noted that a matching perspective is consistent with a life-course developmental perspective. The contingencies of reinforcement and punishment change in accordance with societal expectations regarding appropriate behavior at different ages and life stages. Moreover, according to our theory, early family experience, which may foster oppositional behaviors and fail to develop needed conventional skills, significantly influences success or failure in academic achievement or social relations during the elementary school years. As noted, the empirical evidence shows that the aggressive young child tends to select into friendships with similar peers. According to the matching perspective as illustrated in figure 2.1, these peers will be attractive to the troubled child inasmuch as they are the people most likely to reinforce oppositional behaviors and antisocial tendencies. Thus, individual differences in conduct problems can be linked directly to individual histories of reinforcement and punishment.

In addition, we have argued that differences in emotions, cognitions, and even biological functioning, may be associated with social histories. Punitive experiences, for example, tend to elicit both angry and depressed feelings. In addition, a harsh, punitive home environment may lead to the reasonable expectation of hostile intent on the part of adults and peers outside the home. And the same social disadvantages that may lead to a highly stressed and irritable parent may be associated with inadequate prenatal and postnatal care with the attendant risks for limitations in adequate biological development. These possible linkages between early experience and emotional, cognitive, and biological functioning suggest important mediational processes in relation to later behavior. Central to the argument, however, is the view that individual differences in cognitions, emotions, and biological functioning may be as much a product of environmental contingencies as conventional or antisocial behaviors.

Nevertheless, ours is not a "blank slate" perspective. Sufficient evidence exists to presume that not all children are born with equivalent temperaments or dispositions. Such findings suggest that some parents will have a more difficult socialization task than others. Despite such childhood differences, however, there is no present evidence to suggest that principles of reinforcement and punishment will not play a role in the lives of even difficult children. Ultimately, of course, a rich area of study will be the investigation of statistical interactions between early dispositions and contingencies of multiple sources of reinforcement and punishment in the prediction of antisocial behaviors.

Reciprocity within and Across Social Contexts

Perhaps the most significant contribution of a matching perspective is its illumination of reciprocal processes in social relations and conditions that operate for both children and adults. Within the family, failures in socialization associated with an aggressive, oppositional child will be extremely punishing for parents, who may withdraw from the youth, electing to spend time and effort in relatively more reinforcing activities. A similar scenario may occur with teachers and conventional peers. Across time, the unruly child creates contingencies for conventional others that discourage their attempts to be involved with him or her.

Parents and children are also significantly influenced by contingencies within the larger social environment. Parents without adequate employment who live in high-crime rate areas with poorly funded schools have an extremely difficult task in raising their children. When they fail, their children add to the aggregate-level problems in the community. And yet, even in poor circumstances, when adults come together to enhance social control and educational efforts at the community level, the matching model predicts that neighborhood rates of delinquent acts should decline. Ultimately, the most significant contribution of a matching law approach may involve the implications it has for understanding the reciprocal interplay among micro and macrosocial contexts important for the lives of children and adolescents.

References

Akers, R. L. 1994. *Criminological Theories: Introduction and Evaluation*. Los Angeles, CA: Roxbury Publishing.

Bandura, A. 1977. *Social Learning Theory*. Englewood Cliffs, NJ: Prentice-Hall.

Berkowitz, L. 1989. "Frustration-aggression Hypothesis: Examination and Reformulation." *Psychological Bulletin* 106: 59–73.

Bolger, N., A. DeLongis, R. Kessler, and E. Schilling. 1989. "Effects of Daily Stress on Negative Mood." *Journal of Personality and Social Psychology* 57: 808–18.

Cairns, R. B. 1991. "Multiple Metaphors for a Singular Idea." *Developmental Psychology* 27: 23–26.

Cairns, R. B., and B. D. Cairns. 1991. "Social Cognition and Social Networks: A Developmental Perspective." In *The Development and Treatment of Childhood Aggression*, ed. D. J. Pepler and K. H. Rubi n, 249–85. Hillsdale, NJ: Erlbaum.

Conger, R. D. 1976. "Social Control and Social Learning Models of Delinquent Behavior: A Synthesis." *Criminology* 14: 17–40.

———. 1980. "Juvenile Delinquency: Behavior Restraint or Behavior Facilitation?" In *Theory and Fact in Contemporary Criminology*, ed. T. Hirschi and M. Gottfredson, 131–42. Beverly Hills, CA: Sage.

Conger, R. D., K. J. Conger, G. H. Elder, Jr., F. Lorenz, R. Simons, and L. Whitbeck. 1992. "A Family Process Model of Economic Hardship and Adjustment of Early Adolescent Boys." *Child Development* 63: 526–41.

———. 1993. "Family Economic Stress and Adjustment of Early Adolescent Girls." *Developmental Psychology* 29: 206–19.

Conger, R. D., and G. H. Elder, Jr. 1994. *Families in Troubled Tmes: Adapting to Change in Rural America*. Hawthorne, NY: Aldine Gruyter.

Conger, R. D., X. Ge, G. H. Elder, Jr., F. O. Lorenz, and R. L. Simons. 1994. "Economic Stress, Coercive Family Process, and Developmental Problems of Adolescents." Child Development 65: 541–61.

Conger, R. D., and P. Killeen. 1974. "Use of Concurrent Operants in Small Group Research: A Demonstration." *Pacific Sociological Review* 17: 399–416.

Conger, R. D., G. R. Patterson, and X. Ge. 1995. "It Takes Two to Replicate: A Mediational Model for the Impact of Parents' Stress on Adolescent Adjustment." *Child Development*, 66, 80–97.

Conger, R. D., and M. A. Rueter. In press. "Siblings, Parents, & Peers: A Longitudinal Study of Social Influences in Adolescent Risk for Alcohol Use and Abuse." In *Sibling Relationships: Their Causes and Consequences.*, ed. G. Brody. Norwood, NJ: Ablex Publishing.

Conger, R. D., M. A. Rueter, and J. J. Conger. 1994. "The Family Context of Adolescent Vulnerability and Resilience to Alcohol Use and Abuse." *Sociological Studies of Children*, 6, 55–86.

Crick, N. R., and K. A. Dodge. 1994. "A Review and Reformulation of Social Information-processing Mechanisms in Children's Social Adjustment." *Psychological Bulletin* 115: 74–101.

Dishion, T. J., D. W. Andrews, and L. Crosby. In press. "Antisocial Boys and their Friends in Early Adolescence: Relationship Characteristics, Quality, and Interactional Process." *Child Development.*.

Dishion, T. J., G. R. Patterson, P. C. Griesler.1994. "Peer Adaptations in the Development of Antisocial Behavior: A Confluence Model." In *Aggressive Behavior: Current Perspectives*, ed. L. R. Huesmann, 61–95. New York: Plenum Press.

Downey, G., and J. C. Coyne. 1990. "Children of Depressed Parents: An Integrative Review." *Psychological Bulletin* 108: 50–76.

Egeland, B., E. Carlson, and L. A. Sroufe. 1993. "Resilience as Process." *Development and Psychopathology* 5: 517–28.

Elder, G. H. Jr. 1992. "Life course." In *Encyclopedia of Sociology*, ed. E. Borgatta and M. Borgatta, 1120–30. New York: Macmillan.

Elder, G. H., Jr., and A. Caspi. 1988. "Economic Stress in Lives: Developmental Perspectives." *Journal of Social Issues* 44: 25–45.

Elliott, D. S., D. Huizinga, and S. Menard. 1989. *Multiple Problem Youth: Delinquency, Substance Use, and Mental Health Problems.* New York: Springer-Verlag.

Farrington, D. P., L. E. Ohlin, and J. Q. Wilson. 1986. *Understanding and Controlling Crime: Toward a New Research Strategy.* New York: Springer-Verlag.

Farrington, D. P., and D. J. West. 1990. "The Cambridge Study of Delinquent Development: A Long-term Follow-up of 411 London Males." In *Kriminalitat*, ed. H. J. Kerner and G. Kaiser, 117–38. New York: Springer-Verlag.

Feldman, S. S., and D. A. Weinberger. 1994. "Self-restraint as a Mediator of Family Influences on Boys' Delinquent Behavior: A Longitudinal Study." *Child Development* 65: 195–211.

Gottfredson, M. R., and T. Hirschi. 1990. *A General Theory of Crime.* Stanford, CA: Stanford University Press.

Hamblin, R. L. 1977. "Behavior and Reinforcement: A Generalization of the Matching Law." In *Behavioral Theory in Sociology: Essays in Honor of George C. Homans*, ed. R. L. Hamblin and J. J. Kunkel, 469–502. New Brunswick, N.J.: Transaction Books.

Herrnstein, R. J. 1961. "Relative and Absolute Strength of Response as a Function of Frequency of Reinforcement." *Journal of the Experimental Analysis of Behavior* 4: 267–72.

Hirschi, T. 1969. *Causes of Delinquency.* Berkeley, CA: University of California Press.

Iowa Public Television. 1994. *Surviving the Odds: To Be a Young, Black Male in America.* 8:00–9:00 p.m., April 19.

Kellam, S. G. 1990. "Developmental Epidemiological Framework for Family Research on Depression and Aggression." In *Depression and Aggression in Family Interaction*, ed. G. R. Patterson, 11–48. Hillsdale, NJ: Erlbaum.

Lauritsen, J. L. 1993. "Sibling Resemblance in Juvenile Delinquency: Findings from the National Youth Survey." *Criminology* 31: 387–409.

Loeber, R., and M. Le Blanc. 1990. "Toward a Developmental Criminology." In *Crime and Justice*, ed. M. Tonry and N. Morris, Vol. 12, 375–473. Chicago: University of Chicago Press.

Loeber, R., and M. Stouthamer-Loeber. 1986. "Family Factors as Correlates and Predictors of Juvenile Conduct Problems and Delinquency." In *Crime and Justice*, vol. 7, ed. M. Tonry and N. Morris Chicago: University of Chicago Press.

Lytton, H. 1990. "Child and Parent Effects in Boys' Conduct Disorder: A Reinterpretation." *Developmental Psychology* 26: 683–97.

McDowell, J. J. 1988. "Matching Theory in Natural Human Environment." *The Behavior Analyst* 11: 95–109.

———. 1989. "Two Modern Developments in Matching Theory." *The Behavior Analyst* 12: 153–66.

Melby, J. N., R. D. Conger, K. J. Conger, and F. O. Lorenz. 1993. "Effects of Parental Behavior on Tobacco Use by Young Adolescent Males." *Journal of Marriage and the Family* 55: 439–54.

Moffitt, T. E. 1993. "Adolescence-Limited and Life-course-persistent Antisocial Behavior: A Developmental Taxonomy." *Psychological Review* 100: 674–701.

Parker, J. G., and S. R. Asher. 1993. "Friendships and Friendship Quality in Middle Childhood: Links with Peer Group Acceptance and Feelings of Loneliness and Social Dissatisfaction." *Developmental Psychology* 29: 611–21.

Patterson, G. R. 1982. *Coercive Family Process*. Eugene, OR: Castalia Publishing.
———. 1988. "Family Process: Loops, Levels, and Linkages." In *Persons in Context: Developmental Processes* , ed. N. Bolger, A. Caspi, G. Downey, and M. Moorehouse, 114–51. New York: Cambridge University Press.
———. 1993. "Orderly Change in a Stable World: The Antisocial Trait as a Chimera." *Journal of Consulting and Clinical Psychology* 61: 911–19.
Patterson, G. R., J. B. Reid, and T. J. Dishion. 1992. *Antisocial Boys*. Eugene, OR: Castalia Publishing.
Plomin, R., H. M. Chipuer, and J. M. Neiderhiser. 1994. "Behavioral Genetic Evidence for the Importance of Nonshared Environment." In *Separate Social Worllds of Siblings: The Impact of Nonshared Environment on Development.*, ed. E. M. Hetherington, D. Reiss, and R. Plomin. Hillsdale, NJ: Erlbaum.
Plomin, R., and R. Rende. 1991. "Human Behavioral Genetics." In *Annual Review of Psychology* , ed. M. R. Rosenzweig and L. W. Porter, vol. 42, 161–90. Palo Alto, CA: Annual Reviews, Inc.
Richters, J. E., and P. E. Martinez. 1993. "Violent Communities, Family Choices, and Children's Chances: An Algorithm for Improving the Odds." *Development and Psychopathology* 5: 609–27.
Sampson, R. J., and W. B. Groves. 1989. "Community Structure and Crime: Testing Social-disorganization Theory." *American Journal of Sociology* 94: 774–802.
Sampson, R. J., and J. H. Laub. 1993. *Crime in the Making: Pathways and Turning Points through Life*. Cambridge, MA: Harvard University Press.
Simmons, R. G., and D. A. Blyth. 1987. *Moving into Adolescence: The Impact of Pubertal Change and School Context.*. New York: Aldine de Gruyter.
Simons, R. L., W. J. Beaman, R. D. Conger, and W. Chao. 1993. "Childhood Experience, Conceptions of Parenting, and Attitudes of Spouse as Determinants of Parental Behavior." *Journal of Marriage and the Family* 55: 91–106.
Simons, R. L., C. Johnson, and R. D. Conger. In press. "Corporal Punishment Versus Inept Parenting as an Explanation of Adolescent Adjustment." *Journal of Marriage and the Family*.
Simons, R. L., F. O. Lorenz, C. Wu, and R. D. Conger. 1993. "Social Network and Marital Support as Mediators and Moderators of the impact of Economic Pressure on Parenting." *Developmental Psychology* 29: 368–81.
Simons, R. L., L. B. Whitbeck, W. J. Beaman, and R. D. Conger. 1994b. "The Impact of Mother's Parenting, Involvement by Nonresidential Fathers, and Parental Conflict on the Adjustment of Adolescent Children." *Journal of Marriage and the Family* 56: 356–74.
Simons, R. L., C. Wu, R. D. Conger, and F. O. Lorenz. 1994a. "Two Routes to Delinquency: Differences between Early and Late Starters in the Impact of Parenting and Deviant Peers." *Criminology* 32: 247–76.
Snyder, J., and G. R. Patterson. In press. "Individual Differences in Social Aggression: A Test of a Reinforcement Model of Socialization in the Natural Environment." *The Behavior Analyst.*.
Thornberry, T. P. 1987. "Toward an Interactional Theory of Delinquency." *Criminology* 25: 863–91.
Thornberry, T. P., M. D. Krohn, A. J. Lizotte, and D. Chard-Wierschem. 1993. "The Role of Juvenile Gangs in Facilitating Delinquent Behavior." *Journal of Research on Crime and Delinquency* 30: 55–87.
Thornberry, T. P., A. J. Lizotte, M. D. Krohn, M. Farnworth, and S. J. Jang. 1991. "Testing Interactional Theory: An Examination of Reciprocal Causal Relation-

ships among Family, School, and Delinquency." *Journal of Criminal Law and Criminology* 82: 3–35.

———. 1994. "Delinquent Peers, Beliefs, and Delinquent Behavior: A Longitudinal Test of Interactional Theory." *Criminology* 32: 47–83.

Vuchinich, S., L. Bank, and G. R. Patterson. 1992. Parenting, Peers, and the Stability of Antisocial Behavior in Preadolescent Boys. *Developmental Psychology* 28: 510–21.

Warr, M., and M. Stafford. 1991. "The Influence of Delinquent Peers: What They Think or Do?" *Criminology* 29: 851–66.

Werner, E. E. 1993. "Risk, Resilience, and Recovery: Perspectives from the Kauai Longitudinal Study." *Development and Psychopathology* 5: 503–15.

White, N. M., and P. M. Milner. 1992. "The Psychobiology of Reinforcers." In *Annual Review of Psychology*, ed. M. R. Rosenzweig & L. W. Porter, vol. 43, 443–71. Palo Alto, CA: Annual Reviews, Inc.

Wilson, J. Q., and R. J. Herrnstein. 1985. *Crime and Human Nature*. New York: Simon & Schuster.

3

Stability and Change in
Crime over the Life Course:
A Strain Theory Explanation

Robert Agnew

Strain theory does not play a significant role in recent developmental theories of crime. Such theories are instead dominated by biological and psychological theories and, on the sociological side, by control and social learning theories (e.g., Moffitt 1993, chapter 2 in this volume; Patterson 1992; Sampson and Laub 1990, 1992, 1993, chapter 4 in this volume; Thornberry 1987; Tonry et al. 1991; Warr 1993). The neglect of strain theory by developmental theorists is understandable. Strain theory has been heavily criticized in recent years, and one of the leading criticisms contends that the classic strain theories of Merton (1938), Cohen (1955), and Cloward and Ohlin (1960) are unable to explain trends in crime over the life course (Gove 1985; Greenberg 1977; Hirschi 1969; Matza 1964). While such theories may be able to shed light on the increase in crime in early adolescence, they cannot account for the decrease in crime that begins in late adolescence. If anything, these theories would predict an increase in crime during this period since older adolescents should be more aware of their limited prospects for success (Greenberg 1977; also see Simmons and Rosenberg 1971). Paralleling the attack on strain theory by sociologists, psychologists have seriously challenged the "storm and stress" image of adolescence that once dominated the developmental literature (Lerner and Shea 1982; Petersen 1988; Simmons and Blyth 1987: 3–5). This image is very compatible with strain theory, and its demise may also explain the neglect of strain theory by developmental criminologists.

Greenberg (1977) recognized the limitations of classic strain theory, and developed an integrated strain/control theory specifically designed to explain the peak in crime during adolescence. According to Greenberg, adolescents are subject to much strain because (a) they become very concerned with achieving popularity with peers, but often lack the funds necessary to finance their social activities with peers; (b) they develop a strong desire for autonomy, but their autonomy and self-esteem needs are frustrated by the school system; and (c) males are often "prevented from fulfilling male role expectations," particularly by the school system with its expectations of "docility and submission to authority." As a consequence, adolescents often engage in theft, assert their autonomy and masculinity through criminal activity, and vent their hostility against those who frustrate them. As adolescents enter adulthood, however, they become less concerned with popularity with peers, they acquire legitimate sources of funds, and they experience an increase in autonomy—especially as they leave the school system. Greenberg's theory has never received a proper test, although Hirschi and Gottfredson (1983, 1985) argue that certain data cast doubt on it. They point to the fact, for example, that adolescents with legitimate funds are *more* rather than less likely to steal (see Greenberg's, 1985, response). Perhaps as a result, Greenberg's theory has also been neglected by developmental criminologists in recent years.

Strain theory, however, has recently experienced a revival-with new versions of the theory being developed at the social-psychological and macrolevels (Alder and Laufer 1995). This paper argues that certain of the new strain theories have much to say about the relationship between age and crime, and that they should be part of any developmental theory of crime. In particular, these theories point to new sources of stability and change in crime over the life course, and help better organize existing arguments in this area. The focus is on Agnew's (1992) General Strain Theory (GST). This is the most comprehensive social-psychological strain theory and it has received preliminary empirical support (Agnew and White 1992; Paternoster and Mazerolle 1994). Up to this point, the theory has only been used to explain differences *between individuals* in the level of crime. In this paper, the theory is used to explain trends in crime *within individuals* over time (see Loeber and Le Blanc

1990; Farrington 1986). The theory, in particular, will be used to explain two fundamental facts about crime that have emerged out of the developmental research.

First, much evidence suggests that there are a small group of offenders who engage in crime and other antisocial behavior at a high rate over their life course (Farrington 1986; Moffitt 1993; Olweus 1979; Hirschi and Gottfredson 1983; Gottfredson and Hirschi 1990; Sampson and Laub 1992, 1993; Nagin and Land 1993; Wilson and Herrnstein 1985:240-242; Wolfgang et al. 1972, 1987). Moffitt (1993) refers to these individuals as "life-course persistent" offenders. There is some debate over just how stable the behavior of such individuals is, but most researchers agree that it is reasonably stable and that a central task of any developmental theory is to explain this stability. Several theories have been developed to this end, and in this paper it will be argued that the GST can form a useful supplement to these theories (Sampson and Laub 1992, 1993; Patterson 1992; Patterson et al. 1989; Gottfredson and Hirschi 1990; Wilson and Herrnstein 1985; Caspi et al. 1989; Moffitt 1993; Farrington 1986; Thornberry 1987).

Second, data also suggest that there is another, larger group of individuals whose criminal behavior peaks in mid to late adolescence and declines rapidly thereafter (Farrington 1986; Moffitt 1993; Gold and Petronio 1980; Nagin and Land 1993; Sampson and Laub 1992, 1993; Wilson and Herrnstein 1985). Moffitt (1993) refers to these individuals as "adolescent-limited" offenders. Several theories have also been developed to account for their behavior (Moffitt 1993; Sampson and Laub 1992, 1993; Warr 1993; Greenberg 1977; Thornberry 1987), and the GST will likewise be applied to this issue. There are, of course, additional facts regarding the development of crime that require explanation (see Loeber and Le Blanc 1990; Farrington 1986), but these two are perhaps the most fundamental and well researched.

The paper begins with an overview of GST, and then applies the theory to the explanation of stability and change in criminal behavior.

An Overview of General Strain Theory

GST focuses on *negative relationships with others*: "relationships in which others are not treating the individual as he or she would like to be treated" (Agnew 1992: 50). Such negative relationships increase the likelihood that individuals will experience negative affect, with anger being an especially important reaction. This negative affect creates pressure for corrective action, and crime is one possible response. Crime may be a method for alleviating strain, seeking revenge, or managing negative affect (through illicit drug use).

There are three major types of negative relations or strain: relations where others (1) prevent or threaten to prevent you from achieving positively valued goals (such as popularity with peers or autonomy from adults); (2) remove or threaten to remove positively valued stimuli that you possess (e.g., the loss of a romantic partner); or (3) present or threaten to present you with negatively valued stimuli (e.g., insult or physically assault you). Strain researchers have only focused on the first type of negative relationship, and here strain has been measured primarily in terms of the disjunction between aspirations and expectations. The GST argues that this type of strain would be better measured in terms of the disjunctions between (a) expectations and actual outcomes and (b) just/fair outcomes and actual outcomes. According to GST, negative relationships are ultimately defined from the perspective of the individual. That is, the individual determines whether a particular relationship is negative or aversive. At the same time, the GST argues that certain types of relationships are likely to be experienced as aversive by most individuals.[1] Given this fact, it is possible to develop a list of "those objective situations that might reasonably be expected to cause adversity" among individuals (Agnew 1992: 62).[2]

While certain events are likely to be experienced as aversive by most individuals, GST recognizes that individuals sometimes differ in their appraisal of a given event. Some individuals may cognitively interpret (or later reinterpret) negative relations in ways that minimize their adversity. This is a central theme in the stress literature, and the cognitive reappraisal of aversive events is recognized as a major method of coping. GST lists several cognitive coping strategies in this area (Agnew, 1992: 66–69). Individuals prevented from achieving the goal of monetary success, for example, may cope by lowering the amount of money they desire, claiming that money is unimportant, claiming that other goals are more important than money, exaggerating the amount of money they currently have or expect to have in the future, claiming they are better off than others, focusing on the positive benefits of poverty, or claiming that they are to blame for their poverty. GST contains a discussion of those factors that influence the use of such cognitive coping strategies.

GST also recognizes that there are a variety of ways to cope with events that are interpreted as aversive, and that only some of these coping strategies involve crime. Individuals may engage in several types of behavioral coping, paralleling each of the major types of strain or negative relations. They may seek to achieve positively valued goals, protect or retrieve positively valued stimuli, or terminate or escape from negative stimuli. And their actions in these areas may involve conventional or criminal behavior. Individuals may also engage in emotional coping, in which they act directly on the negative emotions that result from adversity. Emotional coping may involve criminal behavior, as in the use of illicit drugs; or conventional behavior, as in the use of exercise or relaxation techniques. GST also discusses those factors that influence the use of criminal versus noncriminal coping strategies.

GST, then, focuses on three sets of variables: (1) the negative relations experienced by the individual; (2) the individual's appraisal of these negative relations—to what extent are they viewed as aversive (and so contribute to negative affect); and (3) the individual's choice of criminal versus noncriminal coping strategies. These variables are next used to explain stability and change in crime over the life course.

Explaining the Stability of Antisocial/Criminal Behavior

Control and Social Learning Explanations of Stability

As indicated, much data indicate that a small group of offenders engage in high rates of antisocial/criminal behavior over the life course. This stability is most often explained in terms of control and learning theories.

Most theorists begin their explanation of stability by pointing to traits that manifest themselves early in the life of the child. Such traits include impulsivity, hyperactivity, attention-deficit, low intelligence, insensitivity, difficult temperament, minimal tolerance for frustration, and composite traits that incorporate many of these individual traits, such as low "self-control" (Gottfredson and Hirschi 1990; Wilson and Herrnstein 1985; Moffitt 1993; Sampson and Laub 1992, 1993; Tonry et al. 1991). These traits are usually said to be a function of both biological factors and the child's early socialization in the family, although theorists differ in the relative importance attached to biology and socialization (e.g., Wilson and Herrnstein 1985; Gottfredson and Hirschi 1990; Moffitt 1993).

Such traits may affect crime directly, by increasing the individual's propensity to engage in crime. Gottfredson and Hirschi (1990) explain this propensity in terms of control theory, arguing that people with the above traits are less able to restrain themselves from acting on their impulses or desires. Wilson and Herrnstein (1985) explain this propensity in terms of learning theory, arguing that people with the above traits will be more likely to find crime reinforcing. Both Gottfredson and Hirschi and Wilson and Herrnstein argue that once these traits are formed, later changes in the social environment are unimportant except to the extent that they affect the opportunity to commit crime in particular situations (see Nagin and Farrington 1992 for an examination of "persistent-heterogeneity" and "state-dependent" theories).

Other theorists disagree, and argue that these traits may also affect crime indirectly through their effect on the social environment. These indirect effects have been explained in terms of control and learning theories. Certain theorists argue that these traits promote crime by reducing social control: individuals with these traits are less likely to form close attachments to conventional others—such as parents, teachers, and spouses; learn prosocial beliefs and behaviors; do well in school; and obtain rewarding jobs (Moffitt 1993; Sampson and Laub 1993; Caspi et al. 1989). Theorists have also suggested that these traits promote crime by increasing the likelihood that the individual's deviant behavior will be reinforced. Individuals with such traits are more likely to associate with deviant peers and, in a manner described by Patterson (1982, 1992), develop interactional patterns with parents that result in the reinforcement of coercive behavior (Caspi et al. 1989; Sampson and Laub 1993). The impact of such traits has not been explicitly explained in terms of strain theory, although Moffitt (1993), Caspi et al. (1989), and others have advanced explanations compatible with strain theory.

Finally, the stability of crime has been explained in terms of the reciprocal relations between delinquency, social control variables, and social learning variables. Thornberry (1987) is the leading advocate of this position. He argues that these variables are involved in an amplifying loop, such that low social control increases the likelihood of association with delinquent peers and of delinquent behavior, which in turn lead to a further reduction in social control. For most adolescents, this amplifying loop is interrupted by the transition to adulthood—which involves the development of new commitments to conventional activity, such as commitments to work and family. Thornberry, however, argues that this does not happen in all cases. If initial levels of social control are very weak, the adolescent may not develop adult commitments capable of interrupting the loop (1987: 882). According to Thornberry, this is most likely to happen in the case of lower-class individuals, who start out with lower levels of social control and greater levels of exposure to delinquent values, delinquent peers, and delinquent behavior. As a result, they are more likely to become involved in delinquency at an early age, setting the amplifying loop described above in motion and leading to extremely high rates of delinquency. Their ties to conventional society may be so weak by late adolescence that they are unable to break out of the loop. Patterson et al. (1989) draw on social learning theory to make a similar argument. Such arguments are not incompatible with the above emphasis on traits conducive to delinquency: these traits may help explain why some individuals get involved in the amplifying loop described by Thornberry and have trouble breaking out of it (see Sampson and Laub 1993; Moffitt 1993; Caspi et al. 1989). Nevertheless, the work of Thornberry and others suggests that some adolescents may develop stable patterns of delinquency even though they do not possess the above mentioned traits.

The General Strain Theory Explanation of Stability

GST explains the stability of criminal behavior in ways that parallel the above explanations. Like the above theories, GST argues that the stability of crime is partly due to traits that develop early in the life of the child. While such traits may affect self/social control and the reinforcement of crime, they are also important for reasons that are uniquely related to strain theory. In particular, such traits increase the likelihood that individuals will (a) experience negative relationships; (b) interpret these relationships as aversive; and (c) react to this adversity with criminal behavior.

The Concept of Aggressiveness. Certain of these traits were mentioned above, such as hyperactivity, attention deficit, impulsivity, insensitivity, minimal tolerance for frustration, and difficult temperament. Minimal tolerance for frustration and difficult temperament are especially relevant to GST. Those with a minimal tolerance for frustration are more likely to experience environmental stimuli as aversive, showing signs of arousal and distress to a wider range of stimuli than others (Garrison and

Earls 1987; Bates 1980; Compas 1987b: 394, 399; Van Der Boom 1989). Individuals with difficult temperament have been described as moody, fussy, irritable, argumentative, stubborn, and noncompliant (Bates 1980; Tonry et al. 1991; Landy and Peters 1992; Moffitt 1993). As indicated, these traits emerge very early in the life course, and data suggest that they may be the product of both biological factors and early socialization experiences in the family—especially harsh and inconsistent discipline. Further, many of these traits are positively correlated with one another and so are often found in the same individual (Bates 1980; Garrison and Earls 1987; Landy and Peters 1992; Van Der Boom 1989; Wolfe et al. 1992).

Other relevant traits emerge later in childhood, with the individual's problem-solving skills being most relevant to GST. Dodge (1986) lists five steps in effective problem solving: (1) search for cues in the environment; (2) interpret these cues; (3) generate possible responses to the situation; (4) consider the possible consequences of the responses; and (5) enact the chosen response. Individuals differ in their ability to engage in these steps, with data suggesting that delinquents are more deficient in problem-solving skills. Delinquents attend to fewer environmental cues and tend to focus on aggressive cues, more often attribute hostile intentions to the benign or ambiguous acts of others, generate fewer alternative solutions, generate more aggressive responses, fail to recognize the negative consequences of delinquent behavior, and more often lack the social skills to enact prosocial responses (Dodge and Feldman 1990; Dodge and Newman 1981; Hollin 1991; Kazdin 1987; Morton 1987; Landy and Peters 1992; Nasby, Hayden, and DePaulo 1980; Pepler et al. 1991; Slaby and Guerra 1988; Wolfe et al. 1992). It is unclear to what extent biological and social factors contribute to problem-solving skills, although the effectiveness of many problem-solving courses suggests that socialization experiences are of major importance (Hollin 1991; Kazdin 1987; Pepler et al. 1991). Nevertheless, it is undoubtedly the case that traits like impulsivity and intelligence bear a strong relationship to problem-solving skills. These traits have a large impact on the effectiveness of the socialization process (see Moffitt 1993), and these traits directly underlie many problem-solving skills. Individuals who are low in intelligence and high in impulsiveness, for example, will obviously have more difficulty generating alternative solutions to a problem and evaluating the consequences of these solutions.

In sum, many individuals have one or more of the following traits: irritability, minimal tolerance for frustration, hyperactivity, attention deficit, impulsivity, insensitivity to others, and deficient problem-solving skills. For the purposes of theoretical argument, we can classify individuals who score high on these traits as high in *aggressiveness.*

The Impact of Aggressiveness on Crime. GST argues that aggressive individuals are likely to engage in high rates of crime over the life course. Aggressiveness has both direct and indirect effects on crime. Individuals with this trait have a greater propensity to engage in crime, and for that reason they are more likely to respond to a given situation with crime. In particular, their irritability and low tolerance for frustration mean that they are more likely to find a given situation aversive. Their greater tendency to blame adversity on others increases the likelihood that they will react with anger. And this anger, in combination with their limited problem-solving skills, increases the likelihood that they will respond with delinquency. This direct impact of aggressiveness is one reason for the stability of crime.

Aggressiveness also has an indirect effect on crime: individuals with this trait are more likely to be treated negatively by others and the negative affect generated by such treatment increases the likelihood of crime. There are three reasons why aggressive individuals are more likely to be treated negatively. The first reason does not have to do with the causal impact of aggressiveness. As described by Moffitt (1993), many of the traits comprising aggressiveness are partly caused by the aversive behavior of parents or by factors that are linked to the aversive behavior of parents. Moffitt, for example, points out that temperamental traits such as activity level and irritability are partly heritable. So children with these traits will tend to have parents who are "impatient and irritable too" (Moffitt 1993). Children with the traits comprising aggressiveness, then, are more likely to be born and raised in aversive family environments—independent of whatever negative reactions their behavior may elicit. Their behavior will remain stable, then, to the extent that their aversive environment remains stable.

Second, aggressive individuals are more likely to provoke negative reactions from others in a given situation—leading to interactional continuity over the life course (see Caspi et al. 1989, on interactional continuity; also see Moffitt 1993; Sampson and Laub 1993). These negative reactions often anger the aggressive individual and thereby increase the likelihood of crime. Numerous researchers have argued that many of the traits comprising aggressiveness are likely to elicit negative responses from others (Moffitt 1993; Bates 1980; Garrison and Earls 1987; Caspi et al. 1989; Coie et al. 1990). Moffitt argues that children with these sorts of traits are more irritating, less satisfying, and more difficult to discipline. As such, they are likely to be at odds with everyone in their environment. The trait of difficult temperament has been shown to have a negative effect on the quality of mother-infant interaction (Van Der Boom 1989). Children with the above sorts of traits are also more likely to be rejected by peers and to experience problems at school (Coie et al. 1990; Vitaro et al. 1990). And as Caspi et al. (1989) demonstrate, they are more likely to have difficulties with their employers and spouses as well. The stability of criminal behavior, then, is also partly explained by the fact that aggressive individuals are likely to provoke negative reactions from others over the life course.

Third, aggressive individuals are also more likely to become involved or enmeshed in adversive social environments (see Caspi et al. 1989, on cumulative continuity; also see Moffitt 1993; Sampson and Laub 1993). Such individuals are more likely to be rejected by conventional peers, and so are more likely to enter deviant peer groups which—among other things—are characterized by higher levels of conflict (Cairns et al. 1988; Giordano et al. 1986). There is also evidence that such individuals are more likely to obtain less desirable jobs and marry less desirable partners (Caspi et al. 1989).[3] These facts also help explain the stability of criminal behavior over the life course.

It is important to emphasize that the above processes not only increase the likelihood of criminal behavior, they also serve to enhance and maintain the trait of aggressiveness (Landy and Peters 1992). The negative reactions of others may lower one's tolerance for adversity by taxing coping resources, may convince the person that their hostile attributions are correct (see Dodge and Newman 1981; Caspi et al. 1989), and may prevent the person from learning prosocial methods of coping with problems (Morton 1991; Patterson 1982, 1992; Moffitt 1993). This feedback process, as Moffitt and others emphasize, plays a central role in explaining the stability of antisocial behavior—for it helps explain the stability of the trait that underlies antisocial behavior.

To summarize, individuals with the trait of aggressiveness are likely to engage in a high rate of crime over the life course for several reasons.

They are more likely to interpret a given situation as aversive and respond to that adversity with antisocial behavior. They are more likely to be born into aversive family environments and so be the recipients of negative behavior for at least the first part of their lives, they are more likely to provoke negative responses from others in a given situation, and they are more likely to become exposed to aversive environments. Such individuals, in short, are more likely to be subject to the three types of strain identified in GST. They are more likely to have trouble achieving positively valued goals, like popularity with peers and monetary success; to lose those things they value, like friends and good jobs; and to be presented with negative stimuli, like verbal and physical abuse from parents, teachers, and peers. Further, all of these processes serve to maintain and enhance the trait of aggressiveness.

It should be noted that these processes are not inevitable. While many of the components of aggressiveness appear to emerge early in life and be reasonably stable, they are not perfectly stable. As the work of Rutter (1985) and Sampson and Laub (1993) demonstrate, many individuals are able to break out of the cycle of delinquency. This is often accomplished with the aid of a supportive individual, and often happens during periods of major role transitions—such as the start of adulthood. The focus of the present discussion, however, is on those forces promoting the stability of antisocial/criminal behavior.

The Urban Underclass and the Stability of Crime. Aggressiveness is seen as the driving force behind the stability of crime in the above discussion: it increases the likelihood of negative treatment by others and of a criminal response to such treatment. Following the lead of Thornberry (1987), however, we may also argue that some individuals may engage in high rates of crime over the life course even though they are not high in aggressiveness. The environment of the urban underclass is conducive to this outcome, since it is not only lower in control and more criminogenic, but more aversive as well. Further, social and cultural forces may increase the sensitivity of the underclass to certain stimuli and increase the likelihood of a criminal response to these stimuli (see Bernard 1990). As a consequence, such individuals may be more likely to turn to delinquency at an early age. This delinquency may then contribute to a further increase in strain. The delinquent acts of the individual, in particular, are likely to anger others and result in negative treatment by such others. Individuals may be negatively treated by the victims of their delinquency, by parents and others responsible for their behavior, and by others who feel threatened by or upset with their behavior—such as neighbors and peers. The delinquency of the individual may also reduce the likelihood of escape from the underclass. So, like Thornberry (1987), we can argue that delinquency has consequences which contribute to further delinquency, setting an amplifying loop in motion. This argument goes beyond Thornberry, however, by arguing that delinquency may increase strain as well as reduce control and lead to association with delinquent peers.

Explaining the Change in Antisocial/Criminal Behavior

While a small group of individuals engage in high rates of crime over the life course, a much larger group of individuals experience an increase in crime during early to mid-adolescence and a decrease beginning in late adolescence. Numerous explanations have been offered for this fact, although control and social learning explanations once again dominate (Tonry et al. 1991; Sampson and Laub 1990; Farrington 1986; Rowe and Tittle 1977; Warr 1993; Gove 1985; Loeber and Le Blanc 1990; Steffensmeier et al. 1989; Patterson 1992; Thornberry 1987). According to control theory, adolescents are more likely to engage in crime because they are less subject to the familial controls that govern the lives of children but are not yet subject to adult controls. In particular, they are not yet subject to the sanctions of the adult justice system, and have not yet formed close attachments to spouses or strong commitments to work. According to social learning theory, adolescents are more likely to engage in crime because of their increased involvement with delinquent peers. The few empirical studies that have been done in this area tend to confirm that variables like association with delinquent peers, moral beliefs, attachment to family, and commitment to work are able to explain a substantial part of the association between age and crime (Kercher 1987; Rowe and Tittle 1977; Warr 1993; Gold and Petronio 1980; Sampson and Laub 1990, 1993). This section argues that GST can supplement the above explanations, pointing to new variables and shedding additional light on the relationship between age and variables like association with delinquent peers.

According to GST, the peak in crime during adolescence can be explained by changes in (a) the extent of negative relations with others; (b) the tendency to interpret such relations as aversive; and (c) the tendency to cope with adversity through delinquency. For reasons already indicated, aggressive individuals and those in the urban underclass may not experience much change in these variables over the life course. Their individual characteristics and social location lead them to experience negative treatment from others at all ages, and to interpret this negative treatment as aversive and react to it with crime (although adolescence may pose some additional problems). The large majority of adolescents, however, do experience significant changes in these variable.

The Extent of Negative Relations

Loss of Positive Stimuli/Presentation of Negative Stimuli. The adolescent enters a larger and more demanding social world, and does so with the desire to establish autonomy from adults and popularity with the peers who dominate this world. These facts increase the likelihood that adolescents will be treated negatively by others.

Individuals leave elementary school during early adolescence and enter larger, more impersonal, and more diverse secondary schools (Simmons and Rosenberg 1971; Petersen and Hamburg 1986; Simmons and Blyth 1987). They typically change teachers and classmates several times during the day in such schools, which not only dramatically increases the number of relationships—but means that such relationships are less likely to be governed by established patterns of interaction and less likely to be supervised by teachers. Adolescents, then, must assume more responsibility for managing their own social relationships. The greater diversity of individuals they interact with also challenges their role taking and other social skills. Adolescents also find that such schools are more demanding than elementary school. They are subject to more rules, given more work, and graded in a more difficult manner (Petersen and Hamburg 1986; Simmons and Blyth 1987). Adolescents have greater access to their own transportation, which increases their ability to move through their neighborhood and city. This further expands the number and diversity of social relationships. Adolescents dramatically increase the extent to which they interact with others away from their parents and other adults. Adolescents, for example, begin to leave the house on their own in the evening and on weekends. Finally, there is an increase in the size of the peer group, contact with the opposite sex, the level of intimacy with same and opposite sex peers, and association with delinquent peers

(Petersen 1987; Petersen and Hamburg 1986; Lempers and Clark-Lempers 1992; Warr 1993). Interaction with such peers comes to be governed by a more subtle set of social cues. In childhood, for example, peer rejection is a function of highly visible negative behaviors. In adolescence, it is a function of more subtle and differentiated behaviors (Coie et al. 1990). Further, status among peers and others becomes increasingly dependent on the adolescent's competence in several spheres—such as athletics and academics (Coie et al. 1990).

Adolescents, in short, experience a dramatic increase in the size and complexity of their social world. These changes are likely to be stressful in and of themselves, particularly given the fact that they often occur in tandem with major biological changes (Chumlea 1982). More important for our purposes, however, is that these changes increase the likelihood that adolescents will be treated negatively by others. There are more people to negatively treat the adolescent. These people are freer to treat the adolescent in a negative manner, since they are less likely to be under the supervision of adults and their ties to the adolescent may be less strong. Interaction with these people is more demanding in all the senses described above, so there is a greater likelihood that interactions will break down in ways that result in negative treatment.[4] Adolescents, for example, may have difficultly meeting the academic demands of teachers or the emotional demands of romantic partners, with the result being poor grades or severed relationships. Particularly noteworthy is the increased association with delinquent peers. Delinquent peers may increase the likelihood of delinquency for a number of reasons, one of which is that there tends to be more conflict with such peers (Cairns et al. 1988; Giordano et al. 1986). Such conflict may anger or provoke the adolescent, thereby leading to crime. Individuals with delinquent peers may also be more likely to be negatively treated by others outside the peer group. Strain theory, then, may explain part of the effect of delinquent peers on crime.[5]

As adolescents become adults, however, their social world begins to narrow again and they have more control over the nature of this world. Their circle of friends becomes smaller, they usually settle with a single romantic partner, and the number of primary and secondary contacts at their job is likely to be smaller than the number at school. They experience less turnover in friends, romantic partners, and coworkers. And they are much less likely to associate with delinquent peers (Warr 1993).

Further, adults usually have more choice over their associates than adolescents. Adults, for example, typically have some choice over where they will live and work, and who they will marry. This is likely to reduce the probability of negative treatment by one's associates. GST, then, would argue that the reduction in crime starting in late adolescence is partly due to the narrowing of one's social world and the greater choice over one's associates. There are fewer people to treat the adult in a negative manner, and these people are less likely to engage in negative behavior.

Certain data support these speculations. Researchers examining adolescent stress have asked adolescents to describe their "personal problems," the "negative events" they have encountered, the situations or events that have "troubled or worried" them, or the "events that irritate, annoy, or upset" them. The answers inevitably focus on interpersonal problems, typically interpersonal problems with parents, siblings, teachers, friends, and romantic partners (Aneshensel and Gore 1991; Brown et al. 1986; Compas 1987a; Compas et al. 1985; Kohn and Milrose 1993; Stark et al. 1989; Spirito et al. 1991; Larson and Asmussen 1991). Their responses, in particular, fall into the three categories of strain described in the GST. Most such responses seem to involve the presentation of negative stimuli by others. Respondents report that others have negatively evaluated them, disciplined or sanctioned them, pressured them, overburdened them, fought with or got into conflicts with them, and rejected them. In many cases, teenagers will specifically cite certain of the changes noted above as the source of their problems. In a study by Aneshensel and Gore (1991), for example, almost all teenagers who had recently moved to a new school mentioned this move as problematic, claiming that it was difficult to adapt to the new teachers and that they faced higher expectations and more difficult grading. Adolescents also frequently speak of the loss of positively valued stimuli, such as friends and romantic partners (Aneshensel and Gore 1991). And adolescents often mention the failure or anticipated failure to achieve positively valued goals (more below).

The key question, of course, is whether adolescents are more likely to experience negative relations with others than are children and adults. This is a difficult question to answer at present because of the lack of representative surveys that employ comprehensive measures of negative relations. Also, when we survey individuals we are obtaining data on their *perceptions* of negative relations, rather than data on the actual number of *objective* negative relations they have experienced. As will be discussed, there is reason to believe that adolescents may be more likely to perceive negative relations than children. Certain data, however, suggest that negative relations may also be more common among adolescents. Grades become worse during adolescence (Petersen 1987, 1988; Petersen and Hamburg 1986), victimization and association with delinquent peers increase, and certain studies suggest that stressful life events may peak during early and middle adolescence—although these studies typically focus on limited age ranges (Coddington 1972; Larson and Asmussen 1991; Lempers and Clark-Lempers 1992; Newcomb et al. 1981; Compas et al. 1985; Larson and Lampman-Petraitis 1989; Larson and Ham 1993). Further, it should be noted that many of these changes can be tied to the larger, more complex social world of adolescents. Victimization, for example, is more likely in the larger, more diverse schools that adolescents attend (Simmons and Blyth 1987).

The few empirical studies that have tried to account for the relationship between age and crime have not examined variables related to GST, although Gold and Petronio (1980) found that the relationship was partly explained by such variables as poor relationships with parents and negative attitudes toward school. Such variables provide a rough index of negative treatment by others, although they also index level of social control (see Agnew 1995). Further, data from Rutter (1985) and Sampson and Laub (1990, 1993) suggest that crime is most likely to decline among those adolescents who enter satisfying relationships as adults. These data are typically interpreted in terms of social control theory: such relationships increase the costs of crime. They may also index the individual's declining level of strain, however. Finally, as noted above, association with delinquent peers explains a large part of the relationship between age and crime. Such association may contribute to crime, in part, because it is related to an increase in interpersonal conflicts.

Goal Blockage in Adolescence. Traditional strain theories focus on the inability of adolescents to achieve their goals, and the increase in delinquency during adolescence has been explained in terms of goal blockage. The early strain theories focused on the inability of adolescents to achieve long-range goals like monetary success and middle-class status. The focus on such long-range goals, however, made it difficult for such theories to explain the decline in crime in late adolescent; partly as a result, recent strain theories have focused on more immediate goals. One of the most prominent theories in this area is that of Greenberg (1977), and this section relies heavily on his work.

Researchers in both sociology and psychology have pointed to a large number of adolescent goals or "developmental tasks" (Simmons and Blyth 1987: 13–17; Jackson and Bosma 1990; Olbrich 1990). The GST has not focused on any specific goals. The GST argues that individuals tend to pursue a variety of goals, usually focusing on those they are best able to achieve. Any study of goal-blockage, then, should ideally begin by determining what goals the individual considers important—rather than by assuming in advance that certain goals are considered important. At the same time, it is worth noting that many recent researchers have focused their attention on two adolescents goals: autonomy from adults and popularity with peers. Such goals are at the center of Greenberg's (1977) strain theory; autonomy is emphasized in Moffitt's (1993) discussion of "adolescent-limited" offenders; and these goals appear in numerous other explanations of delinquency and developmental accounts of adolescence (e.g., Agnew 1984; Compas and Wagner 1991; Smetana et al. 1991). Adolescents are said to focus on such goals for a variety of reasons (Greenberg 1977), and it should be noted that these goals parallel the changing social circumstances of adolescents described above. Adolescents are beginning to leave the restricted world dominated by parents and elementary school teachers, and they are building a new world that centers around peers.

As has often been noted, however, adolescents are systematically denied the autonomy they desire by adults. While adolescents have more freedom than children, their behavior is still subject to much control—with a broad range of behaviors being prohibited or restricted (see Greenberg 1977; Moffitt 1993; Agnew 1984). The regulations encountered in the school system may be especially difficult to deal with since many of these regulations become *more* strict during adolescence (see Greenberg 1977). Parents, however, may also continue to restrict the freedom of adolescents. Data support these arguments, suggesting that adolescents often demand greater autonomy from parents and teachers, and that they frequently clash with these individuals over issues involving autonomy (Smetana et al. 1991; Petersen and Hamburg 1986; Gold and Petronio 1980; Petersen 1988; Siegel 1982). It should be noted that these clashes usually do not involve "raucous, open conflict" over major issues. This "storm and stress" view of adolescence has faded. Rather, they usually involve clashes over more mundane issues; like doing chores, clothing, appearance, schoolwork, the child's activities, interpersonal relations, and rules regarding such things as bedtime and curfew. In short, they involve clashes over the everyday details of life. Such conflicts generate much emotional tension, however, and they are common. Limited data also suggest that they tend to peak in early to mid-adolescence (Smetana et al. 1991). In the only study to examine the relationship between autonomy and delinquency, Agnew (1984) found that adolescents with a strong need for autonomy were higher in delinquency, with part of the effect of autonomy being mediated by a scale measuring anger/frustration. Agnew (1984), Greenberg (1977), Moffitt (1993) and others argue that the denial of autonomy may lead to delinquency for several reasons. Delinquency may be a means of asserting autonomy (e.g., sexual intercourse or disorderly behavior), achieving autonomy (e.g., stealing money to gain financial independence from parents), or venting frustration against those who deny autonomy.

Data also suggest that adolescents are very concerned about their standing with peers (Newman 1982; Compas and Wagner 1991; Coie et al. 1990). The highly competitive nature of adolescent peer groups, however, makes popularity difficult to achieve for many. Standing with peers is dependent on a number of factors, including social skills, appearance, intelligence, athletic ability, and money to buy clothing and finance social activities. Adolescents deficient in these areas may find themselves rejected by others, and they may turn to delinquency for several reasons. They may seek revenge on those who reject them, turn to theft to finance their social activities (see Greenberg 1977; 1985), turn to drug use to alleviate their negative feelings, and turn to delinquent others who are similarly rejected—indirectly increasing their likelihood of delinquency.

When adolescents become adults, they achieve the autonomy that is often denied them as adolescents. Also, popularity with peers becomes less of a concern. Peers are left behind and new sources of self-esteem emerge (Greenberg 1977). The peak in crime during adolescence, then, may be explained in terms of the goals adolescents pursue. This argument, however, assumes that the goals of autonomy and popularity are not replaced by new goals that are just as difficult to achieve. One might argue, for example, that adults shift their focus to the goal of material success and that they often having trouble achieving this goal. Certain theorists have suggested that this does not happen: that adults lower their aspirations and the importance that they attach to goals like material success (see Shover and Thompson 1992; Tonry et al. 1991: 160). In particular, their increased maturity and experience make them more likely to bring their goals in line with reality. There is limited evidence that aspirations do decline with age (Bachman et al. 1978: 16–18), although more research on the relationship between goal-blockage and age is clearly needed. We currently know little about the absolute and relative importance attached to various goals over the life course, and the extent of goal-blockage experienced.[6]

The Increased Tendency to View the Environment as Adversive

The above discussion focuses on the objective social environment of the adolescent, arguing that there is reason to believe that adolescents are more likely to be treated in a negative manner. There is also reason to believe that adolescents are more likely to define such treatment as aversive. There are several reasons for this, the first of which involve cognitive changes, which make adolescents more aware of their environment. Adolescents, in particular, notice and become upset over things that escape the attention of children. Certain of these cognitive changes are described by Larson and Asmussen (1991: 34–37; also see Rodriguez-Tome and Bariaud 1990):

> with abstract thought teenagers become capable of deeper analysis of social situations; they become sensitive to the thoughts of others, the discrepancy between appearance and reality....The more frequent negative experiences among adolescents may not be a result of an objectively harder, harsher world, but of subjective changes that make it *seem* harder. The adolescents as compared to the preadolescents more often explained their negative emotions in terms of a more distal world, including the feelings of others and anticipated future events. This shift resembles a Piagetian shift from a concrete, here-and-now world to a more abstract, hypothetical, and constructed reality.... The cognitive advances of adolescence lead to the fundamental insight that other people are centers of thinking and feeling. This insight opens the floodgate to sources of anger and anxiety that were not previously perceived. They experience pain through empathic identification with others. They suffer the ups and downs associated with new dimensions of strategic social interactions among peers. Sensitivity to what Suzy told Bob about Jeremy may be beyond the capacity of most fifth graders, yet was a preoccupation of some of our ninth graders.

Other cognitive changes also increase the likelihood that adolescents will experience a given environment as aversive. Larson and Reed (1991) argue that the cognitive growth of adolescents leads them to raise "the ante on what they expect from the world...to impose a more penetrating set of standards on the events and the people around them" (1191: 24). Elkind (1967: 1029–1030) argues that the adolescent passes through an egocentric phase, during which time "he assumes that other people are as obsessed with his behavior and appearance as he is himself." The adolescent also believes that his or her emotional experiences are unique. This egocentrism is said to diminish at ages 15–16, but it may intensify the adolescent's emotional reactions to the environment while in existence. The problems that befall the adolescent, for example, are magnified by the belief that others are also aware of and deeply concerned with them. Finally, certain researchers have found evidence suggesting that adolescents are more likely to blame others for the problems they experience (Spirito et al. 1991; Larson and Asmussen 1991; Dodge and Feldman 1990). Such blame increases the likelihood that adolescents will react to their negative treatment with anger. These later two cognitive changes are important because not only do they increase in adolescence, they also decrease in adulthood. So even if adolescents occupy the same objective social environment as children and adults, there is reason to believe that adolescents will experience this environment as more aversive.

A potential illustration of this fact was provided in a study of young people's perceptions of the stratification system by Simmons and Rosenberg (1971) (also see Seligman et al. 1988). Even though they occupied the same position in the stratification system, teenagers were less likely than children to (a) give favorable ratings to jobs; (b) inflate the prestige level of their father's job and the degree of their parent's success in life; (c) overestimate their own social class; and (d) express optimism about their own personal chances of success. Teenagers were also more likely to perceive economic differences among their peers. Differences in cognitive level are one of the likely explanations for these findings.

Adolescents may also be more likely to experience their environment as aversive because they are more likely to experience several negative events at the same time. Researchers have argued that negative emotional reactions are most likely when individuals experience several negative events at once, and limited data support this proposition (Petersen et al. 1991; Simmons and Blyth 1987; Larson and Ham 1993). The dramatic changes associated with puberty, while not detrimental in and of themselves, may also increase the sensitivity of adolescents to environmental change (see Simmons and Blyth 1987; Petersen 1987).

Finally, adolescents may have a more difficult time engaging in the cognitive reinterpretation of negative events. Adolescents live in a very public world. Much of the negative treatment they receive occurs before an audience, such as classmates or peers. Other negative treatment, although occurring in private, may be shared with peers and so become part of the public sphere. The public nature of adolescent life makes cognitive reinterpretation more difficult since reinterpretations are more likely to be challenged by others. Adolescent peers, in fact, may not only challenge attempts at cognitive reinterpretation, they may regularly remind the adolescent of the negative treatment he or she has suffered. Children and adults live in more private worlds, and so may have an easier time engaging in cognitive reinterpretation. Children probably have limited skills at this form of coping, but parents may assist them by telling them that the negative events they have experienced are not as bad as they think. Adults have much experience with this coping technique.

These arguments find support in several studies, which suggest that adolescents experience higher levels of emotional distress than children and adults (Siegel 1982; Gove 1985; Larson and Asmussen 1991; Petersen and Hamburg 1986; Siddique and D'Arcy 1984; Larson and Reed 1993; also see Mirowsky and Ross 1989). One of the best of these studies was carried out by Larson and Lampman-Petraitis (1989; also see Larson and Ham 1993). They equipped preadolescents and early adolescents with electronic pagers, which were signaled at random times during the day. Respondents were then asked to record their feelings. The early adolescents reported more occurrences of anger, hurt, and worry than did the preadolescents. This higher instance of negative affect was due to (a) a higher instance of perceived negative events and (b) the fact that these negative events had a much larger effect on the emotional state of young adolescents than preadolescents (see Larson and Ham1993).

The Increased Tendency to Cope with Adversity through Delinquency

As argued above, adolescents experience a dramatic increase in the size and complexity of their social world and in their tendency to interpret this world as aversive. At the same time, adolescents are poorly equipped to cope with these changes. Data suggest that adolescents are more likely to cope with adversity in "immature" or maladaptive ways, including delinquency (Compas et al. 1988; Aneshensel and Gore 1991; Hoffman et al. 1992; Rook et al. 1991; Seiffge-Krenke 1990). Certain of these studies, in fact, suggest that their coping efforts exacerbate rather than alleviate their levels of stress. There are several reasons for the greater likelihood of delinquent coping among adolescents.

First, adolescents lack experience at coping. This is not, of course, to claim that children have more experience at coping. Children, however, are under the protection of parents—who cope on their behalf and are a major source of social support. Parents are more likely to be aware of the problems of children, since they supervise children more closely and children are more likely than adolescents to share their problems with parents (Seiffge-Krenke 1990). And parents are more likely to cope for and provide support to children, since they view children as more helpless and fragile than adolescents. As a consequence, adolescents not only confront a much larger and more challenging world, but they must assume much more responsibility for coping with this world. Unfortunately, they have little experience at coping. Many of the coping techniques employed by their parents are unavailable to them, because they lack power or the requisite cognitive skills. Other techniques require practice for effective use. Adolescents, however, typically receive little practice because the changed social circumstances associated with adolescence occur abruptly—often with the transition from elementary to middle or high school. Adolescents may receive increased social support from friends, but as indicated below there is reason to doubt the value of such support. Further, a recent study focusing on adults suggests that social support from friends is less effective than that from family (Jackson 1992). Adolescents, then, often lack the experience and support necessary for effective coping—which increases the likelihood of ineffective coping, including delinquent coping.

Second, coping with strain through nondelinquent means often requires power; power to terminate, alleviate or escape from adverse relations. And as Agnew (1985) argues, one of the distinguishing features of adolescents is that they often lack power and are compelled to remain in relationships they find aversive (although see Agnew 1991). Adolescents "are compelled to live with their family in a certain neighborhood; to go to a certain school; and, within limits, to interact with the same group of peers and neighbors" (Agnew 1985: 156). If any of these contexts is aversive, there is often little that the adolescent can do to legally cope. Except under unusual circumstances, adolescents cannot quit school or change teachers; move to a new neighborhood; leave their family; or impose restraints on parents, teachers, and others. The result is an increase in negative affect and a greater likelihood of delinquent coping. Adolescents, in particular, often end up coping through one of the few sources of power available to them—physical strength. Adults, however, usually have access to legal means of coping. Adults, for example, can move to a new neighborhood, quit their job, or get a divorce. Their greater resources also increase their bargaining power when dealing with others who treat them in a negative manner. Children lack power, but parents typically employ their power in behalf of children (see Marwell's 1966 discussion of "power of agency"). Once again, then, we find that adolescents have less access to nondelinquent means of coping.

Third, not only do adolescents lack access to many nondelinquent modes of coping, but they often find themselves in situations that are conducive to delinquent coping. As previously discussed, they are lower in social control—so the costs of delinquent coping are lower. They are much more likely to associate with delinquent peers, who often encourage the use of delinquent coping. Much of their negative treatment occurs before an audience or becomes known to peers, which increases the pressure to engage in a "face-saving" response, which might involve delinquency. And their tendency to blame others for their adversity increases their anger, which makes a delinquent response more likely. In sum, adolescents are both less able and less disposed to cope with their adversity through nondelinquent channels.

The peak in crime during adolescence, then, is due to an increase in negative relations at this time and an increased tendency to interpret such relations as aversive and react with crime. These arguments obviously apply more to some adolescents than to others. Some adolescents, for example, may experience a smaller increase in negative relations because they attend small high schools in homogeneous communities or they possess personality characteristics that limit their interaction with peers. Likewise, some adolescents may be less disposed to respond to negative treatment with crime because they receive much social support from conventional adults or they have less access to delinquent peers (see Moffitt 1993, for a fuller discussion of these and other variables which may limit the delinquency of adolescents).

Summary and Conclusion

General Strain Theory, then, has much to say about stability and change in crime over the life course. Stability is partly explained in terms of the trait of aggressiveness, which increases the likelihood that individuals will be treated negatively by others, interpret such treatment as aversive, and react to such adversity with crime. And stability is partly explained by the fact that some individuals are born into highly aversive environments. They respond with delinquency, which elicits negative reactions from others and reduces the likelihood of escape from the adversive environment. So strain and delinquency become involved in an amplifying loop, and escape for many is difficult.

The increase in delinquency during adolescence is explained by arguing that adolescents enter a larger and more demanding social world, which increases the likelihood of negative treatment by others. Further, certain of the cognitive and social changes associated with adolescence increase the likelihood that adolescents will find such treatment aversive and cope with it through delinquency.

These arguments differ from the control and social learning explanations that dominate the literature in two ways. First, GST points to certain variables not explicitly considered by these other theories. While the trait of aggressiveness includes most of the traits previously considered in the literature, it also focuses attention on certain traits that have not been accorded a central role by developmental criminologists—such as problem-solving skills. Also, the GST focuses attention on a much broader range of negative relations than have been considered by control and learning theories. While control and learning theorists often examine negative relations between juveniles, parents, and—to a lesser extent— teachers; they seldom focus on negative relations with others—including peers and neighbors; and they rarely examine the broad range of negative life events and life hassles that are central to GST. Further, GST also considers a range of cognitive and social variables that affect the likelihood that social relations will be interpreted as aversive and that aversive relations will be dealt with through delinquency.

Second, GST differs from these other theories in its specification of *intervening processes*. There is some overlap between the independent variables considered by GST, control theory, and social learning theory. All three theories, for example, focus on traits like difficult temperament. In particular, there is much overlap between the traits of aggressiveness and low self-control (see Agnew 1995). Likewise, all three theories focus on negative relations between parents and children, including the use of harsh and inconsistent discipline by parents. The theories differ dramatically, however, when it comes to explaining *why* such variables affect crime. For example, control theorists would argue that negative family relations increase delinquency because they reduce attachment to parents, interfere with the internalization of conventional beliefs, and reduce the likelihood that the child will develop a strong attachment to school. Social learning theorists would argue that these negative relations increase delinquency because they expose the child to coercive models, result in the reinforcement of delinquency, implicitly teach the child that coercive behavior is acceptable in certain circumstances, and increase the likelihood of association with delinquent peers. GST theorists, while acknowledging the validity of these arguments, would also argue that negative relations have another effect. Children subject to harsh and inconsistent discipline are being mistreated on a regular basis. Their punishment is excessive and often undeserved. This fact is likely to anger and frustrate these children, and they may turn to delinquency in an effort to cope. Their delinquency may be a means of escaping from or alleviating their adversity (e.g., running away from home, attacking parents) or managing the negative emotions they are experiencing (e.g., drug use). Agnew (1995) provides a fuller description of the differences between the theories in this area, and describes strategies for testing between the different explanations offered by these theories.

The GST, then, supplements control and social learning theories in explaining the continuity and change in antisocial/criminal behavior: GST points to certain variables not considered by these theories and offers an additional explanation for the effect of variables that are considered by these theories.

Notes

1. This argument finds support in recent research from the stress literature. Compas et al. (1985), for example, asked adolescents to list the major and daily events they had experienced over the previous six months and those they anticipated experiencing in the next six months. They found that 86 percent of the events were similarly rated as positive or negative by 70 percent or more of the subjects. Further, studies generally find that having subjects themselves or independent judges rate the positivity or negativity of events (or the disruption caused

by events) has little effect on empirical findings—each are equally predictive of adjustment measures (Johnson 1986; Newcomb et al. 1981). Finally, both sets of ratings highly correlated with one another (Newcomb et al. 1981).

2. Several such lists have been developed in the stress literature and are in wide use, with the lists varying somewhat according to the age of respondents (for lists focusing on children and adolescents, see Coddington 1972; Compas et al. 1985; Compas 1987a; Kohn and Milrose 1993).

3. Such findings parallel those from the stress literature, which indicates that negative life events are as much a consequence as a cause of negative emotional states (Wagner and Compas 1990:401; Larson and Asmussen 1991; Pearlin 1991; Hetherington and Baltes 1988).

4. One might argue that there are also more people to treat the adolescent in a positive manner. Most of the adolescent's interactions, however, are with fellow adolescents who are likewise struggling to master a larger and more complex social world; it is not clear the positive interactions will increase at the same rate as negative interactions. Further, limited data suggest that positive events do not mitigate or condition the impact of negative events: what matters in explaining delinquency is the number of negative events experienced by the adolescent (see Agnew 1992: 63–64).

5. As Cohen (1965) pointed out many years ago, strain theories tend to neglect the social comparison process. The strain that one experiences is to some extent influenced by the experiences of those around you. Adolescents, as indicated, enter a much larger social world. As such, their realm of social comparison expands greatly. It is unclear what sort of impact this has on strain, but certain theorists have hinted that many of the problems of early adolescents may stem from the fact that they suddenly find that they are "small fish in a big pond" (Petersen and Hamburg 1986; Simmons and Blyth 1987). Adolescents who were previously the "top dog" in their elementary school classes, for example, find that they are among the "bottom dogs" when they enter secondary school.

6. In examining such goal-blockage, one should avoid the tendency to measure strain in terms of the disjunction between aspirations (ideal goals) and expectations (expected goals). As indicated in the GST, strain would be better measured in terms of the disjunctions between (a) expected goals and actual achievement, and (b) just/fair goals and actual achievement. The focus on just/fair goals derives from the equity literature, and this literature may bear a special relevance to autonomy. The dissatisfaction of adolescents may stem not so much from the feeling that they are unable to achieve some ideal level of autonomy, but from the feeling that they are being treated inequitably or unfairly by adults. They are physically adults and are often expected to act like adults, but are denied the privileges of adulthood. Further, they are often asked to make large investments in school and other conventional activities, but the rewards of such investments often carry little value for many adolescents. The source of their dissatisfaction, then, may derive from the disjunction between what is just or fair in their view and their actual treatment.

References

Agnew, R. 1984. "Autonomy and Delinquency." *Sociological Perspectives* 27: 219–40.
Agnew, R. 1985. "A Revised Strain Theory of Delinquency." *Social Forces* 64: 151–67.

Agnew, R. 1991. "Adolescent Resources and Delinquency." *Criminology* 28: 535–66.

Agnew, R. 1992. "Foundation for a General Strain Theory of Delinquency." *Criminology* 30: 47–87.

Agnew, R. 1995. "The Contribution of Social-Psychological Strain Theory to the Explanation of Crime and Delinquency." In *Advances in Criminological Theory, The Legacy of Anomie*, vol. 6, ed. F. Alder and W. Laufer. New Brunswick, NJ: Transaction.

Agnew, R. and H. R. White. 1992. "An Empirical Test of General Strain Theory." *Criminology* 30: 475–99.

Alder, F. and W. Laufer. 1995. *Advances in Criminological Theory, The Legacy of Anomie.*, vol. 6. New Brunswick, NJ: Transaction.

Aneshensel, C. S. and S. Gore. 1991. "Development, Stress, and Role Restructuring: Social Transitions of Adolescence." In *The Social Context of Coping*, ed. John Eckenrode, 55–77. New York: Plenum.

Bachman, J. G., P. M. O'Malley, and J. Johnston. 1978. *Youth in Transition. Volume VI: Adolescence to Adulthood–Change and Stability in the Lives of Young Men.* Ann Arbor, MI: Institute for Social Research.

Bates, J. E. 1980. "The Concept of Difficult Temperament." *Merrill-Palmer Quarterly* 26: 299–319.

Bernard, T. J. 1990. "Angry Aggression among the 'Truly Disadvantaged.'" *Criminology* 28: 73–96.

Brown, J. M., J. O'Keefe, S. H. Sanders, and B. Baker. 1986. "Developmental Changes in Children's Cognition to Stressful and Painful Situations." *Journal of Pediatric Psychology* 11: 343–57.

Cairns, R. B., B. D. Cairns, H. J. Neckerman, S. D. Gest, and J. L. Gariepy. 1988. "Social Networks and Aggressive Behavior: Peer Support or Peer Rejection." *Developmental Psychology* 24: 815–23.

Caspi, A., D. J. Bem, and G. H. Elder. 1989. "Continuities and Consequences of Interactional Styles Across the Life Course." *Journal of Personality* 57: 375–406.

Chumlea, W. C. 1982. "Physical Growth in Adolescence." In *Handbook of Developmental Psychology*, ed. B. B. Wolman, 471–85. Englewood Cliffs, NJ: Prentice-Hall.

Cloward, R. A. and L. E. Ohlin. 1960. *Delinquency and Opportunity.* New York: Free Press.

Coddington, R. D. 1972. "The Significance of Etiologic Factors in the Diseases of Children-II. A Study of a Normal Population." *Journal of Psychosomatic Research* 16: 205–13.

Cohen, A. 1955. *Delinquent Boys.* New York: Free Press.

Cohen, A. 1965. "The Sociology of the Deviant Act: Anomie Theory and Beyond." *American Sociological Review* 30: 5–14.

Coie, J. D., K. A. Dodge, and J. B. Kupersmidt. 1990. "Peer Group Behavior and Social Status." In *Peer Rejection in Childhood*, ed. S. R. Asher and J. D. Coie, 17–59. Cambridge: Cambridge University Press.

Compas, B. E. 1987a. "Stress and Life Events During Childhood and Adolescence." *Clinical Psychology Review* 7: 275–302.

Compas, B. E. 1987b. "Coping with Stress During Childhood and Adolescence." *Psychological Bulletin* 101: 393–403.

Compas, B. E., G. E. Davis, and C. J. Forsythe. 1985. "Characteristics of Life Events During Adolescence." *American Journal of Community Psychology* 13: 677–91.

Compas, B.E., V. L. Malcrane, and K. M. Fondacaro. 1988. "Coping with Stressful Events in Older Children and Young Adolescents." *Journal of Consulting and Clinical Psychology* 56: 405–11.

Compas, B. E. and B. M. Wagner. 1991. "Psychosocial Stress during Adolescence: Intrapersonal and Interpersonal Processes." In *Adolescent Stress: Causes and Consequences,* ed. M. E. Colten and S. Gore, 67–85. New York: Aldine De Gruyter.

Dodge, K.A. 1986. *Social Competence in Children.* Chicago: University of Chicago Press.

Dodge, K. A. and E. Feldman. 1990. "Issues in Social Cognition and Sociometric Status." In *Peer Rejection in Childhood,* ed. S. R. Asher and J. D. Coie, 119–55. Cambridge: Cambridge University Press.

Dodge, K. A. and J. P. Newman. 1981. "Biased Decision-Making Processes in Aggressive Boys." *Journal of Abnormal Psychology* 90: 375–79.

Elkind, D. 1967. "Egocentrism in Adolescence." *Child Development* 38:1025–34.

Farrington, D. P. 1986. "Age and Crime." In *Crime and Justice,* vol. 7, ed. M. Tonry and N. Morris, 189–250. Chicago: University of Chicago Press.

Garrison, W. T. and F. J. Earls. 1987. *Temperament and Child Psychopathology.* Newbury Park, CA: Sage.

Giordano, P.G., S. A. Cernkovich, and M. D. Pugh. 1986. "Friendships and Delinquency." *American Journal of Sociology* 91: 1170–1202.

Gold, M. and R. J. Petronio. 1980. "Delinquent Behavior in Adolescence." In *Handbook of Adolescent Psychology,* ed. J. Adelson, 495–535. New York: John Wiley and Sons.

Gottfredson, M. R. and T. Hirschi. 1990. *A General Theory of Crime.* Stanford, CA: Stanford University Press.

Gove, W. R. 1985. "The Effect of Age and Gender on Deviant Behavior: A Biopsychological Perspective." In *Gender and the Life Course,* ed. A. S. Rossie, 115–44. New York: Aldine.

Greenberg, D. F. 1977. "Delinquency and the Age Structure of Society." *Contemporary Crises* 1: 189–223.

Greenberg, D. F. 1985. "Age, Crime, and Social Explanation." *American Journal of Sociology* 91: 1–27.

Hetherington, E. M. and P. B. Baltes. 1988. "Child Psychology and Life-Span Development." In *Child Development in Life-Span Perspective*, ed. E. M. Hetherington, R. M. Lerner, and M. Perlmutter, 1–19. Hillsdale, NJ: Lawrence Erlbaum Associates.

Hirschi, T. 1969. *Causes of Delinquency.* Berkeley, CA: University of California Press.

Hirschi, T. and M. Gottfredson. 1983. "Age and the Explanation of Crime." *American Journal of Sociology* 89: 552–84.

Hirschi, T. and M. Gottfredson. 1985. "Age and Crime, Logic and Scholarship: Comment on Greenberg." *American Journal of Sociology* 91: 22–27.

Hoffman, M. A., R. Levy-Shiff, S. C. Sohlberg, and J. Zarizki. 1992. "The Impact of Stress and Coping: Developmental Changes in the Transition to Adolescence." *Journal of Youth and Adolescence* 21: 451–69.

Hollin, C. R. 1991. "Cognitive Behavioural Modification with Delinquents." In *Clinical Child Psychology,* ed. M. Herbert, 293–308. Chichester: John Wiley.

Jackson, P. B. 1992. "Specifying the Buffering Hypothesis: Support, Strain, and Depression." *Social Psychology Quarterly* 55: 363–78.

Jackson, S. and H. Bosma. 1990. "Coping and Self in Adolescence." In *Coping and Self-Concept in Adolescence,* ed. H. Bosma and S. Jackson, 1–11. Berlin: Springer-Verlag.

Johnson, J. H. 1986. *Life Events as Stressors in Childhood and Adolescence.* Newbury Park, CA: Sage.

Kazdin, A. E. 1987. *Conduct Disorders in Childhood and Adolescence.* Newbury Park, CA: Sage.

Kercher, K. 1987. "Explaining the Relationship Between Age and Crime: The Biological Vs. Sociological Model." Presented at the annual meeting of the American Society of Criminology, Montreal.

Kohn, P. M. and J. A. Milrose. 1993. "The Inventory of High School Students' Recent Life Experiences: A Decontaminated Measure of Adolescents' Hassles." *Journal of Youth and Adolescence* 22: 43–55.

Landy, S. and R. D. Peters. 1992. "Toward an Understanding of a Developmental Paradigm for Aggressive Conduct Problems During the Preschool Years." In *Aggression and Violence Throughout the Life Span,* ed. R. Peters, R. J. McMahon, and V. L. Quinsey, 1–30. Newbury Park, CA: Sage.

Larson, R. and L. Asmussen. 1991. "Anger, Worry, and Hurt in Early Adolescence: An Enlarging World of Negative Emotions." In *Adolescent Stress: Causes and Consequences,* ed. M. E. Colten and S. Gore, 21–41. New York: Aldine De Gruyter.

Larson, R. and M. Ham. 1993. "Stress and 'Stress and Storm' in Early Adolescence: The Relationship of Negative Events with Dysphoric Affect." *Developmental Psychology* 29: 130–40.

Larson, R. and C. Lampman-Petraitis. 1989. "Daily Emotional States as Reported by Children and Adolescents." *Child Development* 60: 1250–60.

Lempers, J. D. and D. S. Clark-Lempers. 1992. "Young, Middle, and Late Adolescents' Comparisons of the Functional Importance of Five Significant Relationships." *Journal of Youth and Adolescence* 21: 53–96.

Lerner, R. M. and J. A. Shea. 1982. "Social Behavior in Adolescence." In *Handbook of Developmental Psychology,* ed. B. B. Wolman, 503–25. Englewood Cliffs, NJ: Prentice-Hall.

Loeber, R. and M. Le Blanc. 1990. "Toward a Developmental Criminology." In *Crime and Justice: A Review of Research,* vol. 12, ed. M. Tonry and N. Morris, 375–473. Chicago: University of Chicago Press.

Marwell, G. 1966. "Adolescent Powerlessness and Delinquent Behavior." *Social Problems* 14: 35–47.

Matza, D. 1964. *Delinquency and Drift.* New York: John Wiley.

Merton, R. 1938. "Social Structure and Anomie." *American Sociological Review* 3: 672–82.

Mirowsky, J. and C. E. Ross. 1989. *Social Causes of Psychological Distress.* New York: Aldine de Gruyter.

Moffitt, T. E. 1993. "Adolescence-Limited and Life-Course Persistent Antisocial Behavior: A Developmental Taxonomy." *Psychological Review* 100: 674–701.

Morton, T. 1987. "Childhood Aggression in the Context of Family Interaction." In *Childhood Aggression and Violence,* edited by D.H. Crowell, I.M. Evans, and C.R. O'Donnell, 117–58. New York: Plenum.

Nagin, D. S. and D. P. Farrington. 1992. "The Onset and Persistence of Offending." *Criminology* 30: 501–23.

Nagin, D.S. and K. C. Land. 1993. "Age, Criminal Careers, and Population Heterogeneity: Specification and Estimation of a Nonparametric, Mixed Poisson Model." *Criminology* 31: 327–62.

Nasby, W., B. Hayden, and B. M. DePaulo. 1980. "Attributional Bias Among Aggressive Boys to Interpret Unambiguous Social Stimuli as Displays of Hostility." *Journal of Abnormal Psychology* 89: 459–68.

Newcomb, M. D., G. J. Huba, and P. M. Bentler. 1981. "A Multidimensional Assessment of Stressful Life Events Among Adolescents: Derivation and Correlates." *Journal of Health and Social Behavior* 22: 400–415.

Newman, P. R. 1982. "The Peer Group." In *Handbook of Developmental Psychology*, ed. B. B. Wolman, 526–36. Englewood Cliffs, NJ: Prentice-Hall.

Olbrich, E. 1990. "Coping and Development." In *Coping and Self-Concept in Adolescence*, ed. H. Bosma and S. Jackson, 35–47. Berlin: Springer-Verlag.

Olweus, D. 1979. "Stability of Aggressive Reaction Patterns in Males: A Review." *Psychological Bulletin* 86: 852–57.

Paternoster, R. and P. Mazerolle. 1994. "An Empirical Test of General Strain Theory." *Journal of Research in Crime and Delinquency* 31: 235–63.

Patterson, G.R. 1982. *Coercive Family Process.* Eugene, OR: Castalia.

Patterson, G. R. 1992. "Developmental Changes in Antisocial Behavior." In *Aggression and Violence Throughout the Life Span*, ed. R. D. Peters, R. J. McMahon, and V. L. Quinsey, 52–82. Newbury Park, CA: Sage.

Patterson, G. R., B. D. DeBaryshe, and E. Ramsey. 1989. "A Developmental Perspective on Antisocial Behavior." *American Psychologist* 44: 329–35.

Pearlin, L. I. 1991. "The Study of Coping: An Overview of Problems and Directions." In *The Social Context of Coping*, ed. J. Eckenrode, 261–76. New York, Plenum.

Pepler, D.J., G. King, and W. Byrd. 1991. "A Social Cognitively Based Social Skills Training Program for Aggressive Children." In *The Development and Treatment of Childhood Aggression*, ed. D. J. Pepler and K. H. Rubin, 361–79. Hillsdale, NJ: Lawrence Erlbaum.

Petersen, A. C. 1987. "The Nature of Biological-Psychosocial Interactions: The Sample Case of Early Adolescence." In *Biological-Psychosocial Interactions in Early Adolescence,* ed. R. M. Lerber and T. T. Foch, 35–61. Hillsdale, NJ: Lawrence Erlbaum.

Petersen, A. C. 1988. "Adolescent Development." *Annual Review of Psychology* 39: 583–607.

Petersen, A. C. and B. A. Hamburg. 1986. "Adolescence: A Developmental Approach to Problems and Psychopathology." *Behavior Therapy* 17: 480–99.

Petersen, A. C., R. E. Kennedy, and P. Sullivan. 1991. "Coping with Adolescence." In *Adolescent Stress: Causes and Consequences*, ed. M. E. Colten and S. Gore, 93–110. New York: Aldine De Gruyter.

Rodriguez-Tome, H. and F. Bariaud. 1990. "Anxiety in Adolescence: Sources and Reactions." In *Coping and Self-Concept in Adolescence*, ed. H. Bosma and S. Jackson, 167–86. Berlin: Springer-Verlag.

Rook, K., D. Dooley, and R. Catalano. 1991. "Age Differences in Workers' Efforts to Cope with Economic Distress." In *The Social Context of Coping,* ed. J. Eckenrode, 79–105. New York: Plenum.

Rowe, A. R. and C. R. Tittle. 1977. "Life Cycle Changes and Criminal Propensity." *Sociological Quarterly* 18: 223–36.

Rutter, M. 1985. "Resilience in the Face of Adversity." *British Journal of Psychiatry* 147: 598–611.

Sampson, R. J. and J. H. Laub. 1990. "Crime and Deviance Over the Life Course: The Salience of Social Bonds." *American Sociological Review* 55: 609–27.

Sampson, R. J. and J. H. Laub. 1992. "Crime and the Life Course." *Annual Review of Sociology* 18: 63–84.

Sampson, R. J. and J. H. Laub. 1993. *Crime in the Making.* Cambridge, MA: Harvard University Press.

Seiffge-Krenke, I. 1990. "Developmental Processes in Self-Concept and Coping Behavior." In *Coping and Self-Concept in Adolescence,* ed. H. Bosma and S. Jackson, 49–68. Berlin: Springer-Verlag.

Seligman, M. E. P., L. P. Kamen, and S. Nolen-Hoeksema. 1988. "Explanatory Style Across the Life Span: Achievement and Health." In *Child Development in Life-Span Perspective,* ed. E. M. Hetherington, R. M. Lerner, and M. Perlmutter, 91–114. Hillsdale, NJ: Lawrence Erlbaum Associates.

Shover, N. and C. Y. Thompson. 1992. "Age, Differential Expectations, and Crime Desistance." *Criminology* 30: 89–104.

Siddique, C. M. and C. D'Arcy. 1984. "Adolescence, Stress, and Psychological Well-Being." *Journal of Youth and Adolescence* 13: 459–73.

Siegel, O. 1982. "Personality Development in Adolescence." In *Handbook of Developmental Psychology*, ed. B. B. Wolman, 537–48. Englewood Cliffs, NJ: Prentice Hall.

Simmons, R.G. and D. A. Blyth. 1987. *Moving into Adolescence.* New York: Aldine De Gruyter.

Simmons, R. G. and M. Rosenberg. 1971. "Functions of Children's Perceptions of the Stratification System." *American Sociological Review* 36: 235–49.

Slaby, R. G. and N. G. Guerra. 1988. "Cognitive Mediators of Aggression in Adolescent Offenders: 1. Assessment." *Developmental Psychology* 24: 580–88.

Smetana, J. G., J. Yau, A. Restrepo, and J. L. Braeges. 1991. "Conflict and Adaptation in Adolescence: Adolescent-Parent Conflict." In *Adolescent Stress: Causes and Consequences*, ed. M. E. Colten and S. Gore, 43–65. New York: Aldine De Gruyter.

Spirito, A., L. J. Stark, N. Grace, and D. Stamoulis. 1991. "Common Problems and Coping Strategies Reported in Childhood and Early Adolescence." *Journal of Youth and Adolescence* 20: 531–44.

Stark, L. J., A. Spirito, C. A. Williams, and D. C. Guevremont. 1989. "Common Problems and Coping Strategies I: Findings with Normal Adolescents." *Journal of Abnormal Child Psychology* 17: 203–21.

Steffensmeier, D. J., E. A. Allan, M. D. Harer, and C. Streifel. 1989. "Age and the Distribution of Crime." *American Journal of Sociology* 94: 803–31.

Thornberry, T.P. 1987. "Toward an Interactional Theory of Delinquency." *Criminology* 25: 863–91.

Tonry, M., L. E. Ohlin, and D. P. Farrington. 1991. *Human Development and Criminal Behavior.* New York: Springer-Verlag.

Van Der Boom, D. C. 1989. "Neonatal Irritability and the Development of Attachment." In *Temperament in Childhood,* ed. G. A. Kohnstamm and J. E. Bates, 299–318. Chichester, England: John Wiley.

Vitaro, F., C. Gagnon, and R. E. Tremblay. 1990. "Predicting Stable Peer Rejection from Kindergarten to Grade One." *Journal of Clinical Child Psychology* 19: 257–64.

Wagner, B. M. and B. E. Compas. 1990. "Gender, Instrumentality, and Expressivity: Moderators of the Relation Between Stress and Psychological Symptoms During Adolescence." *American Journal of Community Psychology* 18: 383–406.

Warr, M. 1993. "Ages, Peers, and Delinquency." *Criminology* 31: 17–40.

Wilson, J. Q. and R. J. Herrnstein. 1985. *Crime and Human Nature.* New York: Touchstone.

Wolfe, D. A., C. Wekerle, and R. McGee. 1992. "Developmental Disparities of Abused Children: Directions for Prevention." In *Aggression and Violence Throughout the*

Life Span, ed. R. D. Peters, R. J. McMahon, and V. L. Quinsey, 31–51. Newbury Park, CA: Sage.

Wolfgang, M., R. Figlio, and T. Sellin. 1972. *Delinquency in a Birth Cohort.* Chicago: University of Chicago Press.

Wolfgang, M., T. P. Thornberry, and R. Figlio. 1987. *From Boy to Man, From Delinquency to Crime.* Chicago: University of Chicago Press.

4

A Life-Course Theory of Cumulative Disadvantage and the Stability of Delinquency

Robert J. Sampson and John H. Laub

Although often lumped together, longitudinal and developmental approaches to crime are not the same. Longitudinal research invokes a methodological stance—collecting and analyzing data on persons (or macrosocial units) over time. Ironically, however, one of the objections to existing longitudinal research has been that it often looks like, or produces results equivalent to, cross-sectional research (Gottfredson and Hirschi 1987). Critics of longitudinal research have a valid point—many studies simply investigate between-individual relationships using a static, invariant conception of human development. For example, showing an "effect" of social class at time one on crime at time two requires a longitudinal design, but substantively such an effect says nothing about within-individual change, dynamic or sequential processes, or whether in fact "time" really matters. Hence longitudinal studies often borrow the tools of cross-sectional analysis but do not inform about how individuals progress through the life course. Perhaps most important, until recently longitudinal research has labored under the trinity of dominant crimino-

We thank Terry Thornberry for helpful comments on a previous draft. This paper stems from an ongoing project using the archives of Sheldon and Eleanor Glueck, and draws in part from our recent book *Crime in the Making: Pathways and Turning Points Through Life*. Financial support from the Russell Sage Foundation (grant #998.958) is gratefully acknowledged.

logical theories—strain, control, and cultural deviance—all of which are inherently static in their original conceptualization. It is little wonder that the mismatch of static theory with longitudinal data has produced unsatisfactory results.

By contrast, developmental approaches are inextricably tied to dynamic concerns and the unfolding of biological, psychological, and social processes through time. Rutter and Rutter (1993) propose an admittedly "fuzzy" but nonetheless useful definition of development as "systematic, organized, intra-individual change that is clearly associated with generally expectable age-related progressions and which is carried forward in some way that has implications for a person's pattern or level of functioning at some later time" (1993: 64). Development is thus focused on systematic change, especially how behaviors set in motion dynamic processes that alter future outcomes.

With respect to crime, Loeber and LeBlanc (1990: 451) argue that "developmental criminology" recognizes both continuity and within-individual changes over time, focusing on "life transitions and developmental covariates...which may mediate the developmental course of offending." This strategy has also been referred to as a "stepping stone approach" where factors are time ordered by age and assessed with respect to outcome variables (see Farrington 1986). A similar orientation can be found in interactional theory (Thornberry 1987), which embraces a developmental approach and asserts that causal influences are reciprocal over the life course.

In this paper, we take seriously the conceptions of time and systematic change implied by a developmental approach. We do so with reference to a particularly vexing problem that has led to much debate in criminology—continuity (or stability) in criminal behavior. As reviewed below, there is evidence that antisocial and criminal behaviors are relatively stable over long periods of the life course. Yet while most criminologists can agree on the basic facts, the implications of this stability are contentious. Namely, the fact of stability can be interpreted from both a developmental and a time-invariant, static perspective. Our purpose is to lay out these competing viewpoints on the issue from the perspective of our recent theoretical framework on age-graded informal social control (Sampson and Laub 1993). We specifically propose that sources of continuity stem in large part from developmental processes that we term "cumulative disadvantage" (Sampson and Laub 1993; Laub and Sampson

1993). The idea of cumulative disadvantage draws on a dynamic conceptualization of social control over the life course, integrated with the one theoretical perspective in criminology that is inherently developmental in nature—labeling theory.

Evidentiary Backdrop

The facts appear straightforward. For some time now research has shown that individual differences in antisocial behavior are relatively stable over time. For example, Olweus's (1979) review of sixteen studies on aggressive behavior revealed "substantial" stability—the correlation between early aggressive behavior and later criminality averaged .68 (1979: 854–55). Loeber (1982) completed a similar review of the extant literature in many disciplines and concluded that a "consensus" has been reached in favor of the stability hypothesis: "children who initially display high rates of antisocial behavior are more likely to persist in this behavior than children who initially show lower rates of antisocial behavior" (1982: 1433). In addition to earlier classic studies (e.g., Glueck and Glueck 1930, 1968; Robins 1966), more recent works documenting stability in delinquent behavior across time include West and Farrington (1977), Bachman et al. (1978), and Wolfgang et al. (1987).

The linkage between childhood delinquency and adult outcomes is also found across domains that go well beyond the legal concept of crime (e.g., excessive drinking, traffic violations, marital conflict or abuse, and harsh discipline of children). Huesmann et al. (1984) report that aggression in childhood was related not just to adult crime but marital conflict, drunk driving, moving violations, and severe punishment of offspring. Other studies reporting a coalescence of delinquent and "deviant" acts over time include Glueck and Glueck (1968), Robins (1966), and West and Farrington (1977). As Caspi and Moffitt (1993: 2) note, continuities in antisocial behavior have also been replicated in nations other than the United States (e.g., Canada, England, Finland, New Zealand, and Sweden) and with multiple methods of assessment (e.g., official records, teacher ratings, parent reports, peer nominations). Taken as a whole, these different studies across time, space, and method yield an impressive generalization that is rare in the social sciences.

To be sure, behavioral stability in criminal conduct is not perfect or inevitable. As we have reviewed elsewhere, there are considerable discontinuities in crime throughout life that must be explained (Sampson and Laub 1992). For example, while studies do show that antisocial behavior in children is one of the best predictors of antisocial behavior in adults, "most antisocial children do not become antisocial as adults" (Gove 1985: 123; see also Robins 1978). Similarly, Cline (1980: 669–670) concludes that there is far more heterogeneity in criminal behavior than previous work has suggested, and that many juvenile offenders do not become career offenders. For these reasons we view intra-individual change and "turning points" as integral to developmental theories of criminal behavior (Laub and Sampson 1993). Nonetheless, we restrict our attention in this article to an explanation of the stability of delinquency from a developmental framework.

The Developmental Status of Criminological Theory

How might criminological theory explain behavioral stability? The simple answer is that the question has been largely ignored by criminologists despite the long-standing evidence. Especially from a sociological framework, criminologists have not paid much attention to the developmental implications of early antisocial behavior and its stability through time and circumstance (Sampson and Laub 1992). This is not surprising, however, since traditional criminological theory is decidedly nondevelopmental in nature. Take, for example, the three dominant perspectives on crime—control, strain, and cultural deviance. Each of these perspectives seeks to explain why some individuals engage in crime and not others—a between-individual mode of inquiry.[1] Thus each tends to assign causal priority to the *level* of competing variables (e.g., degree of attachment to parents vs. delinquent definitions) among individuals, which are then tested for relative effects with cross-sectional designs (see Thornberry 1987 for a similar discussion).

When the evidence on stability has been seriously considered by criminologists, static explanations also predominate (for an overview see Sampson and Laub 1993). These generally involve the interpretation of stability as arising from a "latent trait" that is time invariant (e.g., extroversion, low IQ). But if a trait is time-invariant, do we need to follow persons longitudinally? Gottfredson and Hirschi (1990: 237) answer this very question in the negative and criticize developmental criminology for neglecting its own evidence on the stability of personal characteristics.

Specifically, Gottfredson and Hirschi (1990) interpret stability from the viewpoint of a personality trait—low self-control—that causes crime at all ages. In other words, Gottfredson and Hirschi's theory posits a trait of low self- control that differs among individuals but remains constant over time within a given person. Since within-individual change is excluded from the theory by definition, they view behavioral change as "illusory" or "alleged" (Hirschi and Gottfredson 1993: 51).[2]

The implications for a developmental strategy are profound. As Nagin and Farrington (1992: 501) trace them: "Once relevant time-stable individual differences are established, subsequent individual experiences and circumstances will have no enduring impact on criminal (or noncriminal) trajectories." The time-invariant or static viewpoint argues therefore that stability in crime over the life course is generated by population *heterogeneity* in an underlying criminal propensity that is established early in life and remains stable over time (see also Wilson and Herrnstein 1985). Precisely because individual differences in the propensity to commit crime emerge early and are stable, childhood and adult crime will be positively correlated. It then follows that the correlation between past and future delinquency is not causal but spurious because of population heterogeneity. The hypothesized sources of early propensity cover a number of factors, but in addition to self-control leading candidates in the criminological literature include temperament, IQ, and hyperactivity (Wilson and Herrnstein 1985).

A time-invariant or static interpretation is perhaps understandable when considered along with the larger intellectual history of developmental research. Following what Dannefer (1984) terms the "ontogenetic" model, the dominant view of human development has been one of "maturational unfolding" irrespective of context. That is, the environment is seen as the stage on which life patterns are played out—one that has no real bearing on the structure of development.[3] Hence developmental approaches almost always look to the early childhood years as the shaper of all that follows. In an incisive essay, the psychologist Jerome Kagan (1980: 44) argues that this strategy represents a "faith in connectedness" where notions of stability comport with larger ideas on the universe as a rational order undisturbed by arbitrariness, contingency, and situation. He suggests that the assumption of stability of structures goes back to "the Greek notion that immutable entities lay behind the diversity and cyclicity in nature's rich display" (1980: 45). Kagan even asserts that a widespread faith in connectedness by Western scholars has led developmentalists to be "permissive regarding the validity of supporting facts, and eager for any evidence that maintains the belief" (1980: 44). Like the existentialists who vigorously challenged the notion of continuity of experience, emphasizing instead the freedom of choice to abrogate one's past, Kagan (1980: 53) views the hypothesis of a static, unbroken trail from childhood to adulthood as fundamentally flawed and rooted in philosophical belief rather than scientific fact.

Whatever the epistemological underpinnings, the dominant criminological theories of the last three decades—strain, control, and cultural deviance—have also been treated as largely static in their predictions. This is not to say that they are devoid of developmental *implications* (see especially Thornberry 1987; Loeber and Le Blanc 1990), only that the leading theoretical trio is rooted in "between-individual" rather than temporal thinking. Yet as we shall now see, there is one theoretical tradition, currently in eclipse, that was formed with developmental processes in mind.[4]

Labeling Theory Reconsidered

As Loeber and Le Blanc (1990: 421) have argued, labeling theory is the only criminological theory that is truly developmental in nature because of its explicit emphasis on processes over time. Although labeling theorists have addressed a number of diverse issues, of particular relevance for developmental theories of criminal behavior is the attention drawn to the potentially negative consequences of being labeled for understanding subsequent behavior. For example, Lemert (1951) maintained that societal reactions to primary deviance may create problems of adjustment that foster additional deviance or what he termed "secondary deviance."

In general, labeling theorists have conceptualized this process as the "stigmatizing" and "segregating" effects of social control efforts (Paternoster and Iovanni 1989: 375). As Lemert has explained: Primary deviance is assumed to arise in a wide variety of social, cultural, and psychological contexts, and at best has only marginal implications for the psychic structure of the individual; it does not lead to symbolic reorganization at the level of self-regarding attitudes and social roles. Secondary deviation is deviant behavior, or social roles based upon it, which becomes means of defense, attack, or adaptation to overt and covert problems created by the societal reaction to primary deviation. In effect, the original "causes" of the deviation recede and give way to the central importance of the disapproving, degradational, and isolating reactions of society (Lemert 1972: 48).

Labeling may thus lead to an alteration of one's identity, exclusion from "normal routines" or "conventional opportunities," and increased contact with and support from deviant subgroups. All three, in turn, may lead to further deviance. Contrary to past characterizations of labeling theory, Paternoster and Iovanni emphasize the contingent nature of these developmental processes (1989: 375–381; see also Tittle 1975). Similar to historical sociologists' concerns with contingency and "path dependency" (Aminzade 1992), they stress that "we should not expect labeling effects to be invariant across societal subgroups" (1989: 381). Paternoster and Iovanni also note that the "stigmatizing and exclusionary effects" of labeling "act as intervening variables in the escalation to secondary deviance" (1989: 384).

The role of the criminal justice system in the labeling process is especially important. Garfinkel (1956) describes this process as a "status degradation ceremony." From a developmental perspective, formal degradation ceremonies like those surrounding felony trials are most salient with respect to later behavioral outcomes. For example, successful degradation ceremonies that lead to felony convictions may increase the probability of negative job outcomes in later life. As Becker argues, the designation of "deviant" or "criminal" often becomes a "master status" whereby "the deviant identification becomes the controlling one" (1963: 33–34). The concept of a deviant career thus suggests a stable pattern of deviant behavior that is sustained by the labeling process (Becker 1963: 24–39). In a similar vein, Schur (1971) refers to this process as *role engulfment*.

In a recent review of the empirical research on labeling theory, Paternoster and Iovanni (1989) argue that the "secondary deviance hypothesis" has not been adequately tested. In large part this is because the complexities of labeling theory have not been fully explicated in extant research. In particular, Paternoster and Iovanni (1989: 384) contend that "by failing to consider the requisite intervening effects, the bulk of these studies do not constitute a valid test of labeling theory." From a developmental perspective, it is also notable that the follow-up periods in most tests of labeling have been quite short and rarely include the developmental transition from adolescence to adulthood (but see Farrington et al. 1978). For example, a common scenario has been to test the effects of police contacts or court referrals on future delinquency *within* the juvenile career (see e.g., Thomas and Bishop 1984; Smith and Paternoster 1990).

Recent research by Link (1982; 1987; Link et al. 1989; 1987) on mental health may provide guidance for criminologists interested in alternative conceptualizations of labeling theory compared to those found in criminology (see also Paternoster and Iovanni 1989). Link developed a "modified labeling theory," which like Paternoster and Iovanni, moves beyond simplistic statements about the direct effects of labeling and provides a specification of the intervening mechanisms and developmental process. Building on Scheff's (1966) labeling theory, Link argues that official labeling and subsequent stigmatization generate negative consequences regarding social networks, jobs, and self-esteem in the lives of mental patients (see Link et al. 1989).

The first step in this model is a focus on beliefs about devaluation and discrimination. The key idea is that individuals (patients and nonpatients) internalize societal conceptions and beliefs about mental illness. The result is that "patients' expectations of rejection are an outcome of socialization and the cultural context rather than a pathological state associated with their psychiatric condition" (Link et al. 1989: 403). The second step is official labeling through contact with treatment providers. This step is important because the label applied at the individual level personalizes societal beliefs about devaluation and discrimination towards patients. The third step in Link's model focuses on the patients' responses to their stigmatizing status, including secrecy and withdrawal. The fourth step emphasizes the consequences of the stigma process on patients' lives. Although potentially beneficial, secrecy and withdrawal may also have negative consequences for individual patients by limiting life chances. This effect is consistent with the idea of secondary deviation as developed by Lemert (1951). The fifth and final step in the process is vulnerability to future disorder. As a result of earlier processes, patients may suffer from poor self-esteem, diminished network ties, and experience unemployment (or underemployment) as a result of their own and others' reaction to their label. These deficits increase the risk of further disorder in the future.

Link and his colleagues have demonstrated empirical support for this modified conception of labeling processes (see Link 1982; 1987; Link et al. 1989; 1987). Most important for our purposes is the finding that labeling has negative consequences in the lives of psychiatric patients regarding work status, income, friendships, family relations, and mate selection. Link's program of research steers attention away from static and "deterministic" aspects of labeling and focuses instead on the more subtle—and clearly indirect—consequences of labeling for later behavior. This emphasis is consistent with a developmental, stepping-stone perspective. In fact, Link (1982: 203, n.2) notes that labeling effects are produced "incrementally," and should be thought of as "a series of reinforcing conditions." While it may be the case (as critics of labeling theory have long contended) that the labeling of deviance is initially the result of actual differences in behavior (see e.g., Gove 1980), this fact is not inconsistent with the notion that such labeling may causally influence the later direction of developmental trajectories over the life course.

Despite its obvious affinity to a life course, developmental framework, labeling theory has rarely been viewed from this perspective. For the most part, research on labeling has consisted of cross-sectional studies or panel studies entailing modest follow-up periods *within* rather than *across* developmental phases. With their focus on deviant identity and "psychic change," labeling analysts have also undertheorized the role of social structural constraints. As described more below, structural effects of labeling may emerge through social allocation mechanisms that have nothing to do with a redefinition of the self or other social-psychological processes that operate within the individual. In particular, the structural consequences of labeling during adolescence (e.g., long-term incarceration as a juvenile) on later adult outcomes have not been fully incorporated into extant labeling theory. Although we suspect much more is at work in the form of ideological resistance, these lacunas have no doubt contributed to the received wisdom that labeling theory is "discredited." We think otherwise, and thus turn to an integration of the dynamic aspects of labeling theory with social control theory, and then apply this perspective to findings of stability produced by criminological research. As a backdrop, we first provide a brief overview of the social control portion of our theory.

Extending an Age-Graded Theory of Informal Social Control

The central idea of social control theory—that crime and deviance are more likely when an individual's bond to society is weak or broken—is an organizing principle in our theory of social bonding over the life course

(Sampson and Laub 1993). The life course has been defined as "pathways through the age differentiated life span" (Elder 1985: 17), in particular the "sequence of culturally defined age-graded roles and social transitions that are enacted over time" (Caspi et al. 1990: 15). Two central concepts underlie the analysis of life course dynamics. A *trajectory* is a pathway or line of development over the life span such as worklife, parenthood, and criminal behavior. Trajectories refer to long-term patterns of behavior and are marked by a sequence of transitions. *Transitions* are marked by life events (e.g., first job or first marriage) that are embedded in trajectories and evolve over shorter time spans (see also Elder 1985: 31–32).

Following Elder (1985), we differentiate the life course of individuals on the basis of age and argue that the important institutions of both formal and informal social control vary across the life span. However, we emphasize the role of age-graded informal social control as reflected in the structure of interpersonal bonds linking members of society to one another and to wider social institutions (e.g., work, family, school). Unlike formal sanctions that originate in purposeful efforts to control crime, informal social controls "emerge as by-products of role relationships established for other purposes and are components of role reciprocities" (Kornhauser 1978: 24).

Although traditional control theory (e.g., Hirschi 1969) is static, we believe its integration with the life course framework may be used to understand the dynamics of both continuity and change in behavior over time. In particular, a major thesis of our work is that social bonds in adolescence (e.g., to family, peers, and school) and adulthood (e.g., attachment to the labor force, cohesive marriage) explain criminal behavior regardless of prior differences in criminal propensity—that age-graded changes in social bonds explain changes in crime. We also contend that early (and distal) precursors to adult crime (e.g., conduct disorder, low self-control) are mediated in developmental pathways by key age-graded institutions of informal and formal social control, especially in the transition to adulthood (e.g., via employment, military service, marriage, official sanctions).

In uniting continuity and change within the context of a sociological understanding of crime through life, a major concept in our framework is the dynamic process whereby the interlocking nature of trajectories and transitions generate *turning points* or a change in life course (Elder 1985:

32). Adaptation to life events is crucial because the same event or transition followed by different adaptations can lead to different trajectories (Elder 1985: 35). That is, despite the connection between childhood events and experiences in adulthood, turning points can modify life trajectories—they can "redirect paths." For some individuals, turning points are abrupt—radical "turnarounds" or changes in life history that separate the past from the future (Elder et al. 1991: 215).

For most individuals, however, we conceptualize turning points as "part of a process over time and not as a dramatic lasting change that takes place at any one time" (Pickles and Rutter 1991: 134; Rutter 1989; Clausen 1993). The process-oriented nature of turning points leads to a focus on incremental change and age-related progressions and events, which carry forward or set in motion dynamic processes that shape future outcomes (Rutter and Rutter 1993: 64). In our theoretical model, turning points may be positive *or* negative because they represent "times of decision or opportunity when life trajectories may be directed on to more adaptive or maladaptive paths" (Rutter and Rutter 1993: 244). As Rutter and Rutter recognize, "Life-span transitions have a crucial role in the processes involved, strengthening emerging patterns of behavior or providing a means by which life trajectories may change pattern" (1993: 109; see also Maughan and Champion 1990: 310). This variability results because life transitions do not have the same impact on everyone. For instance, getting married may be beneficial or deleterious depending on "*when* a person marries, *whom* a person marries, the *quality* of the relationship formed and whether or not *changes* in social group and life patterns are involved" (Rutter and Rutter 1993: 356, emphasis in the original). Although not usually thought of as such, some turning points are thus negative, serving to exacerbate early trajectories of antisocial conduct.

Cumulative Disadvantage

We believe that a developmental conceptualization of labeling theory, integrated with the age-graded theory of informal social control previously outlined, provides an alternative way of thinking about trait-based interpretations of behavioral stability. Consider first an often neglected fact about stability. As reviewed by Rutter and Rutter (1993: 77–79), psychological traits usually thought of as having the greatest biological basis—e.g., activity level and temperament—in fact show relatively low stability from childhood to adulthood. By contrast, even though aggression is arguably less likely than these studied traits to result from biological differences, it shows the *highest* stability.

Why should this be so? A clue is that aggression is a social behavior that, by definition, involves interpersonal interaction. Moreover, aggression and conduct disorder often generate immediate and harsh responses by varying segments of society compared to most personality traits. As we shall elaborate, aggression tends to foster physical counterattacks, teacher and peer rejection, punitive discipline, parental hostility, and harsh criminal justice sanctions. The common feature to all these responses is retaliation and attempts at control and domination.

Logically, then, the fact that much delinquency starts early in the life course implies that retaliatory efforts to suppress it also begin early. These repressive efforts accrete incrementally over time to produce developmental effects. Specifically, we argue that antisocial children replicate their antisocial behavior in a variety of social realms in part because of the differing reactions that antisocial behavior brings forth (Caspi 1987). Maladaptive behaviors are "found in interactional styles that are sustained both by the progressive accumulation of their own consequences (cumulative continuity) and by evoking maintaining responses from others during reciprocal social interaction (interactional continuity)" (Caspi et al. 1987: 313, emphasis added). The combination of interactional and cumulative continuity over time is thus inherently a social process.

Invoking a state dependence argument (see Nagin and Paternoster 1991), our theory incorporates the causal role of prior delinquency in facilitating adult crime through a process of "cumulative disadvantage." The state dependence component implies that committing a crime has a genuine behavioral influence on the probability of committing future crimes. In other words, crime itself—whether directly or indirectly—causally modifies the future probability of engaging in crime (Nagin and Paternoster 1991: 166). Although this role is potentially direct, we emphasize a developmental model where delinquent behavior has a systematic attenuating effect on the social and institutional bonds linking adults to society (e.g., labor force attachment, marital cohesion). For example, delinquency may spark failure in school, incarceration, and weak bonds to the labor market, in turn increasing later adult crime (Tittle 1988: 80). Serious sanctions in particular lead to the "knifing off" (Moffitt 1993) of future opportunities such that labeled offenders have fewer options for a conventional life.

The cumulative continuity of disadvantage is thus not only a result of stable individual differences in criminal propensity, but a dynamic process whereby childhood antisocial behavior and adolescent delinquency foster adult crime through the severance of adult social bonds. From this view, similar to what Thornberry (1987) has termed interactional theory, weak social bonding serves as a mediating and hence causal sequential link in a chain of adversity between childhood delinquency and adult criminal behavior. We further believe that this process of cumulative disadvantage is linked to four key institutions of social control—family, school, peers, and state sanctions.

Family

The importance of family management and socialization practices (e.g., monitoring and supervision, consistent punishment, and the formation of close social bonds among parents and children) for explaining crime and delinquency has been well established (see e.g., Loeber and Stouthamer-Loeber 1986: 29). When considering the role of families and crime, however, criminologists generally view childrearing in a static framework that flows from parent *to* child. This static view ignores the fact that parenting styles are also an adaptation to children in a process of reciprocal interaction. An example of interactional continuity in the family is when the child with temper tantrums provokes angry and hostile reactions in parents, which in turn feeds back to trigger further antisocial behavior by the child. In support of this idea, there is evidence that styles of parenting are very sensitive to these troublesome behaviors on the part of children.

Lytton (1990) has written an excellent overview of this complex body of research, which he subsumes under the theoretical umbrella of "control systems theory." This theory argues that parent and child display reciprocal adaptation to each other's behavior level, leading to what Lytton calls "child effects" on parents. One reason for these child effects is that reinforcement does not work in the usual way for conduct disordered children. As Lytton (1990: 688) notes, conduct disordered children "may be underresponsive to social reinforcement and punishment." Hence normal routines of parental childrearing become subject to disruption based on early antisocial behavior—i.e., children themselves differentially engender parenting styles likely to further exacerbate antisocial behavior.

The behavior that prompts parental frustration is not merely aggressiveness or delinquency, however. Lytton (1990: 690) reviews evidence showing a connection between a child being rated "difficult" in preschool (e.g., whining, restlessness, strong-willed resistance) and the child's delinquency as an adolescent—a relation that holds independent of the quality of parents' childrearing practices. For example, Olweus (1980) showed that mothers of boys who displayed a strong-will and hot temper in infancy later became more permissive of aggression, which in turn led to greater aggressiveness in middle childhood. Moreover, there is experimental evidence that when children's inattentive and noncompliant behavior is improved by administering stimulant drugs, their mothers become less controlling and mother-child interaction patterns are nearly normalized (Lytton 1990: 688). All of this suggests that parenting, at least in part, is a reaction to children's temperament, especially difficult ones.

Although rarely studied directly, it seems likely that delinquent behavior and other deliberate violations of parental authority spark retaliation in the form of harsh physical punishment and, in some cases, parental abuse. In turn, child abuse and violent punishment have been linked to later violent offending on the part of victims (Widom 1989). To the extent that children's appraisals of themselves are powerfully influenced by negative parental labeling (Matsueda 1992), the consequences of violent interactional styles, parent-child conflict, and violent punishment for later life are potentially quite large.

In any case, our point is that interactional continuity begins in the family. This is not a simultaneous relationship at one point in time so much as a reinforcing cycle that builds over time to further increase the probability of antisocial behavior (see also Thornberry 1987: 869). In Nagin and Paternoster's (1991) terminology, this process captures the state dependence effect of prior delinquency on future crime.

School and Peers

Many years ago, the Gluecks observed that poor school attachment may be a consequence of misbehavior more than a cause (1964: 23). Teachers may be particularly sensitive to unruly and difficult children, leading to rejection of the child or at least a strained teacher-student relationship. This rejection undermines the attachment of the child to the school, and ultimately, the child's performance in the school. More recent evidence on the reciprocal relationship between delinquency and school attachment has been uncovered in research by Liska and Reed (1985), Olweus (1983), and Thornberry et al. (1991).

Similar processes have been revealed for peer interactions. For instance, children who are aggressive are more likely to be rejected by their peers compared with less aggressive children (see Cairns and Cairns 1992; Coie et al. 1991; Dodge 1983; Patterson et al. 1989). This process creates a vicious cycle of negative interactions and is consistent with Caspi's (1987) idea of interactional continuity. Dishion and his colleagues (1991) have also found that poor family practices, peer rejection, and academic failure at age ten increased the likelihood of involvement with antisocial peers at age twelve. In this sense, peer rejection and the deviant peer group contribute to the maintenance of antisocial behavior through mid-adolescence (see also Thornberry et al. 1994). Although further discussion is beyond the scope of this article, the existing evidence thus suggests that the reciprocal interactional dynamics of teacher and peer rejection contribute to the continuity of aggression and other forms of delinquent behavior.

Criminal Justice and Institutional Reaction

Cumulative disadvantage is generated most explicitly by the negative structural consequences of criminal offending and official sanctions for life chances. The theory specifically suggests a "snowball" effect—that adolescent delinquency and its negative consequences (e.g., arrest, official labeling, incarceration) increasingly "mortgage" one's future, especially later life chances molded by schooling and employment. For example, it has long been the case that many jobs formally preclude the hiring of ex-prisoners (Glaser 1969: 233–238). Experimental studies have also shown that employers are reluctant to consider ex-offenders as potential employees (Boshier and Johnson 1974; Dale 1976; Finn and Fontaine 1985).

The stigma associated with arrest and conviction extends to membership in trade unions, "bonding" applications, and licensing restrictions (see Davidenas 1983). For example, many trade unions deny membership to ex-offenders (Dale 1976: 324), while the standard commercial blanket bond contains a provision that nullifies coverage if employers have knowingly hired any person with a criminal record (Dale 1976: 326). The result is that ex-offenders are barred from employment where bonding is required (e.g., security guards, hotel workers). Of course, these are precisely the sort of low-skilled jobs that are compatible with the educational and work-history profiles of most offenders.

The licensing of government-regulated private occupations yields even more structural constraints on the reintegration of ex-offenders. As an example, in only four states can an ex-offender work as a barber without interference by the state licensing agency because of criminal conduct (Dale 1976: 330). Although there is considerable state-by-state variation, licensing boards bar ex-offenders from literally hundreds of other occupations, including apprentice electrician, billiards operator, and plumber (Singer 1983: 246 and Dale 1976). Again, these seem to be primary "escape routes" from a disadvantaged past were it not for the criminal record.

Arrest, conviction, and imprisonment are clearly stigmatizing, and those so tarnished face structural impediments to establishing strong social ties to conventional lines of adult activity—regardless of their behavioral predispositions (see also Schwartz and Skolnick 1964; Thornberry and Christenson 1984; Burton et al. 1987). Drawing on the thesis of cumulative disadvantage, there is thus support for hypothesizing that incarceration has negative effects on job stability and employment in adulthood (see especially Bondeson 1989; Freeman 1991). The logic of this theoretical perspective in turn points to a possible *indirect* role of delinquency and official sanctioning in generating future crime.

Although long-term assessments are rare, there is some developmental evidence that bears on this thesis. As part of a larger project, we have analyzed the natural histories originally gathered by Glueck and Glueck (1950 1968) of 500 delinquents and 500 control subjects matched on age, IQ, ethnicity, and neighborhood deprivation (see Sampson and Laub 1993 for details). To test the cumulative disadvantage thesis, we examined the role of job stability at ages seventeen–twenty-five and twenty-five–thirty-two as an intervening link between incarceration and adult crime. In doing so we controlled for theoretically relevant factors in the etiology of job stability. As Gottfredson and Hirschi (1990) argue, those individuals with low self-control and tendencies toward crime are also the same individuals likely to have unstable histories in employment and other conventional lines of activity. Accordingly, we controlled for official arrest frequency, unofficial delinquency, and sample attrition risk. Moreover, previous research (e.g., Robins 1966; Vaillant 1983) in conjunction with our own qualitative analysis revealed the important role of drinking in understanding patterns of job stability—heavy or abusive drinkers tend to either drift from job to job or be fired from their jobs at a rate much higher than nondrinkers. Excessive drinking that began in adolescence (age nineteen or younger) was thus also controlled. Finally, we used empirical methods that took into account persistent unobserved heterogeneity in criminal behavior (Nagin and Paternoster 1991).

Using this multimethod, multimeasure approach, we found that length of juvenile incarceration had the largest overall effect on later job stability—regardless of prior crime, excessive adolescent drinking, and exclusion risk. Even though all the delinquent boys were incarcerated at some point, those incarcerated for a longer period of time had trouble securing stable jobs as they entered young adulthood compared to delinquents with a shorter incarceration history. Since unofficial propensity to deviance, sample selection bias, drinking, unobserved heterogeneity, and prior criminal history were controlled (the latter influencing the length of confinement), it seems unlikely that the result is spurious.

Our analyses also underscored the deleterious role that incarceration may play in developmental trajectories of employment in later periods of adulthood (ages twenty-five–thirty-two). Length of incarceration in both adolescence *and* young adulthood had significant negative effects on job stability at ages twenty-five–thirty-two (Sampson and Laub 1993: 167–168). These results are noteworthy not only because confounding "propensity" factors were taken into account (e.g., crime and drinking), but also for the long-term negative consequences of juvenile incarceration independent of adult incarceration (Laub and Sampson 1994). Apparently, the structural disadvantages accorded institutionalized adolescents are so great (e.g., through dropping out of high school, record of confinement known to employers) that their influence lingers throughout adult development. We tested the idea of cumulative effects by also examining the duration of incarceration from adolescence (< seventeen) through the transition to young adulthood (ages seventeen–twenty-five). As the total time served in juvenile and adult correctional facilities increased, later job stability decreased (controlling for prior record and unofficial deviance).

Although limited, the data thus suggest that looking only at the direct effects of official sanctions is misleading. Length of incarceration—whether as a juvenile or adult—has little direct bearing on later criminal activity when job stability is controlled. This does not imply unimportance, however, for there is evidence that the effect of confinement may be indirect and operative in a developmental, cumulative process that reproduces itself over time (see also Hagan and Palloni 1990). Consistent with the theoretical idea of cumulative continuity and state (duration) dependence (Nagin and Paternoster 1991; Featherman and Lerner 1985), incarceration appears to cut off opportunities and prospects for stable employment later in life. This "knifing off" has important developmental implications—job stability and also marital attachment in adulthood are significantly related to changes in adult crime (Sampson and Laub 1993: ch. 7). Namely, the stronger the adult ties to work and family, the less crime and deviance among both delinquents and controls. Therefore, even if the direct effect of incarceration is zero or possibly even negative (i.e., a deterrent), its indirect effect may well be criminogenic (positive) as structural labeling theorists have long argued.

Other Evidence

Although infrequently studied over significant periods of human development, there is additional evidence of cumulative continuity arising from state sanctions and the attenuation of social bonds to employment. Based on the Cambridge Study in Youth Development, Farrington (1977) found that convictions increased the probability of future offending. Using the same longitudinal data, research by Nagin and Waldfogel (1992) supports the cumulative continuity thesis in showing a destabilizing effect of convictions on the labor market prospects of London boys. More recently, and again using the Cambridge data, Hagan (1993) has shown that delinquency increases the probability of future unemployment, regardless of prior differences in criminal propensity. Thornberry and Christenson (1984) have similarly shown a lagged positive effect of criminal involvement on future adult unemployment, controlling for prior propensities to unemployment.

In perhaps the most impressive set of findings, Richard Freeman has analyzed the National Longitudinal Survey of Youth (NLSY) to estimate effects of jail time, probation, conviction, and arrests (charges) on whether individuals were employed (and for how many weeks) for each year from 1980 to 1988. Control variables included sociodemographic characteristics (e.g., education, region, age) and self-reported use of drugs and alcohol. Net of these factors, Freeman's results showed that serious involvement with the criminal justice system had large long-term effects on employment. Specifically, men in jail as of 1980 had lower employment in all succeeding years than other men with comparable characteristics (Freeman 1991: 11). Similar results obtained for the number of weeks worked in the years previous to the interview follow-up. Interestingly, there was no effect of conviction but very large effects for jail time. As Freeman concludes: "The relation between incarceration and employment is "causal" rather than the result of fixed unobserved personal characteristics that are correlated with crime and employment: proportionately fewer youths who had been incarcerated worked years afterward than did nonincarcerated youths with similar initial employment experiences" (1991: 1).

Freeman also investigated these relationships using the Boston Youth Survey of out-of-school young men conducted during the height of the Boston labor market boom in the 1980s. To adjust for individual differences, Freeman's analyses controlled for age, race, education, grades in school, living arrangements, public housing, marital status, religious attendance, household size, alcohol use, and gang membership. Similar to the NLSY findings, his results showed that criminal offending and sanction experiences—especially jail time—severely restricted future opportunities in the labor market. In fact, Freeman's multivariate analyses "confirm that having been in jail is the single most important deterrent to employment" (1991: 13). This result held up when unobserved heterogeneity in individual differences in employment proclivities were controlled.

Freeman's consistent research findings from very different samples underscore the fact that we do not necessarily need to assume that personal "identities" change as a result of labeling and state sanctions. Rather, we take a more rational choice approach that focuses on endogenous decisions about the utility of labor market participation and adherence to conventional norms (see also Cook 1975). In other words, once severe sanctions like incarceration have been imposed, labor market decisions take on new meaning—especially when weighed against the opportunities provided by the innovation and expansion of drug economies in recent years (Freeman 1991: 22). From this view, labels work cumulatively through the structural transformation of one's stake in conformity to conventional society.

Structural Location and Continuity

To this point we have examined how involvement in delinquent behavior and criminal sanctioning during the transition from adolescence to young adulthood constrains subsequent development. Although this is certainly a developmental issue, Jessor et al., (1991: 252) argue "that there might well be very different outcomes of the same attribute, depending on the stage of the life course, the time in history, the particular cultural and social context, and the relevant aspects of the larger social setting." In their recent longitudinal study, Jessor and his colleagues (1991) found that despite continuity in problem behavior from adolescence to young adulthood, there was little evidence of "spillover" effects into other areas of adult life (e.g., work, education, family, friendships, and mental health). For this sample, delinquency does not appear to be a major handicap with respect to adult outcomes. However, the participants of Jessor et al.'s study (1991: 268) consisted largely of middle-class youth drawn from a "normal" sample.

Along similar lines, Hagan's (1991) research suggests that the deleterious effect of adolescent deviance on adult stratification outcomes is greatest among lower class boys, especially as mediated by police contacts. Middle-class boys who escaped the negative consequences of official labeling did not suffer impairment in adult occupational outcomes as a result of their adolescent delinquency. Avoiding the snares of arrest and institutionalization thus provided opportunities for prosocial attachments among middle-class youth to take firm hold in adulthood.

Recent experimental research on domestic violence provides even more compelling evidence of the interaction of structural location and sanctions. Randomized experiments in Milwaukee, Miami, Colorado Springs, and Omaha all revealed that arrest reduced repeat violence among the employed but *increased* it among the unemployed (Sherman 1992; 1993: 10). In other words, sanctioning tends to aggravate crime when administered in populations with low "stakes in conformity." Much like Braithwaite's (1989) theory of reintegrative shaming, Sherman (1993) argues that stigmatizing punishment among the disaffected works only to increase "defiant" recidivism. In particular, he posits that criminal justice sanctions provoke future defiance of the law when offenders have weak social bonds to both sanctioning agents and the wider community.

These studies suggest that the concepts of knifing off and cumulative continuity are most salient in explaining the structurally constrained life chances of the disadvantaged urban poor. In other words, cumulative disadvantage, state-dependence, and location in the class structure appear to interact. Among those in advantaged positions that provide continuity in social resources over time, both nondelinquents and delinquents alike are presumably not just more motivated, but better able structurally to establish binding ties to conventional lines of adult activity (Laub and Sampson 1993: 307). If nothing else, incumbency in prosocial middle-class roles provides advantages in maintaining the status quo and counteracting negative life events (e.g., being fired). Legal deterrents work better here, reducing future offending as classical theory suggests they should (Sherman 1992).

Among the disadvantaged, things seem to work differently. Deficits and disadvantages pile up faster, and this has continuing negative consequences for later development in the form of "environmental traps" (Maughan and Champion 1990: 308). Perhaps most problematic, the process of cumulative disadvantage restricts future options in conventional domains that provide opportunities for social "interdependence" (e.g., stable employment) while simultaneously encouraging options within subcultures that "reject the rejectors" (Braithwaite 1989: 102). Maughan and Champion (1990: 308) argue that this process takes on the characteristics of a "conveyor belt" that is extremely difficult to manage or jump off—especially for the disadvantaged. Thus one cannot ignore the effects of larger social contexts (social structure and living conditions) on development (Rutter and Rutter 1993: 34–37).

Implications

Our synthesis of cumulative disadvantage and state dependence recasts in a structural and developmental framework the original contentions of labeling theory that official reactions to primary deviance (e.g., arrest) may create problems of adjustment (e.g., unemployment) that foster additional crime in the form of secondary deviance (e.g., Lemert 1951; Becker 1963). Similar to Becker's concept of a deviant career sustained by the labeling process, Hagan and Palloni (1990) suggest that continuity in delinquent behavior may result from a structural imputation process that begins early in childhood (see also Tittle 1988: 78–81; Laub and Sampson 1993). Indeed, the stability of behavior may reflect more the stability of social *response* than the time-invariance of an individual trait. As we have argued, aggression is a social behavior embedded in ongoing social interactions with salient others.

Taking a similar position, Dannefer (1987: 216) argues that most developmental research is too quick to attribute continuity to time-stable traits and social-psychological processes rather than "structured mechanisms of social allocation producing similar differentiating tendencies in successive cohorts." The channeling of prior differences and the tendency toward cumulation of both advantage and disadvantage is so general that it has been referred to as the "Matthew effect"—"To him who hath shall be given; from him who hath not shall be taken away that which he hath" (see Dannefer 1987: 216). The Matthew effect underscores what Smith (1968) has called "vicious and benign circles" of development. Or as John Clausen puts it—"early advantages become cumulative advantages; early behaviors that are self-defeating lead to cumulative disadvantages" (1993: 521).

Patterson (1993) has offered the most telling metaphor for understanding the developmental risks of cumulative disadvantage—the "chimera." Patterson and his colleagues (1989) have examined the developmental course of antisocial behavior and delinquency across a developmental trajectory involving family, school, and peers. Their model consists of a series of action-reaction sequences across the developmental stages of early childhood, middle childhood, and late childhood and adolescence. Patterson argues that antisocial behavior leads to a "cascade" of secondary problems (e.g., school failure, peer rejection, depressed mood, and involvement with deviant peers) and he is quite explicit that "for problems produced at later stages, antisocial behavior is only an indirect determinant" (Patterson and Yoerger 1993: 145).

Appropriately, then, Patterson (1993) refers to the antisocial trait as a "chimera"—a hybrid where qualitative shifts in problem behavior (e.g., academic failure, peer rejection, etc.) as well as new forms of antisocial behavior (e.g., substance abuse) are "grafted" onto a core antisocial trait. From our perspective, the grafting process, the "piling up" of disadvantage, and the resultant chimera of a persistent criminal career is likely to interact with race and structural location (Hagan 1991; Jessor et al. 1991;

Thornberry 1987). Namely, there is increasing evidence that the probability of adolescent risks becoming transmuted into adverse adult circumstances is greatest among those in disadvantaged racial and economic positions.

On a final note, we stress that our theorizing of cumulative continuity and the causal role of salient life experiences in adulthood does not negate the potential importance of self- selection and individual differences. By distinguishing self-selection from cumulative continuity we incorporate the independent effects of both early delinquency (or individual propensity) and the dimensions of adult social bonding on adult crime. This distinction is consistent with recent research on homophily in social choices across the life course. As Kandel et al. (1990: 221) state: "although individual choices are made, in part, as a function of the individual's prior attributes, values, and personality characteristics, involvement in the new relationship has further effects and influences on that individual." Similarly, Rutter et al. (1990) and Quinton et al. (1993) found homophily in the choice of marital partners but also a substantial effect of marital cohesion and stable family life that held after taking planning of marriage partners into account. We found a similar phenomenon in our re-analyses of the Gluecks' data (see Sampson and Laub 1993; Laub and Sampson 1993).

An important roadblock to integrating trait-based models with life-course theory is thus conceptual and turns on what we believe is an incorrect interpretation of homophily. To assume that individual differences influence the choices one makes in life (which they certainly do), does not mean that social mechanisms emerging from those choices can then have no causal significance.[5] Choices generate constraints *and* opportunities that themselves have effects not solely attributable to individuals. As situational theorists have long pointed out, the same person—with the same attributes and traits—acts very different in different situations. For these reasons, the integration of rational choice, situational, and social control theories with a life-course perspective that respects yet is not reducible to individual differences seems a promising avenue of future advances in criminological theory (see also Nagin and Paternoster 1993).

Notes

1. Even if we grant the argument that strain and cultural deviance theories are macro-level in nature (e.g., Bernard 1987), most applications still pose static

questions (e.g., whether between-societal differences in crime rates are associated with variations in income inequality).
2. It is with no small irony that stability can only be established with longitudinal data, yet its existence had led to static explanations.
3. Life-span developmental psychology does incorporate historical change, although developmental processes are still usually treated as invariant *within* cohorts (Dannefer 1984: 105).
4. One might also argue that social learning theory is developmental in nature, since it deals with processes that unfold over time. Still, the causal variables emphasized in social learning theory to date (e.g., deviant peers) tend to be static just like those in strain, control, and cultural deviance. Perhaps this is not surprising given the theoretical compatibility of social learning and cultural deviance theories (see Kornhauser 1978). In any event, the developmental cast of social learning theory, although beyond the scope of this paper, deserves consideration in future theoretical work.
5. We should also note that even homophily, though usually attributed to self selection, is profoundly shaped by structural constraints beyond the pale of individual choice (see generally Blau 1977).

References

Aminzade, Ronald. 1992. "Historical Sociology and Time." *Sociological Methods and Research* 20: 456–80.

Bachman, Jerald, Patrick O'Malley, and Jerome Johnston. 1978. *Youth in Transition, Volume VI: Adolescence to Adulthood—Change and Stability in the Lives of Young Men*. Ann Arbor, MI: University of Michigan Press.

Becker, Howard. 1963. *Outsiders: Studies in the Sociology of Deviance*. New York: Free Press.

Bernard, Thomas. 1987. "Testing Structural Strain Theories." *Journal of Research in Crime and Delinquency* 24: 262–80.

Blau, Peter. 1977. *Inequality and Heterogeneity*. New York: Free Press.

Bondeson, Ulla V. 1989. *Prisoners in Prison Societies*. New Brunswick, NJ: Transaction Publishers.

Boshier, Roger, and Derek Johnson. 1974. "Does Conviction Affect Employment Opportunities?" *British Journal of Criminology* 14: 264–68.

Braithwaite, John. 1989. *Crime, Shame, and Reintegration*. Cambridge: Cambridge University Press.

Burton, Velmer, Francis Cullen, and Lawrence Travis. 1987. "The Collateral Consequences of a Felony Conviction: A National Study of State Statutes." *Federal Probation* 51: 52–60.

Cairns, Robert B., and Beverly Cairns. 1992. "The Sociogenesis of Aggressive and Antisocial Behavior." In *Facts, Frameworks, and Forecasts: Advances in Criminological Theory*, vol. 3, ed. Joan McCord, 157–91. New Brunswick, NJ: Transaction Publishers.

Caspi, Avshalom. 1987. "Personality in the Life Course." *Journal of Personality and Social Psychology* 53: 1203–13.

Caspi, Avshalom, and Terrie E. Moffitt. 1993. "The Continuity of Maladaptive Behavior: From Description to Understanding in the Study of Antisocial Behavior." In *Manual of Developmental Psychopathology*, ed. Dante Cicchetti and Donald Cohen. New York: Wiley, forthcoming.

Caspi, Avshalom, Glen H. Elder, Jr., and Ellen S. Herbener. 1990. "Childhood Personality and the Prediction of Life-Course Patterns." In *Straight and Devious Pathways from Childhood to Adulthood*, ed. Lee Robins and Michael Rutter, 13–35. Cambridge: Cambridge University Press.

Caspi, Avshalom, Glen H. Elder, Jr., and Daryl J. Bem. 1987. "Moving Against the World: Life-Course Patterns of Explosive Children." *Developmental Psychology* 23: 308–13.

Coie, J. D., M. Underwood, and J. E. Lochman. 1991. "Programmatic Intervention with Aggressive Children in the School Setting." In *The Development and Treatment of Childhood Aggression*, ed. D. J. Pepler and K. H. Rubin, 389–410. Hillsdale, NJ: Erlbaum.

Clausen, John. 1993. *American Lives: Looking Back at the Children of the Great Depression*. New York: Free Press.

Cline, Hugh F. 1980. "Criminal Behavior over the Life Span." In *Constancy and Change in Human Development*, ed. Orville G. Brim Jr. and Jerome Kagan, 641–74. Cambridge: Harvard University Press.

Cook, Philip J. 1975. "The Correctional Carrot: Better Jobs for Parolees." *Policy Analysis* 1: 11–54.

Dale, Mitchell. 1976. "Barriers to the Rehabilitation of Ex-Offenders." *Crime and Delinquency* 22: 322–37.

Dannefer, Dale. 1984. "Adult Development and Social Theory: A Paradigmatic Reappraisal." *American Sociological Review* 49: 100–16.

———. 1987. "Aging as Intracohort Differentiation: Accentuation, the Matthew Effect, and the Life Course." *Sociological Forum* 2: 211–36.

Davidenas, J. 1983. "The Professional License: An Ex-Offender's Illusion." *Criminal Justice Journal* 7: 61–69.

Dishion, Thomas J., Gerald R. Patterson, M. Stoolmiller, and M. L. Skinner. 1991. "Family, School, and Behavioral Antecedents to Early Adolescent Involvement with Antisocial Peers." *Developmental Psychology* 27: 172–80.

Dodge, Kenneth A. 1983. "Behavioral Antecedents of Peer Social Status." *Child Development* 54: 1386–99.

Elder, Glen H., Jr. 1985. "Perspectives on the Life Course." In *Life Course Dynamics*, ed. Glen H. Elder Jr., 23–49. Ithaca: Cornell University Press.

Elder, Glen H. Jr., Cynthia Gimbel, and Rachel Ivie. 1991. "Turning Points in Life: The Case of Military Service and War." *Military Psychology* 3: 215–31.

Farrington, David P. 1977. "The Effects of Public Labeling." *British Journal of Criminology* 17: 112–25.

———. 1986. "Stepping Stones to Adult Criminal Careers." In *Development of Antisocial and Prosocial Behavior*, ed. Dan Olweus, Jack Block, and Marian Radke-Yarrow, 359–84. New York: Academic Press.

Farrington, David P., S. G. Osborn, Donald West. 1978. "The Persistence of Labelling Effects." *British Journal of Criminology* 18: 277–84.

Featherman, David, and Richard Lerner. 1985. "Ontogenesis and Sociogenesis: Problematics for Theory and Research about Development and Socialization Across the Lifespan." *American Sociological Review* 50: 659–76.

Finn, R. H., and P. A. Fontaine. 1985. "The Association between Selected Characteristics and Perceived Employability of Offenders." *Criminal Justice and Behavior* 12: 353–65.

Freeman, Richard. 1991. "Crime and the Employment of Disadvantaged Youth." Cambridge: Harvard University, National Bureau of Economic Research.

Garfinkel, Harold. 1956. "Conditions of Successful Degradation Ceremonies." *American Journal of Sociology* 61: 420–24.

Glaser, Daniel. 1969. *The Effectiveness of a Prison and Parole System*. Abridged edition. Indianapolis: Bobbs-Merrill Co.

Glueck, Sheldon, and Eleanor Glueck. 1930. *500 Criminal Careers*. New York: A.A. Knopf.

———. 1950. *Unraveling Juvenile Delinquency*. New York: Commonwealth Fund.

———. 1964. *Ventures in Criminology*. Cambridge: Harvard University Press.

———. 1968. *Delinquents and Nondelinquents in Perspective*. Cambridge: Harvard University Press.

Gottfredson, Michael, and Travis Hirschi. 1987. "The Methodological Adequacy of Longitudinal Research on Crime." *Criminology* 25: 581–614.

Gottfredson Michael, and Travis Hirschi. 1990. *A General Theory of Crime*. Stanford: Stanford University Press.

Gove, Walter R. 1980. *The Labeling of Deviance: Evaluation of a Perspective*. 2d ed. Beverly Hills, CA: Sage.

———. 1985. "The Effect of Age and Gender on Deviant Behavior: A Biopsychosocial Perspective." In *Gender and the Life Course*, ed. Alice S. Rossi, 115–44. New York: Aldine.

Hagan, John. 1991. "Destiny and Drift: Subcultural Preferences, Status Attainments, and the Risks and Rewards of Youth." *American Sociological Review* 56: 567–82.

———. 1993. "The Social Embeddedness of Crime and Unemployment." *Criminology* 31: 465–91.

Hagan, John, and Alberto Palloni. 1990. "The Social Reproduction of a Criminal Class in Working-Class London, Circa 1950–1980." *American Journal of Sociology* 96: 265–99.

Hirschi, Travis. 1969. *Causes of Delinquency*. Berkeley: University of California Press.

Hirschi, Travis, and Michael Gottfredson. 1993. "Commentary: Testing the General Theory of Crime." *Journal of Research in Crime and Delinquency* 30: 47–54.

Huesmann, L. Rowell, Leonard D. Eron, Monroe M. Lefkowitz, and Leopold O. Walder. 1984. "Stability of Aggression over Time and Generations." *Developmental Psychology* 20: 1120–34.

Jessor, Richard, John E. Donovan, and Frances M. Costa. 1991. *Beyond Adolescence: Problem Behavior and Young Adult Development*. Cambridge: Cambridge University Press.

Kagan, Jerome. 1980. "Perspectives on Continuity." In *Constancy and Change in Human Development*, ed. Orville G. Brim Jr. and Jerome Kagan, 26–74. Cambridge: Harvard University Press.

Kandel, Denise, Mark Davies, and Nazli Baydar. 1990. "The Creation of Interpersonal Contexts: Homophily in Dyadic Relationships in Adolescence and Young Adulthood." In *Straight and Devious Pathways from Childhood to Adulthood*, ed. Lee Robins and Michael Rutter, 221–41. New York: Cambridge University Press.

Kornhauser, Ruth. 1978. *Social Sources of Delinquency*. Chicago: University of Chicago Press.

Laub, John H., and Robert J. Sampson. 1993. "Turning Points in the Life Course: Why Change Matters to the Study of Crime." *Criminology* 31: 301–25.

———. 1994. "The Long-Term Effect of Punitive Discipline." In *Coercion and Punishment in Long-Term Perspectives*, ed. Joan McCord. Cambridge: Cambridge University Press (forthcoming).

Lemert, Edwin. 1951. *Social Pathology*. New York: McGraw-Hill.

————. 1972. *Human Deviance, Social Problems, and Social Control.* 2d ed. Englewood Cliffs, NJ: Prentice Hall.

Link, Bruce. 1982. "Mental Patient Status, Work, and Income: An Examination of the Effects of a Psychiatric Label." *American Sociological Review* 47: 202–15.

————. 1987. "Understanding Labeling Effects in the Area of Mental Disorders: An Assessment of the Effects of Expectations of Rejection." *American Sociological Review* 52: 96–112.

Link, Bruce, Francis Cullen, James Frank, and John F.Wozniak. 1987. "The Social Rejection of Former Mental Patients: Understanding Why Labels Matter." *American Journal of Sociology* 92: 1461–1500.

Link, Bruce, Francis Cullen, Elmer Struening, Patrick Shrout, and Bruce Dohrenwend. 1989. "A Modified Labeling Approach to Mental Disorders: An Empirical Assessment." *American Sociological Review* 54: 400–423.

Liska, Allen, and Mark Reed. 1985. "Ties to Conventional Institutions and Delinquency: Estimating Reciprocal Effects." *American Sociological Review* 50: 547–60.

Loeber, Rolf. 1982. "The Stability of Antisocial Child Behavior: A Review." *Child Development* 53: 1431–46.

Loeber, Rolf, and Magda Stouthamer-Loeber. 1986. "Family Factors as Correlates and Predictors of Juvenile Conduct Problems and Delinquency." In *Crime and Justice*, vol. 7, ed. Michael Tonry and Norval Morris, 29–149. Chicago: University of Chicago Press.

Loeber, Rolf, and Marc Le Blanc. 1990. "Toward a Developmental Criminology." In *Crime and Justice*, volume 12, ed. Michael Tonry and Norval Morris, 375–437. Chicago: University of Chicago Press.

Lytton, Hugh. 1990. "Child and Parent Effects in Boys' Conduct Disorder: A Reinterpretation." *Developmental Psychology* 26: 683–97.

Matsueda, Ross. 1992. "Reflected Appraisals, Parental Labeling, and Delinquency: Specifying a Symbolic Interactionist Theory." *American Journal of Sociology* 97: 1577–1611.

Maughan, Barbara, and Lorna Champion. 1990. "Risk and Protective Factors in the Transition to Young Adulthood." In *Successful Aging*, ed. Paul Baltes and M. Baltes, 296–331. Cambridge: Cambridge University Press.

Moffitt, Terrie E. 1993. "Life-course Persistent and Adolescence Limited Antisocial Behavior: A Developmental Taxonomy." *Psychological Review* 100: 674.

Nagin, Daniel, and Raymond Paternoster. 1991. "On the Relationship of Past and Future Participation in Delinquency." *Criminology* 29: 163–90.

————. 1993. "Enduring Individual Differences and Rational Choice Theories of Crime." *Law and Society Review* 27: 201–30.

Nagin, Daniel and David P. Farrington. 1992. "The Stability of Criminal Potential From Childhood to Adulthood." *Criminology* 30: 235–60.

Nagin, Daniel, and Joel Waldfogel. 1992. "The Effects of Criminality and Conviction on the Labour Market Status of Young British Offenders." Unpublished manuscript. Pittsburgh: Carnegie Mellon University.

Olweus, Dan. 1979. "Stability of Aggressive Reaction Patterns in Males: A Review." *Psychological Bulletin* 86: 852–75.

————. 1980. "Familial and Temperamental Determinants of Aggressive Behavior in Adolescent Boys." *Developmental Psychology* 16: 644–60.

————. 1983. "Low School Achievement and Aggressive Behavior in Adolescent Boys." In *Human Development: An Interactional Perspective*, ed. David Magnusson and Vernon L. Allen, 353–65. New York: Academic.

Paternoster, Raymond, and Leeann Iovanni. 1989. "The Labeling Perspective and Delinquency: An Elaboration of the Theory and an Assessment of the Evidence." *Justice Quarterly* 6: 359–94.

Patterson, Gerald R. 1993. "Orderly Change in a Stable World: The Antisocial Trait as a Chimera." *Journal of Consulting and Clinical Psychology* 61: 911-19.

Patterson, Gerald R., and Karen Yoerger. 1993. "Developmental Models for Delinquent Behavior." In *Mental Disorder and Crime*, ed. Sheilagh Hodgins, 140–72. Newbury Park, CA: Sage.

Patterson, Gerald R., Barbara D. DeBaryshe, and Elizabeth Ramsey. 1989. "A Developmental Perspective on Antisocial Behavior." *American Psychologist* 44: 329–35.

Pickles, Andrew, and Michael Rutter. 1991. "Statistical and Conceptual Models of 'Turning Points' in Developmental Processes." In *Problems and Methods in Longitudinal Research: Stability and Change*, ed. David Magnusson, Lars Bergman, Georg Rudinger, and Bertil Torestad, 133–65. New York: Cambridge University Press.

Quinton, David, Andrew Pickles, and Barbara Maughan, and Michael Rutter. 1993. "Partners, Peers, and Pathways: Assortative Pairing and Continuities in Conduct Disorder." *Development and Psychopathology* 5: 763–83.

Robins, Lee N. 1966. *Deviant Children Grown Up.* Baltimore: Williams and Wilkins.

———. 1978. "Sturdy Childhood Predictors of Adult Antisocial Behavior: Replications from Longitudinal Studies." *Psychological Medicine* 8: 611–22.

Rutter, Michael. 1989. "Pathways from Childhood to Adult Life." *Journal of Child Psychology and Psychiatry* 30: 25–31.

Rutter, Michael, D. Quinton, and J. Hill. 1990. "Adult Outcomes of Institution-reared Children: Males and Females Compared." In *Straight and Devious Pathways from Childhood to Adulthood*, ed. Lee Robins and Michael Rutter, 135–57. New York: Cambridge University Press.

Rutter, Michael, and Marjorie Rutter. 1993. *Developing Minds: Challenge and Continuity Across the Life Span.* New York: Basic Books.

Sampson, Robert J., and John H. Laub. 1992. "Crime and Deviance in the Life Course." *Annual Review of Sociology* 18: 63–84.

———. 1993. *Crime in the Making: Pathways and Turning Points Through Life.* Cambridge: Harvard University Press.

Scheff, Thomas H. 1966. *Becoming Mentally Ill.* Chicago: Aldine.

Schur, Edwin M. 1971. *Labeling Deviant Behavior.* New York: Harper and Row.

Schwartz, Richard, and Jerome Skolnick. 1964. "Two Studies of Legal Stigma. In *The Other Side: Perspectives on Deviance*, ed. Howard Becker, 103–117. New York: Free Press.

Sherman, Lawrence. 1992. *Policing Domestic Violence.* New York: Free Press.

———. 1993. "Defiance, Deterrence, and Irrelevance: A Theory of the Criminal Sanction." *Journal of Research in Crime and Delinquency* 30: 445–73.

Singer, Richard. 1983. "Conviction: Civil Disabilities." In *Encyclopedia of Crime and Justice*, ed. Sanford Kadish, 243–48. New York: Free Press.

Smith, Brewster. 1968. "Competence and Socialization." In *Socialization and Society*, ed. John Clausen, 270–320. Boston: Little Brown.

Smith, Douglas, and Raymond Paternoster. 1990. "Formal Processing and Future Delinquency: Deviance Amplification as Selection Artifact." *Law and Society Review* 24: 1109–31.

Thomas, Charles, and Donna Bishop. 1984. "The Effect of Formal and Informal Sanctions on Delinquency: A Longitudinal Comparison of Labeling and Deterrence Theories." *Journal of Criminal Law and Criminology* 75: 1222–45.

Thornberry, Terence P. 1987. "Toward an Interactional Theory of Delinquency." *Criminology* 25: 863–91.

Thornberry, Terence P., and R.L. Christenson. 1984. "Unemployment and Criminal Involvement: An Investigation of Reciprocal Causal Structures." *American Sociological Review* 49: 398–411.

Thornberry, Terence P., Alan J. Lizotte, Marvin D. Krohn, Margaret Farnworth, and Sung Joon Jang. 1991. "Testing Interactional Theory: An Examination of Reciprocal Causal Relationships among Family, School, and Delinquency." *Journal of Criminal Law and Criminology* 82: 3–35.

———. 1994. "Delinquent Peers, Beliefs, and Delinquent Behavior: A Longitudinal Test of Interactional Theory." *Criminology* 32: 47–84.

Tittle, Charles. 1975. "Deterrents or Labeling?" *Social Forces* 53: 399–410.

———. 1988. "Two Empirical Regularities (maybe) in Search of an Explanation: Commentary on the Age-Crime Debate." *Criminology* 26: 75–86.

Vaillant, George E. 1983. *The Natural History of Alcoholism*. Cambridge: Harvard University Press.

West, Donald J., and David P. Farrington. 1977. *The Delinquent Way of Life*. London: Heinemann.

Widom, Cathy S. 1989. "The Cycle of Violence." *Science* 244: 160–66.

Wilson, James Q., and Richard Herrnstein. 1985. *Crime and Human Nature*. New York: Simon and Schuster.

Wolfgang, Marvin E., Terence P. Thornberry, and Robert Figlio. 1987. *From Boy to Man: From Delinquency to Crime*. Chicago: University of Chicago Press.

5

A Symbolic Interactionist Theory of Role-Transitions, Role-Commitments, and Delinquency

Ross L. Matsueda and Karen Heimer

Recent criminological research has emphasized the importance of viewing crime and delinquency within the framework of the life-course or life-span development (Hagan and Palloni 1988; Elliott, Huizinga, and Menard 1989; Loeber and Le Blanc 1990; Sampson and Laub 1992, 1993; Farrington 1992). A life-course perspective opens new puzzles and questions for the study of deviance, such as the role of pathways, trajectories, and life-course transitions in deviance, hypotheses about duration-dependent processes, questions about ontogenetic versus sociogenic causal mechanisms, and issues in modeling longitudinal data. The empirical research on these topics suggest that trajectories, pathways, and transitions are important, and that a general theory of crime should incorporate a life-course view (Sampson and Laub 1992, 1993; Farrington 1992; Hagan and Wheaton 1993). This chapter explores the potential contribution of symbolic interactionism to a life-course theory of crime. We argue that such a view provides a theory of the meaning of life-course transitions and a situational theory of the mechanisms by which such transitions translate into criminal acts. It also provides a slant on

This paper is based on research supported in part by grants from the National Science Foundation SBR-9311014 and the Central Investment Fund for Research Enhancement, University of Iowa. We thank Kathleen Anderson for research assistance and helpful comments and Terence P. Thornberry for helpful comments and suggestions.

the ontogenetic-sociogenic debate, and can help specify duration-dependent hypotheses about crime. The remainder of this chapter is divided into three parts: First, we briefly review the importance of a life-course perspective in crime and delinquency, highlighting important issues, theoretical questions, and tentative empirical findings. Next, we sketch a symbolic interactionist approach to crime in the life course. Third, we apply the theory to three stages of the life course: early child development, adolescence, and adulthood.

Life Course, Development, and Crime

Life-course perspectives generally view life events in the context of life stages, transitions, turning points, and pathways, which are embedded in social institutions (Elder 1985). According to Elder (1985), pathways or trajectories refer to long-term trends or patterns of events, such as occupational careers or family trajectories. In contrast, transitions refer to short-term changes that can redirect a trajectory, such as getting married, becoming divorced, or entering the labor force. For example, Sampson and Laub (1993) argue that it is not life transitions per se that affect criminality, but rather the extent of informal social control associated with such transitions that lead to changes in crime. That is, life events effect change in crime by influencing the strength of social ties, which reflect investments in institutional relationships or social capital (Laub and Sampson 1993).

A parallel approach has been applied to crime under the term "developmental criminology" (Loeber and Le Blanc 1990). Again, the proposal is to view crime in developmental terms, refining concepts of age-of-onset, age-of-termination, and cumulative frequency with dynamic concepts: activation refers to early development after onset, including acceleration, diversification, and stabilization; aggravation refers to developmental sequences and escalation of criminality; and desistance refers to deceleration, specialization, and ceiling effects. It follows that the parameters of change in crime, and by implication the parameters of criminal career models, are all summary statistics of the concept of an individual hazard rate, the instantaneous probability or propensity to engage in illegal behavior (Hagan and Palloni 1988). A useful definition of development in crime is a duration-dependent hazard rate of criminality, where duration dependence means the rate of change is dependent on time, i.e., is nonconstant or nonstationary (e.g., Featherman and Lerner 1985). From this view, not all change in crime is developmental; rather, change in crime is developmental when the hazard rate is changing with time, such as the waiting time in the prior state of the same event, or the waiting time in the state of some other event. For example, if the likelihood of crime declines as individuals age, or increases the longer one is a member of a delinquent gang, then crime is developmental. Conversely, if the likelihood of crime is the same regardless of age, length of time in a delinquent gang, or any other duration-dependent mechanism, then crime is not developmental. We begin with the premise that crime is developmental. Moreover, development can be age-graded, history-graded, or event-graded.

Sampson and Laub's Theory of Informal Social Control

Applied to crime and delinquency, the life-course approach has fallen center stage amidst controversy in criminology (Hagan and Palloni 1988). In perhaps the most promising program of research on deviance within the life course, Sampson and Laub (1990, 1992, 1993; Laub and Sampson 1993) specify a theory of informal social control. Their theoretical view combines low self-control theory and social control theory: criminal behavior is due in large part to a stable trait of childhood antisocial propensity, which causes adult deviance and adult problems with conventional institutions like education, family, military, and employment. But net of antisocial propensity, they argue that adult ties to conventional institutions and individuals reduce adult criminality. For Sampson and Laub, it is not education, marriage, or employment per se that is important, but rather the level of commitment and attachment to those conventional roles. Here they draw parallels between adult social bonds and Coleman's (1990) concept of social capital. Their empirical results find that early childhood antisocial behavior is linked to adult deviant behavior as well as adult social bonding—marital attachment, job stability, and occupational commitment. Moreover, net of child antisocial behavior, marital attachment and job stability (but not occupational commitment) affect adult crime and the time to desistance from crime (Sampson and Laub 1993).

In both their theoretical discussions and their empirical tests, Sampson and Laub consider three important issues: the roles of ontogenesis and sociogenesis (Dannefer 1984); the existence of heterogeneity and state dependence (Nagin and Paternoster 1991); and the need to specify and test duration-dependent mechanisms (Featherman and Lerner 1985). Specifically, they recognize the role of ontogenesis (individual development), but clearly specify a sociogenic theory of development and crime that focuses on social processes (see also Loeber and Le Blanc 1990; Elliott et al. 1989). They thus avoid the "fallacy of ontogenetic reductionism," in which socially organized developmental phenomena are reduced to individual ontogenetic causes (Dannefer 1984). Moreover, Sampson and Laub acknowledge that continuity in crime can be explained by individual differences that remain stable over time (population heterogeneity), or by changes directly brought on by an earlier criminal event (state dependence). Finally, they specify and test duration-dependent hypotheses about the time to crime given their theoretical model (1993: 171–78).

Sampson and Laub's work has set an important theoretical and research agenda for examination of crime in the life course. Nevertheless, we believe that a symbolic interactionist perspective can augment their theoretical argument in two important ways. First, by relaxing the assumptions made by control theories that the motivation for crime is constant across persons, that subcultures are impotent, and that only conventional culture matters, a symbolic interactionist theory can provide a more complete and nuanced theory of the content of culture—one that specifies a theory of the meaning of social roles, and links the life course to criminal and deviant subcultures. Second, by providing a situational theory of action, interactionism can stipulate how the dynamics of the immediate situation are linked to social roles, meanings, and behaviors, and how individual propensities (personality) are socially reconstituted in interactions. Third, the theory of meaning within interactions specifies a dialectical relationship between the life course and interaction: social interaction is conditioned by the life course, which at the same time, is socially constituted in interactions.

A Symbolic Interactionist Framework

Symbolic interactionism is a useful framework for developing a life-course theory of crime for several reasons. First, unlike structural functionalism, which underlies anomie and social control theories of crime, symbolic interactionism does not take a static view of society, social organization, and social order. Instead, interactionism builds on the philosophical position of American Pragmatism, beginning with a process model of society: society consists of an ongoing process of interactions, which fit together and constitute social organization and social order. Such a model is compatible with a life-course perspective that begins with a dynamic view of individual, group, and societal biographies. Second, symbolic interactionism takes a clear and consistent position on the ontogenetic-sociogenic debate. We follow George Herbert Mead's (1934) view of "biosocial man," in which the impulses, instincts, and genotypes of human biological organisms are translated into behavior through a social process consisting of interaction with others. Third, life-course perspectives emphasize the importance not only of role-transitions, but also of the meanings of such transitions to individuals (Elder 1985). Symbolic interactionism provides an explicit theory of meaning and a way of linking roles to meanings, identities, and subcultures (Stryker 1980). Finally, symbolic interactionism can stipulate specific mechanisms of population heterogeneity and state dependence within a unified framework. Thus, we can apply these mechanisms to crime without having to resort to ad hoc mixing of contradictory theories, like social control and labeling. To specify the mechanisms explicitly requires a brief review of a symbolic interactionist view of crime. We build upon statements made by Matsueda (1992) and Heimer and Matsueda (1994) in applying the principles to life-course issues.

Culture and Subcultures

Symbolic interactionism rejects the assumptions of sociology's structural functionalists, and criminology's social control theorists, that society consists of a single moral order and that subcultures are irrelevant to the motivation of crime and delinquency (Kornhauser 1978; Hirschi 1969). Instead, interactionists assume that pluralist societies consist of a diversity of perspectives organized along lines of communication. These perspectives at times crystalize into distinct social worlds, in which groups organize around a common set of concerns and viewpoints. These subcultures can give rise to new ways of solving problems or adapting to the environment. At the same time, they can give rise to a parochialism that generates deviant behavior from the standpoint of other groups.

A dominant culture in pluralist societies consists of the intersection of various perspectives, and is socially constituted in interaction. In general, a dominant culture consists of norms, beliefs, and behavior patterns that facilitate success in conventional realms and proscribe deviant and criminal behavior. In a market economy, various forms of capital investment increase the likelihood of individual market success, including investments in human capital, such as schooling and job training (Becker 1964), social capital, which inheres in social relations such as obligations and expectations, information channels, and norms (Coleman 1990), and cultural capital, defined as competence in elite status cultures, including elite attitudes, behaviors, and habits (Bourdieu 1977). These forms of capital are resources that can be translated into material rewards through conventional institutions. Moreover, capital investments should reduce the likelihood of criminality by increasing conventional role commitments, identities, and reference groups, and by reducing incentives for crime.

Furthermore, within criminal subcultures, one can speak of rudimentary criminal counterparts to conventional culture.[1] That is, success in a criminal subculture may be increased by investing in criminal counterparts to human, social, and cultural capital. Thus, members of these subcultures might gain greater monetary returns, prestige, and status through investing in criminal skills, training, obligations, information channels, norms, attitudes, and habits. Because such structures and norms foster behavior proscribed by the larger social system—which mobilizes resources to combat the behavior—they will remain comparatively rudimentary, weak, and ineffectual relative to conventional structures. Nevertheless, in contrast to disorganization and control theorists, we do not view these structures and cultures as entirely impotent (Matsueda 1988). For individuals unable to attain success in conventional ways, criminal structures may be important determinants of crime (e.g., Cloward and Ohlin 1960). We use the term "criminal capital" to refer to forms of human, social, and cultural capital that foster returns to criminal behavior. Both conventional and criminal capital investments vary across the life course and are critical variables in explaining the timing and sequence of behaviors and roles. We argue that investments in various forms of capital and the resulting decisions based on those investments are in part conditioned by taking the role of significant others in problematic situations.

Social Process and Transactions: Role-Taking

Symbolic interactionism assumes that society is an ongoing process of social transactions, consisting of interactions between two or more individuals. Transactions are built up by participants' adjustments to each other and their situations. When adjustments are smooth and routine, they occur without self-consciousness. When they are temporarily blocked, the situation becomes problematic and the individuals engage in role-taking, solving the problematic situation by taking the role of others, viewing themselves as objects from the standpoint of others, and considering alternative lines of action from the standpoint of others (Mead 1934). When an act or impulse is blocked by a physical or social barrier, an emotion is released, and the impulse is transformed into an image, including a plan of action and the anticipated reactions of others to the action. This image is then reacted to by another impulse, which either follows the plan into overt behavior, combines the plan with another, or blocks the plan, causing the situation to remain problematic. Mead (1934) referred to the image as the "me," the reacting impulse as the "I," so that cognition is an internal dialogue or conversation between two phases of the self, the "I" and the "me." This process continues until the problem is solved or the transaction ends. Once the problem is solved, the "me" is incorporated into the self in memory, and can be called up in future problematic situations. When problematic situations are solved repeatedly in similar ways, they become less problematic, and behavior becomes more habitual, nonreflective, and scripted (Matsueda 1992; Heimer and Matsueda 1994). Specifically, consistent with some psychological research, situations that are encountered repeatedly become routine and do not trigger deep cognitive processing; behavior, therefore, appears relatively "mindless" and unfolds in a scripted fashion (Shiffrin and Schneider 1977; Langer 1989). Thus, successive solutions to problematic situations—solutions that are rewarded, to use the terms of social learning theories, leads to continuity in behavior—whether legal or illegal—across similar situations. For example, within turf gangs, violence may be automatic and nonreflective, whereas within a church choir, violence would rarely result and only after considerable reflection.

The self, then, is the critical locus of social control, and consists of a dialectical relationship between the "I" and the "me." The "me" consists of the portion of the self rooted in one's organized groups; the "I" consists of impulses, some of which are socially conditioned. Moreover, the "I" contains a variable element of novelty or emergence, so that the response of the "I" can never be predicted perfectly by the "me."

From this standpoint, criminal acts refer to specific directions of ongoing behaviors. The probability of such behaviors occurring is a function of the situation into which interactants self-select, and the contributions of each interactant to the direction of that behavior. Those contributions in turn are a function of the individual biographical histories of each interactant relevant to criminality. This includes stable views of the self (as a criminal or conformist) from the standpoint of others, attitudes and motives about crime, and anticipated reactions of others toward crime (Heimer and Matsueda 1994).

Role-Commitment and Differential Social Control

Because the self consists of a dialectic between the "I" and the "me," behavior is patterned, but not completely determined. Stability in the self results from stability in the organization of attitudes in the "me," or the generalized other, which leads to continuity in behavior within individuals. This organization of the self results from participation in organized groups, which implies that those individuals who participate in similar organized groups will display similarities in behavior relevant to the particular group. For example, youths who participate in delinquent peer groups are likely to take the role of delinquents when considering whether to engage in delinquent behavior. If role-taking involving this generalized other repeatedly solves problematic situations, the delinquent group is likely to constitute an important element of a youth's "me" and the youth is likely to become increasingly committed to the group, which becomes an important generalized other. Thus, self-control is social control because social organization enters behavior through the process of taking the role of the other (Matsueda 1992).

With respect to unlawful behavior it is important to emphasize that social control varies in strength *and* meaning. In a pluralistic society, members participate in multiple groups, which vary not only in the degree to which they control the behavior of a given member, but also in the meaning or content of control—either encouraging or dissuading criminal behavior through the process of role-taking. Therefore, social control of criminal versus conventional behavior is a process of differential social control—either toward conventional or criminal habits and solutions to problematic situations (Matsueda 1992; see also Elliott et al. 1989). Differential social control includes stable views of the self (as a criminal or conformist) from the standpoint of others, attitudes and motives about crime, and anticipated reactions of others to crime (Heimer and Matsueda 1994).

Identity theorists have specified testable generalizations to capture this process by which participation in groups leads to certain forms of behavior (McCall and Simmons 1978; Stryker 1980). Identity theory proposes that commitment to a specific role in an organized group increases the likelihood that the group will serve as a generalized other in problematic situations. The symbolic interactionist concept of role-commitment entails notions of "side-bets" (Becker 1960) or the cost of giving up meaningful relationships with others (Stryker 1968), and contains both a cognitive base (commitment) and a socioemotional base (attachment) (Burke and Reitzes 1991). The greater the rational or emotional cost of jeopardizing a role, the greater the commitment to the role. Role commitments, then, are an important element of social capital: they constitute the structure of social networks and imply obligations, expectations, information, and norms.

Commitment to roles is linked to the self through identities, an important feature of the stable self. Here, the self is viewed as a system of hierarchically organized role-identities. The most important, salient, or prominent identities are those that correspond to roles that have received greater investments by the individual (Stryker 1968, 1980; McCall and Simmons 1978). These identities are built up fundamentally through ongoing processes of interaction: through participation in organized groups leading to recurrent role-taking involving those groups, commitments to group roles are built up, and corresponding identities established. The identity becomes more salient or prominent, increasing the likelihood that it will be the basis of future behavior, in part because the corresponding behaviors have become habitualized, and in part because the identity becomes relevant to an increasingly broader range of situations. Thus, over time, as behavior becomes routinized, the "I" recedes in importance and a wider range of problems are resolved from the standpoint of a specific role-identity or generalized other. Turner (1978) used the term, "role-person merger," to refer to this situation in which the person becomes so identified with a specific role that he or she seeks to enact the role even when it may be inappropriate. Under these circumstances, behavior is routinized, the "I" is relatively dormant, and change is unlikely. This view of stability and change in the self helps explain life-course transitions. But also relevant to that explanation are biological differences.

A Biosocial View of Human Behavior

Most symbolic interactionists, following Blumer (1969) and others, have ignored the role that genetic, biological, and constitutional factors play in behavior, and instead have assumed that social processes are sufficient to account for behavior. We take a different view, beginning with Mead's view of humans as biosocial organisms (see also Shibutani 1961).[2] In this view, genetics alone do not determine criminality—i.e., there is no crime gene—but inheritance does play an important role in the process leading to crime, operating indirectly through social interaction. This view is generally consistent with twin and adoption studies of crime. Twin studies show that correlations between delinquency of identical twins (e.g., .70) are consistently higher than those of fraternal twins (e.g., .50), suggesting that both genetics and shared environments play an important role in acounting for behavior (e.g., Rowe 1983). Adoption studies show that the criminality of adoptees resembles the criminality of biological parents slightly more than that of adoptive parents (e.g., Mednick, Gabrielli, and Hutchings 1984). Although these studies have been criticized on methodological grounds (e.g., Walters and White 1989; Gottfredson and Hirschi 1990), it is hard to deny that inheritance plays some role (Walters and White 1989; Plomin 1986).

But what are the specific mechanisms by which genes influence criminal behavior? Scarr and McCartney (1983) argue that the way in which genetic traits influence behavioral outcomes is by affecting the environment. They identify three mechanisms by which genotypes *select* environments: (1) passively, in which parents select environments of their children (because parents' genotypes are correlated with children's genotypes, the result is a correlation between child's genotypes and environment); (2) evocatively, in which the physical and social environment responds to a child's genotypes; and (3) actively, in which a child's genotype directly selects the environment. Moreover, these are age-dependent effects: passive selection is emphasized in infancy, when parents determine a child's environment; and active selection is increasingly empha-sized in adolescence and adulthood.

This conception of the interplay between genetics and environments can be consistent with an interactionist framework. From an interactionist standpoint, human beings are biosocial organisms that adjust to chang-ing environments; the ability to engage in self-reflective behavior—in which the attitudes of organized groups enter behavior—is the highest evolutionary form of adjustment because it gives humans the capacity to change the environment to which they must adjust. Thus, human beings are born with genotypes, constitutions, and temperaments, but these do not directly determine behavior. Instead, they restrict the range of behav-iors possible, and affect the likelihood that certain environments are se-lected. The most important element of the environment is role-taking, in which adjustments to the environment are self-conscious. In the case of infants and young children, parents help determine environments in part unintentionally, due to their structural limitations (e.g., resources), and in part intentionally, as they exercise their discrimination, tastes, and values. The physical and social environment selected will affect a child's behavior by circumscribing the child's social transactions. But the environment's response to the child's constitution and evolving social self is more critical. Here the self emerges through reciprocal role-taking in social transactions. From an interactionist standpoint, the evocative and active mechanisms of selecting environments are not discrete. Rather, they emerge jointly out of interaction: the self is built up from appraisals of oneself by others, and the self in turn actively selects future lines of action to adapt to present problematic situations.

An example of how a genetic characteristic affects criminality is given in Caspi, Elder, and Bem's (1987) work on child temper tantrums. This work shows how early child temper tantrums can lead to later problems in life (e.g., downward occupational mobility, erratic work lives, and divorce) through one of two mechanisms: cumulative continuity, in which the maladaptive behavior selects individuals into negative environments (e.g., dropping out of school) that perpetuate the maladaption; and inter-actional continuity, in which reciprocal interaction with the environment leads to sustained maladaptive behaviors. From an interactionist stand-point, these two mechanisms derive from a continuous social process, in which reciprocal role-taking produces a self that selects future environ-ments. Thus, early child tantrums can lead to criminality through a labeling process: temperamental outbursts lead to problems in conventional settings, like preschool and kindergarten, causing adults to discipline and label the child as a troublemaker or problem-child, which alters the child's views of self, increasing the likelihood of sustained troublesome behavior. This, in turn, can increasingly channel a child into situations conducive to deviance, foreclose conventional opportunities, and leave the child with a deviant identity.

Symbolic Interaction, Life Course, and Delinquency

Symbolic Interaction and the Life Course

We can use a symbolic interactionist framework to examine delinquency within the life course. The most important phases of the life course include infancy, childhood, adolescence, and adulthood. Within these phases are age-graded or development-graded social roles including the roles of dependent child, student, adolescent peer, employee, criminal, spouse, parent, military employee, etc. When viewed within a person and across time, these roles trace out life-course trajectories for individuals.

From an interactionist standpoint, there exists a dialectical relationship between the life course—consisting of age-graded and developmentally graded organized social roles—and social interactions (Wells and Stryker 1986). On the one hand, the life course, like other aspects of social organization, is constituted in social interaction; on the other hand, social interactions are in part conditioned by the life course. But how exactly is behavior conditioned by the life course, and how exactly is the life course constituted in interaction? We can posit two mechanisms: (1) an endogenous process in which actors consider aspects of the life course in carrying out meaningful, self-conscious behavior; and (2) an exogenous social structuring that may or may not condition the consciousness of actors.

Drawing on our earlier discussion of role-taking within problematic situations and Mead's theory of temporality, we can specify an endogenous process by which the life course is constituted. One can think of features of the life course as abstract objects whose meaning is constituted in social interactions. Although we can speak of a life course as an objective phenomenon existing independent of consciousness, it is an indefinite object; what is important in behavior is the specific meaning of features of the life course as constituted in interactions. Thus, an individual's biographical history—including the content of identities, definitions of situations, and role-expectations—is limited by his or her specific life-course roles, transitions, and trajectories. In the process of engaging in meaningful action, individuals take the role of the other, call up elements from the past to solve problematic situations in the present in light of future consequences. When individuals consider aspects of their biographical past or consider the future consequences of action that have implications for future role-transitions and trajectories, they are taking into self-conscious consideration features of the life course. For example, a high school dropout may consider whether he wants to pursue drug dealing as a major source of income, or instead delay gratification, take a low-paying conventional job, and attend an evening trade school. The decision may involve considering the attitudes of peers toward drug dealing, the risks and future potential involved, as well as imagining the probability of garnering a high paying job after completing trade school, and the meaning of such a job. The life course as a whole consists in part of the aggregation of interactions such as these that involve self-conscious attention to some of its constituent features.

But the life course also is constituted partly exogenously in interactions, without self-consciousness. When the features of a nonproblematic situation—including role relationships of interactants, the objective opportunities to engage in behavior, such as crime, and the resources available to interactants—are age-graded or developmental, they directly constitute the life course in social interaction. Finally, the life course also constrains social interaction, and thus behavior. Here age-graded or development-graded roles affect behavior by delimiting opportunities, and affecting the generalized other and identities by affecting communication networks, peer associations, and subcultural affiliation.

Role Transitions and Crime

The life course can be viewed as a series of transitions, representing choice points, or branches in a time-ordered tree diagram. Each choice made at one point opens up opportunities and choices at a future time point, as well as closing off other opportunities (Atchley 1975; Wells and Stryker 1986). For example, dropping out of high school reduces the likelihood of obtaining a job that requires a college degree, while increasing the likelihood of pursuing criminal careers, such as dealing drugs. For our purposes, an important distinction is between conventional and criminal roles. Conventional roles entail predominantly law-abiding behavior; when crime is called for, it is exceptional and transient. Criminal roles entail predominantly law-abiding behavior as well; but it also includes criminal behavior as a major defining feature. For example, most of the day-to-day behavior of persons occupying the roles of pimp or drug dealer is law-abiding behavior, but nevertheless the roles are defined by sustained criminal role expectations of organizing prostitution and selling drugs, respectively. Most acts of crime are probably transient rather than role behavior.

A symbolic interactionist perspective can help explain why some individuals undergo life-course transitions at particular times, while others do not, and how such transitions may affect the probability of illegal behavior. According to interactionism, role transitions and continuity are each an outcome of social interaction. That is, within social transactions, individuals self-select into social roles—including age-graded roles—and are selected by social groups into social roles. Most importantly, self-selection and other selection into roles occurs simultaneously in social interaction.

At an abstract level of explanation, we can specify the major determinants of role-continuity versus role-transition, given a decision point between two or more age-graded social roles. This entails factors that push one out of a social role and factors that pull one into another role. These determinants include the context of the decision, particularly its location in social structure; and the factors that affect the direction of role-taking, including impulses, habits, commitments, reference groups, attitudes, and anticipated reactions. The immediate context of the decision conditions the outcome by framing possible objective alternatives. Here, structural position, defined by access to resources and power in society, becomes important. The greater the resources and power, the greater the range of alternative roles, and the greater the likelihood of selecting a role that maximizes tangible rewards and minimizes aversive outcomes. An individual located in an advantaged social class with greater human capital (education, experience, and skills) and social capital (network connections, obligations and authority, norms and sanctions, and information) will have access to a wider range of social roles, such as high-paying desirable jobs, than a lower-class person lacking capital. By determining the objective possibilities, social structure will exert a direct effect on the likelihood of individual role-transitions. This holds for criminal as well as conventional roles. For criminal roles, criminal capital—network connections, information, and obligations associated with criminal subcultures—are particularly important (Letkemann 1973; Steffensmeier 1986).

In addition to these direct effects, structural location may affect role-transitions indirectly. Here symbolic interactionism can help specify selection mechanisms. From an interactionist standpoint, social structure conditions alternatives, but selection into a role is dependent on perceptions of alternatives and their meanings, which are formed through role-taking in interactions. People are likely to remain in roles if they do not perceive the opportunity to change, even if opportunity exists objectively. Here the situation does not become problematic, and people will continue engaging in habitual behavior associated with existing roles. However, once alternative roles are under consideration, the situation becomes problematic and persons engage in role-taking. The outcome of this role-taking process will be affected by the relative meanings of the present and prospective roles. These meanings, in turn, are determined by perceived appraisals by others, salience of the role-identities, and strength of habits and attitudes corresponding to the roles. It follows that role-continuity is more likely for individuals who have experienced a restricted range of roles, a restricted set of generalized others, and a restricted range of information about new roles.

Selection into roles is often a joint transaction carried out between two or more individuals. For example, employment is typically a joint decision between employer and employee (Sørensen and Kalleberg 1981), college entrance is a joint decision between student applicants and college admission committees, and entrance into professional crime rings is often a joint process of inquiry and recruitment (Sutherland 1937; Letkemann 1973). Similarly, selection out of roles can also be a joint decision: for example, the decision to divorce or separate at a particular time is often determined jointly by spouses, or the decision to leave a criminal organization may be a joint decision among members. In each case, the transaction entails role-taking, as interactants take the role of the other in a process of developing a joint definition of the situation, and work toward a given outcome. The outcome will be governed by the emergent dynamics of the interaction, in which interactants consider the perspectives of the other in light of the immediate circumstances, drawing upon past experiences to fit behavior together and attain a future objective.

Individuals lacking qualities or skills that social roles require will be unlikely to be selected into such roles. Through the interactional process of being denied entrance into various roles, the individual is likely to adjust by externalizing failure, devaluing the role, or internalizing failure, and blaming himself. They may have no alternatives to less-desirable positions, and may also develop a preference for such positions. The clearest example of this is given by Gottfredson and Hirschi (1990), who argue that persons who are impulsive, unskilled, unable to plan or delay gratification, and preoccupied with risk-taking are unlikely to succeed at conventional activities, such as school, jobs, and family life, and at the same time unable to control their criminality. But for Gottfredson and Hirschi (1990), the effects of life-course transitions are spuriously related to criminal behavior: each is entirely determined by a stable individual personality trait they term "low self control." We argue that selection into life-course events such as high school dropout, unemployment, and divorce may result from an interactional process that reflects in part prior individual characteristics—including mutable elements of the self—but that those events and their attendant roles directly effect criminality by changing opportunities, resources, reference groups, and therefore, elements of the self that in part selected the events in the first place (Thornberry 1987). Thus, there may be a long-term tendency toward cumulative continuity, in which individual characteristics select for roles and events which reinforce those characteristics (Caspi, et al. 1987).

Social roles may have disparate effects on criminal behavior depending on the specific role and the type of criminal offense examined. Here a simple typology of social roles is useful: (1) social roles that are overwhelmingly conventional (e.g., schoolteacher); (2) social roles that typically include specific forms of criminal behavior (e.g., college fraternity member); and (3) criminal roles in which some form of sustained crime is a defining characteristic (e.g., gang member). Net of individual characteristics, conventional social roles can affect crime in several ways. The most important mechanism is through their effects on reference groups, generalized others, and perspectives. Reference groups are often attached to social roles in that the group supports the behavior and expectations of the role. Thus, repeated positive interaction with a reference group corresponding to a role will increase one's commitment to the role. For example, employment in a firm brings the employee into contact with other employees who serve as a reference group. Role commitment, in turn, will on average reduce the likelihood of behaviors that may be inconsistent with the role or even jeopardize the role, such as crime (e.g., Sampson and Laub 1992). But the effect of commitment on crime may be contingent on the meaning of the role in relation to crime. For example, developing a committed marriage to a criminal spouse may increase the likelihood of criminal behavior. Having a child may have very different meanings for an impoverished inner-city family than an affluent family. These different meanings may be consequential for crime. For the impoverished family, having a child may increase pressure for welfare fraud or theft, whereas for the affluent family, having a child may increase commitment to the family unit. Some conventional social roles may carry expectations or tolerances for certain forms of criminal behavior, such as employee theft, embezzlement, or violations of affirmative action laws. Here, developing a commitment to the role may reduce the likelihood of crime in general, while increasing the likelihood of a specific role-related criminal act.

In contrast, criminal roles operate very differently. Because sustained criminal behavior is a defining characteristic of the role, increased commitments will increase those role-specific offenses, net of the individual characteristics that selected for the role. Role-commitments are built up through interacting with other members of the criminal group and successfully committing criminal acts (Elliott, Huizinga, and Ageton 1985; Elliott, et al. 1989). Again, the meaning of the role is critical, which explains why some roles select for certain crimes, like insider-trading or embezzlement, and not others, like gang violence. Criminal roles may affect one's general attitudes toward deviant behavior, and thus generalize to other forms of crime as well. The meaning of the role entails how one sees oneself from the standpoint of significant others, attitudes toward the role, and role-expectations, and operates through the process of role-taking. Continuity in and commitment to criminal roles are also affected by interactions with conventional society, which may reinforce the role through negative labeling. For example, convicted criminals have difficulties returning to conventional society because of the stigma of their status (e.g., Irwin 1970). Negative labeling may make it difficult to find employment, increasing the likelihood of resuming a criminal role.

That is, net of individual characteristics that handicap them on the labor market, the negative reactions to their prior criminal roles may contribute to cumulative continuity.

Role Trajectories and Duration-Dependent Mechanisms

For a theory of crime to take a developmental or life-course approach, it must specify not only the effects of roles and transitions on crime, but also specify duration-dependent causal mechanisms (Featherman and Lerner 1985). One way of framing this discussion is to follow Daniel Nagin's (Nagin and Paternoster 1991; Nagin and Farrington 1992) lead and apply Heckman's (1981) distinction between state dependence versus population heterogeneity to crime (see also Sampson and Laub 1993). Heckman (1981) argued that continuity in events, like spells of unemployment or poverty, can be explained by individual differences that remain stable over time (population heterogeneity) or by changes directly brought about by the earlier event, like changes in preferences, constraints, or prices (state dependence). Nagin and his colleagues apply this to crime, noting that persistent criminality can be due to individual characteristics that select for crime (heterogeneity), like low self-control, biological characteristics, or relatively stable structural characteristics like social class, as well as mechanisms that result from the *event* of committing a crime, such as secondary deviance, specific deterrence, and social learning.[3] They find support for state dependence and rule out inertia or mere habit (Nagin and Paternoster 1991), but elsewhere find more support for heterogeneity over state dependence (Nagin and Paternoster 1992).[4]

State dependence can be further decomposed into two components identified by Caspi et al. (1987): cumulative continuity, in which maladaptive behavior increasingly channels an individual into environments that sustain the behavior; and interactional continuity, in which maladaptive behavior is responded to by others (in reciprocal social interaction) in ways that maintain the behavior (see also Sampson and Laub 1993). The former refers to a sorting process into structural positions, while the latter refers to sorting into interactional sequences. We argued above that a symbolic interactionist perspective implies that both selection into social roles (due to individual heterogeneity) and the social role itself (state dependence) should affect subsequent role transitions and behavioral outcomes, like crime and deviance. Moreover, the mechanism by which individuals select into roles and positions is the self, which itself is in part socially constituted in interactions. This is consistent with Moffitt's (1993) view that life-course persistent delinquents may begin with neuropsychological deficits and temperament problems, which selects them into structural positions conducive to labeling and antisocial behavior, and results in interactions in which they fail to learn prosocial alternatives. She suggests that adolescence-limited delinquents tend to imitate the delinquent acts of life-course persistent peers in an effort to establish autonomy and maturity. Our view is also consistent with Sampson and Laub's (1993) findings that adult social roles affect adult criminality net of childhood delinquency, temperament, and low self control, and contrasts with the position of Gottfredson and Hirschi (1990) who argue that stability in crime should be the result of heterogeneity in the form of the trait of low self-control.

Within this framework, we can specify duration-dependent hypotheses. One source of hypotheses stems from variation in the process of selection into social roles. Selection can vary in the degree to which it is systematic versus random. Thus, selection is often very systematic as previously discussed, a process of interaction involving self-selection and other-selection. But at other times, selection into roles can be the result of stochastic processes, in which other-selection is minimal and self-selection is either minimal or dominated by the "I," the impulsive component of the self. We can hypothesize that the stronger the systematic component of the selection process, the greater the correspondence between the individual's characteristics (including temperament, constitution, impulses) and social self (including one's generalized other), and the social role. The result is that subsequent commitment to the role will be stronger, increasing role-continuity over time. Conversely, the stronger the stochastic component of selection, the greater the discontinuity between individual characteristics and the social role. The result is that the individual is less likely to fit in with reference groups associated with the new role, less likely to come to identify with the role, and therefore, more likely to seek a role change. Duration in the role will be short. This process would be even more extreme in the unlikely case in which systematic selection produces mismatches between individual and role.

Similarly, when the selection into social roles is primarily self-selection rather than other-selection, there should be a greater fit between the self and the role, and a greater motivation to develop a commitment to the role. This should increase the duration of the role. Of course, the mere fact of self-selection does not guarantee a fit between an individual and a role; this hypothesis holds only net of other qualifications, skills, and attributes for the role. Conversely, when selection is primarily other-selection, the individual may not fit as well (because others do not have access to full information on the biographical history of the individual) and may be less-motivated to stay in the role. For example, a youth who selects into a delinquent gang because he has strongly aspired to gain the status of a gang member is more likely to stay in the gang than someone who was uninterested in the gang, but was selected out of propinquity. The first youth is more likely to fit in with the gang, adopt its perspective, and fulfill its role-expectations.

Net of the individual characteristics (heterogeneity) that selected an individual into the role, a variety of events occur that affect commitment to the role and, thus, duration (state dependence). The most important is a change in reference groups. This in turn leads to changes in the self as viewed from the standpoint of others, increasing the likelihood of role-behavior and commitment to the role. Thus, a transition into a subcultural delinquent role may increase negative labeling by conventional institutions, increase status and identities based on subcultural norms and behavior, and perhaps increase objective opportunities to perform the new role-behavior. Finally, the consequences of role-specific behaviors will affect role continuity and commitment: positive psychic and material returns from a criminal role will increase identification with the role, while negative returns will decrease identification.

It follows that, all else constant, the longer the waiting time in a conventional or criminal role, the greater the likelihood of commitment and the lesser the likelihood of change. In other words, if we define an individual hazard rate of role-continuity as a latent variable representing the propensity to remain in the role per unit of time, the hazard averaged across individuals should increase with duration in the role. This is because there will be greater time for interactions based on the role, performance of role-behavior, and communications with a role-specific reference group. The result is that the self will increasingly become tied to the role. But for those individuals who are mismatched to the role, interactions and role-performance will be negative, resulting in the opposite effect. Mismatched individuals will have short role-durations, as they seek to exit the role. Moreover, the longer they remain in the role (are unsuccessful in exiting), the greater the negative interactions and the greater the likelihood of a role-transition. Thus, the effect of role-duration on the hazard or a role-transition is conditional on being mismatched to the role. Furthermore, even for those well-matched, at some point increase in commitment will be offset by countervailing processes, such as reaching a saturation point of interest, reaching a point of diminishing returns, or reaching a point in which the physiological effects of aging begin to hamper adequate role-performance and therefore, attainment of rewards. The result is that, on average, hazards for role-continuity will begin to decline increasingly over time, causing the aggregate of hazards to trace out a curve that resembles the age-crime curve: a sharp increase early in the role, followed by a slow decline over time. Of course, a role-transition can involve exiting a role and entering a new role(s), or adding a new role(s) to one's constellation of role-relationships. Regardless of whether one exits the original role when entering a new role(s), such transitions involve a process of competing risks among possible roles. Thus, individual role-trajectories are summary statements of individual hazard rates of competing risks among social roles, which from our standpoint, are socially constituted in interactions. And, as Hagan and Palloni (1988) show, the age-crime curve is an aggregate of individual trajectories of criminality versus other social roles. We can examine these trajectories by examining their constituents: age-graded or development-graded role transitions through the life course. These transitions typically occur during major life stages: childhood, adolescence, and adulthood.

Child Development and Antisocial Behavior

Interaction, Identity Formation, and
Deviant Behavior in Early Childhood

Social control rests on the ability to take the role of the other, which requires the acquisition of language, or significant symbols that call out the functionally identical response in self and others (Miller 1973). After young children have developed language skills, an important development with respect to antisocial behavior is the learning of the significant symbol, the directive, "No," which distinguishes appropriate and inappropriate behavior from the standpoint of others. In addition, the social self begins to emerge through rudimentary role-taking, in which children begin to label and differentiate themselves from others (Hewitt 1987). As children experience a wider range of situations, particularly those outside the family setting (e.g., preschool or play with other children), their ability to take the perspectives of others improves (Denzin 1972). Role-taking now takes the form of play-acting, in which children perform discrete roles serially, such as playing mother, doctor, nurse (Mead 1934). At this stage, the child is not cognizant of the larger social group in which the role is embedded and takes the role of the other without considering relationships to larger social groups, such as the family or hospital staff. Social control, then, at the age of three or four, consists of a serial process of considering the reactions of concrete significant others, like mother, father, best friend, teacher, and so on. The identities that emerge at this stage are restricted largely to gender identity, body image, and personal characteristics (Keller, Ford, and Meacham 1978). Such embryonic identities are unstable, changing easily with situational context. Nevertheless, they can set up patterns of self-reflection that extend throughout the life course (Demo 1992). Indeed, the identities that begin to form during the preschool years can be consequential for future roles and identities. It follows that young children who become accustomed to seeing themselves as "bad kids" or "troublemakers" through the eyes of others are likely to perceive negative appraisals from others as they age, which can increase the chances for forming a delinquent identity in later years.

By the time children are five or six years old, their cognitive capabilities have matured to the point where they can view situations from the perspectives of a variety of others, including teachers, peers, and parents, and anticipate the reactions of others to certain lines of action (Entwistle, et al. 1987). Their developing cognitive capabilities also allow for the emergence of a stable set of attitudes toward the self by this time, which we can think of as the "core" self-concept (Demo 1992). Research shows that children who have developed a core self-image as a "bad kid" through taking the roles of their parents, teachers, and peers are more likely than children who view themselves as "good kids" to intentionally break rules at home and school because misbehavior is consistent with their identities (Matsueda 1992). Misbehavior, of course, perpetuates others' appraisals and reflected appraisals as a "bad kid," increasing the chances of future deviance (Matsueda 1992). Conversely, children who have come to see themselves as "good kids" through the eyes of others will be relatively unlikely to violate rules and norms, prompting further appraisals by others and reflected appraisals as a good kid and making future rule violation less likely. This labeling process occurring early in life can lead to self-fulfilling prophecies.

From our perspective, labeling of children does not occur in a vacuum but reflects objective characteristics of children, like abilities, temperaments, and constitutions. For example, intelligent, sociable preschoolers tend to have more positive interactions with caretakers than other children, which can produce positive labels and self-images (MacKinnon and King 1988). The relationship between objective characteristics and interactional environments reflects a three-pronged selection process (e.g., Scarr and McCartney 1983). First, when children are very young, parents likely play a large role in creating the association between characteristics and interactional environments—parents presumably share with their children genotypes related to intelligence and sociability and therefore select environments for their children that to some extent are "matched" to such characteristics. Second, intelligent, sociable children may themselves evoke positive responses from others because of the value given to these characteristics in our culture. By contrast, less intelligent, reticent children may evoke fewer positive responses and more negative responses. Third, bright, sociable children may themselves seek out positive interactions with others. The outcome is that intelligent and sociable children are more likely to find themselves in social environments that reward these attributes and accordingly begin to develop corresponding identities. By contrast, less intelligent, less socially skilled, and temperamental children may receive negative sanctions rather than rewards for these attributes, and thus, develop negative identities.

We can imagine that parents will channel temperamental children into interactions that reinforce such tendencies, and that temperamental children will evoke negative responses from others and will themselves initiate or select into interactions in which others perceive them to be "difficult children" or "troublemakers." Indeed, research finds that temperamental, aggressive children who are not socially responsive tend to evoke coercive and erratic responses from parents, which increases antisocial behavior (Keller and Bell 1979; Patterson 1982; Lytton 1990; Patterson, Reid, and Dishion 1992). We argue that such responses to children increase negative labeling, which can set in motion a self-fulfilling prophecy leading to behavioral trajectories that "move against the world," including later delinquency (see Caspi, et al. 1987; Moffitt 1993). A similar process may account for the greater likelihood of future delinquency among children with attention-deficit disorders (Moffitt 1990; White, et al. 1990). In short, characteristics that lead to selection into particular environments during early childhood can have implications for labeling and reflected appraisals. When reflected appraisals from a variety of sources converge on a common self-image, they become a core part of self and thus, have significant consequences for future trajectories of deviance versus conformity.

Another clear example of the selection process is the influence of sex on interactional environments. Parents view and treat infants differently on the basis of sex from the time they are born, thereby creating different social environments for males and females and initiating the formation of gender identity (see Cahill 1980). After gender identity emerges, children become active agents in gender role construction by seeking out situations in which they test and learn to express gender identity. Also, the biological fact of being male or female evokes quite different reactions and expectations from the others with whom children interact, such as families, teachers, and peers (see Goffman 1977; Cahill 1980). As in the case of ability and temperament, this three-pronged selection process leads to the formation of gender identity. Because our culture defines female antisocial behavior more negatively than male antisocial behavior, strong gender identity should reduce the chances of future delinquency among females but not males (Schur 1983; Heimer, 1996).

Such selection processes are conditioned by social structure. Parents with greater access to financial resources can mitigate the negative consequences for their temperamental children. And, differences in parenting styles across social class are likely consequential when parents select environments for their children based on children's attributes, like intelligence, sociability, or attention-deficit disorders.

Consequently, abilities, temperaments, constitutions, and social structure influence selection into interactional environments, which influence children's reflected appraisals, definitions of deviance, and anticipated reactions for deviance. For example, selection into an environment in which parental supervision is lax can attenuate the learning of moral principles from parents and increase the learning of antisocial motives from peers. Research provides partial support for this argument: (1) Difficult children, with histories of temper tantrums, are supervised less closely than other children and are more likely to break rules and laws (Sampson and Laub 1993: 91); and (2) selection processes result in less supervision for boys than girls and hence, higher rates of male than female delinquency (Jensen and Eve 1976; Hagan, Simpson, and Gillis 1987). The weaker supervision of boys and temperamental children increases delinquency by reducing the learning of conventional morals and enhancing the learning of delinquent definitions from peers. Also, the stronger the emotional connection between parent and child, the more likely the child is to consider the parent's reactions to delinquency— which presumably would be negative, averaged across persons—when they negotiate definitions of situations through role-taking (Heimer and Matsueda 1994; see also Hewitt, 1989:118).

Overall, we can specify a developmental hypothesis based on the discussion in this section. In early childhood, the negotiation of antisocial definitions of situations are influenced largely by impulses of the "I" and concrete others who are present in the immediate situation, but not abstract others who are not present. So, in a group of peers playing aggressively, children will be apt to behave similarly regardless of potential reactions by parents. By middle childhood (ages of nine to eleven), children's cognitive capabilities have developed sufficiently to allow them to grasp the notion of multiple explanations for behavior (Demo 1992). Here the child can recognize multiple and perhaps competing definitions of rule and norm-violating behaviors. Thus, children negotiate definitions of situations by simultaneously considering the perspectives of a variety of others, such as parents, teachers, and peers, who may be physically absent.

Generalized Others, Social Networks, Peer Groups, and Delinquency

By middle childhood, then, youths are capable of taking the perspectives of generalized others or reference groups. During the game stage of the development of self, a child is able to take the role of an abstract organized group, locate him or herself within the group, and consider the attitudes, rules, and expectations relating the child to other group roles. Mead's (1934) favorite example of the game is a baseball game, in which a pitcher must hold the attitudes of all incumbents of positions, including the batter, the catcher, the managers, and the other fielders. He is able to take the role of the abstract group, including the rules, norms, and expectations to organize the various roles. Involvement in antisocial peer groups has parallel consequences. Thus, the member of an antisocial peer group will be more likely to engage in group delinquency because the generalized other is organized around deviant behavior. As the child participates in increasingly diverse and broad groups, its generalized other broadens and diversifies. Continuity in generalized others (the "me") results in stability in self. But, the self also changes over time with changes in group participation and novel solutions (the "I") to problematic situations.

Children's generalized others likely reflect the perspectives of both families and peers, which at times conflict (Hewitt 1989:118; Heimer and Matsueda 1994). By middle childhood, however, the influence of peer groups is intensified and the influence of parents wanes (Thornberry, et al. 1991; Demo 1992). Peer interactions become crucial contexts for children's interpretations of their worlds, resulting in peer cultures that are essential for the development of the knowledge and skills necessary to participate in the adult world. In short, peers become at least as important as adults in the socialization process (Corsaro 1992:162).

From a symbolic interactionist perspective, peer groups are essential to antisocial behavior during childhood and adolescence because they shape identities and communicate cultural definitions of deviance. Once again, selection is important. Although parents influence selection into peer groups through supervision (Matsueda and Heimer 1987), selection by the peer groups and self-selection become more important by middle and late childhood. Thus, highly aggressive boys are rejected by conventional peer groups (Dishion 1990) and are likely to associate with other antisocial children (Dishion, et al. 1991; Vuchinich, Bank, and Patterson 1992). They are less likely to consider the perspectives of conventional peer groups and are more likely to take the role of the antisocial peer group in problematic situations. Consequently, these youths will continue to react to difficult situations aggressively and their antisocial and aggressive behavior will appear stable over time. When selection into deviant peer groups is systematic rather than random, stability in antisocial behavior may be due in large part to preexisting individual differences, or heterogeneity.

At other times, selection can be stochastic. For example, youths may be "falsely accused" of being troublemakers in school or fortuitously sorted into an antisocial peer group. If such stochastic processes lead youths to enact deviant or antisocial roles, the mere fact of role-occupancy *itself* can create stability in antisocial behavior through processes producing state dependence. By virtue of their group status, these youths may be further labeled as troublemakers, come to identify with the delinquent group, and learn delinquent attitudes and values.

Similarly, when youths select into peer groups that are organized against law violation, taking the role of these groups produces attitudes and identities that conflict with antisocial behavior. Again, such selection may be based on strong matching between the characteristics of youths and conventional groups and at other times may be approximately random. Strong selection into these groups would occur when youths have learned to conform to the expectations of authority figures, when youths' scholastic performance is encouraged and they develop commitments to academics, or when other characteristics of youths are strongly compatible with those of peer groups organized against delinquency. Interestingly, gender plays a strong role here. Boys' peer groups are integrated by the excitement derived from rule-violation, while girls' groups are integrated by sharing intimacies and secrets with each other (Thorne and Luria 1986). Boys gain status in their peer groups through the display of "toughness" and "coolness," while girls gain status through their physical appearances, social skills, and academic success (Adler, Kless, and Adler 1992). Consequently, girls are more likely than boys to select into groups that are organized against antisocial behavior.

Finally, the more systematic the role selection, the greater the match between the individual and the group, and therefore, the greater the future role-commitments and role-continuity. And, the longer the duration in a role, the greater the future continuity—until a major triggering event occurs. This is because the identities formed in interaction with groups become stable over time, persons are motivated to maintain stable self-images, and consequently, seek further interaction with these groups. It is also because other reference groups, such as parents and teachers, label youths, reducing the chances of transitions out of peer group roles. And, role transitions also become more difficult the longer one enacts a role because behavior becomes scripted, automatic, and nonreflective (Heimer and Matsueda 1994). This suggests that youths who have developed strong conventional or deviant role-identities will be likely to continue such trajectories during adolescence unless some major events occur to alter such trajectories. Other youths may be more susceptible to transitions across deviant and conventional groups.

Adolescence, Delinquency, and Youth Crime

Pubertal change is often viewed as an important trigger in the transition from childhood to adolescence. Indeed, adolescence is commonly seen as a period in which biological changes dramatically outpace social development, thus requiring great social adjustment. In addition, the transition from childhood to adolescence also involves a transition from elementary school to middle school and high school environments. These major biological and social changes create stress and contribute to the "difficulties" of adolescence (Simmons and Blyth 1987). One of the major adjustments that occurs during this period is the development of a stable identity (Erikson 1968) that allows the youth to align previous conceptions of self with current social, physical, and physiological changes. This requirement causes adolescents to be unusually egocentric and preoccupied with the evaluations and thoughts of their significant others and reference groups (Elkind 1967).

Understanding adolescence, then, requires a perspective that acknowledges the importance of biological as well as social development. A symbolic interactionist perspective can recognize both. From this viewpoint, biological tendencies, such as those accompanying puberty, set the context in which social interactions unfold. Indeed, physical and hormonal changes can create impulses, needs, or desires, which trigger role-taking; yet, the potency of such impulses is determined by the *meaning* that they are given when youths take themselves as objects from the perspectives of others (see Simmons and Blyth 1987). Thus, biological factors shape behavior principally through reflective thought, in which they are defined and examined by the individual.

This means that the dramatic physical and physiological changes that occur during this period create impulses or needs that are symbolized in identity crises, preoccupation with appraisals by others, and psychological stress, which in turn prompt delinquency when role-taking suggests that impulses and needs may be satisfied by delinquency. Physiological changes will have the largest impact on identity crises, reflected appraisals of self, and stress when they are "off-time." For instance, children that mature earlier or later than their peers must negotiate identities in light of off-time hormonal changes, growth spurts, voice changes, and the development of acne. Given that most youths emancipate from parents during this time (Montemayor 1983), the peer group becomes an especially important generalized other for giving meaning to physical changes (or lack of change). In some cases, the meaning given to maturational processes increases the chances of delinquency. Youths who experience early growth spurts may feel more comfortable interacting with older peers, who are of similar physical size, and may be more willing to engage in delinquency if this translates into acceptance by the group. For example, Caspi et al. (1993) find that early onset of pubertal changes (menarche) increases adolescent female delinquency in coed schools but not all-girl schools. They hypothesize that girls experiencing early menarche in coed schools associate with older delinquent boys, who influence them into delinquency. This mechanism does not occur in all-girl schools, since girls lack opportunities to associate with older boys. We would argue that the association and learning process entails role-taking with a reference group of older boys. In general, the important arenas for role-taking during adolescence are the school and peer group (e.g., Demo 1992).

Student Roles and the Social Organization of the School

Since the advent of mandatory education and child labor laws, the role of student and the social institution of the school have become central to the lives of adolescents, and thus, constitute a primary arena in which identities are formed (Coleman 1961; Greenberg 1977; Platt 1977). The social organization of the school, as a haven of development and learning, has a positive impact on the identities of most youths. For instance, the school provides youths with opportunities to develop academic skills within the classroom and social skills within extracurricular activities, such as organized sports, band, special interest, and leadership groups. When youths have experienced repeated successes in these arenas earlier in childhood, they will have developed identities premised on commitments to student roles, which they seek to maintain during adolescence. Consequently, the trajectories of conventional students, initiated in previous years, can continue into adolescence when youths continue to work for good grades and become further involved in extracurricular activities (Schafer and Polk 1967; Wiatrowski, Hansell, Massey, and Wilson 1982). These youths are relatively unlikely to adopt delinquent lines of action when they consider the perspectives of their teachers, other committed students, and the school (Heimer and Matsueda 1994).

By contrast, when youths have failed in the classroom or in extracurricular activities, they are less likely to view themselves positively from the perspectives of teachers and schools. Indeed, poor performance in the classroom and the absence of positive experiences with extracurricular activities can have devastating consequences for self-esteem, given the importance of the school and student roles during adolescence. This can be exacerbated when poor performance leads to failure to be promoted to the next grade and the youth is off-time in terms of age-graded transitions in comparison to peers. Under these circumstances, we can expect weak commitment to student roles, lack of motivation to perform well academically, and generally, alienation from school. Teachers are likely to view these youths in a negative light, which youths perceive through role-taking. This, in turn, heightens alienation and increases the chances of selection into groups of other alienated students (Menard and Morse 1984) in an attempt to repair a damaged identity (Kaplan 1980). In groups of similarly alienated peers, then, youths encourage one another to "reject the rejecters" (Sykes and Matza 1957), and innovate attitudes and behaviors that are counter to those supported by the school. When confronted with problematic situations, these youths are more likely than committed students to jointly negotiate delinquent lines of action.

The outcome of this labeling process can be seen in studies of academic tracking in schools. Students assigned to college tracks perform better and have a greater chance of high school graduation, even when factors that account for initial selection into track (e.g., ability) are controlled (Gamoran and Mare 1989). Net of social class and ability, students assigned to low and average ability tracks are viewed more negatively by teachers and classmates, have lower aspirations, have more negative self-images, are more alienated, and are more likely to drop out than their high track counterparts (e.g., Oakes 1985; Schafer and Olexa 1971). From an interactionist perspective, students in lower tracks are more likely than those in higher tracks to form reflected appraisals as poor students, which can be expected to hinder the development of strong commitments to academic roles and schooling. These youths, then, are more likely drop out of school and more likely to select into peer groups that encourage law violation. The general practice of ranking students may cause identity problems for students ranked on the bottom. In some ways, schools, like total institutions, seek to break down the identities youth bring to school, and reconstitute them in ways consistent with the ideology of achievement and the social control requirements of the school (Goffman 1961). Ironically, the degradation ceremonies in schools often exacerbate the problems of control, causing threats to identity and encouraging rebellion to restore self-images (Greenberg 1977).

Other aspects of the social organization of schooling contribute to alienation from conventional school roles. The first of these stems from our cultural definitions of adolescence, which emphasize conflicting values like moral maturity versus social irresponsibility, social concern versus egocentrism, and laudable ideals versus childish misbehavior (Kett 1977). While we expect *children* to be obedient, we expect *adolescents* to begin exercising their own judgement at some times, but yet not at others. Such contradictions are embodied in the social organization of the school. For example, through policies such as hall passes, bathroom monitoring, and dress codes, the school strips youths of autonomy and denies them the opportunity to demonstrate moral and social responsibility (Greenberg 1977). This presents a dilemma for youths when they take the perspective of the school in general, and specific teachers in particular: they are aware that the school simultaneously expects maturity and immaturity from them. Concretely, this means that when youths encounter novel situations, the likely social consequences for any given line of action will be unclear—sometimes responsibility and independence may be rewarded, and at other times, it may be negatively sanctioned. When the consequences for behavior are unclear, the likelihood of deviant behavior increases.

Social class can condition the interactionist process linking the school, role-taking, and delinquency. For instance, based on his study of working class British students, Willis (1977) argues that working-class cultural capital—norms, values, skills, speech patterns, demeanor, and practices—is devalued in schools, which instead reward and value middle-class cultural capital. Indeed, some argue that the typical language patterns used in schools are compatible with middle class but not working-class socialization, thereby communicating to youths a devaluing of working-class cultural capital from the outset (Meehan 1992). Through taking the role of teachers and the school itself, working-class youngsters become aware that their cultural capital is not valued highly and that success in the school setting would be difficult. Youths then act upon this knowledge by selecting into oppositional peer groups, which reproduce and revel in working-class culture and reject the academic achievement orientation of the school (Cohen 1955; Willis 1977). Eventually, the peer group becomes a much more important generalized other than teachers and schools, and these youths engage in activities that produce skills associated with working class rather than middle-class jobs. Finally, the emergent normative codes of oppositional peer groups may promote rejection of other middle-class values, such as the value given to private property, which increases the chances of delinquency among working class youths (Cohen 1955).

Peer Roles and the Social Organization of Peer Groups

Within adolescent peer groups, attention is largely focused on acceptance, status, and group solidarity (Corsaro and Eder 1990). Gossip and evaluation of group members becomes a primary activity, reinforcing membership and definitions of appropriate behavior from the perspective of the group (Eder and Enke 1991). Indeed, daily interactions with peer groups allow youths to constitute norms about appearance, friendship, sexuality, and achievement, which youths subsequently consider through role-taking when they negotiate identities and lines of action. In this way, peer groups are an important source of social control during adolescence.

In addition to reinforcing group solidarity and controlling members' behaviors, a common theme in adolescent peer groups is resistance and rebellion against adult rules (Wulff 1988). Reactance against adult authority may be due to the inherent contradictions in adolescence, such as pressures to conform and exert independence. Because it affords youths with autonomy and personal control, such reactance may be a "universal feature of peer culture" during adolescence (Corsaro and Eder 1990). Thus, when youths consider the perspectives of peer groups, they are quite likely to rebel against rules. And, because delinquency represents an extreme form of resistance to authority, peer group processes may explain part of the peak in crime during adolescence (Warr 1993). These arguments are consistent with the empirical finding that association with delinquent peers is a robust and powerful predictor of law violation during adolescence (e.g., Warr and Stafford 1991; Elliott and Menard in press; Matsueda and Heimer 1987).[5] Moreover, delinquent peers can increase the likelihood of delinquency via role-taking by fostering identities as troublemakers and transmitting definitions favorable to delinquency (Heimer and Matsueda 1994).

But what determines selection into delinquent peer groups? A critical factor is prior behavior. Indeed, deviant youths actively seek out similar peers (Billy and Udry 1985) and, therefore, actively shape their own future role-taking and delinquent behavior (Heimer and Matsueda 1994). Other social psychological factors contribute to the selection of peer groups: youths who are strongly committed to student roles, whose families disapprove of law violation, and whose parents offer warm and supportive emotional environments will be less likely to select into delinquent groups (Elliott, et al. 1985, 1989; Thornberry, et al. 1991).

Structural features of community organization also affect selection into delinquent peer groups. For instance, the opportunity structures of communities—such as the opportunities for getting a good education and landing a job that pays well—are consequential for the emergence of delinquent groups and gangs (Vigil 1985; Hagedorn 1985; Sullivan 1989; Hagan 1991). Specifically, when opportunities for economic success through legitimate avenues are not available, youths may adapt by forming deviant subcultures (Cohen 1955; Cloward and Ohlin 1960). Youths who live in communities where legitimate opportunities are blocked and delinquent gangs are common are more likely to interact with and take the perspectives of persons who favor law violation as a way to satisfy needs. Thus, a structural feature of communities—the availability of educational and occupational opportunities—is consequential for the formation of delinquent groups, which in turn, influence role-taking and delinquency.

Cultural features of communities also may be consequential for delinquent group formation and role-taking. In structurally disadvantaged communities where adults do not sanction delinquency, crime can come to be defined as an acceptable mechanism for generating income or acceptable "work" (Sullivan 1989). In some structurally disadvantaged communities, characteristics such as toughness, smartness, and machismo become valued cultural capital, which can be translated into status in subcultures and lead to delinquency (see Miller 1958; Vigil 1985). Entrance into gangs can then involve a matching process, focused on norms of toughness, risk-taking, courage, honor, and negative attitudes toward law enforcement (Horowitz 1983). Once a tradition of delinquent groups is established in a community, the likelihood that other youths will come into contact with such groups, and consider their perspective through role-taking, is increased. And, there may be significant pressures to affiliate with gangs in communities where long-standing traditions exist.

For example, many youths are recruited into gangs by older siblings or other relatives and move through the gang in a series of age-graded cliques. Indeed, gang membership often is viewed as indicating commitment to the larger community, neighborhood, and even ethnic group (Vigil 1985).

Adulthood, Adult Roles, and Crime

Adulthood marks a series of significant changes for individuals, as they take on more responsibility, develop commitments to adult social roles, and accomodate to the effects of physiological aging. At the same time, however, the transition to adulthood is marked by continuity with adolescence. Patterns of behavior in adolescence trace a trajectory that influences the transition to adulthood by affecting access to resources, selection into adult roles, and consequently the likelihood of adult crime. The most important adult roles, family and work, are important for criminality in two ways: as causal forces that affect criminal behavior net of individual characteristics, and as noncausal states that are spuriously correlated with criminality due to causal characteristics of individuals selecting both crime and adult roles.

Family Roles: Marriage and Parenthood

Conventional wisdom suggests that getting married and becoming a parent will have a negative effect on criminality. Some research supports this proposition that marriage reduces crime and antisocial behavior (Gibbens 1984; Rand 1987), although the effect may be age-graded, applying more to delayed than early marriages (West 1982; Farrington 1986). Sampson and Laub (1993) argue that the key to adult criminality is the degree of bonding to conventional institutions, which operate to control individual behavior. They find that criminality is affected not by marriage per se, but instead by attachment to spouse, measured by attitudes toward marital responsibility, attitudes about the conjugal relationship, and the absence of divorce, separation, and desertion. Similarly, Quinton et al. (1993) find that having a supportive spouse reduces adult criminality for both males and females (see also Pickles and Rutter 1991).

From our perspective, the important dimension of adult family roles is the meaning of the role to spouses, particularly as it is relevant to criminality. For most individuals, the greater the commitment to spousal and parent roles—including a greater respect for the institution of marriage, a greater affection for and attachment to family members, and a stronger investment in familial activities—the lower the likelihood of criminality, since crime entails the risk of jeopardizing the functioning of the family. When confronted with opportunities for crime, the family is likely to enter role-taking as a generalized other. Committed family members are likely to take the role not only of family members, but the role of the family as a conventional institution intertwined with other institutions, and are thereby unlikely to jeopardize the family through crime. In contrast, individuals who lack commitments to family roles are less likely to share the family as a generalized other, and thus, less likely to be controlled by the family. For example, some members of the urban underclass have little belief in the sanctity of the family and little commitment to the roles of parent and spouse, and thus are vulnerable to criminalistic influences. Commitment to parenthood is perhaps the most important family influence on crime. Because crime is so counternormative and carries serious sanctions, nearly all committed parents desire that their children refrain from most crimes, particularly serious crimes. Such desires will affect their attitudes and behaviors, as they seek to be positive influences and role models, which in turn will reduce the likelihood of their own criminality.

Although commitment to family roles—a conventional set of roles—will on average reduce the likelihood of criminality, there are instances in which commitment to family roles *increases* the likelihood of crime. For example, in the relatively uncommon case in which spouses together commit crimes such as robbery, greater commitment to the spousal unit may increase the likelihood of a commitment to crime. Indeed, it is conceivable that a spouse who holds criminalistic attitudes may influence a straight spousal partner into crime. We hypothesize that such an effect, if it exists, would operate through role-taking: the straight partner would learn criminal attitudes from their spouse by taking the role of the other and considering him or herself from their standpoint. Thus, husbands holding criminalistic attitudes may influence the criminality of their wives. Sampson and Laub (1993), however, found that the opposite does not occur: deviant wives do not significantly affect the deviance of their husbands, when marital attachment is controlled. Given the gender differences in power and types of deviance, this finding is perhaps not surprising.

Any examination of the effects of family roles on parents' criminality must consider the possibility that preexisting individual characteristics or prior experiences select for both family roles and criminality, which could render the association spurious. A number of empirical studies have examined the development of family roles, which typically occurs in early adulthood through an assortative mating process in which persons are matched to cohabitation or marriage partners. These studies show that people tend to select partners based on homogamy or similarity of experience, including similarities in educational attainments, occupational status, religious preference, and deviance (e.g., Kandel 1990), with recent trends suggesting that education is replacing religion (Kalmijn 1991; Mare 1991). Thus, high school educational experiences are consequential not only for occupational attainments but also for selection of marriage partners. For example, youths who drop out of school, engage in deviance and delinquency, land unskilled low-paying jobs are likely to marry partners with similar experiences. In the previous section, we argued that youngsters who have difficulty in schools, are negatively labeled by teachers, and become alienated from schools are more likely to affiliate with similarly disenfranchised peers (including delinquent peers). Consequently, they are more likely to have self-images premised on membership in marginal and deviant youth groups, and more likely to move into unskilled, low-paying jobs and select mates with similar problems. This homogamy in mate selection may reflect propinquity, restricted structural opportunities to find other mates, or the desire to validate identities that emerged during adolescence. Either way, continued interaction with a similarly disenfranchised spouse will constrain family resources, reinforce deviant identities, and lead to a greater likelihood of deviance, marital instability, and divorce. By contrast, when homogamy is based on success in school and the labor market, spouses will likely have greater resources at their disposal, and stronger identities stressing family and work roles. This should foster marital stability and conformity.

These arguments receive some support from longitudinal research on the life trajectories of temperamental children. Specifically, research finds that men with histories of temperamental behavior during childhood are less likely to succeed in educational and occupational realms, and more likely to experience unhappy marriages. Women with histories of temperamental behavior during childhood are more likely to marry unsuccessful husbands and experience unhappy marriages (Caspi et al. 1987; Elder, Caspi, and Downey 1986). Such husbands may also be at risk for more crime. Quinton et al. (1993) find homophily in deviance across the life course: those who exhibit conduct problems in childhood tend to select deviant nonsupportive partners. Moreover, they find that homophily in deviance is explained not by direct selection, but rather a series of events. Childhood conduct disorders select for deviant peers and lack of planning—and early out-of-wedlock pregnancy in girls—all of which increase the likelihood of selecting a deviant partner or spouse.

But what about the case of heterophily? Theoretically, we would expect that under certain conditions, spouses may influence each other's criminality. A criminal could be pushed into conformity by a law-abiding spouse if the spouse is highly influential, determined, and endowed with sufficient material resources, and if the criminal is receptive to change. We would argue that a process of change would entail changing the content of the criminal's role-taking and identity by changing his or her reference groups and generalized others. A similar process would account for the perhaps rarer case in which a noncriminal takes up crime after being influenced by a criminalistic spouse. Some research supports the notion of spousal influence. Quinton et al. (1993) find that although there is great continuity in deviance—child conduct disorders are highly correlated with adult maladaptation—a supportive nondeviant spouse can create significant discontinuities in deviance (see also Pickles and Rutter 1991). They find this effect for both males and females. However, Sampson and Laub (1993) fail to find evidence that deviant wives bring about deviance in conforming husbands.

The timing of transitions into or out of family roles may be critical to one's life chances and criminality. For example, teenage pregnancy can result in material needs that are beyond reach, or curtail one's educational attainment. The difficulty of such off-time transitions varies dramatically by context. When accompanied by substantial investments in social capital—such as a supportive spouse, a supportive kinship network, an adequate income, and advanced education and career opportunities—teenage pregnancy may pose few additional problems, and thus, be unrelated to criminality. In contrast, in the absence of social capital—no spouse or kinship, few marketable skills, and an inadequate income—and in the presence of other risk factors—such as a delinquent history, explosive temper, or history of drug use—teenage pregnancy can lead to

continuous problematic situations. Such problems may increase the likelihood of crime.

From an interactionist perspective, the stigma of these off-time, early
transitions to parenthood can solidify deviant or marginalized identities
developed during earlier life stages and, thus, increase alienation from
other conventional roles, such as legitimate work roles, and encourage
entry into less legitimate roles, such as welfare and even criminal roles.
This implies that the high rates of school drop out, teenage pregnancy,
unemployment, welfare dependency and crime among the urban underclass
(Wilson 1987) may involve trajectories of commitments to deviant identities and roles that begin early in the life course, continue through adulthood, and are ultimately rooted in structural conditions.

Work Roles: Labor Force Attachment

This discussion suggests that family roles operate in conjunction with
occupational and work roles to affect the likelihood of crime. From an
interactionist perspective, it is the *meaning* of work that is most relevant
to role-taking, identity, and deviance. When work means more than simply having a job, when it is tied to a career and a long-term commitment,
when it leads to reference groups that disdain crime, and when it brings
prestige and status and thus self-esteem and a positive identity, it can be
an important restraint from crime. Conversely, when work is merely a
temporary dead-end source of spending money, bringing little prestige
and esteem, and not affecting one's reference groups, it may have little or
no restraining effect on crime. Further complicating matters, work sometimes means an opportunity to commit crimes, such as employee theft or
embezzlement.

A number of studies find an empirical relationship between adult employment and desistance from crime: those parolees who succeed in the
labor market are less likely to recidivate (e.g., Cook 1975). Sampson
and Laub (1993) find that, net of childhood antisocial behavior, job stability (employment status, stability of recent employment, and work habits) affects adult desistance from crime, not jobs per se. Uggen (1992)
finds that, net of background factors and employment variables, job quality
reduces criminal recidivism among adult offenders. From our perspective, job quality, employment status, recent job stability, and work habits
on the job are important dimensions of the meaning of work to individu-

als. This meaning is tied to structural opportunities, the objective characteristics of jobs, reference groups, and individuals's histories of role-taking. Thus, based on reference groups and prior role-taking, a dead-end blue-collar job may mean frustration and failure to one person, and success and a reasonable livelihood to another. Although recent survey research controls for several variables that may affect both crime and employment, estimates of the work-crime relationship could still be biased due to selectivity. Individuals who select into good jobs may have a lower criminal propensity than those who select into poor jobs or no jobs at all. That is, it may be that work is related to crime not because of the experience of having a job, but rather because of the systematic ways individuals are sorted into various jobs.

This sorting or selection mechanism is often viewed as a matching process, in which prospective employees are matched to prospective jobs by employers (Sørensen and Kalleberg 1981). Clearly, the attributes and backgrounds of individuals are critical for this sorting process. Those individuals who have greater endowments, greater investments in human capital (such as years of schooling, educational credentials, and job skills), and greater social capital (such as the obligations, expectations, information channels, and norms derived from network ties), will have greater employment prospects than individuals lacking those attributes. Such investments and attributes develop early in the life course through family socialization, peer influences, and school experiences. Thus, youth who are committed to trajectories of conventional roles—educational and law-abiding peer roles—will be likely to invest in conventional human and social capital, and thereby increase their employment prospects. Youth who are committed to deviant roles—drug use and delinquent roles—are more likely to invest in criminal capital, such as developing peer networks of delinquency, crime, and drug acquisition and use. They will be less attractive to employers because they lack the positive traits signalled by conventional capital, and possess negative traits signalled by criminal capital. Research on the labeling process finds that the stigma of a criminal record makes it difficult for ex-offenders to find employment (for a discussion see Sampson and Laub's chapter in this volume).

On the other side of the equation, employers' preferences are driven by their perceptions of worker skills and abilities, but also by structural characteristics that affect demand for specific forms of labor. For example, primary sector firms are likely to have internal labor markets, which causes employees to compete over vacancies rather than wages, insulates them somewhat from neoclassical market competition, and increases their returns to human capital as more extensive on-the-job training accentuates returns (Dickens and Lang 1985). In contrast, workers in secondary sector jobs are more vulnerable to market competition, earn lower wages, are less rewarded for human capital investments, and are more likely to end up stuck in dead-end jobs. In short, the quality of and remuneration from jobs is determined not only by individual human and social capital investments, but also structural conditions, such as access to primary sector positions. Such determinants suggest a systematic selection process into jobs, which could bias estimates of the work-crime relationship in nonexperimental data.

Some research has controlled for selectivity directly using randomized controlled experiments (see Uggen et al. 1992). The National Supported Work Demonstration Project randomly assigned subjects to a control group versus an experimental group that received jobs. Subjects were drawn from three unemployed groups at risk for crime: ex-offenders who had been incarcerated, ex-addicts who had been treated in a drug treatment facility, and youth who dropped out of school, half of whom had been arrested. A three-year follow-up revealed that, overall, the treatment was effective for ex-addicts, but not youth dropouts or ex-offenders. Moreover, there was a treatment by age-interaction effect: among ex-addicts and ex-offenders older than 35 years of age, experimentals were less likely than controls to have been arrested in the three-year follow-up period (Piliavin and Gartner 1984). The negative finding concerning younger offenders is consistent with follow-up evaluations of the Jobstart Demonstration Project (Cave and Doolittle 1991). The null overall findings may be due to the meaning of the jobs assigned to experimentals. The jobs were low-paying, uninteresting, and offered little mobility—in short, typical secondary-sector jobs—and thus, work may have been viewed as a temporary, inadequate source of economic support, while crime was viewed as a more exciting, better-paying alternative for younger offenders (Piliavin and Gartner 1984: 200). The positive experimental finding for older subjects suggests that the timing of life-course transitions may be critical to their effects on crime. Moreover, it illustrates the interaction between biological and social determinants of crime. Older offenders are physiologically slower, weaker, and less-dexterous, and perhaps are more likely to become burned out from crime than their younger counterparts. For these reasons, they are on the declining side of the age-crime curve—on average they are more likely to desist from crime. This average decrease means that they will have less support for crime as they have fewer criminals in their reference groups. At an advanced age, jobs may provide a particularly attractive alternative to crime, thereby increasing the rate of desistance.

But having a job does not always exert a negative effect on crime. Indeed, depending on the meaning of work, the organization of work can be intimately intertwined with crime. For example, some studies estimate that over seventy-five percent of employees in legitimate jobs are involved in some form of employee theft (Henry 1981; Comer 1985). At times, stealing from a business is justified or tolerated as a "perk" to employees or as a cost simply passed on to customers (Ditton 1977). In another example, Arnold and Hagan (1992) argue that lawyer misconduct results from three structural factors: pressures to deviate due to inexperience combined with job expectations; a stratification system in which lawyers are solo practitioners at the bottom; and macroeconomic recessions. Moreover, they find that careers of misconduct unfold through interaction and labeling between offender and prosecution. Similarly, studies of embezzlers find that embezzlement often results from a financial problem and verbalizations that justify the behavior while allowing the embezzler to maintain a favorable self-image (e.g., Cressey 1973). Studies of corporate crime typically find illicit acts of corporations result from structural incentives to violate the law, organizational structures of the firm that diffuse responsibility, and a corporate culture of crime in which corporate actors justify illicit activity (e.g., Sutherland 1949; Clinard and Yeager 1980; Coleman 1987). Finally, the intertwined nature of criminal and legitimate roles, which varies by meaning, is illustrated by the case of housewives. This role excludes women from the paid labor force and thereby reduces opportunities for crimes such as employee theft, corporate crimes, and some street crimes (Simon 1976). At the same time, it increases opportunities for other crimes, such as welfare fraud, which they may view as a way of accommodating to the role of child caretaker (Steffensmeier and Cobb 1981).

Joblessness and Criminal Capital

Commitment to criminal roles in adolescence and early adulthood restricts future opportunities for legitimate employment and increases the chances for unemployment, largely by restricting networks that offer access to legitimate jobs (Hagan 1993). Such a process can escalate over time: early involvement in crime can restrict success in the labor market and foster continued crime, which further restricts labor market options (Sullivan 1989). From an interactionist perspective, when crime is a primary source of income for long periods of time, reference groups increasingly become less conventional and more criminal, and thus role-transitions to legitimate work become more difficult and less likely. This may correspond to "life-course persistent" offenders described by Moffitt (1993). These individuals, such as professional thieves and "rounders," become increasingly committed to criminal roles and identities over time and are unlikely to change direction in trajectories (Sutherland 1937; Letkemann 1973).

When labor market success is impeded by deficits in human, social, or cultural capital, role-taking may lead to identities, goals, and morality favoring property and street crimes as viable solutions to financial problems. For example, when individuals are isolated from legitimate job opportunities, as in some urban ghettos, crimes like drug dealing may be defined as an acceptable way to earn a living (Anderson 1990). Indeed, norms can emerge that justify criminal enterprises even when legitimate work opportunities exist. In secondary labor markets, for instance, individuals often participate in legitimate work while "moonlighting" in criminal enterprises (Holzman 1983; Sullivan 1989). When individuals are committed to roles in both legitimate and criminal groups, role-taking and identities will reflect these dual commitments. Indeed, these commitments can be quite compatible. For example, young men who work in legitimate auto garages by day and also work stripping stolen cars in chop-shops by night (Sullivan 1989), are likely to form identities centered on the common features of the activities—automotive work—and deemphasize the legal-illegal dimension. Here the illegal role may be viewed as an extension of the legal counterpart.

In communities where such criminal traditions exist, we can speak of social and cultural capital that fosters success and mobility in illegal enterprises (Cloward and Chlin 1960). Thus, success in illegal markets, either in terms of monetary returns or prestige of illegal "occupations," (Matsueda et al.1992), is determined by one's embeddedness in the criminal world. Those criminals with greater ties to criminal networks are more likely to acquire skills and experiences that facilitate returns from illegal activity and reduce the risk of sanction (Sullivan 1989; Letkemann 1973; Åkerström

1985; Reuter 1983). Through interactions with other members of a criminal world, they are likely to acquire criminal capital—the criminal argot, insider's information, and attitudes—that may increase their subcultural status (Åkerström 1985). Perhaps the extreme case of such processes surrounds organized crime families, which may contain specific cultural schemas and extensive network structures (Cressey 1969; Reuter 1983). Moreover, such embeddedness may in turn hamper the individual's success in conventional labor markets (Hagan 1991, 1993).

Prison experiences make transitions to conventional roles even more difficult. Again, length of time in the role is important: the longer periods of incarceration, the higher the probability of future crime and the lower the likelihood of transitions to legitimate work roles (Sampson and Laub 1993). While some reentering criminals may prefer to avoid legitimate roles, others will have little choice due to their criminal label. Here, net of prior propensities, negative labeling and stigmatization of official criminals, combined with reduced conventional social capital, will hamper efforts to obtain stable employment and resume stable family roles (Irwin 1970). The process of stigmatization and labeling operates through a role-taking process, in which societal members attribute stereotypical characteristics to criminals, such as having poor character, being likely to recidivate, and being dangerous. The result may be a return to those criminal subcultures that led to incarceration in the first place.

Conclusion

This chapter has argued that symbolic interactionism can provide a fruitful way of examining crime and delinquency throughout the life course. The interactionist perspective developed here has several important features. First, it assumes a biosocial view of human behavior such that behavior occurs at the intersection between biological and environmental processes. Second, it specifies specific ways in which ontogenetic mechanisms are constituted in interactions with others. Third, it emphasizes the importance of criminal and deviant counterparts to conventional culture and organization, including criminal capital. Fourth, it implies several duration-dependent mechanisms linking social roles and criminal behavior through the major life-course transitions from childhood to adolescence and finally, to adulthood.

Notes

1. We use the terms, "deviant subcultures" or "criminal subcultures" to refer to subcultures in which some forms of deviance or crime are widespread, tolerated, or even encouraged. Thus, we would argue that certain crimes are tolerated or the laws proscribing them are neutralized in infracultures and encouraged in contracultures (see Matsueda et al. 1992).

2. Mead's pragmatism begins with the theory of evolution, which for him, stipulated a life process in which individual organisms are adjusting to a changing environment to sustain a species. Genetic mutations are emergent (novel) adjustments (solutions) to problems posed by the environment. Reflective thinking by human beings represents the highest level of evolution, because it allows the organism to control its behavior and environment self-consciously. The novel element of reflective behavior, originating in the response of the "I" is an efficient emergent adjustment to a problem posed by a changing environment.

3. State dependence refers to being in a state, which has a duration. Criminal acts typically have very little duration. Nevertheless, one can use the concept of state dependence by treating criminal acts as discrete indicators of an unobservable state of readiness or propensity to commit crimes.

4. The contradictory results may be due to differences in datasets or more specifically the variables included in the models, and outcome variables used. Nagin and Paternoster (1991) use two waves of the National Youth Survey, which uses self-reported delinquency on adolescents and include a vector of 16 exogenous variables (e.g., peer effects, family background, violence and drugs) known to have strong effects on delinquency. It could be that these 16 variables capture most of the between-person within-time variation in delinquency, leaving the heterogeneity component trivial in size. Nagin and Farrington (1992) use 11 waves of Farrington's London Cohort Data, which uses conviction as an outcome and four substantive variables (IQ, parental child rearing, parental criminal record, and daring) in addition to age. The large unobserved heterogeneity component could be the result of the four variables capturing only modest between-person, within-time variation in crime, and the fact that no covariates are included to capture the effects of processing by the criminal justice system on convictions.

5. Control theorists argue that the correlation between delinquent peers and delinquency is spurious, a reflection of the selection into peer groups, rather than a causal relationship (e.g., Gottfredson and Hirschi 1990). Following Robins (1966), Sampson and Laub (1993) interpret their extraordinarily large correlations between delinquency and delinquent peers ("virtually coterminous") to be spurious due to selection into peer groups. The argument is based on comparing the large correlations of delinquency between peers and modest correlations of delinquency between siblings. If the peer correlations are due to causation and not selection, then sibling correlations should also be high, since there is no possibility of self-selection. We believe, however, that the premise could be faulty: it is likely that siblings simply do not have as strong an influence on youth compared to peers. A more plausible interpretation, consistent with findings of Elliott and Menard (in press), is that the correlation partly reflects causation and partly reflects selection.

References

Adler, Patricia A., Steven J. Kless, and Peter Adler. 1992. "Socialization to Gender Roles: Popularity among Elementary School Boys and Girls." *Sociology of Education* 65: 69–87.

Åkerström, Malin. 1985. *Crooks and Squares*. New Brunswick, NJ: Transaction Press.

Anderson, Elijah. 1990. *Streetwise: Race, Class, and Change in an Urban Community*. Chicago: University of Chicago Press.

Arnold, Bruce L., and John Hagan. 1992. "Careers of Misconduct: Prosecuted Professional Deviance Among Lawyers." *American Sociological Review* 57: 771–80.

Atchley, R. 1975. "The Life Course, Age Grading, and Age Linked Demands for Decisions Making." In *Life-Span Developmental Psychology: Normative Life Crises*, ed. N. Datan and L. Ginsberg, 261–78. New York: Academic Press.

Becker, Gary S. 1964. *Human Capital*. New York, National Bureau of Economic Research: Columbia University Press.

Becker, Howard S. 1960. "Notes on the Concept of Commitment." *American Journal of Sociology* 66: 32–40.

Billy, John O. G. , and J. Richard Udry. 1985. "Patterns of Adolescent Friendships and Effects on Sexual Behavior." *Social Psychology Quarterly* 48: 27–41.

Blumer, Herbert. 1969. *Symbolic Interactionism: Perspective and Method*. Englewood Cliffs, NJ: Prentice-Hall.

Bourdieu, Pierre. 1977. "Cultural Reproduction and Social Reproduction." In *Power and Ideology in Education*, ed. J. Karabel and A. H. Halsey, 487–511. New York: Oxford University Press.

Burke, Peter J., and Donald Reitzes. 1991. "An Identity Theory Approach to Commitment." *Social Psychology Quarterly* 54: 239–51.

Cahill, Spencer E. 1980. "Directions for an Interactionist Study of Gender Development." *Symbolic Interaction* 3: 123–38.

Caspi, Avshalom, Glen H. Elder, Jr., and Daryl J. Bem. 1987. "Moving Against the World: Life-Course Patterns of Explosive Children." *Developmental Psychology* 23: 308–13.

Caspi, Avshalom, Donald Lynam, Terrie E. Moffitt, and Phil A. Silva. 1993. "Unraveling Girls' Delinquency: Biological, Dispositional, and Contextual Contributions to Adolescent Misbehavior." *Developmental Psychology* 29: 19–30.

Cave, George, and Fred Doolittle. 1991. *Assessing Jobstart: Interim Impacts of a Program for School Dropouts*. New York: Manpower Demonstration Research Corporation.

Cloward, Richard A., and Lloyd E. Ohlin. 1960. *Delinquency and Opportunity*. New York: Free Press.

Clinard, Marshall B., and Peter C. Yeager. 1980. *Corporate Crime*. New York: Macmillan.

Cohen, Albert K. 1955. *Delinquent Boys*. Glencoe, IL: Free Press.

Coleman, James S. 1990. *Foundations of Social Theory*. Cambridge, MA: Harvard University Press.

———. 1961. *The Adolescent Society*. Glencoe, IL: Free Press.

Coleman, James W. 1987. "Toward an Integrated Theory of White-Collar Crime." *American Journal of Sociology* 93: 406–39.

Comer, Michael J. 1985. *Corporate Fraud*. London: McGraw-Hill.

Cook, Phillip J. 1975. "The Correctional Carrot: Better Jobs for Parolees." *Policy Analysis* 1: 11–54.

Corsaro, William A. 1992. "Interpretive Reproduction in Children's Peer Cultures." *Social Psychology Quarterly* 55: 160–77.

Corsaro, William A., and Donna Eder. 1990. "Children's Peer Cultures." *Annual Review of Sociology* 16: 197– 220.

Cressey, Donald R. 1969. *Theft of the Nation: The Structure and Operations of Organized Crime in America*. New York: Harper and Row.

———. 1973. *Other People's Money: A Study in the Social Psychology of Embezzlement*. Belmont, MA: Wadsworth.

Dannefer, Dale. 1984. "Adult Development and Social Theory: A Paradigmatic Reappraisal." *American Sociological Review* 49: 100–16.

Demo, David H. 1992. "The Self-Concept over Time: Research Issues and Directions." *Annual Review of Sociology* 18: 303–26.

Denzin, Norman K. 1972. "The Genesis of Self in Early Childhood." *Sociological Quarterly* 13: 291–314.

Dickens, William T., and Kevin Lang. 1985. "A Test of Dual Labor Market Theory." *American Economic Review* 75: 792–805.

Dishion, Thomas J. 1990. "The Family Ecology of Boys' Peer Relations in Middle Childhood." *Child Development* 61: 874–92.

Dishion, Thomas. J., Gerald R. Patterson, M. Stoolmiller, and M. L. Skinner. 1991. "Family, school, and behavioral antecedents to early adolescent involvement with antisocial peers." *Developmental Psychology* 27: 172–80.

Ditton, Jason. 1977. *Part-Time Crime*. New York: Macmillan.

Eder, Donna ,and Janet Lynn Enke. 1991. "The Structure of Gossip: Opportunities and Constraints on Collective Expression Among Adolescents." *American Sociological Review* 56: 494–508.

Elder, Glen H., Jr. 1985. "Perspectives on the Life Course." In *Life Course Dynamics*, ed. Glen H. Elder, Jr., 23-49. Ithaca: Cornell University Press.

Elder, Glen H., Jr., Avshalom Caspi, and Geraldine Downey. 1986. "Problem Behavior and Family Relationships: Life Course and Intergenerational Themes." In *Human development and the Life Course: Multidisciplinary Perspectives*, ed. A. B. Sorenson, F. E. Weinert, and L. R. Sherrod, 293–340. Hillsdale, NJ: Lawrence Erlbaum Associates.

Elkind, D. 1967. "Egocentrism in Adolescence." *Child Development* 38: 1025–34.

Elliott, Delbert S., David Huizinga, and Suzanne Ageton. 1985. *Delinquency and Drug Use*. Beverly Hills: Sage.

Elliott, Delbert S., David Huizinga, and Scott Menard. 1989. *Multiple Problem Youth: Delinquency, Substance Use, and Mental Health*. New York: Springer-Verlag.

Elliott, Delbert S., and Scott Menard. In press. "Delinquent Behavior and Delinquent Friends: Temporal and Developmental Patterns." In *Some Current Theories of Deviance*, ed. J. D. Hawkins. Newbury Park, CA: Sage.

Entwistle, D. W., K. L. Alexander, A. M. Pallas, and D. Cadigan. 1987. "The Emergent Academic Self-Image of First Graders: Its Response to Social Structures." *Child Development* 58: 1190–1206.

Erikson, Erik H. 1968. *Identity: Youth and Crisis*. New York: Norton.

Farrington, David P. 1986. "Unemployment, School Leaving, and Crime." *British Journal of Criminology* 26: 335–56.

Farrington, David P. 1992. "Explaining the Beginning, Progress, and Ending of Antisocial Behavior from Birth to Adulthood." Pp. 253–86 in *Facts, Frameworks, and*

Forecasts: Advances in Crimiological Theory, vol. 3, edited by J. McCord. New Brunswick, NJ: Transaction.

Featherman, David, and Richard Lerner. 1985. "Ontogenesis and Sociogenesis: Problematics for Theory and Research about Development and Socialization across the Lifespan." *American Sociological Review* 50: 659–76.

Gamoran, Adam, and Robert D. Mare. 1989. "Secondary School Tracking and Educational Inequality: Compensation, Reinforcement, or Neutrality?" *American Journal of Sociology* 94: 1146–83.

Gibbens, T. C. N. 1984. "Borstal Boys After 25 Years." British Journal of Criminology 24: 49–62.

Goffman, Erving. 1961. *Asylums*. Garden City, New York: Anchor.

———. 1977. "The Arrangement between the Sexes." *Theory and Society* 4: 301–31.

Gottfredson, Michael, and Travis Hirschi. 1990. *A General Theory of Crime*. Palo Alto: Stanford University.

Greenberg, David F. 1977. "Delinquency and the Age Structure of Society." *Contemporary Crises: Crime, Law, and Social Policy* 1: 189–223.

Hagan, John. 1991. "Destiny and Drift: The Risks and Rewards of Youth." *American Sociological Review* 56: 567–82.

———. 1993. "The Social Embeddedness of Crime and Unemployment." *Criminology* 31: 465–91.

Hagan, John, and Alberto Palloni. 1988. "Crimes as Social Events in the Lifecourse: Reconceiving a Criminological Controversy." *Criminology* 26: 87–100.

Hagan, John, John Simpson, and A. R. Gillis. 1987. "Class in the Household: A Power-Control Theory of Gender and Delinquency." *American Journal of Sociology* 92: 788–816.

Hagan, John and Blair Wheaton. 1993. "The Search for Adolescent Role Exits and the Transition to Adulthood." *Social Forces* 71: 955–80.

Hagedorn, John M. 1985. *People and Folks: Gangs, Crime and the Underclass in a Rustbelt City*. Chicago: Lakeview Press.

Heckman, James. 1981. "Statistical Models for Discrete Panel Data." In *Structural Analysis of Discrete Panel Data with Econometric Applications*, eds. Charles F. Manski and David McFadden, 114–78. Cambridge, MA: MIT Press.

Heimer, Karen. 1995. "Gender, Race, and the Pathways to Delinquency: An Interactionist Explanation." Pp. 140–73 in *Crime and Inequality*, eds. J. Hagan and R. Peterson. Stanford, CA: Stanford University Press.

Heimer, Karen 1996. "Gender, Interaction, and Delinquency: Testing a Theory of Differential Social Control." *Social Psychology Quarterly* 59: 39–61.

Heimer, Karen, and Ross L. Matsueda. 1994. "Role-Taking, Role-Commitment, and Delinquency: A Theory of Differential Social Control." *American Sociological Review* 59: 365–90.

Henry, Stuart. 1981. *Can I Have it in Cash?* London: Astragal Books.

Hewitt, John P. 1989. *Self and Society: A Symbolic Interactionist Social Psychology*. Boston: Allyn and Bacon.

Hirschi, Travis. 1969. *Causes of Delinquency*. Berkeley: Free Press.

Holzman, Harold R. 1983. "The Serious Habitual Property Offender as 'Moonlighter': An Empirical Study of Labor Force Participation Among Robbers and Burglars." *Journal of Criminal Law and Criminology* 73: 1774–92.

Horowitz, Ruth. 1983. *Honor and the American Dream: Culture and Identity in a Chicano Community*. New Brunswick, NJ: Rutgers University Press.

Irwin, John. 1970. *The Felon.* Englewood Cliffs, NJ: Prentice-Hall.

Jensen, Gary F. and Raymond Eve. 1976. "Sex Differences in Delinquency: An Examination of Popular Sociological Explanations." *Criminology* 13: 427–48.

Kalmijn, Matthijs. 1991. "Shifting Boundaries: Trends in Religious and Educational Homogamy." *American Sociological Review* 56: 786–800.

Kandel, Denise, Mark Davies, and Nazli Baydar. 1990. "The Creation of Interpersonal Contexts: Homophily in Dyadic Relationships in Adolescence and Young Adulthood. In *Straight and Devious Pathways from Childhood to Adulthood*, ed. Lee Robins and Michael Rutter, 221–41 New York: Cambridge University Press.

Kaplan, Howard B. 1980. *Deviant Behavior in Defense of Self.* New York: Academic.

Keller, B. and R. Q. Bell. 1979. "Child Effects on Adults' Method of Eliciting Altruistic Behavior." *Child Development* 50: 1004–10.

Keller, A., L. H. Ford, and J. A. Meacham. 1978. "Dimensions of Self-Concept in Pre-School Children." *Developmental Psychology* 14: 483–99.

Kett, Joseph F. 1977. *Rites of Passage: Adolescence in America, 1977 to the Present.* New York: Basic.

Kornhauser, Ruth R. 1978. *Social Sources of Delinquency.* Chicago: University of Chicago Press.

Langer, Ellen J. 1989. "Minding Matters: The Consequences of Mindless-Mindfulness." In *Advances in Experimental Social Psychology*, vol. 22, ed. L. Berkowitz, 137–73. San Diego, CA: Academic.

Laub, John H., and Robert J. Sampson. 1993. "Turning Points in the Life Course: Why Change Matters to the Study of Crime." *Criminology* 31: 301–25.

Letkemann, Peter. 1973. *Crime as Work.* Englewood Cliffs, NJ: Prentice-Hall.

Loeber, Rolf ,and Marc Le Blanc. 1990. "Toward a Developmental Criminology." In *Crime and Justice*, vol. 22, ed. Michael Tonry and Norval Morris, 375–437. Chicago: University of Chicago Press.

Lytton, Hugh. 1990. "Child and Parent Effects in Boys' Conduct Disorder: A Reinterpretation." *Developmental Psychology* 26: 683–97.

MacKinnon, C. E., and D. King. 1988. "Day Care: A Review of Literature, Implications for Policy, and Critique of Resources." *Family Relations* 37: 229–36.

Mare, Robert D. 1991. "Five Decades of Educational Assortative Mating." *American Sociological Review* 56: 15–32.

Matsueda, Ross L. 1988. "The Current State of Differential Association Theory." *Crime and Delinquency* 34: 277–306.

———. 1992. "Reflected Appraisals, Parental Labelling, and Delinquency: Specifying a Symbolic Interactionist Theory." *American Journal of Sociology* 97: 1577–1611.

Matsueda, Ross L., Rosemary Gartner, Irving Piliavin, and Michael Polakowski. 1992. "The Prestige of Criminal and Conventional Occupations." *American Sociological Review* 57: 752–70.

Matsueda, Ross L. and Karen Heimer. 1987. "Race, Family Structure and Delinquency: A Test of Differential Association and Social Control Theories." *American Sociological Review* 52: 826–40.

McCall, George J., and John L. Simmons. 1978. *Identities and Interaction.* New York: Free Press.

Mead, George H. 1934. *Mind, Self and Society.* Chicago: University of Chicago.

Mednick, S. A., W. F. Gabrielli, and B. Hutchings. 1984. "Genetic Influences in Criminal Convictions: Evidence from an Adoption Cohort." *Science* 224: 891–94.

Meehan, Hugh. 1992. "Understanding Inequality in Schools: The Contribution of Interpretive Studies." *Sociology of Education* 65: 1–20.

Menard, Scott, and Barbara J. Morse. 1984. "A Structuralist Critique of the IQ-Delinquency Hypothesis: Theory and Evidence." *American Journal of Sociology* 89: 1347–78.

Miller, David L. 1973. *George Herbert Mead: Self, Language and the World.* Chicago: University of Chicago Press.

Miller, Walter 1958. "Lower Class Culture as a Generating Milieu of Gang Delinquency." *Journal of Social Issues* 14: 5–19.

Moffitt, Terrie E. 1990. "Juvenile Delinquency and Attention Deficit Disorder: Developmental Trajectories from Age 3 to 15." *Child Development* 61: 893–910.

———. 1993. "Adolescent-Limited and Life-Course-Persistent Antisocial Behavior: A Developmental Taxonomy." *Psychological Review* 100: 674–701.

Montemayor, R. 1983. "Parents and Adolescents in Conflict: All Families Some of the Time and Some Families Most of the Time." *Journal of Early Adolescence* 3: 83–103.

Nagin, Daniel S. and David P. Farrington. 1992. "The Stability of Criminal Potential From Childhood to Adulthood." *Criminology* 30: 235–60.

Nagin, Daniel S. and Raymond Paternoster. 1991. "On the Relationship of Past and Future Delinquency." *Criminology* 29: 163–90.

Oakes, Jeannie. 1985. *Keeping Track: How Schools Structure Inequality.* New Haven: Yale University Press.

Patterson, Gerald R. 1982. Coercive Family Process. Eugene, OR: Castalia.

Patterson, Gerald R., John B. Reid and Thomas J. Dishion. 1992. *Antisocial Boys: A Social Interactional Process.* Eugene, OR: Castalia Publishing Co..

Pickles, Andrew, and Michael Rutter. 1991. "Statistical and Conceptual Models of 'Turning Points' in Developmental Processes." In *Problems and Methods in Longitudinal Research: Stability and Change*, ed. David Magnusson, Lars Bergman, Georg Rudinger, and Bertil Torestad, 133–65, New York: Cambridge University Press.

Piliavin, Irving and Rosemary Gartner. 1984. "The Impacts of Supported Work on Ex-Offenders." In *The National Supported Work Demonstration,* ed. R.G. Hollister, P. Kemper, and R.A. Maynard, 172–204. Madison, WI: University of Wisconsin Press.

Platt, Anthony M. 1977. *The Child Savers: The Invention of Delinquency.* Chicago: University of Chicago Press.

Plomin, Robert. 1986. *Development, Genetics, and Psychology.* Hillsdale, NJ: Lawrence Erlbaum.

Quinton, David, Andrew Pickles, Barbara Maughan, and Michael Rutter. 1993. "Partners, Peers, and Pathways: Assortative Pairing and Continuities in Conduct Disorder." *Developmental Psychopathology* 5: 763–83.

Rand, Alicia. 1987. "Transitional Life Events and Desistance from Delinquency and Crime." In *From Boy to Man: From Delinquency to Crime*, ed. Marvin Wolfgang, Terence P. Thornberry, and Robert M. Figlio, 134–62. Chicago: University of Chicago Press.

Reuter, Peter. 1983. *Disorganized Crime: Illegal Markets and the Mafia.* Cambridge, MA: MIT Press.

Robins, Lee. 1966. *Deviant Children Grown Up.* Baltimore: Williams and Wilkins.

Rowe, David. 1983. "Biometrical Genetic Models of Self-Reported Delinquent Behavior: A Twin Study." *Behavior Genetics* 13: 473–89.

Sampson, Robert J., and John H. Laub. 1990. "Crime and Deviance over the Life Course: The Salience of Adult Social Bonds." *American Sociological Review* 55: 609–27.

———. 1992. "Crime and Deviance in the Life Course." *Annual Review of Sociology* 18: 63–84.

———. 1993. *Crime in the Making: Pathways and Turning Points through Life.* Cambridge: Harvard University Press.

Scarr, Sandra , and Kathleen McCartney. 1983. "How People Make Their Own Environments: A Theory of Genotype—Environment Effects." *Child Development* 54: 424–35.

Schafer, Walter E., and Carol Olexa. 1971. *Tracking and Opportunity: The Looking Out Process and Beyond.* Scranton: Chandler Publishing Co.

Schafer, Walter E., and Kenneth E. Polk. 1967. "Delinquency and the Schools." In *Task Force Report: Juvenile Delinquency and Youth Crime,* 222–27. Washington, D.C.: Government Printing Office.

Schur, Edwin M. 1983. *Labeling Women Deviant.* New York: McGraw-Hill.

Shibutani, Tamotsu. 1961. *Society and Personality.* Englewood Cliffs, NJ: Prentice-Hall.

Shiffrin Richard M., and Walter Schneider. 1977. "Controlled and Automatic Human Information Processing: II. Perceptual Learning, Automatic Attending, and a General Theory." *Psychology Review* 84: 127–90.

Simmons, Roberta G., and Dale A. Blyth. 1987. *Moving Into Adolescence: The Impact of Pubertal Change and School Context.* New York: Aldine de Gruyter.

Simon, Rita. 1976. *Women, Crime and Criminology: A Feminist Critique.* London: Routledge and Kegan Paul.

Sørensen, Aage B., and Arne L. Kalleberg. 1981. "An Outline of a Theory of the Matching of Persons to Jobs." In *Sociological Perspectives on Labor Markets,* ed. I. Berg , 49–74. New York: Academic Press.

Steffensmeier, Darrell J. 1986. *The Fence: In the Shadow of Two Worlds.* Totowa, NJ: Rowman and Littlefield.

Steffensmeier, Darrell J., and Michael J. Cobb. 1981. "Sex Differences in Urban Arrest Patterns, 1934–79." *Social Problems* 29: 37–50.

Stryker, Sheldon. 1968. "Identity Salience and Role Performance: The Relevance of Symbolic Interaction Theory for Family Life." *Journal of Marriage and the Family* 30: 558–64.

———. 1980. *Symbolic Interactionism.* Menlo Park, CA: Benjamin/Cummings.

Sullivan, Mercer L. 1989. *"Getting Paid": Youth Crime and Work in the Inner City.* Ithaca: Cornell University Press.

Sutherland, Edwin H. 1937. *The Professional Thief.* Chicago: University of Chicago Press.

———. 1949. *White Collar Crime: The Uncut Version.* New Haven, CT: Yale University.

Sykes, Gresham M., and David Matza. 1957. "Techniques of Neutralization: A Theory of Delinquency." *American Sociological Review* 22: 664–70.

Thornberry, Terence P. 1987. "Toward an Interactional Theory of Delinquency." *Criminology* 25: 863–91.

Thornberry, Terence P., Alan J. Lizotte, Marvin D. Krohn, Margaret Farnworth, and Sung Joon Jang. 1991. "Testing Interactional Theory: An Examination of Reciprocal Causal Relationships Among Family, School and Delinquency. *Journal of Criminal Law and Criminology* 82: 3–35.

Thorne, Barrie, and Zella Luria. 1986. "Sexuality and Gender in Children's Daily Worlds." *Social Problems* 33: 176–90.

Turner, Ralph H. 1978. "The Role and the Person." *American Journal of Sociology* 84: 1–23.

Uggen, Christopher. 1992. "Innovators, Retreatists, and the Conformist Alternative: A Job Quality Model of Work and Crime." Paper presented at the 1992 annual meetings of the American Sociological Association, Pittsburgh, PA.

Uggen, Christopher, Irving Piliavin, and Ross L. Matsueda. 1992. "Jobs Programs and Criminal Desistance." Paper presented at the Conference on the Potential of Publicly Funded Jobs Programs, Urban Institute, Washington, D.C.

Vigil, James Diego. 1985. *Barrio Gangs.* Austin, TX: University of Texas Press.

Vuchinich, Samuel, Lew Bank, and Gerald R. Patterson. 1992. "Parenting, Peers, and the Stability of Antisocial Behavior in Preadolescent Boys." *Developmental Psychology* 28: 510–21.

Walters, Glenn D., and Thomas W. White. 1989. "Heredity and Crime: Bad Genes or Bad Research? (Review of the Literature). *Criminology* 27: 455–85.

Warr, Mark. 1993. "Age, Peers, and Delinquency." *Criminology* 31: 17–40.

Warr, Mark, and Mark Stafford. 1991. "The Influence of Delinquent Peers: What They Think or What They Do?" *Criminology* 29: 851–66.

Wells, L. Edward and Sheldon Stryker. 1986. "Stability and Change in Self Over the Life Course." In *Life Span Development and Behavior,* vol. 7, ed. P. B. Baltes, D. L. Featherman, and R. M. Lerner, 191–229. Hillsdale, NJ: Lawrence Erlbaum.

West, Donald J. 1982. *Delinquency: Its Roots, Careers, and Prospects.* London: Heinemann.

White, Jennifer L., Terrie E. Moffitt, Felton Earls, Lee N. Robbins, and Phil A. Silva. 1990. "How Early Can We Tell? Predictors of Childhood Conduct Disorder and Adolescent Delinquency." *Criminology* 28: 507–33.

Wiatrowski, Michael D., Stephen Hansell, Charles R. Massey, and David L. Wilson. 1982. "Curriculum Tracking and Delinquency." *American Sociological Review* 47: 151–60.

Willis, Paul E. 1977. *Learning to Labor.* London: Routledge and Kegan Paul.

Wilson, William J. 1987. *The Truly Disadvantaged: The Inner City, the Underclass, and Public Policy.* Chicago: University of Chicago Press.

Wulff, Helena. 1988. *Twenty Girls: Growing Up, Ethnicity, and Excitement in a South London Microculture.* Stockholm: University of Stockholm Press.

6

A Generic Control Theory of the Criminal Phenomenon: The Structural and Dynamic Statements of an Integrative Multilayered Control Theory

Marc Le Blanc

Introduction

Over the last forty years, criminology has not witnessed any major theoretical innovations. Numerous theories were available: social disorganization, strain, control, cultural deviance, differential association, social learning, labelling, deterrence, and so on. In addition, these theories were elaborations of ideas of nineteenth-century theorists such as Quetelet, Durkheim, Marx, and Tarde. Over the last four decades, we have witnessed enormous theoretical activities that take the form of theoretical elaboration, integration or modelling. This situation is particularly true of Hirschi's bonding theory; a theory formulated in 1969.

Bonding theory is an elaboration of the more general control perspective. Control theories have been presented by such theorists as Thrasher (1927), Freud (1963), Reiss (1951), Nye (1958), and Reckless (1961), to name a few. While these theorists outlined different constructs, they

Research for this paper was supported by Conseil de la recherche en sciences humaines du Canada and a Killam Fellowship.

Parts of this paper were presented at the 1993 Meeting of the American Society of Criminology.

accepted the same basic assumptions concerning human nature (see Empey 1978 and Kornhauser 1978, discussions). Over the last few decades, bonding theory has become, and remains, the most prominent, empirically based criminological theory for the explanation of juvenile delinquency. During that same period, criminology was also entering a new era of theoretical questioning in which the theoretical perspective was viewed as more important than the content or structure of the theory. Social control, radical, structural, social learning, cultural deviance, labelling, deterrence, rational choice, and so on are theoretical perspectives that discuss guidelines for understanding the criminal phenomenon. In that context of competing of perspectives, empirically oriented criminologists pursued two research directions: testing bonding theory and confronting that theory with existing theories.

In the first direction, empirical studies of control theory were numerous; Kempf (1993) reports more then seventy investigations. However, studies that made an exact replication of bonding theory with the variables employed by Hirschi were few. In addition, a situation of near anarchy in the operationalization of key concepts characterized the verification of bonding theory. This anarchy meant that researchers referred to the constructs of the theory, but without a clear consensus on the measures to operationalize them. In the second direction, there were numerous attempts to integrate bonding theory with other theories, particularly differential association or social learning theory, but mainly at the level of empirical model building. This approach gave rise to controversy about the usefulness of theoretical integration, as shown in *Theoretical Methods in Criminology* (Meier 1985) and at the Albany Conference on Theoretical Integration (Messner et al. 1989). Because there was much more interest in empirical modelling, the content of the theory was not a major focus of attention. As a consequence, bonding theory remained stagnant for nearly twenty years. Neither the internal consistency nor the structure of the theory was the object of major challenges from empirical data. We had to wait until 1990 for a major elaboration of the foundations of bonding theory and an extension of its constructs by Gottfredson and Hirschi.

During that period, neither bonding theory nor other criminological theories addressed straightforwardly the question of the explanation of continuity and change in offending over time or the question of changes in bonding during the life course. Only labelling theory, particularly Lemert's (1951) theory of primary and secondary deviance, and learning theory, particularly Sutherland's differential association theory (Sutherland and Cressey 1960) and Akers' (1973) comprehensive social learning theory, are clearly developmental. Other theories did not explore the developmental implications of their discursive statements. Only very recently have criminologists begun to include a developmental perspective in their theory (see the special issue on theory published in *Criminology*, 25,4; and Loeber and Le Blanc 1990).

In this paper, we want to follow two of the possible roads to theory development, integration and elaboration. We will start by distinguishing different types of theoretical activities, particularly integration, elaboration, and modelling. Afterwards, we will define levels of explanation of the criminal phenomenon: crime, criminal and criminality. Starting from these layers of the criminal phenomenon, we elaborate an integrative multilayered control theory. This paper proposes a static and a dynamic formulation of our generic theory. We define the components of the theory and their organization in a particular structure. We also state the theory from a process point of view.

Preliminaries

Theoretical Elaboration, Integration, and Modelling

In criminology during the 1960s, the term "integration" designated an integration of different theoretical perspectives or the simultaneous consideration of data from multiple disciplines, especially sociology and psychology. This definition of integration was shared by scholars in North America and Europe, for example Mannheim (1965), Wolfgang and Ferracuti (1967), and Szabo et al. (1968), among others. Two decades later, however, the term integration no longer referred to an interdisciplinary integration. Johnson (1979) and Elliott et al. (1985) reduced its scope to an integration of sociological theories and the Albany Conference on Theoretical Integration (Messner et al. 1989) confirmed that tendency. Because of this unfortunate change in the meaning of the term theoretical integration, it is now necessary to distinguish clearly among types of theoretical activity. Criminologists perform three major types of theoretical activities: elaboration, integration and modelling.

Elaboration is the development or expansion of an existing theory. As compared to an initial theory, elaborated theory has the following characteristics according to Wagner and Berger (1985): it has a similar structure; it applies to a similar phenomenon; it is more comprehensive, more rigorous, more precise; and it is empirically more adequate. Hirschi's bonding theory possesses all these characteristics in relation to Durkheim's initial statement of the importance of the bond to society (1895, 1934). However, elaboration is an unusual activity in contemporary criminology. DeFleur and Quinney (1966) used set theory to formalize and extend Sutherland's differential association theory. Empey and Lubeck (1971) relied on formal rules to develop their axiomatic theory of lower-class delinquency, an elaboration of strain theory. Concerning bonding theory, there is only one comprehensive attempt at elaboration through formalization, Le Blanc and Caplan's (1993) formal statement using Gibbs' method (1985). There are also some discursive elaborations of bonding theory (for example, Catalano and Hawkins 1986; Le Blanc and Caplan 1993; Thornberry, 1987). Theoretical elaboration can also take the form of a multilayered theory as defined by Lenski (1988). In this case, the theorist derives special theories from a general theoretical statement. We have proposed this type of elaboration for bonding theory under the denomination of middle-range family control (Le Blanc 1992), school control (Le Blanc et al. 1992, 1993) and constraints theories (Le Blanc 1995).

Integration, the second type of theoretical activity, is the formulation of a theory that incorporates separate notions into a new whole. Theoretical integration implies for Wagner and Berger (1985) a new structure for the theory and additional predictions. For Thornberry (1989: 52), theoretical integration is "the act of combining two or more sets of logically interrelated propositions into a larger set of interrelated propositions, in order to provide a more comprehensive explanation of a particular phenomenon." In criminology, and particularly in the area of bonding theory, we can distinguish three different kinds of theoretical integration: unification, combination and incorporation.

Unification concerns the levels of explanation of the phenomenon considered. In this case, a common conceptual framework applies to the micro and macro levels of explanation, for example crime and criminality. Pearson and Weiner (1985) propose a social learning theory unification, while Gottfredson and Hirschi (1990) develop a control one.

Combination involves the amalgamation of different orienting theoretical strategies such as social control, social learning, labelling, or other theories within a particular branch of a discipline such as sociological criminology. There are numerous such combination of social control theory with other unit theories, most often social learning or differential association theory (Conger 1976; Matsueda 1988; Catalano and Hawkins 1986; Reid 1989) and the most comprehensive attempt along these lines is by Elliott et al. (1985, 1989) using social control, social learning and strain theories.

Incorporation uses notions from different branches of a discipline to formulate a new theory; for example, notions from biological, sociological or psychological criminology are amalgamated. Constructs of control theory have been affiliated with biological constructs by Arnold and Brungardt (1983), Denno (1985) and Udry (1988) and with psychological constructs by Le Blanc et al. (1988) and Gottfredson and Hirschi (1990).

Modelling, the third type of theoretical activity, has become the prevalent theoretical activity in criminology during the last few decades. According to Hanneman (1988), it is the development of a system of propositions about a set of data that is a statistical description of an explanation of a phenomenon. There are many empirical models of social control theory. Most of the verifications of Hirschi's theory reviewed by Kempf (1993) are of this nature, as are many of the elaborations and integrations previously cited. Each model distinguishes itself by the constructs involved, by their measurement, by the type of sample used, or by all three of these characteristics. No model is the object of a replication on a different set of data. The mere existence of these numerous models corresponds to the situations of theory proliferation, theory competition and theory variation describe by Wagner and Berger (1985).

In this paper, we perform two types of theoretical activity—integration and elaboration—and leave for another paper the question of empirical modelling. The generic control theory that we propose is integrative in the classical sense; it uses constructs originating from different disciplines. In that sense it is an integrative incorporation. It is also an integrative unification because it applies to the three levels of definition and explanation of the criminal phenomenon—criminality, criminal and crime. This approach to the elaboration of control theory is based on the following rationale. First, there is currently no precise formulation of control theory for some of the levels of the criminal phenomenon. And second, there is currently no developmental formulation of control theory.

The Criminal Phenomenon, Levels of Definition, and Explanation[1]

The objective of this section is to specify the levels of the delinquency phenomenon that a multilayered integrative criminological theory must be able to address. The French criminologist Jean Pinatel (1963), in a masterful effort to define the bases of criminology, was the first to propose that criminologists should distinguish among three levels of the criminal phenomenon, namely criminality, criminal and crime. Each level has its own perspectives, its own rationales and its own methods (see Le Blanc and Fréchette 1989, for an elaborated discussion). Figure 6.1 sketches these levels of definition and explanation of the criminal phenomenon.

Pinatel defines criminality as the sum of infractions committed at a given time and place. It occurs on a societal scale and is influenced by demographic, economic or political factors. Criminality is not an individual criminal propensity as defined by Gottfredson and Hirschi (1990). Their definition of criminality introduced more confusion than clarity in criminology. Based on Pinatel's definition, the dependent variable is the rate of criminality for a particular geographical and social unit and for a specific period. The independent variables are indicators of the state of a society (differential social organization in Sutherland's terms, Sutherland and Cressey 1960), characteristics of a community (social disorganization in the Chicago school terms, Shaw and McKay 1969), dimensions of effective community control (Bursik and Grasmick 1993), or indicators of the functioning of an institution (school organization characteristics for example, Gottfredson and Gottfredson 1985).

The second level, the criminal, refers to the transgressor and includes a study of the transgressor's personal characteristics, as well as of the factors that influence the formation and evolution of his personality. This level of the criminal phenomenon corresponds to the expression of individual offending, as suggested by Blumstein et al. (1986). The dependent variable is any descriptive index of the criminal career, such as participation, frequency, onset, or duration, or any developmental measures, such as activation, aggravation or desistance (Le Blanc and Fréchette 1989). The independent variables are personal characteristics of an individual, such as the biological capacity and the personality, or social indicators such as the relationship with the environment, the bond to society in Hirschi's terms (1969), social class, and so on.

FIGURE 6.1
Levels of Definition and Explanation of the Criminal Phenomenon

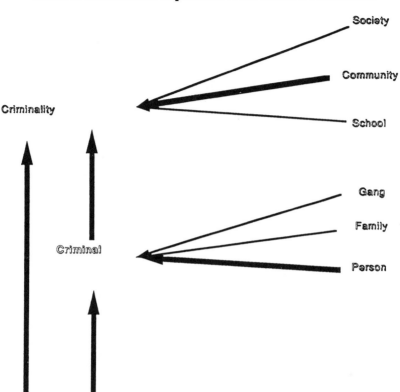

The third level of interpretation, is the crime itself. The criminal event has a beginning, a development and an end, and the task of criminology is to ascertain the factors or mechanisms that cause its appearance. At that level the dependent variable is any characteristics of specific offences. The independent variables are characteristics of the situation, such as routine activities (Cohen and Felson 1979) or other variables of the rational choice model of Cusson (1983) or Clarke and Cornish (1985).

American criminologists recently rediscovered this basic criminological rule, that there are various levels of definition matched with various levels of explanation (Hirschi 1979, 1989; Short 1985, 1989). However, the emphasis of criminological research has been mainly on two levels, criminality and criminal, just as Sutherland had suggested much earlier (Sutherland and Cressey 1960). This basic rule is far from being followed in the discourse of criminologists (see Le Blanc and Fréchette 1989, for examples). However, a number of more recent authors, for example Arnold and Brungardt (1983), Pearson and Weiner (1985), Short (1989), Cullen (1985), and Gottfredson and Hirschi (1990), take into account the need to specify the level of definition when elaborating their theoretical propositions for the explanation of the criminal phenomenon. In this paper, the terms crime, criminal and criminality are used inclusively, referring to the criminal phenomenon at whatever age, including children and adolescent offending as well as adult criminal activity.

Accepting that there are three levels of the criminal phenomenon implies that there are corresponding levels of explanation that are distinct and matched to them. Psychologists generally distinguish three levels— the milieu, the person, and the situation—and tend to use the more complex ecological classification of Bronfenbrenner (1979). For their part, sociologists tend to refer to society, community and institutions. As shown in figure 6.1, these levels of explanation match the levels of the criminal phenomenon. In consequence, each level of explanation is principally pertinent to a particular level of definition. In addition, to respect the logic of the ecological fallacy and the fallacy of reductionism, explanatory variables of one level do not explain the dependent variable of another level. Societal variables may affect the person and his milieu, however only person variables can influence directly individual offending and person variables cannot affect the rate of criminality directly. The same logic applies to the levels of crime and criminal. Figure 6.1 also implies that the levels of definition and explanation may have some relationships with each other. Crimes are constituent parts of the criminal and criminality, while criminality includes individual offending. Explanatory variables are constantly interacting and, it is also implicit from a dynamic point of view, that levels of definition and explanation reciprocally influence each other over time. Time is then conceived as a spiral as illustrated in figure 6.10. At a specific time, the characteristics of a person and of his community, associated with previous behavior, will partially determine subsequent behavior that, in turn, will modify the characteristics of the person and of his community. From the levels of definitions and explanation of the criminal phenomenon presented in figure 6.1, there can be at least seven layers in the explanatory theory. In this paper, we will limit discussion to three strata: the community, the person, and the act. These explanatory layers call for a multilayered theory. Each level of definition and explanation is autonomous. However, a particular level includes other levels. Each level has its own set of explanatory factors, notwithstanding the fact that crime is part of individual offending and criminality and that individual offending is part of criminality.

Lenski (1988, p. 168) defines a multilayered theory as "one in which a broadly inclusive general theory establishes a covering principle from which a series of more limited special theories can be derived." Lenski applies that definition to various subsets of societies. We propose to apply it to the levels of definition and explanation of the criminal phenomenon. A broadly inclusive general theory is what Wagner and Berger (1985) call an orienting strategy; it discusses guidelines for understanding crime, what notions to include and how to relate them to each other. In criminology, there are many such orienting strategies: social control, radical, structural, social learning, cultural deviance, labelling, deterrence, rational choice, and so on. These limited theories are unit theories, as defined by Wagner and Berger (1985). They present and evaluate a plausible body of theoretical statements offered to explain a particular layer of the criminal phenomenon. In this article, we develop both a general control theory and a set of limited theories about crime, criminal and criminality; this set of theories constitutes a multilayered control theory of the criminal phenomenon.

The Integrative Multilayered Control Theory, the Structural Statement[2]

In this section, we present the structure of the generic control theory. We define the constructs and relationships among them. We start with a comprehensive statement of the integrative multilayered control theory. We then state the theory for the three levels the criminal phenomenon.

A Generic Control Theory

Control theory dates back to the nineteenth-century idea that the family is the cause of delinquency (Empey 1978). This idea is also linked to Quetelet's (1835: 95) statement that "This fatal propensity appears to be developed in proportion to the intensity of the physical power and passions of man.... The intellectual and moral development...subsequently weaken the propensity to crime...." Hirschi (1969) limits the notion of control to Durkheims's definition of the bond to society as expressed in Durkheim's "Le suicide" (1897). Kornhauser (1978) sets the origin of a more elaborated version of control theory with Thrasher (1927), and with Shaw and McKay (1969), while Empey (1978) emphasizes Freud's psychodynamic formulation. Nevertheless, much of the recent literature forgets formulations that preceded Hirschi's statement. Precursors and followers of Hirschi would probably agree with Empey's statement that the core of control theories is (1978: 207): "...their emphasis upon the idea that delinquent and conformist behavior is a function of the ability of the child to control his antisocial impulses. They start from the assumption that children require training if they are to behave socially. Delinquent behavior will result either if a child lacks the ability for effective training or because he has been trained badly." This statement fits particularly well Durkheim's definition of control in his 1934 book *L'éducation morale* and the last version of control theory that introduces the notion of low self-control (Gottfredson and Hirschi 1990). As currently formulated, control theory only applies to the second level of the criminal phenomenon, the criminal. We propose to elaborate this theory for the other two levels, crime and criminality.

Our general control theory of the criminal phenomenon states that, *in a favorable environment and setting, control mechanisms operate efficiently and change in harmony with social expectations, and as a consequence, conformity results and maintains itself over time.* Conversely, in an unfavorable context, control mechanisms are insufficient and inappropriate and the criminal phenomenon emerges and persists.

We use the term control according to its third literal definition in Webster's dictionary (245, 3b): "one that controls" or "a mechanism used to regulate and guide the operation of a system." The term control then refers to the definition of the central notion that Gibbs proposes for sociology (1989: 23): "...control is *overt* behavior by humans in belief that (1) the behavior increases the probability of some subsequent condition and (2) the increase or decrease is desirable." For Gibbs, the commission or the omission of an act is overt behavior. Overt behavior manifests itself in several forms: inanimate things,[3] human and nonhuman organisms, self-controls and external controls—proximal, sequential, or social. Gibbs argues that this notion of control is central for sociology and for all the behavioral and social sciences. Gibbs' definition of control is compatible with its literal definition: the exercise of restraining and directing influences. This definition has two main advantages. First, this definition keeps us away from the strictly individual level formulation of the definition of control by Durkheim and others, that is the bond to society and internal and external constraints used during the socialization process. Second, its level of abstration facilitates the formulation of our control theory at the three levels of definition of the criminal phenomenon. Individuals, communities and events can produce behaviors—acts, circumstances or conditions—that are purposive and desirable. Bonds and constraints, as defined in the Durkheimian tradition, are only one type of such overt behaviors.

Gibb's notion of control is also central to psychology. For example, Lytton (1990) uses the umbrella of control system theory to review the literature on child development and Horowitz (1987) proposes a structural/behavioral control model of development. This notion of control is also dominant in criminology. For bonding theorists, attachment and supervision are forms of such regulating mechanisms. We could also argue that an arrest, the perceived certainty of a sanction or opportunities are forms of restraining influences for subsequent offending; they are constructs proposed by labelling, deterrence and strain theorists. Favorable and unfavorable definitions for differential association theorists and reinforcements for learning theorists are also controls because they are directing influences on criminal behavior.

Our generic theory identifies four categories of control mechanism: bonding, unfolding, modelling and constraining. Two types of context modulate these mechanisms, the environment and the setting. Each category of control mechanism and each type of context[4] represent numerous factors that have a potential impact on one particular level of the criminal phenomenon. The definitions of the control mechanisms are the following.

Bonding refers to the various ways by which individuals are held together in a community or interpersonally. Unfolding is the natural growth and development toward a desirable state, the growth of a community, or the development of the person according to values and expectations. Modelling is the existence of patterns than can shape conformity, opportunities that are available in a community and to individuals. Constraining refers to the regulation of conformity through various direct and indirect restraints; these restraints are limits defined by a community or imposed by the social network of the person. These mechanisms simultaneously and causally interact to produce conformity. They also have their own life or ontogeneity. This theory is systemic in the sense that it defines a structure, a sequence between the components, as well as directional relationships between the components including reciprocal or feedback effects. Figures 2 illustrate this generic theory with unidirectional and bidirectional arrows. It is also a dynamic theory because over time there is continuity and change within the mechanisms as well as because of their mutual influences. Figure 6.2 illustrates change by the superimposed boxes.

The structure of the theory, the relative position of the mechanisms in figure 6.2, indicates the direct and indirect impacts of the various mechanisms of control relative to the criminal phenomenon. The relative position of the mechanisms of control depends on the principle of prerequisites and on the distinction between continuity and change. The theory states that there are exogenous or contextual factors that do not have a direct impact on the criminal phenomenon; they are the environment and the background. The mechanisms of control mediate their impact. Two of these mechanisms of control, bonding and unfolding, are prerequisites or remote sets of factors, their impact is indirect on the criminal phenomenon. They are the foundations of the control mechanisms.

Without bonds, models cannot be significant and constraints cannot operate. As a consequence, an unbounded community or individual cannot be sensitive to direct controls or influenced by the available models. In addition, since the unfolding mechanism refers to a desirable state, this definition of what ought to be necessarily precedes the influence of available models and constraints, what is available as direct controls. Figure 6.2 also states that the bonding and the unfolding mechanisms modulate the criminal phenomenon through the mechanisms of modelling and constraining. These mechanisms are proximal causes of the criminal phenomenon. Models and constraints are more specific to the space-time dimension and tend to change frequently. They are not the more permanent dimensions of control such as bonding and unfolding. Figure 6.2 also states that the bonding and the unfolding mechanisms are in a situation of reciprocal causation at any given time. The modelling and the constraining mechanisms are in the same situation, a causal order cannot be established theoretically or empirically at a specific time.

FIGURE 6.2
Control Theory of the Criminal Phenomenon

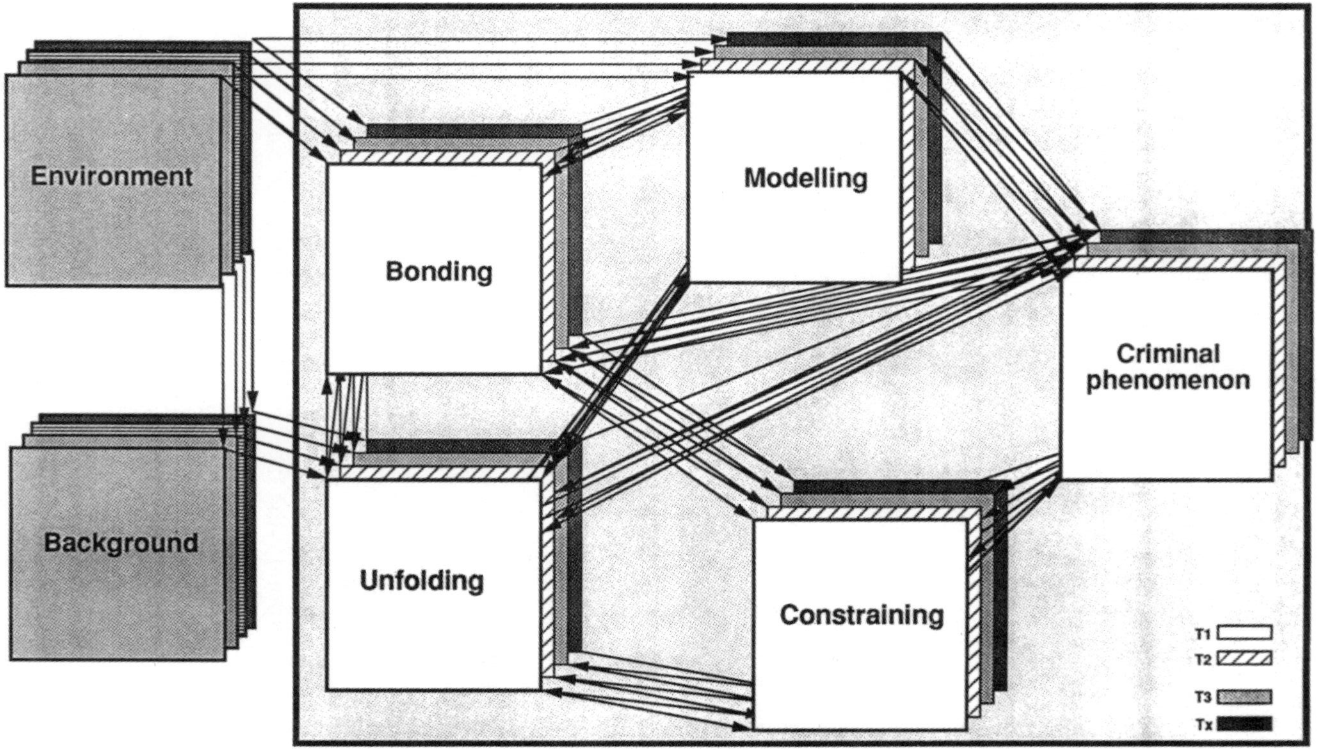

In sum, the bonding and unfolding mechanisms are both the foundation of and the continuity component of control; the modelling and constraining mechanisms are catalysts of conformity and are the changeable dimensions of control. Even in that context, we postulate that the four mechanisms of control are in a synergistic relation. They interact to produce an overall level of control of the criminal phenomenon. This synergy is particularly the result of the reciprocal relation between the bonding and the unfolding mechanisms and the reciprocal relation between the modelling and the constraining mechanisms.

We intend to demonstrate that this structure of the theory applies to the three levels of the criminal phenomenon. In a multilayered theory, the components have to be present at all the levels of definition and explanation of the criminal phenomenon. There is isomorphy in the mechanism of control at the layers of the crime, criminal and criminality. In this paper, we want to show that there are isomorphic constructs in the criminological literature for the various levels of definition and explanation. Let us formulate the integrative control theory at the level of individual offending. We start at this level because it is the layer for which control theory is most complex. The level of the criminal is also in-between the micro level, the crime, and the macro level, the criminality. Then we will present a sketch of the theory at the other levels of the criminal phenomenon.

A Control Theory of Individual Offending [5]

Reiss' (1951) statement of control theory proposed a distinction between social and personal control. Hirschi's formulation of control theory (1969) did not include psychological variables, but this deficiency is overcome with the introduction of the notion of self-control by Gottfredson and Hirschi (1990). Our initial elaboration of control theory involved such a construct (Le Blanc and Biron 1980), while our most recent version incorporates the six components enumerated earlier, namely social ties, entry into the adolescent role, psychological functioning, social constraints, social status and gender (Le Blanc et al. 1988; Le Blanc and Caplan 1993). Figure 6.3 describes the integrative personal control theory. *At the individual level, conformity to conventional standards of behavior occurs and persists, on one hand, if an appropriate level of allocentrism exists and the bond to society is firm and, on an other hand, if constraints are appropriate and models of pro-social behavior are available. This personal and social regulation of conformity is conditioned by the biological capacities of the person and his position in the social structure.* Alternatively, offending emerges and continues when egocentrism persists, when the social bond is tenuous, when constraints are insufficient and deviant models are abundant. These causes of offending will be more potent when the individual has some biological deficiencies and when he comes from the lower social class. We can now define the components of this theory represented in figure 6.3.

Social Status

The position of the individual in the social structure is the first contextual condition that affects the development of the bond to society and exposure to prosocial influences. Hagan (1988) is the most prominent recent North-American proponent of this position and Walgrave (1992) uses the term social vulnerability to refer to that contextual set of factors. Criminology has constantly documented that, if the person lives in a deteriorated community and if his socioeconomic status is low, his probability of becoming criminal and of having a criminal career is much higher (Blumstein et al. 1986). The impact of belonging to certain ethnic or racial groups is similar. It is also well known that in these milieus there exist various subcultures of deviance that support deviant patterns of behavior and more occasions are present for offending in these communities (see, for example, Cloward and Ohlin 1960). Such social conditions are indirect causes of offending, as shown in figure 6.3. This relationship appears in studies about the impact of the family, school systems, and their combination (see for example, Laub and Sampson 1988; Sampson and Laub 1993; Le Blanc 1992; Le Blanc et al. 1992) on self-reported and official delinquency (Le Blanc 1994).

Biological Capacities

Arnold and Brungardt (1983) were the first to introduce the construct of biological capacity in a control theory of offending. Studies document that biological deficiencies, such as the nature of the functioning of the central nervous system, testosterone, and so on (Hodgins 1985; Moffit 1990; Knoblich and King 1992; Blackburn 1993) and a difficult temperament (Wilson and Herrnstein 1985) are conditions that limit the pos-

FIGURE 6.3
Control Theory at the Level of the Criminal

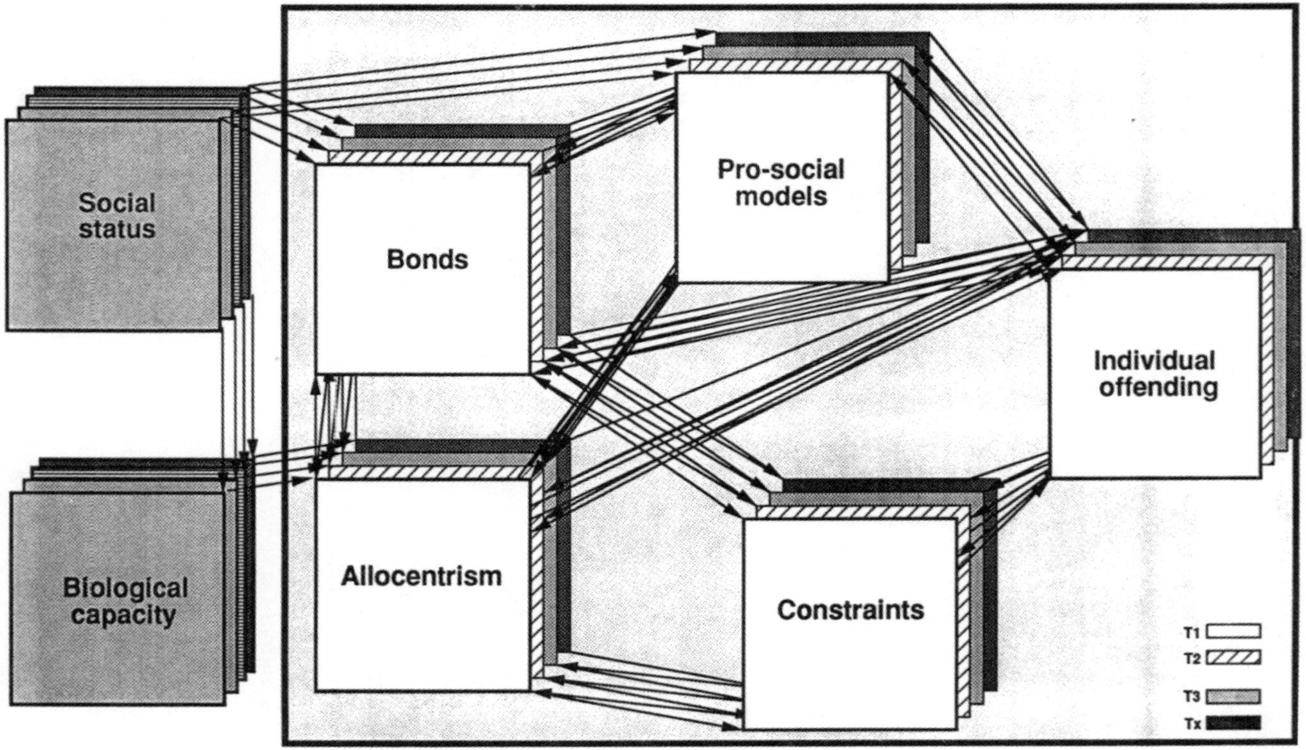

sibilities for the development of personality. Sampson and Laub (1993) define this last set of factors as child effects and they show that they are distal explanations of adult offending. In our personal control theory, such deficiencies will affect the development of allocentrism in the person and, in particular, should affect the cognitive development of the individual (IQ and moral development). The egocentric and cognitively primitive individual will be more likely to be criminal and to persist in offending. Such factors are indirect causes of conformity and offending as shown in figure 6.3.

Bond to Society

Following Hirschi (1969), the numerous replications of his theory (Kempf 1993), and its formalization (Le Blanc and Caplan 1993), we can state that an individual's bond to society manifests itself towards several institutions constituting the different spheres of the person's world. Three institutions receive particular emphasis for the adolescent: family, school, and peers. For adults, these institutions are marriage, work and peers. The person relates to these institutions through two avenues: attachment to persons and commitment to institutions. The development of the bond to society may be more difficult when the person lives in adverse socioeconomic conditions and when she is highly egocentric and less able cognitively.

The most important element of the bond to conventional society is the individual's attachment to persons. The importance of this element lies in the number of persons in society that can lead to an individual's attachment. There are at least three categories of such figures: parents or spouse, peers, and persons in positions of impersonal authority. Attachment to persons is part of the framework of the social norm that states what ought to be. The theory assumes that if a person is sensitive to the opinions of others, then he feels an obligation to abide by their norms. Consequently, the internalization of norms depends on the individual's attachment to persons and attachment to persons favors the acceptance of societal constraints such as parental discipline, school or work sanctions. Attachment to conventional persons acts as a major deterrent to the commission of criminal acts. The stronger this tie, the more likely the person will consider them when and if he envisages committing a crime. This attachment to persons also counters the impact of criminal influ-

ences: a weak or broken attachment to persons increases the susceptibility to deviant and criminal influences. The theory defines the process
through which attachment to persons reduces the commission of crimes
and criminal influences. That is, the person's level of attachment to conventional individuals determines his level of attachment to peers and to
persons in positions of impersonal authority. The cumulative impact of
these attachments protects the person against criminal influences and
discourages occasional and persistent offending.

The second element of the bond is commitment to institutions such as
school, religion, work, or success. Commitment refers to an attitude of
acceptance of an institution, an affective investment in education, work,
religion, and so on. If such commitments are strong, deviant behavior is
costly. Therefore, when a person faces the temptation to commit a crime,
he must evaluate the costs of his behavior relative to the investments he
has made. The assumption underlying the idea of commitment to institutions is that the attitudinal investment of most persons seriously affects
the decision to commit criminal acts. Commitment is a constraint on
offending and a protection against criminal influences since they would
jeopardize the person's possibility of realizing the fruits of his investment. This suggests that the person is committed to conformity not only
by his present investments but also by what he hopes to achieve.

Allocentrism

A comprehensive and integrative perspective for the explanation of offending cannot rule out individual differences. The criminological literature documents the importance of individual differences in the emergence
and development of individual offending (Feldman 1978; Kornhauser 1978;
Wilson and Herrnstein 1985; Fréchette et Le Blanc 1987; Blackburn 1993).
While there are a large variety of psychological theories, only one has a
common set of postulates with social control theories. As shown by Empey
(1978), it is the psychodynamic perspective. Freud developed the postulates that children are originally antisocial and that socialization occurs
through successive stages. We could easily argue that Piaget's (1967) theory
of intellectual development and Kohlberg's (1976) theory of moral development are part of the control family. Bonding theorists are now considering psychological dimensions more explicitly. Gottfredson and Hirschi
(1990), for example, propose the construct of low self-control as an inte-

gral part of control theory. In our view, this construct is a very limited selection of the possible psychological traits that are associated with individual offending. It refers to vulnerability to the temptation of the moment; individuals with low self-control are impulsive, insensible, physical, risk-taking, short-sighted, and nonverbal.

Allocentrism is the movement away from the natural egocentrism of the individual. It manifests itself by a genuine consideration of what surrounds a person; it is the disposition to think about others and to behave in relation to them. This egocentrism-allocentrism axis of the development of humans (see Lerner 1986) serves to synthesize the personality dimensions associated with offending. We propose this construct to represent psychological control as a complement to Hirschi's social control theory (Le Blanc and Biron 1980; Le Blanc et al. 1988). This is in accordance with the classic conception of the explanation of offending that stresses the importance of psychological variables (Wolfgang and Ferracuti 1967, among others).

A review of the literature in this domain convinced us that two major lines of complementary thought need to be part of our integrative psychological control theory (Fréchette and Le Blanc 1987). The first stems from developmental theories and lead us to consider the level of psychic development, which means the level of progression from a primitive toward a rich psychic life manifested by a certain level of allocentrism. Allocentrism manifest itself in terms of movement from self-centered to "decentered" states on social, affective, moral, relational, and cognitive dimensions. The decentered person is no longer limited in outlook to his own activities and needs. The second line of research made it possible to identify a great number of personality traits that correlate with delinquent conduct. We synthesized them under the notion of the egocentric personality, a deficient psychological functioning because it focuses excessively on the self. The egocentric personality has five distinguishing traits: hyposociality (inability to cope with the demands and constraints of social life), negativeness (hostile attitude toward others), insecurity (malaise and strong feelings of discomfort), primitiveness (rudimentary manner of functioning; giving strict priority to personal needs), and cognitive deficiencies (a lag in intellectual and moral development). This cohesive structure constitutes the framework for the psychic support of individual offending. Personal isolation emerges as the main characteristic of serious delinquency; in other words, the most determining negative influence is withdrawal from intimate human contact. A multidimensional structure directly supports that isolation. This structure involves hyposociality, which seems to be the most powerful element, and negativeness; insecurity, primitiviness, and cognitive deficiencies strengthen these influences.

Figure 6.3 indicates that the normal development of allocentrism favors the establishment of a solid bond to society, receptivity to social constraints, and preference for prosocial influences, and, finally, conformity to conventional standards of behavior. However, the levels of allocentrism and cognitive development are dependent on individual biological capacity. Allocentrism improves over time and then counters the continuation of individual offending.

Constraints

Following Durkheim's (1895, 1934) classic distinction between norms, defined as rules of law and moral values, and discipline, characterized as monitoring and punishment, we propose that there are two major sources of restraint when an individual envisages a crime, internal and external constraints (see the full elaboration of the constraint component in Le Blanc 1995).

External constraints are of two categories, formal and informal. Labelling theorists fully elaborate the formal external constraint perspective (see Shoemaker 1990), while bonding theorists develop the informal social reaction point of view (see Le Blanc and Caplan 1993). Labelling theory states that the imposition of the official label of criminal, following criminal activity, favors the development of a criminal self-image and the emergence of new and more serious forms of criminal activities. Bonding theorists recognize that both very low and very high levels of parental control are least effective in bringing about conformity. They also argue that both strict and punitive or lax and erratic discipline increase the level of conduct problems. Direct parental control variables (supervision and discipline) are related to offending during adolescence even when attachment to parents and family context (family structure, marital relations, parental deviance, and so on) are controlled statistically (Le Blanc 1992). In the school domain, contrary to the family domain, external constraint, as compared to bonding, is the best explanation of adolescent and adult offending (Le Blanc 1994).

Bonding theorists elaborate the notion of internal constraint under the concept of beliefs (Hirschi 1969) and under the concept of perceived certainty and severity of sanctions, a notion borrowed from deterrence theorists (see Paternoster 1987). The first notion refers to the person's belief in conventional standards of behavior, that is, the extent to which he believes he should obey the rules of society. The person's beliefs act as a moral obstacle to the commission of crimes. The less a person believes he should obey the rules of society, the greater is the probability that he will commit crimes. However, there is ample variation in the attitude of respect toward the rules of society; many persons feel no moral obligation to conform. Four types of belief are potentially important: the acceptance of the normative system, the use of neutralization techniques, the legitimacy of rules imposed by parents, and by controlling institutions (Le Blanc and Caplan 1993). Perceptual deterrence theory postulates an inverse relationship between the perceived certainty and severity of sanctions and offending. Empirical tests of this hypothesis are numerous but the results are still inconclusive (Le Blanc 1995).

As represented in figure 6.3, individual receptivity to social constraints depends on the quality of the person's bond to society, the level of development of his allocentrism and on the presence of strong prosocial influences. These constraints are one of the last protections against individual offending. When constraints are age-inappropriate, erratic or absent, they are direct and proximal causes of individual offending as shown in our previous studies (Le Blanc et al. 1988; Le Blanc 1992, 1993, 1995; Le Blanc et al. 1992, 1993).

Prosocial Influences

Tarde (1924) introduced a modelling explanation of delinquency, which was later developed by Sutherland (Sutherland and Cressey 1960). Modelling is an important cause of adolescent delinquency according to numerous studies (see Elliott et al. 1985, 1989; Thornberry et al. 1994). A central assumption of classical control theories is that companionship with delinquents is an incidental by-product of the quality of the bond to society. This assertion suggests that the relationship between delinquent companions and offending is spurious. However, after testing this hypothesis with his data and reviewing numerous other studies, Hirschi (1969) revised his bonding model to state that delinquent companions have a direct or causal impact on the commission of crimes. Furthermore, after formalizing Hirschi's theory we proposed that a weak or broken bond to society leads to the acquisition of delinquent friends and directly affects the level of offending (Le Blanc and Caplan 1993). In the latest revision of bonding theory, Gottfredson and Hirschi (1990) suggest that low self-control leads to street life and to the membership in a deviant group. These factors, in turn, lead to a more frequent offending.

The delinquent friend represents, in part, the person's exposure to criminal influences. A person, however, is exposed to criminal influences through a variety of other sources: deviant subcultures that are present in his community, television and video viewing, parental deviance and criminality, routine activities, spouse's deviance, and so on. Figure 6.3 states that the person's receptivity to criminal influences depends on the quality of his bond to society, the development of his allocentrism and the tightness of the constraints imposed by himself or others. Thus the receptivity to criminal influences is a direct and proximal cause of individual offending as shown by numerous criminological studies (see particularly Elliott et al. 1985, 1989; Thornberry et al. 1991, 1994; Sampson and Laub 1993).

The Structure of the Personal Control Theory

The structure of the theory, as indicated by the relative position of the mechanisms in figure 6.3, depends on the principle of developmental prerequisites and on the distinction between continuity and change as in the structure of the generic control theory.

As shown by Zazzo's (1979) magisterial synthesis, animals and humans have two primary needs, self-conservation and integration into their species. Animals and humans inherit these two needs. First, the primary need for self-conservation has a biological origin and is the source of personal traits. As a result, the biological context of our theory contains a set of distal factors for explaining conformity. They, however, give birth to the unfolding mechanisms, named allocentrism, that are closer explanations of conformity. This mechanism implies that from his temperament the person develops his character and personality in interaction with his environment. World views define the goals of this development in a social and cultural context—the setting in our theory—and biological capacities limit the attainment of these expectations. Second, the primary need of integration to its species leads to bonding, which grounds the individual in a social and cultural milieu. This sociocultural context of the bond is a remote set of factors for conformity while the quality of the bond has a more direct impact on conformity. In our general theory, the bonding and the unfolding mechanisms are in a situation of synergy. This situation is similar at the level of the criminal (figure 6.3). In causal modelling terms, bonds and allocentrism are in a situation of reciprocal causation; no one-way causal sequence is justifiable between these components of the theory. They are developmental prerequisites of conformity. They are also continuous primary needs during the life course.

This is not the case for the modelling and constraining mechanisms. During the life course, models and constraints change with the evolution of society. Models—attitudinal and behavioral demands of society for children, adolescents and adults—are constantly changing over time and with age. During the life course, constraints are also transformed; for example external controls have priority early in the life course while internal controls gain dominance later in the life course (see for example Durkheim 1934; Nye 1958). As a consequence, figure 6.3 states that prosocial models and constraints are results of the bonding and allocentrism mechanisms; they are proximal causal factors of conformity. They operate in synergy, as the bonding and unfolding mechanisms do. In figure 6.3, reciprocal arrows represent synergy.

Figure 6.3 also implies causal and retroactive effects. Arrows from one superimposed box of a mechanism to the next one of another mechanism (in fact from one time to a later time) represent a causal impact. By definition, a causal effect follows the sequence proposed by the structure of the theory. In contrast, a retroactive effect runs in the opposite direction of the sequence defined by the structure of the theory. An example of a retroactive effect is the impact of the modelling mechanism at one time on the bonding mechanism at the subsequent time, and so on for all other mechanisms. An other example of such retroactive effects is the impact of previous individual offending on the subsequent state of bonding, unfolding, modelling, and constraining. Figure 6.3 also implies that individual offending will sequentially display the same type of effect on the modelling and constraining mechanisms and on the bonding and allocentrism mechanisms.

We began the elaboration of our multilayered control theory at the level of the individual. We stated that the personal and social regulation of conformity is conditional to the biological capacities of the person and his position in the social structure. This regulation of conformity is the result of the interaction of proximal mechanisms, such as constraints and prosocial models of behavior, and distal mechanisms, such as the development of allocentrism and bonds to society. Synergy results from the interactions between these set of factors. In the next section, we move to the level of criminality, another layer of the criminal phenomenon. We elaborate our community control theory with the logic used for our personal control theory.

A Control Theory of Criminality

Kornhauser (1978) argues convincingly that the social disorganization perspective is basically a control theory, even if it is primarily about community disorganization. She indicates that this theoretical perspective has an overwhelming emphasis on community context even if it does sometimes specify the influence of coordinate individual level variables. She demonstrates that social disorganization theory includes the major components of a control theory: the strength of social bonds as the foundation of control, the importance of direct controls, the weakness of culture, and defective socialization to cultural values. Her model is based on three constructs: exogenous variables (economic status, mobility, heterogeneity), cultural disorganization, and social disorganization. She specifies the relationships between the exogenous variables and the structural and cultural community organization without stating clearly the connection between these two forms of community organization. Our version of community control elaborates on this base. Figure 6.4 represents our control theory at the level of explanation of the community.

The dependent variable is the rate of criminality in a particular community at a specific moment and its evolution over time. This rate refers either to an overall rate or to rates of specific types of criminal acts. The independent variables, as in the individual level of control theory, comprise six constructs: social structure, setting, social organization, cultural organization, opportunities, and direct controls. These constructs represent respectively the environment and the setting contexts, the bonding, the modelling, the unfolding and the constraining mechanisms of the generic control theory. Thrasher (1927) and Shaw and McKay (1969) proposed some of these constructs and Kornhauser (1978) and Sampson

FIGURE 6.4
Control Theory at the Level of the Criminality

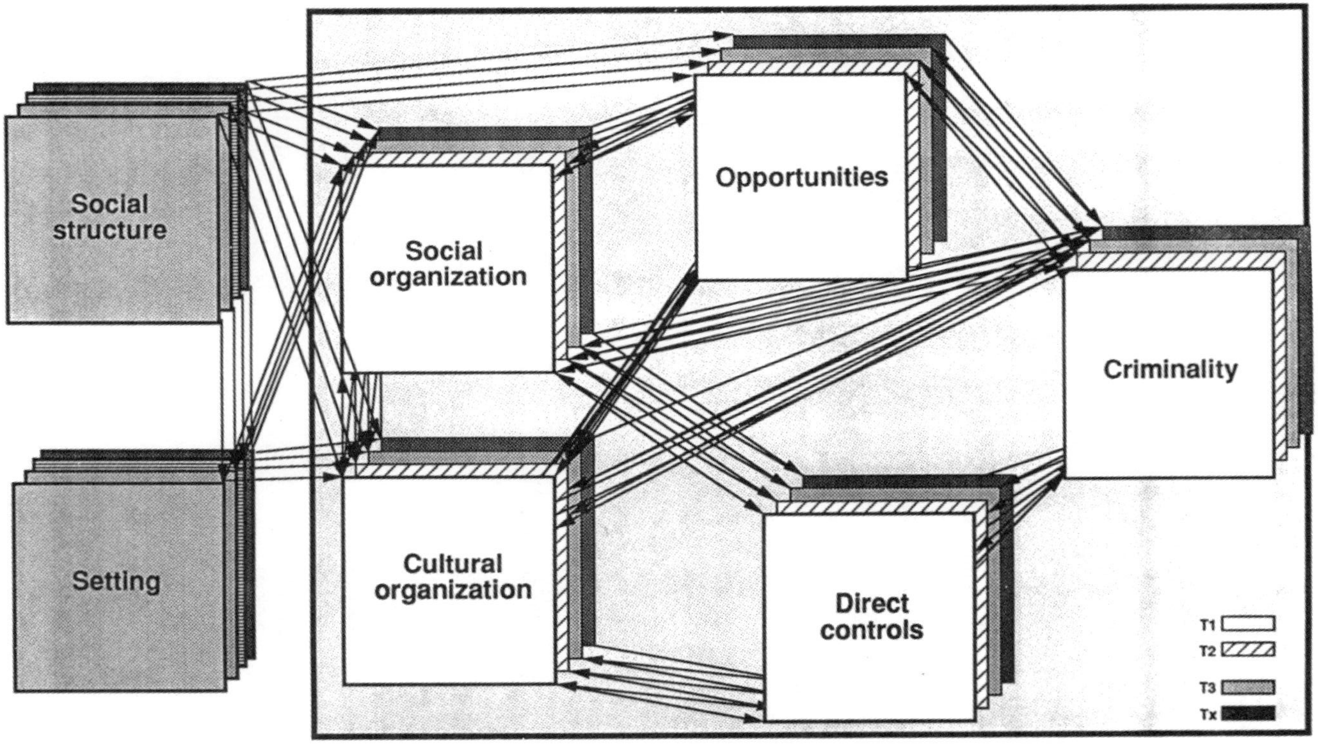

(1991) elaborate upon them. Bursik and Grasmick (1993) stress the intervening aspect of community social organization constructs between the social structure and criminality.

Our community control theory assumes that *a high rate of conformity to conventional standards of behavior persists in a community when the social organization is sound and the cultural organization robust, when direct controls are efficient, and when there are sufficient legitimate opportunities. This regulation of conformity is conditional on the quality of the setting and on the position of the community in the more general social structure.* Alternatively, a high rate of criminality will exist when social and cultural disorganization are persistent, when direct controls are inappropriate and when deviant subcultures and opportunities are present. These causes of a high rate of criminality in a community will be more efficient in a physically deteriorated setting and when the social status of the community is low. The rate of conformity will vary over time and between communities according to changes in the position of the community in the social structure and the quality of the setting and to variations in the levels of social and cultural organization, direct controls and opportunities. We begin by outlining the content of each of these communities constructs before we discuss the structure of the theory.

Social Structure

The definition of the social structure appears under different terms in different theories: exogenous variables for Kornhauser (1978), the population dimension for Figueira-McDonough (1991) and urbanization for Wikström (1990). Bursik and Grasmick (1993) define this dimension as the socioeconomic composition of the community, the residential stability of the residents and the racial and ethnic heterogeneity of the neighbourhood. This construct parallels the concept of social structure in the individual level theory. Since the seminal studies of Shaw and McKay (1969) numerous studies have documented that rates of criminality are higher in communities that display lower social status and higher poverty and that these communities are heavily populated by immigrants (see Kornhauser 1978; Wikström 1990; and Bursik and Grasmick 1993, reviews).

Figure 4 states that a disadvantaged social context favors social and cultural disorganization, the presence of illegitimate opportunities, and inappropriate direct controls (see also Wikström, 1990, for a formulation of these statements based on a more extensive literature review). Sampson (1993) shows the indirect impact of the social structure on the rate of criminality through the social organization dimension. A change in the position of the community in the social structure may also affect formal and informal social controls and the rate of criminality in that community (Bursik and Grasmick 1993).

Setting

The setting is the isomorphic construct to biological capacity at the level of the individual. It is defined traditionally in criminology by density and crowding (Figueira-McDonough 1991) and by the physical deterioration of the inner city (Kornhauser 1978). It could now also involve such characteristics as the level of pollution by substances (such as lead and so on), traffic, noise, and so on. The impact of the setting on criminality has long been documented (Shaw and McKay 1969; Kornhauser 1978, and others). We can state that the characteristics of the setting of a community provide a context that favors or disfavors community control over criminality. Figure 6.4 states that a physically deteriorated and a very low or a very high density setting encourages social and cultural disorganization. Such a setting also favors the use to direct controls (Figueira-McDonough 1991). A change in the setting, gentrification for example, could only indirectly modify the rate of criminality over time through community control.

Social Organization

Social disorganization traditionally refers to the weakness of informal networks; it is the loss of community control over members and the erosion of informal networks (see Sampson 1988, 1991). Sampson (1992) highlights three major dimensions of community social organization: the ability of a community to supervise and control teenage peer groups, the quality of local friendship and acquaintanceship networks, and the rate of local participation in formal and voluntary organizations. Said in an other way, social disorganization is the inability of organizations, groups and individual members of a community to solve their common problems collectively (Shoemaker 1990). Bursik and Grasmick (1993), for their part, refer to the quality of primary relational networks (intimate informal primary groups: family, friends, neighbors) and the strength of secondary relational networks (broader local interpersonal networks and the interlocking of local institutions). All these authors are clearly referring to a bonding mechanism between members of a community, that is, ties between the members of a community that are some sort of community attachment and commitment. These are similar mechanisms compared to the individual bonding mechanism that we defined at the previous level of explanation of the criminal phenomenon.

Figure 6.4, based on the reviews by Kornhauser (1978) and Bursik and Grasmick (1993), stresses that the social structure of the community (socioeconomic composition, residential stability and ethnic heterogeneity) affects the level of social disorganization. It also indicates, in accordance with lower-class theories (Cohen 1955; Cloward and Ohlin 1960), that when social disorganization is high various deviant subcultures exist in the community. Social disorganization will increase cultural disorganization (Kornhauser 1978), reduce formal controls (see Figueira-McDonough 1991) and increase the opportunities for crime (Wikström 1990). Variations in social organization over time should also modify the rate of criminality.

Cultural Organization

The distinction between structure and culture has long been established in sociology, particularly by Parsons. Following that direction, various notions are present in the criminological literature that refer to cultural organization. There is Sutherland's constructs of economic and political individualism (Sutherland and Cressey 1960), Sellin's (1938) notion of culture conflict, Merton's (1957) anomie construct, and Angel's (1947) social integration notion (cultural, normative, communicative). The term cultural disorganization, proposed by Kornhauser (1978), seems particularly appropriate to represent these notions and the unfolding mechanism. The definition of this mechanism stresses the growth and development of a community toward a desirable state. Cultural disorganization, for Kornhauser, refers to the attenuation of societal cultural values as controls. The desirable state for any society is the presence of robust and influential cultural values.

According to Kornhauser (1978), the physical deterioration of slum areas, their low economic status, their cultural heterogeneity, and the mobility of the residents are responsible for the presence of both the diversity and the obsolescence of subcultures in the community. These factors also account for the instability and narrow scope of community culture and the irrelevance of societal culture. This situation impedes communication and obstructs the quest for common values and as a result there is an attenuation of subcultural, communal and societal cultural values in these communities. The cultural organization-disorganization continuum at the level of the community has a common feature with the egocentrism-allocentrism continuum at the level of the individual. The continuum defines a desirable state for the development of a community or an individual.

Figure 6.4, following existing empirical evidence, proposes that social and cultural disorganization will increase in deteriorated settings and in heterogeneous, mobile and low social status communities. It also postulates that these two disorganization constructs are related reciprocally to each other. This position is probably the most conservative one, notwithstanding the fact that Kornhauser (1978) limits herself to a nonrecursive model and states that cultural disorganization causes social disorganization. Since there is no clear empirical evidence nor solid theoretical reasons to support this limited position, we will postulate reciprocal causality or synergy. Social and cultural disorganization will support the emergence of various subcultures (Kornhauser 1978; Bursik and Grasmick 1993) and they will encourage the development of formal social control (Figueira-McDonough 1991, reports that there is an inverse relationship between social disorganization and direct controls). Over time, modifications in cultural disorganization should indirectly imply changes in the rate of criminality.

Opportunities

In a deteriorated setting and a low socioeconomic status community, various deviant models and numerous illegitimate opportunities will be available to adolescents. Such a relationship has been masterly described by Cloward and Ohlin (1960). Bursik and Grasmick (1993) use the construct of neighborhood opportunities and argue that neighborhood processes affect routine activities and gang behavior and, in turn, the community level of criminality.

Our notion of opportunities is more comprehensive. It includes the subcultures, their representative gangs, and corresponding illegal markets (stolen goods businesses, drugs, prostitution, and so on). However, it also involves black markets, such as undeclared work, and deficiencies in resources for conventional activities, such as work, playgrounds, sports organizations, art classes, and so on. Our notion of opportunities also refers to the large availability of suitable targets for crimes because of the deficiencies in social and cultural organization and formal and informal direct controls. All these categories of community opportunities offer deviant models to persons living in such a community. The existence of these illegitimate opportunities and the scarcity of legitimate opportunities will encourage the use of repressive direct controls and they will sustain a high rate of criminality as illustrated in figure 6.4. Changes in the level of such opportunities over time should correspond to equivalent changes in the rate of criminality.

Direct Controls

Kornhauser (1978, p.74) defines direct controls as "…purposive efforts to ensure conformity or limit deviance.…" Hunter (1985: 233) proposes three levels of such control. The private level refers to relationships among friends; friends accomplish such control through the withdrawal of sentiment, social support and mutual esteem. The parochial level of direct control points to the broader set of local interpersonal networks of neighbors, and interlocking of local institutions, such as voluntary organizations, stores, schools, churches. The public level involves the ability of the community to secure public goods and services (health services, social services, policing, and so on) that various outside agencies allocate to the community.

Bursik and Grasmick (1993) document with their literature review that the level of direct control directly affects the criminality rate. In turn, the level of direct private, parochial and public controls depends on the level of social disorganization. In the same vein, Figueira-McDonough (1991) concludes from her review of the literature that social disorganization will be a central cause of criminality because of the intervention of direct controls or the transfer of many control functions from primary groups to formal organizations. In such a case, law enforcement agencies will be more present and repressive, and there will also be a proliferation of agencies and programs in the domains of school, personal counselling, professional training, health services, and so on. Figure 6.4

states that direct controls are a proximal cause of the rate of criminality and the presence of various subcultures and illegitimate opportunities reinforces the community's propensity to crime.

The Structure of the Community Control Theory

We argue that an integrative community control theory contains six constructs: social structure, setting, social organization, cultural organization, opportunities and direct controls. In addition, based on past theoretical statements and empirical studies, we proposed many interdependencies between these constructs. However, we did not justify the particular sequence of constructs represented in figure 6.4. Let us see if the principle of prerequisite and the distinction between continuity and change apply to community control as they do for personal control.

There is a total consensus among the specialists of community control that the social structure of the community (socioeconomic status, heterogeneity and mobility) and its setting (particularly if it is physically degraded) are exogenous factors to community processes. These sets of variables directly influence the social and cultural organization of the community, the nature of available opportunities, and the nature of direct controls. In consequence, these authors conclude that the social structure and the setting of a community do not have a direct impact on the rate of criminality.

The following assumption can be made concerning the relative position of the constructs of social and cultural organization of the community, opportunities and direct controls. Communities, like humans, have two primary needs, self-conservation and integration to the larger society. First, the primary need of self-conservation has its origin in the setting of the community and its social structure and it is the main source of community organization. As a result, the setting and social structural contexts of our theory are distal sets of factors for conformity. They, however, encourage the bonding (social organization) and the unfolding (cultural organization) mechanisms that are closer explanations of conformity but not direct explanations. These mechanisms imply that, from a particular setting and a specific position in the social structure, the community develops its social and cultural organization. Second, the primary need for the integration of the community into the larger society leads also to community organization. In our general control theory, the bonding and the unfolding mechanisms are in a situation of synergy and no ordering is justifiable between these components of the theory. They are growth prerequisites of conformity. There is also a consensus among authors that the available opportunities and the nature of direct controls are consequences of the social and cultural organization of the community.

The two primary needs of communities, self-conservation and integration, are always present during history. This is not the case for the modelling (opportunities) and constraining (direct controls) mechanisms. Over time, the models change and the constraints alter with the evolution of the community and the larger society. Models—attitudinal and behavioral exemplars—are constantly changing in history through fashions and growth. For example, gangs of today are different from gangs of previous decades (see Spergel 1990). During history, constraints have been transformed from repressive to humanitarian (Van Dijk 1989, documents these changes). As a result, figure 6.4 states that the modelling and the constraining mechanisms are influenced by the bonding and unfolding mechanisms, they are proximal causal factors of conformity. The structure of the theory proposed by figure 6.4 is another application of the principle of growth prerequisite and of the distinction between continuity and change. Figure 6.4 also indicates that this theory is dynamic and interactional. Development is represented by superimposed boxes in this figure. Reciprocal and directional arrows represent interactions.

A Control Theory of Crime

An event control theory has common grounds with a personal control theory and a community control theory. Hirschi (1986), for his part, argues convincingly that there is no fundamental opposition between rational choice and control perspectives. He states that they share the same image of man as a self-seeking individual. In addition, even if the corresponding models emphasize different criminal phenomenon, the criminal event and the criminal, they are complementary for that reason. Bursik and Grasmick (1993), for their part, state that the routine activities and the social disorganization approaches complement each other. They argue that community dynamics relate naturally to the offender/target/capable guardian convergence so important for routine activities theory. In addition, with the help of the theoretical and empirical literature, they show that there is a complex series of interdependencies between the components of community control and routine activities, on one part, and the convergence of a target and an offender, on the other.

In sum, a criminal event is a function of the community in which it takes place and of the individual who commits it. In these circumstances, it is natural to move to the micro level of definition and explanation of the criminal phenomenon with a control perspective. The discursive statement of our integrative event control theory is the following. Offense control theory assumes that *conformity to conventional standards of behavior in a specific situation occurs when routine activities are conventional, when self-control is high, when there is no occasion for the perpetration of a criminal act, and when guardianship is reliable. This regulation of conformity is conditional on the quality of community and personal controls.* Alternatively, a crime is likely when the person's self-control is low, when his routine activities are unconventional, when there are numerous occasions to commit crimes and when possible targets are unprotected. These causes of the perpetration of an offense will be more potent when the person has a high propensity for crime (low personal control) and lives in a disorganized community (low community control). Over time, the variations in the quality of the offense control mechanism change the probability of the commission of a crime. Figure 6.5 represents this theoretical statement.

The dependent variable is a particular criminal event. This event has various characteristics (the nature of the crime; the mechanics of the perpetration of the act: planning, use of instruments, accomplices, and so on; the psychological reaction before, during and after the event). Le Blanc and Fréchette (1989) define these components of a criminal event and study changes in them during the life span. The explanatory constructs of community control, personal control, self-control, routine activities, occasions and guardianship are isomorphic with the constructs of the other two levels of the criminal phenomenon. Personal and community controls represent the structural factors or the exogenous variables. Routines' activities delineate the bonding mechanism, the self-control component manifests the unfolding mechanism, the occasions construct defines the modelling mechanism, and the guardianship dimension represents the constraining mechanism.

As represented in figure 6.5, we propose that a person's routine activities will primarily be away from the household when the person's bond to

FIGURE 6.5
Control Theory at the Level of the Crime

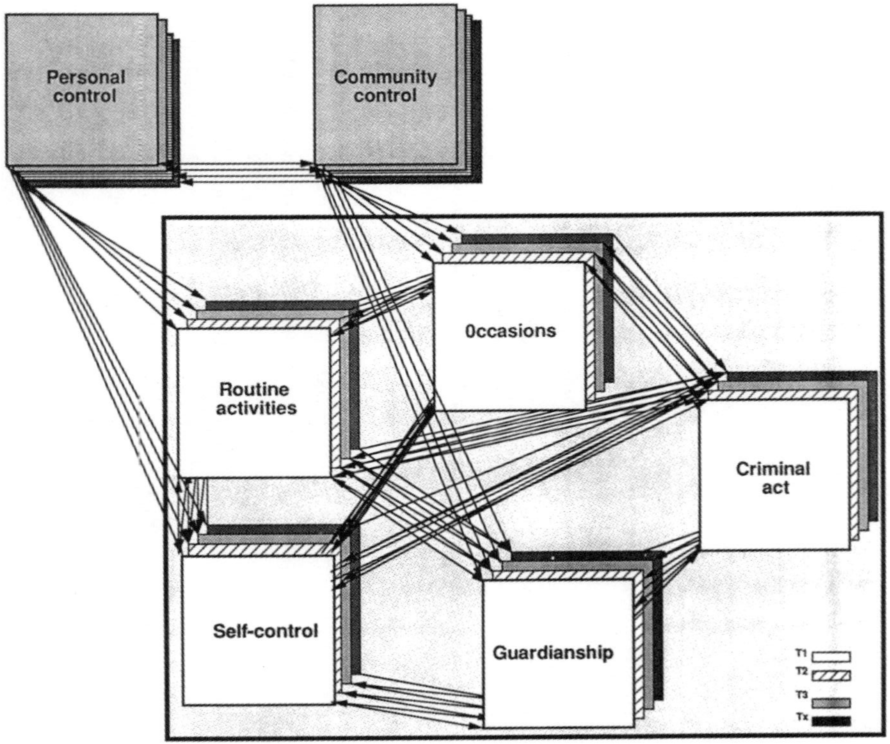

society is tenuous and his self-control will be low when he is highly ego-centric. Figure 6.5 also states that when community control is low there are numerous occasions to commit crimes and less guardianship. We also postulate that when routine activities tend to take the potential offender away from home there will be more occasions to commit crimes and that when self control is low the occasion will appear more interesting and the guardianship will be underestimated. Crime more likely occur when all these factors are active. Our integrative offense control theory relies greatly on Felson's (1986) discussion of the relationships between criminal choices, routine activities, indirect control, ecology, and social control theories. Figure 6.5 also represents the interdependencies between the constructs from a dynamic point of view—the superimposed boxes, and in an interactional perspective—the directional and bidirectional arrows.

Community Control

Community control involves four processes, social organization, cultural organization, legitimate opportunities and increased formal control. The social structure and the setting of a particular community modulate these processes. Figure 6.6 states that the quality of community control influences indirectly the perpetration of specific crimes through the proliferation of occasions and unstable guardianship. Poor community control will increase the probability of the perpetration of a criminal act.

Felson's (1986) discursive statement of the links between routine activities and other theoretical perspectives recognizes the importance of community control for the proliferation of opportunities for predatory crimes. He states (123) that "a tight community...offers little opportunity for common exploitative crime." For their part, Bursik and Grasmick (1993), reviewing the literature, argue that changes in the social structure of the community, in the household composition for example, will increase available targets and diminish guardianship. As a consequence, we propose that the level of community control will determine the availability of occasions to commit crimes and will diminish the number of persons, physical protection devises, or specific situations that can act as capable guardians.

Personal Control

There are bridges between personal and event control. Clarke and Cornish's (1995) criminal involvement model includes many classic con-

trol theory constructs. For example, they include, in the background factor box, upbringing, cognitive style, and so on; in the previous experience box, they retain moral attitudes, contact with law enforcement
agencies, and so on; and, in the perceived solution box, they refer to
involvement in legitimate and illegitimate activities. These constructs refer
to some types of indirect and direct controls. Felson (1986) also explicitly cites bonds to society, an aspect of our construct of personal control,
in his elaborated model of the criminal event. He calls the bond the handle-
unhandle potential offender. As a consequence, rational choice and routine activities theorists recognize that the level of personal control is an
important exogenous variable when the perpetration of a crime is possible and considered.

Figure 6.5 states that the level of personal control indirectly affects
the convergence of the available target and the inclined offender. This
indirect impact can occur through routine activities for Felson (1986) or
the reaction to chance events and the readiness of the potential perpetra-
tor for Clarke and Cornish (1985).

Routine Activities

The construct of routine activities refers to habitually enacted public
activities. This construct focuses particularly on individual life-style
(Hindelang et al. 1978) or the daily activity patterns that disperse the
person away from his family (Felson and Gottfredson 1984) and household situation (Cohen and Felson 1979). According to routine activity
theory, these activities will bring the person in contact with numerous
targets or occasions for the commission of a crime, and, particularly,
contact with unproperly guarded targets. The construct of involvement
in conventional activities, borrowed from Hirschi's theory (1969), is
complementary to this construct of routine activities. It incorporates public
and private, institutional and noninstitutional activities. The involvement
process states that the greater the involvement of the person in conventional activities, the less time he has to engage in deviant acts and the less
chance of exposure to the temptation of crime. When defining offending
as an activity, the emphasis is on the nature of the conventional activity
as oppose to the quantity of conventional activities. With this position,
five types of activities are presumably important. These institutional and
non-institutional activities revolve around the family (or the spouse and

children), peers, leisure, school or work, and loitering. These types of activities are important since, according to Hirschi's results (ours also Fréchette et Le Blanc 1987) school-related activities inhibit criminal activities, whereas the adolescent's loitering, participation in work and in leisure activities positively correlate with offending (which may not be the case for adults). The other two types of involvement, activities with parents (or later on with a spouse) and peers (particularly if they are conventional) are a protection against the commission of criminal acts.

Figure 6.5 introduces a construct of routine activities that covers this entire range of activities. The model states that the dominance of public and noninstitutional routine activities will increase the number of occasions to commit crime and the number of contacts with unguarded targets. In turn, unconventional routine activities are supported by deficient personal and community controls. Conversely, private and institutional routine activities will decrease the number of occasions to commit a crime and the number of contacts with unguarded possible targets. Changes in routine activities over time could modify the probability of the commission of a criminal act and also could result in a transfer from one type of criminal offense to another type of offense.

Self-Control

Gottfredson and Hirschi (1990: 87) define self-control as "the idea that people differ in the extend to which they are vulnerable to the temptation of the moment." They characterize people with low self-control as "...impulsive, insensible, physical, risk-taking, short-sighted, and nonverbal" (90). For their part, Clarke and Cornish (1985) introduce similar notions with what they call previous experiences and learnings (direct and vicarious experience of crime, foresight and planning, and so on), reactions to chance events (easy opportunities, need for cash, drugs, and so on) and readiness to commit a crime. The egocentric person is also describe as an impulsive individual (Fréchette and Le Blanc 1987). For us, Gottfredson and Hirschi's (1990) construct of low self-control should be part of the event control theory rather than the personal control theory. We made this choice because the notion of egocentric personality, defined earlier on, is much more comprehensive than the above definition of self-control. As in our conception, Eysenck's (1977) definition of personality includes impulsivity as a subtrait of a larger dimension, extroversion.

Figure 6.5 indicates that low self-control will persist when the person's bonds to society are tenuous, when he is egocentric, when prosocial influences are weak and when constraints feeble. The person will then be more likely to prefer routine activities that offer excitement and thrill, which will, in turn, increase the number of occasions for the perpetration of a criminal act. Individuals with low self-control will also be more likely to evaluate guardianship as inefficient. As a result, the probability of the occurrence of a criminal event will be higher.

Occasions

The Chicago school teaches criminologists that in crime-prone communities there are numerous occasions for the commission of criminal acts. Cohen and Felson's (1979) routine activity theory uses the construct of suitable targets to represent the possibilities to commit a crime. According to Clarke and Cornish (1985), the individual makes a rational choice about the suitability of the target; he evaluates the degree of effort involve, the amount and immediacy of the reward, the likelihood and severity of punishment, and the moral costs. We expect that the more a target seems suitable, the higher the probability of the commission of the offense, particularly if the person's self-control is low and his activities public and noninstitutional. Figure 6.5 also states that the presence of numerous suitable targets in a community is a proximal cause of the commission of a crime.

Guardianship

In Cohen and Felson's (1979) routine activity theory, three elements are necessary for the commission of a criminal act: a likely criminal, a suitable target, and the absence of a capable guardian against crime. A capable guardian can be a person, a physical protection device, or a specific situation. The risk of victimization literature is eloquent on the relationship between guardianship and the perpetration of crimes (see Bursik and Grasmick 1993, review 73–80). Figure 6.5 indicates that the absence of guardianship is a proximal cause of a crime and that a situation is likely to be perceived as such when the person has low self-control, when his routine activities are predominantly unconventional, and when there are suitable targets.

The Structure of the Event Control Theory

We argue that an integrative event control theory needs six constructs: community control, personal control, routine activities, self-control, occasions and guardianship. We also propose many connections between these constructs. However, the theoretical statements and the empirical studies at this level are rare and they are not always explicit about these interdependencies. As a consequence, our event control theory rests on shakier grounds then the community control and the personal control parts of our control theory. However, the principles of context and prerequisites and the distinction between continuity and change can help us speculate on the structure of the integrative event control theory as we did at the other two layers of our control theory.

The most pertinent hypothesis is that the level of community and personal controls are contextual factors to the criminal event. Personal control directly affects the choice of routine activities and the level of self-control. Community control directly determines the availability of occasions for the commission of a crime and the quality of guardianship. However, these contextual variables do not have a direct impact on the commission of a crime. Community control and personal control are contextual prerequisites of a criminal event. As a result, at this level of explanation, the contextual factors originate from two levels of explanation of the criminal phenomenon—community control from the level of criminality and personal control from the level of the criminal. This is a major difference from what we proposed earlier. Then, the contextual factors were of the same level of explanation. At the level of the criminal event there is then a convergence of all the factors, community, personal and event, to determine the probability of a specific crime.

Concerning the position of the constructs of routine activities and self-control and the constructs of occasions and guardianship, we can make the following assumption. First, the decision to commit a crime is made if the person is available and ready. The primary condition of availability has its origin in routine activities and relates to the primary need of self-conservation or the adaptation of the individual to the sustenance activities of a community. Second, the level of self-control also represents a primary condition of readiness and relates to the primary need of integration or involvement in a specific situation. In our general control theory, the bonding and the unfolding mechanisms are in a situation of reciprocal causation, no orderings exist between these components of the theory. Their influence is synergistic and they are prerequisites to conformity. As a consequence, appropriate routine activities and high self-control will diminish the convergence between the offender, suitable targets and unguarded premises.

The two primary conditions of a criminal event, which are more stable individual propensities, are the availability of the individual for crime through appropriate routine activities and the readiness of the person through low self-control. This is not the case for the modelling (occasions) and constraining (guardianship) mechanisms. During periods of the day or the week, occasions and the guardianship change. As a consequence, figure 6.6 states that the bonding and the unfolding mechanisms are catalysts for the modelling and the constraining mechanisms, which are viewed as proximal causes of conformity. The structure of the theory proposed by figure 6.5 is another application of the principle of prerequisite and of the distinction between continuity and change. Figure 6.5 also indicates that this theory is, synergistic, dynamic and interactional. Reciprocal relations represent synergy in this figure. Superposed boxes show dynamics. In addition, retroactive and directional arrows represent interactions.

The Three-Layered Control Theory, a Generic Perspective

The central notion of our theory is control. We define control as the exercise of restraining and directing influences over the criminal phenomenon. We propose that in appropriate contexts control will be tighter and in harmony with expectations, and, as a consequence, conformity will result. The restraining and directing influences are the result of four mechanisms: bonding, unfolding, modelling and constraining. The simultaneous consideration of these four mechanisms and of their contexts constitute a theoretical elaboration and combination, as define earlier in this paper. Our theoretical statement is an expansion of existing theories and a mixture of various control constructs. Our theory is an amalgamation of psychological and sociological control theory, of its bonding and constraint components. The proposed system of control of the criminal phenomenon is an open system because it exchanges energy with other systems. The mechanisms of control involve synergy because they combine their action to regulate the criminal phenomenon. This complex open system of control of the criminal phenomenon is subject to the laws of thermodynamics about the conservation of energy (a system neither creates nor destroys energy during any process) and equilibrium (during an irreversible process, entropy always increases).

We then specified our control theory for three layers of the criminal phenomenon, criminality, criminal, and crime. Our community control theory assumes that a high rate of conformity to conventional standards of behavior exists when social organization is sufficient, when cultural organization is influential, when direct controls are efficient, and when there are adequate legitimate opportunities. This regulation of conformity is conditional on the quality of the setting and on the position of the community in the social structure. Our personal control theory reasons that a person's conformity to conventional standards of behavior is present when allocentrism grows, when the bond to society is solid, when the constraints are adequate, and when pro-social influences are strong. This personal and social governance of conformity is conditional on the biological capacity of the person and on his or her position in the social structure. Finally, our offense control theory proposes that criminal acts are unlikely when routine activities are conventional, when self-control is high, when there is no occasion for the commission of crimes, and when guardianship is reliable. This regulation of conformity is conditional on the quality of community control and the level of personal control.

Figure 6.6 represents the interdependencies among these three layers of our control theory. This theory is interactional because it includes the two categories of interactions that Thornberry (1987) defines as necessary for such a theoretical statement. Reciprocal effects, the first condition of this perspective, are the large arrows. They show that for a specific moment in time community control has a global impact on personal and event control, that personal control has an impact on community control and event control, and that event control has an impact on community control and personal control. Figure 6.6 also shows that events are part of criminality and offending, while the criminal career is an integral part of criminality. Causal effects, the second characteristic of an interactional theory, is stressed by the impact of community control at time 1 on personal control at time 2 and by the impact of personal control at time 2 on community control at time 3, and by all the arrows between personal, event and community controls that go from one period of time to another one. Our theory is also

FIGURE 6.6
Interdependencies between the Specific Layers of Control Theory

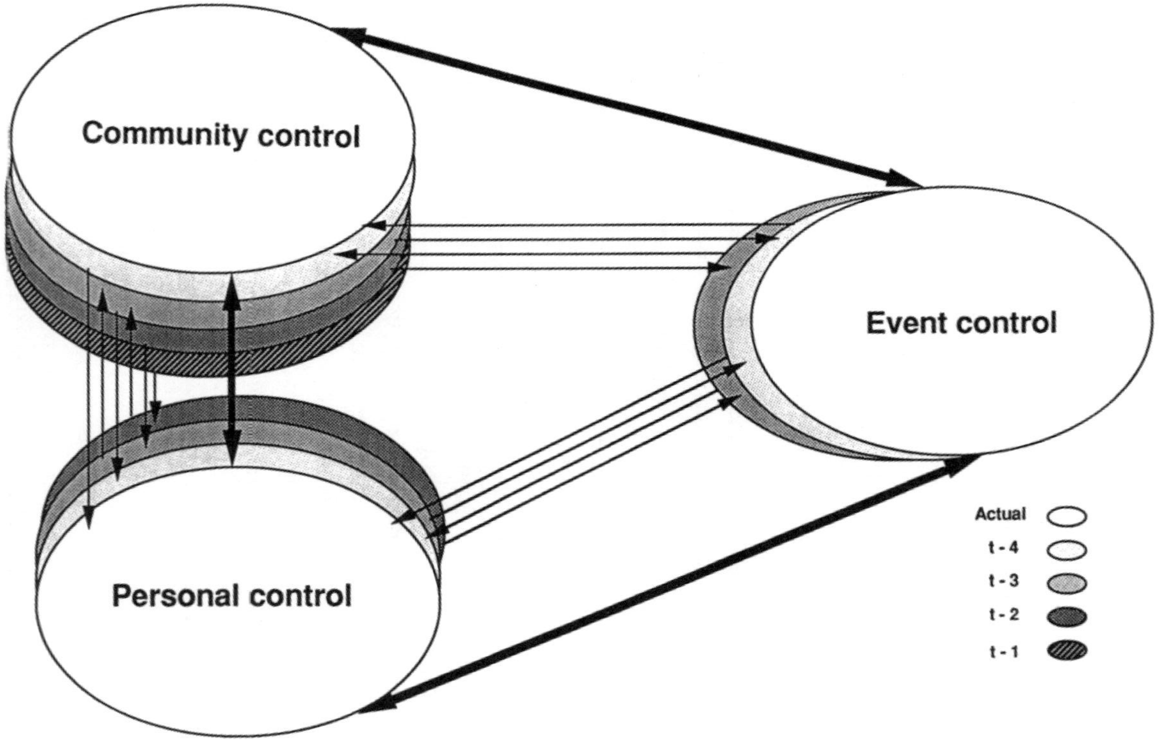

systemic because figure 6.6 implies that there are synergistic and retro-active relations. Synergy is represented by bidirectional arrows between community and personal controls when event control is the focus of explanation. Retroactive effects are included because event control at a specific point in time affects community and personal control at the next point in time.

Figure 6.6 also indicates that these interactions take place in two con-texts. First, there are contextual prerequisites to some categories of con-trol. We propose that a certain level of community control always exists before a particular level of personal control develops. Communities have a history, while persons have a life course during a specific historical period. Conversely, a certain level of personal control always exists be-fore the perpetration of a crime becomes possible. Persons are states, while events are situations. In figure 6.6, this context of interaction is represented by the absence of an oval at time 1 for personal control, while time 1 community control influences time 2 personal control. Con-versely, there is no time 2 oval for the event control while time 2 personal control influences time 3 event control.

Second, the context in which these interactions grow is sensitive to dependent on initial conditions; this is the butterfly effect of chaos theory (Gleick 1987). This principle states that complex systems are unstable and that small differences in input can produce overwhelming differ-ences in output. Nagin and Farrington's (1992a, b) papers on the impact of the age of onset and prior delinquency on subsequent offending sup-ports the position that, at least in part, initial offending determines sub-sequent criminal activity (see also Sampson and Laub 1993). In figure 6.6, the superimposed ovals picture this phenomenon. These sets of ovals state, for example, that an initial level of personal control will, in large part, determine the subsequent level of personal control. In our models of family control (Le Blanc 1992), school control (Le Blanc et al. 1992) and constraints (Le Blanc 1995), the correlations of all the control vari-ables with themselves at a subsequent point in time are stronger than the reciprocal (a correlation with another variable measured at the same point in time) or causal (a correlation with other variables measured at a later point in time) correlations. This is also the case in Thornberry et al.'s (1991, 1994) and Patterson et al.'s (1992) analyses.

Figures 6.7, 6.8 and 6.9 move us farther in the direction of theoretical unification. They specify some of the relationships among the three strata of the criminal phenomenon. We use three figures to report these relationships because a single figure would be too complex and difficult to read. In each figure, there are six categories of factors that are represented at each level of definition of the criminal phenomenon: grounds (setting, biological capacity), milieus (social position of the community, social status of the individual or his family), expectations (cultural organization, allocentrism, self-control), social conditions (social organization, social bonds, routine activities), restraints (direct controls, internal and external constraints, guardianship), and situations (legitimates opportunities, pro-social influences, occasions). These factors are arranged according to their proximity to the dependent variables. In order, they are predisposing factors (grounds and milieus), precipitating factors (desirable states and conditions) and triggering factors (restraints and situations).

Figure 6.7 reports interdependencies between community and personal control. Figure 6.8 presents relationships between the constructs of personal and event control. Finally, figure 6.9 shows the impact of community control on event control. In these figures, we represent only reciprocal effects (bidirectional relation between two variables at the same point in time) and recursive (unidirectional relations between two variables measured at the same point in time). State dependence (a correlation between the same variable at two points in time), causal (a relationship between a variable measured at one point in time and a different variable measured at another point in time) and retroactive (the impact of the dependent variable at time 1 on independent variables at time 2) effects are not presented in these figures to facilitate the understanding of our multilayered control theory. However, it should be assumed that they exist, as stated earlier.

Very few theoretical statements and even fewer empirical studies have discussed interdependencies between community control and personal control constructs. Kornhauser (1978: 69) synthesizes Shaw and McKay's theory in a graph where social disorganization implies weak controls and, on the basis of these weak controls, youths become delinquent with or without the influence of organized crime and delinquent companions. Kornhauser then elaborates the Shaw-McKay theory, stating that cultural disorganization implies a loss of direct external control by the family and the resulting defective socialization produces weaker direct internal control. She also indicates that social disorganization implies that the

FIGURE 6.7

Interdependencies between Community Control and Personal Control

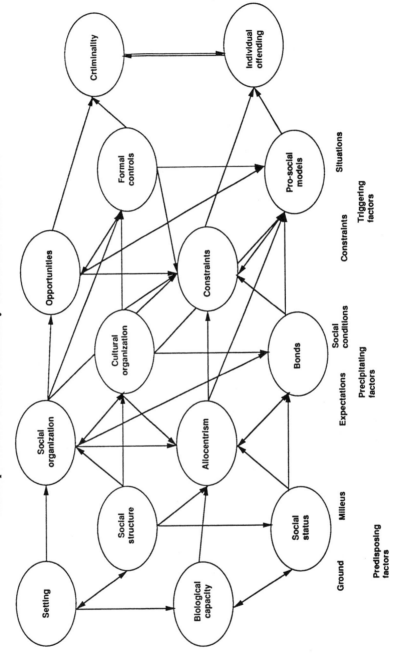

attachment and commitment of the child, as well as the instrumental bond to institutions, will be attenuated and, as a consequence, direct control will suffer at school and in the family. Empirical studies, such as Krohn (1986), Simcha-Fagan and Schwartz (1986), Gottfredson et al. (1991) and Lizotte et al. (1993), conclude that the direct impact of community variables on individual offending is marginal. However, there is a clear indication that social disorganization variables have an indirect impact on offending. For example, Sampson (1993) shows that community-level differences in social cohesion and indirect controls do have significant effects on individual-level variations in offending, deviant attitude and association with delinquent peers through family management techniques.

Consequently, figure 6.7 proposes the following theoretical statements of interdependencies between community level and individual level constructs. The nature of the community setting (density, space, quality of air, and so on) affects the biological capacity of individuals. The social structure of the community limits the range of both individual and family social and ethnic status in a particular community. The community level of cultural organization restricts expectations for the development of the individual in terms of the social bond and allocentrism, while the level of social organization narrows the possibilities of individual development, bonding and unfolding mechanisms. The available pro-social influences for individuals are dependent on the range of legitimate and illegitimate opportunities and on the level of social organization in the community. Finally, cultural expectations and opportunities mould internal constraints while external constraints depend on the quality of the social organization and the nature of direct controls in the community. In sum, community level constructs are contextual factors of individual level constructs.

There are very few theoretical statements and empirical studies of the relationships between community and offense constructs. Reviewing this scant literature, Bursik and Grasmick (1993) suggest that the convergence of a suitable target, a motivated offender and the absence of a guardian is a function of the model of routine activities that, in turn, depends on the social structure of the community. Wikström (1990) observes that urbanization implies weaker social control, greater opportunities for crime, more motivated offenders and more criminal events. Figure 6.8 presents the postulated relationships between the community

FIGURE 6.8
Interdependencies between Community Control and Event Control

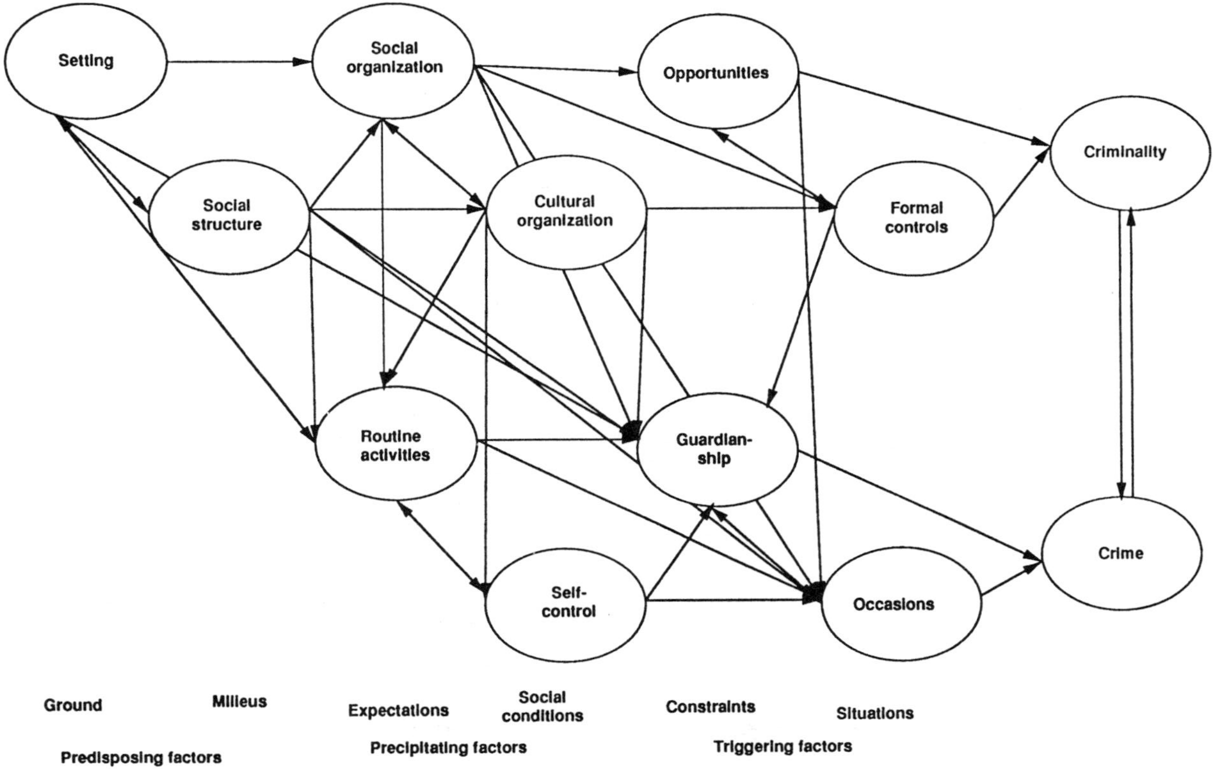
Setting
Social organization
Opportunities
Criminality
Social structure
Cultural organization
Formal controls
Routine activities
Guardian-ship
Crime
Self-control
Occasions
Ground
Milieus
Expectations
Social conditions
Constraints
Situations
Predisposing factors
Precipitating factors
Triggering factors

FIGURE 6.9

Interdependencies between Personal Control and Event Control

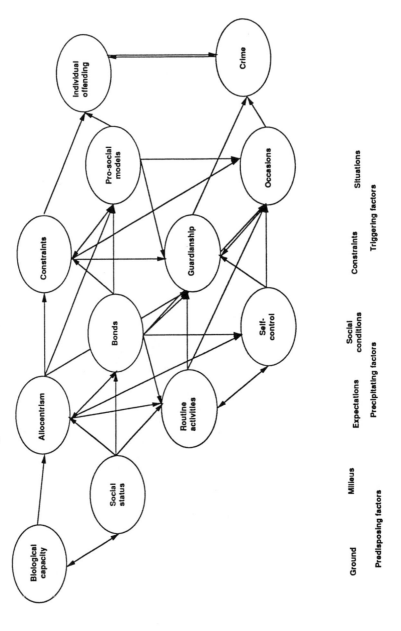

control and offense control constructs. The pattern of routine activities of an individual is the product of the characteristics of the setting, the social structure and the social and cultural organization of the community where the person lives. Cultural expectations and informal controls influence his particular level of self-control. Occasions for the perpetration of crimes increase with the deterioration of the setting, weak social organization, diverse illegitimate opportunities, and in low status communities. Finally, guardianship diminishes when informal control is poor and direct control omnipresent.

There are some theoretical statements and empirical studies about the connections between the community and the personal layers. However, there is virtually nothing in the literature concerning interdependencies between the individual and the event layers. Clarke and Cornish (1985) and Felson (1986) discuss the impact of some individual variables on the decision to commit a crime. Felson proposes that the bond to society is important in that decision. Potential offenders with low social bonds tend to overestimate the suitability of a target and underestimate the capacity of the guardian. Clarke and Cornish offer a complex sequential involvement theory to explain this. Background factors associated with previous experiences, learning and needs influence the way in which the individual evaluates and perceives possible solutions. In turn, the decision to perpetrate a crime depends on the individual's reaction to chance events and his readiness to commit an offense. Figure 6.9 elaborates our generic control theory on these grounds.

The choice of routine activities depends on the quality of the bond to society. Individuals with weaker bonds will favor public and noninstitutional activities. The level of self-control decreases for people who remain egocentric on the egocentric-allocentric continuum. Guardianship is more likely evaluated as deficient if the individual is egocentric and unbounded to society. The temptation of the occasion will increase with the weaknesses of the bond and of the constraints, and with the exposure to antisocial influences.

The Generic Control Theory, a Dynamic Statement

Until now, this discursive statement of our generic control theory has defined the constructs and the structure of their interdependencies. It is now time to propose a developmental statement of our multilayered control theory. We will start by an evaluation of the consideration given by existing criminological theories to continuity and change. We will then define our contextual and developmental perspective. Subsequently, we will distinguish between the course of development and developmental processes.

Are There Developmental Theories in Criminology?

Most criminological theories are not developmental in nature. They do not discuss the dynamics of continuity and change of the criminal phenomenon over time. In addition, when they internally carry a developmental perspective, criminologists rarely interpret them in that way. Labelling and learning theories are exceptions but their tests are rarely longitudinal.

Labelling theory, and particularly Lemert's (1951) theory of primary and secondary deviance, is a dynamic theory. Briefly, Lemert's theory states that when an individual is labelled deviant because of some antisocial behavior, that label is a major cause for behaviors that emerge as part of a deviancy amplification process. Differential association theory (Sutherland and Cressey 1960) can also be interpreted in a developmental manner because its central thesis is that criminal behavior is learned over time. Akers' (1973) social learning theory also falls in that category. However, these authors refer to learning that happens during a short time span rather than the whole life course.

Strain and cultural deviance theories imply a temporal process of involvement in offending. For example, Cohen's (1955) theory stated that the contrast between working-class socialization and middle-class values of success leads first to failure in school, then to low self-esteem, then to school dropout and association with delinquent peers, then to a reaction formation and, finally, to a delinquent status.

Control theory, as stated by Hirschi (1969), would probably not be interpreted in a developmental manner by its author. However, attachment, commitment, and so on, are clearly bonds that are formed progressively through interaction with others and society, rather than being considered *de novo* psychosocial states during adolescence. The most recent formulation of control theory by Gottfredson and Hirschi (1990) also negates a developmental perspective. These authors basic position is that there is a stable criminal propensity, low self-control, that explain a life course of offending.

Recent integrated models, such as Elliott et al.'s (1985, 1989) have done little to enhance our knowledge of the ordering of causal factors, aside from confirming that past delinquency is the most powerful predictor of future delinquency. One problem with many of these models is the short span of time considered, generally a few years between measures (Elliott et al. 1985, 1989; Le Blanc et al. 1988; Thornberry et al. 1991, 1992; and others). Integrated theories (see Messner et al. 1989) have not adopted a developmental perspective because they failed to emphasize processes over time or temporal ordering and changes in causal factors with age. Some new criminological models, however, are clearly sequential because they do propose a specific time ordering of causal factors for a longer time span (Farrington 1986; Le Blanc and Fréchette 1989; Hawkins et al. 1986; Kaplan 1984; Thornberry 1987; West 1982).

Still, the ordering of factors often merely refers to certain classes of factors as operating at specific age periods while other factors are active at another age, rather than being based on distinct developmental processes. For example, Thornberry (1987) proposed an interactional theory that links dynamic constructs to the person's position in the social structure. He argues that controls, learning, and delinquency are reciprocally related over the person's life cycle, and that they may be conceptualized developmentally with different variable contents and structures at different age periods and phases of life. For instance, commitment may be conceptualized as commitment to school during adolescence and commitment to work during young adulthood.

We can conclude from this brief summary that theorists in criminology generally do not explore all the developmental implications nor exploit all the potential dynamic strengths of their theories. Only very recently have they formulated theories that include a developmental perspective. We believe that the time is ripe to further these endeavors through our generic control theory. To do so, we will use the frameworks provided by theoretical developmental psychology and chaos theory.

A Contextual and Developmental Perspective

According to Lerner (1986), the mechanistic, organismic and contextual theoretical perspectives about development could be described in the following way. The mechanistic position stresses that the laws of natural science apply to other disciplines, that the reduction of a phenomena to its fundamental units is necessary, that the same laws apply to all levels of study, that the focus should be on quantitative changes and that these changes are additive. In comparison, the organismic perspective emphasizes that the organism must be studied as a whole, that at each level of phenomenal organization there is an emergence of new phenomena, that phenomena grow such that later forms of organization cannot be reduced to earlier ones, and that changes are qualitative, discontinuous, multiplicative, and interactive. The main proposition of the contextual theoretical perspective is that every phenomenon is historic. Constant changes at all levels of analysis characterize life and embeddedness of each level with all others is a particularity of human phenomena. This position is particularly relevant to our definition of the criminal phenomenon and the layers of our control theory.

Crime is embedded in criminality and individual offending, and criminals are constituent parts of the crime rate. Event control is part of personal and community control, and personal control is a component of community control. Figure 6.10 represents embeddedness by arrows going from event control to personal control and so on and shows change by the spirals. In the contextual perspective, development is also probabilistic. This means that the influence of the changing context on the trajectory of development is partly uncertain and that development must be defined in terms of "...organism-context reciprocal, or dynamic-interactional relations" (Lerner 1986: 69). However, the organization and the internal coherence of the organism limit the probabilities of different trajectories. These principles are also those of the chaos theoretical perspective in science (Glieck 1987; Briggs and Peat 1989). This scientific perspective talks about structured randomness, complex systems, nonlinear dynamics, and inner rhythms.

In sociology, Fararo (1989) develops that line of thinking under the notion of dynamic social systems and formalizes his theory in terms of the mathematics of nonlinear dynamics. In our formulation of control theory, a crime is probable in the context of a specific level of personal control and community control. Individual offending will continue in the context of a specific community.

According to the contextual perspective on development, we can state that the level of community control, of personal control, and of event control is specific to a particular time and space. According to chaos theory (see Briggs and Peat 1989), we can state that changes at one layer of control will affect changes at the other layers of control; there is a coevolution of the changes at the various layers of control. Spirals in figure 6.10 represent this phenomenon of coevolution. Changes in event control will modify the level of personal control and community control and vice versa. Arrows from one spiral to the others in figures 6.6 and 6.10 represent those interdependencies. In addition, we can state that the level of community control depends upon and influences societal control, that the level of personal control determines and results from the level of community control, and so on. Studies that we cited in the previous section document these statements.

Whatever the level of explanation of the criminal phenomenon, we propose that the fundamental developmental trajectory reflects the orthogenic principle state by Werner (1957: 126). "...whenever development occurs it proceeds from a state of relative globality and lack of differentiation to a state of increasing differentiation, articulation, and hierarchic integration." Psychologists will easily accept that proposition (see Lerner's review 1986) and sociologists will also recognize the pertinence of that statement for societal change (Boudon 1984; Caplow 1988) and community change (see the studies of Bursik 1986, for Chicago and Schuerman and Kobrin 1986, for Los Angeles). However, criminologists still dispute the application of that principle to the development of individual criminal activity (Le Blanc 1993b). Users of transition matrices argue for the randomness of offenses, while developmentalists claim that there are developmental stages of offending.

The evolution toward more complexity is governed by two principles: sensitivity to the initial condition and probabilistic epigenesis. Criminologists have demonstrated that past criminal activity explains subsequent offending. The results of Elliott et al. (1985, 1989), Nagin and Farrington (1992a, b), Patterson et al. (1992), Jessor et al. (1991), Sampson and Laub (1993), and others are eloquent about this phenomenon of amplification. Chaos theorists refer to the consequences of sensitivity to the initial condition as the "Butterfly effect" (Glieck 1987). Offending is not the only variable affected by that principle; a significant proportion of the explained variance of explanatory variables—attachment to parents, commitment to education, association with delinquent peers, and others—is accounted for by the past level of those same variables (for a few examples see Le Blanc et al. 1992; Le Blanc 1992, 1993a; Thornberry et al. 1991, 1992). Superimposed boxes in figures

6.3 to 6.6 represent this developmental mechanism. As a consequence, each subsystem is partly self-organizing and self-perpetuating. This is the case for the bonding, unfolding, modelling and constraining systems and their subsystems. Concerning the principle of probabilistic epigenesis, our results about individual offending (Le Blanc and Fréchette 1989) and Patterson's data (1992) about problem behavior clearly show that there are some normative stages but that the outcome of individual behavioral development is only probable, never certain. Some individuals will pass through all stages, some will not; some individuals will start at the initial stage and some will not. Developmental sequences are hierarchic rather then embryonic.

Finally, development is interactional as proposed by some criminologists (see Thornberry 1987, Le Blanc et al. 1988) and contextual developmentalists (see Lerner 1986). As represented in figures 6.3 to 6.6 and 6.10, the development of event, personal and community control implies interactions. Interactions take various forms: reciprocal interdependencies among constructs at a specific time; causal relationships between constructs over time, such that constructs that will become alternatively independent and dependent variables; state dependencies for each construct; and, retroactives, the impact of the criminal phenomenon on the four control mechanisms. These retroactive effects have two possible consequences, amplification or regulation of the criminal phenomenon.

The Course of Development

After reviewing the principles that govern the dynamics of control of the criminal phenomenon, either event, personal or community, it is necessary to specify the nature of the course of development. In our developmental criminology paradigmatic paper (Loeber and Le Blanc 1990) and in our analysis of individual offending (Le Blanc and Fréchette 1989), we relied on Wohlwill's (1973) developmental analysis of child behavior and applied some of his ideas to the study of the development of individual offending. We argue, in this section, that we can apply the methods used for the study of within-individual change to the study of the course of event and community control. The course of control can take the form of either quantitative and qualitative change, a distinction fundamental for developmentalists and specialists of social change.

Quantitative changes are usually termed trends at the community level of analysis and growth curves at the individual level of analysis. For example, quantitative changes refer to variations in the percentage of immigrants, of single-parent families, and so on, for communities, to changes in height, attachment, neuroticism, and so on for individuals, and, to variations in the value of goods stolen, in physical harm, and so on, at the level of the event.

Loeber and Le Blanc (1990) propose that these quantitative changes should be assessed in at least three ways and they supply, for each type of quantitative change, numerous examples in the domain of individual offending. First, quantitative changes are the degree of change on the scale that measures any construct of our control theory. Second, quantitative changes correspond to the direction of change, is there progression or regression. Finally, quantitative changes also refer to the rate of change, or the velocity, i.e., the relationship between the degree of change and time. We could measure the degree, direction and velocity of change in the structure of the community, for example variation in the racial heterogeneity of the community, in its social organization, for example changes in participation in voluntary organization, in its direct control, for example the number of police patrols, and so on for the other constructs of the community control theory. We could assess the degree, direction and velocity of change in attachment, egocentrism, number of delinquent friends, and so on for the other constructs of the personal control theory. We could describe the degree, direction and velocity of change in guardianship, the availability of targets, and so on for the others constructs of the event control theory.

Qualitative changes are a more complex problem. They refer to something new, something that is different from what went before, something that is more complex according to the orthogenetic principle. These changes in nature are habitually subdivided in a developmental sequence that comprises a certain number of stages. When sociologists talk about industrial, postindustrial, developing, and postmodern societies, they refer implicitly to such stages. When social ecologists talk about a community moving from a middle-class status to a working-class status, from a racial minority status to a racial majority status, from a homogeneous underclass status to a gentry status, and so on, they define implicitly stages of development. When psychologists talk about sensorimotor or preoperational intelligence, about oral, anal or phallic functioning, conventional or postconventional reasoning, and so on, they refer explicitly to stages. In each of these examples, sociologists and psychologists call attention to a universal developmental sequence divided into a limited number of stages. We assume that a normative developmental sequence exists for the community, individual and event constructs of our generic control theory.

Concerning individuals, there are numerous theories and empirical studies that show that developmental stages exist and that they are related to age. For example, there are psychosexual (Freud 1905), cognitive (Piaget 1967), moral (Kohlberg 1976), psychosocial (Erickson 1972), peer relations (Oden 1988), external control (Durkheim 1934), and play (Berk 1989) developmental sequences to name a few domains and the principal theorists. In addition, according to Loeber and Le Blanc review's (1990), there is growing evidence that there are stages of development of such problem behaviors as drug use and criminal activity. We think that if we were to apply this line of thinking and research to community change and event change we would probably identify developmental sequences as well.

At the level of analysis of events, there is probably a sequence in planning and organization of crimes, for example between a forged check to a sophisticated credit card fraud, from an unplanned breaking and entry to a professional one, from events of bully behavior during childhood to gang fights during adolescence and wife battering later on. At the community level, there are probably successive periods when the socioeconomic status and ethnic heterogeneity of a neighborhood changes. For example, with respect to the process of gentrification neighborhoods could change from being homogeneous with respect to lower socioeconomic status and minority group composition, to being quite heterogeneous with a mixture of statuses and ethnicities, to being homogeneous with respect to higher socioeconomic status and majority group composition as the process of gentrification is completed.

Contrary to the position of many developmental stage theorists, a developmental sequence does not imply an embryonic course. Every individual or community does not go through all the stages. Research data show that the course is usually hierarchic, however. People start at different stages and move through a different number of stages. It is particularly the case for individual offending as showed by Le Blanc and Fréchette (1989). We postulate that it is also the case for every construct of the multilayered control theory defined either for its community, personal and event layers. The consequence of the hierarchic course is the possibility of numerous trajectories.

Loeber and Le Blanc (1990) also propose that this hierarchic course on a universal developmental sequence can be specified according to what Wohlwill (1973) calls conservation, synchrony and paths. They review the literature and show that these notions apply to individual offending. The conservation notion assesses individuals' retention of certain offense types while moving to a new stage in offending (retention) or the addition of new offense types to the already existing crime mix (innovation). The notion of synchrony examines the probability that individuals will make the transition on various dimensions of personal control (attachment, allocentrism, constraints, and so on) from one stage to an adjacent stage within a given period. Finally, paths are particular trajectories on a developmental sequence that individuals follow over a time. These formulations of conservation, synchrony and paths refer to personal control.

Concerning community control, they can be stated in the following way. Conservation assesses the retention of certain forms of community control—social organization, cultural organization, available opportunities or direct controls—while moving to another stage of community control or retention of a certain form of criminality while moving to another form. Synchrony refers to the probability that a community will simultaneously make the transition to new stages of complexity on its social organization, cultural organization, available opportunities, direct control, and criminality. Finally, paths are particular trajectories for various communities on the normative developmental sequence.

Qualitative changes imply a developmental sequence of stages. In turn, the consequence of the existence of these stages is the presence of critical periods at the intersections of these stages, periods when the system of control is in a state of disequilibrium. Figure 6.10 shows these transitions by the intersections of the spirals. Classical developmentalists call these periods transitions (see Lerner's review, 1986); some criminologists refer to them as turning points (Sampson and Laub 1993), while others use the notions of drift (Matza 1957) or strain (Cohen 1955); behaviorists define these transitions as learning that represents a change in the behavioral repertoire of an organism (see Lerner 1986); while chaos theorists name them bifurcations (Glieck 1987; Briggs and Peat 1989). For all these authors, turbulence and chaos characterize these critical periods. The course of development, because of the difficulty or ease of the transitions, can manifest sleeper effects (Kagan and Moss 1962), abrupt changes (Flavell 1971) and ceiling effect (Le Blanc and Fréchette 1989).

The Developmental Processes

The developmental course of the criminal phenomenon involves both quantitative and qualitative changes. Along the qualitative course, there are some facilitating mechanisms such as activation, escalation and decline. These processes characterize the course of criminality and individual offending. The distribution of individual offending according to age is a clear indication of the existence of a cycle of offending. Our empirical study (Le Blanc and Fréchette 1989) and our review (Loeber and Le Blanc 1990) show that criminal activity emerges and is activated through an acceleration of the frequency of offending, a diversification of the types of offenses committed, and a stability of offending across time. In addition, individual offending becomes increasingly severe for persistent offenders, they move from minor offenses, to average and to major property offenses, then to serious personal offenses. Finally, there is a gradual desistance through a deceleration of the frequency of offenses, a de-escalation and a diminution of the variety of offenses committed. Le Blanc and Fréchette (1989) state these processes in mathematical terms.

We also believe that it is possible to show that the nature of criminality in a specific community changes under the impact of the same processes. For example, activation manifests itself through the emergence of adolescent gangs and the arrival of a criminal population in a particular community. Aggravation occurs during a period when adult criminal organization become more structured, and compete for the distribution of illicit services (prostitution, drugs, and so on). Finally, decline manifests itself when juvenile gangs are no longer fashionable, when illicit services move to other areas, and when criminal organizations age. As a result, the developmental processes of activation, escalation and decline could apply to the levels of the criminal phenomenon and the control mechanisms.

Community, personal and event control are also the object of quantitative and qualitative change. Along the qualitative course, there are processes that facilitate transitions from one stage to another and from one state to another one. These processes are maturation, adaptation, socialization or learning. The first process, maturation, refers to the natural growth and differentiation that characterize every system over time. Chaos theorists (see Glieck 1987) would suggest that the internal clock of communities and individuals is geared toward more control. Jessor et al. (1991), Sampson and Laub (1993) and Le Blanc and Fréchette (1993e) show that with time personal control increases. Concerning communities, there are no study that document such internal clock. However, an impressionistic analysis of a large city over a long period of time indicates that some communities die, that is, they are completely replaced by commercial and industrial activities; other communities move through different levels of conventional and unconventional control, that is, they are conventional for a period, then become disorganized under subcultural control, and then return to conventional levels of control. This process can require decades to unfold for individual communities.

The second process, adaptation, refers to the way an organism adapts through the integration of new external elements or through structural change to fit with the environment. Control is also the result of successive adaptations. For example, a community integrates a new group of immigrants or adapts to changes in land use and individuals adapt to a new wife, a new job, the birth of a child, and so on.

The third process, socialization or learning is, according to Lerner, "a relatively permanent change in behavioral potentiality that occurs as a result of reinforced practice" (1986: 411). The impact of this learning process on offending refers to differential association (Sutherland and Cressey 1960) and social learning (Akers 1973) for criminologists. A community can also enlarge its repertoire through a prevention program that increases guardianship for example. Reinforcements operate as attractors in chaos theory (Glieck 1987; Briggs and Peat 1989). Attractors are magnetic points that structure a phenomenon.

Through these processes, development can appear either chaotic or ordered. Chaotic development would imply anarchy or an unruled system, a system in which different factors that operationalize control would independently and irregularly produce the criminal phenomenon. Ordered development would be deterministic; it would involve a hierarchic system with a specific set of rules, that are both necessary and sufficient causes to explain the phenomenon. Our presentation of the dynamics of control—its quantitative and qualitative course and its processes—implies an "heterarchic" system to use the term proposed by Schwartz and Ogilvy (1979). A system of control characterized by mutual constraints and influences and by various orderings. Such a system is governed by several rules, not only by one rule.

A Representation of the Dynamics of Control

Figure 6.10 represents the dynamics of control of the criminal phenomenon. This figure integrates the mechanisms of the course of development and the developmental processes to the structure of the generic control theory of the criminal phenomenon. The dynamics of control are of two categories. First, figure 6.10 represents continuity and change over time; in that case, the figure must be read from the bottom to the top of the page. Second, figure 6.10 also shows the interactions between the layers of control; in that case, the figure must be read horizontally.

The vertical reading of figure 6.10 implies that we think in terms of continuity and change. The arrow on the left side of the figure indicates time and time refers to minutes and hours in the event control spiral, to days, weeks, months, and years in the personal control spiral, and to years and decades in the community control spiral. Each spiral represents a layer of the criminal phenomenon and, as a consequence, a type of control. The personal control-individual offending spiral is specified in figure 6.3 and formulated in section 2.2. The community control-criminality spiral is defined in figure 6.4 and discussed in section 2.3. The event control-crime spiral is depicted in figure 6.5 and presented in section 2.4. These spirals are metaphors that represent the mechanisms we proposed to specify the course of development of the criminal phenomenon. Orthogenesis is showed by the time dimension that is associated with the spirals. The beginning of the spirals represents the initial condition, while the rest of the spirals introduces the sensitivity to the initial condition. The independent spirals are there to indicate that event control, personal control, and community control are self-organizing phenomena. Coevolution is indicated by the placement of the spirals on three dimensions. Finally, along each spiral there are probabilistic quantitative and qualitative changes.

The horizontal reading of figure 6.10 implies that we think in terms of interdependencies between the layers of control of the criminal phenome-

FIGURE 6.10
A Generic Control Theory of the Criminal Phenomenon,
A Dynamic Statement

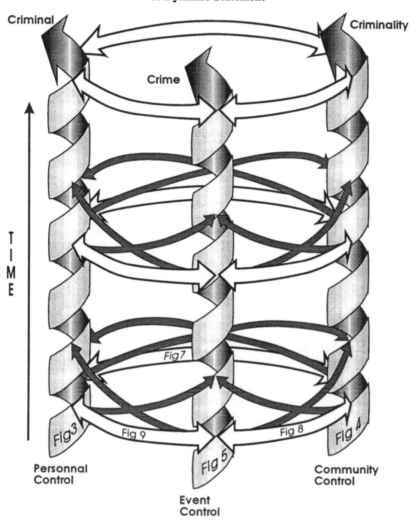

non. These interdependencies are of two categories: synergistic and interactional. In our discursive statement of our theory, synergy implied
embeddedness and reciprocal relations between the layers of control. In
figure 6.10, embeddedness is represented by the fact that the crime spiral
is placed between the criminal and the criminality spirals. This position

indicates that an offense is a constituent part of individual offending and of the rate of criminality and that individual offending is part of criminality. The reciprocal relations between the layers of control were specified in section 2.5. In Figure 6.10 these interactions are shown by the large arrows, each arrow indicates the figure that elaborates these interdependencies, specifically figures 6.7, 6.8 and 6.9. Synergy is represented in figure 6.10 by three plateaus of large arrows. Synergy also exists at all points along the time dimension and, as a consequence, the generic control of the criminal phenomenon looks like a torus attractor such as those proposed by chaos theorists to represent continuity and change (see Briggs and Peat 1989).

Figure 6.10 also represents the interactional perspective of our control theory. The discursive statement of our generic control theory identifies various types of relations: reciprocal, causal, state dependent, and retroactive. Large arrows indicate reciprocal relations, while thin arrows show causal relations and retroactives. These thin arrows emerge from intersections in the spirals to indicate critical periods in the course of the criminal phenomenon. The use of spirals implies state dependency. A discursive statement of the relations showed in figure 6.10 would be the following. Insufficient community control and tenuous personal control will diminish the level of event control of a person and a crime is more likely to be be committed. Conversely, the commission of a crime will alter the actual level of personal control for that person and modify the actual level of control in his community. Notwithstanding these relationships that exist between layers of control, there is also some independence within layers such that there are changes relative to the initial condition. In addition, a change in a person's level of event control, will alter his subsequent level of personal control and the subsequent level of control in his community. A change in community control will also affect the subsequent level of personal and event control for the person. Finally, a change in the level of a person's personal control will affect the subsequent level of event control for that person and the following level of control in his community. Notwithstanding these changes, the level of the criminal phenomenon also modifies the subsequent level of control. In figure 6.10, these reciprocal, causal relations, state dependencies and retroactive effects are represented for two specific moments. In fact, these interactions exist all along the time dimension.

Conclusion

Our control theory of the criminal phenomenon is a theoretical elaboration. The theory covers three levels of definition and explanation of the criminal phenomenon and it specifies the relationships among the explanatory constructs of these levels. The three layers of the control theory rest upon four assumptions about human nature and social order. The first assumption is that humans are unsocialized at birth and during the life course socialization is never perfect. These conditions favor the emergence and maintenance of a criminal propensity in the individual. The second assumption is that a social order always implies some consensus on values and informal and formal mechanisms of interactions. However, social order is always transient. The third assumption is that communities and individual are self-serving and have mutual influences on each other. The fourth assumption is that the event, the individual and the community influence each other as much as they are influenced by forces internal to each of these dimensions.

Our control theory is also integrative. It combines constructs from various disciplines and from many theories. The scope of this integration is wide. This integration is also conceptual according to the definition proposed by Liska et al. (1989). We construct our theory assuming that different words and terms are different for different theorists but that their theoretical meanings and operational definitions are similar. For example, our construct of exposure to pro-social influences incorporates the construct of delinquent companions of other theories.

Another characteristic of our theory is its isomorphy. The similarity of structure, from one level of the criminal phenomenon to the others, increases the clarity of our theory. We propose six constructs: two categories of exogenous factors and four mechanisms: bonding, unfolding, modelling and constraining to be used throughout the theory. This characteristic of our theory corresponds to the view of nature propose by chaos theory. Gleick's (1987) review documents the fractal nature of the universe, while Butz (1992) argues that the self is also fractal. Because of this structure, our multilayered control theory is parsimonious but not simplistic.

Finally, our control theory is developmental. We define a contextual perspective that allows for developmental principles like orthogeny, sensitivity to the original state and epigenetic probability. The course of change has as quantitative dimensions but is mainly qualitative and non-linear. There are also specific processes to regulate these qualitative changes.

As presented here, this formulation of our multilayered control theory has several deficiencies. One deficiency concerns its generic and discursive status. The statement of our control theory is not yet specific enough and additional work is needed to facilitate an operational formulation of the theory. A theory is also never complete before a formal test identifies its logical inconsistencies. A formalization of the individual level control theory exists (Le Blanc and Caplan 1993), but the same operations should take place for community and event control and our generic control theory as a whole. Only then, will it be possible to discuss its testability and start empirical tests. However, numerous test of specific elements of our control theory do exist in the criminological literature.

Notes

1. This section is, in part, an abstract of pages 9 to 12 in Le Blanc and Fréchette (1989).
2. This section of the paper is a thorough revision of the theoretical section of a chapter (Le Blanc 1993a) and of our presentation at the 51st Meeting of the American Society of Criminology in Phoenix.
3. "Attempted inanimate control is overt behavior by a human.... An inanimate thing may be a solid object, an observable substance, or an unobservable substance..." Gibbs (1989: 43).
4. The terminology introduced in criminology by Hagan (1994) can also be applied to the notions in our theory: The contexts are physical and human capital; bonding and unfolding mechanisms are social and cultural capital.
5. This section of the paper is a summary of previous papers: Le Blanc and Biron 1980; Le Blanc 1983; Le Blanc et al. 1988; Le Blanc et al. 1990.

References

Akers, R. L. 1973. *Deviant Behavior, a Social Learning Approach.* Belmont: Wadsworth Publishing Co.

Angel, R. C. 1947. "The Social Integration of American Cities of More Than 100,000 Population." *American Sociological Review* 12: 335–342.

Arnold, W. R. and T. Brungardt. 1983. *Juvenile Misconduct and Delinquency.* Boston: Houghton Mifflin.

Berk, L. 1989. *Child Development.* Boston: Allyn and Bacon.

Blackburn, R. 1993. *The Psychology of Criminal Conduct: Theory, Research and Practice.* Toronto: Wiley.

Blumstein, A. J. Cohen, J. A. Roth and C. A. Visher. 1986. *Criminal Career and "Career Criminals."* Washington: National Academy Press.

Boudon, R. 1984. *La Place du Désorde.* Paris: Presses Universitaires de France.

Briggs, J. and F. D. Peat. 1989. *Turbulent Mirror.* New York: Harper and Row.

Bronfenbrenner, U. 1979. *The Ecology of Human Development.* Cambridge: Harvard University Press.

Bursik, R. J. 1986. "Ecological Stability and the Dynamics of Delinquency." In *Crime and Justice: An Annual Review. Communities and Crime,* ed. A. J. Reiss and M. Tonry, 35–66. Chicago: University of Chicago Press.

Bursik, R. J. and H. Grasmick. 1993. *Neighborhoods and Crime: The Dimensions of Effective Community Control.* New York: Lexington Books.

Bursik, R. J. and J. Webb. 1983. "Community Change and Patterns of Delinquency." *American Journal of Sociology* 88: 24–42.

Butz, M. R. 1992. "The Fractal Nature of the Development of the Self." *Psychological Reports* 71: 1043–63.

Caplow, T. 1988. ":The Comparative Charting of Social Change in Advanced Industrial Societies." *European Studies Newsletter XVII*(5): 1–6.

Catalano, R. F. and J. D. Hawkins. 1986 *"The Social Development Model: A Theory of Antisocial Behavior."* Paper Presented at the Safeco Lectureship on Crime and Delinquency, University of Washington.

Clarke, R. V. and D. B. Cornish. 1985. "Modelling Offender's Decisions: A Framework for Research and Policy." In *Crime and Justice: An Annual Review,* ed. M. Tonry and N. Morris. Chicago: University of Chicago Press.

Cloward R. A. and L. E. Ohlin. 1960. *Delinquency and Opportunity: A Theory of Delinquent Gangs.* New York: Free Press.

Cohen, A. K. 1955. *Delinquent Boys: The Culture of the Gang.* New York: Free Press.

Cohen, L. E., and M. Felson. 1979. "Property Crime Rates in the United States: A Macrodynamic Analysis 1947–1977, with Ex Ante Forecasts for the Mid-1980," *American Journal of Sociology* 86: 90–118.

Conger, R. 1976. "Social Control and Social Learning Models of Delinquency: A Synthesis." *Criminology* 14(1): 17–40.

Cornish, D., and R. Clarke. 1986. Introduction. In *The Reasoning Criminal, Rational Choice Perspectives of Offending,* ed. D. B. Cornish and R. V. Clarke. New York: Springer-Verlag.

Cullen, F. T. 1985. *Rethinking Crime and Deviance Theory: The Emergence of a Structuring Tradition.* Ottawa: Rowman & Allanheld.

Cusson, M. 1983. *Delinquency, Why?* Toronto: University of Toronto Press.

DeFleur, M. L., and R. Quinney. 1966. "A Reformulation of Sutherland's Differential Association Theory and a Strategy for Empirical Verification." *Journal of Research in Crime and Delinquency* 3(1): 1–22.

Denno, D. H. 1985. "Sociological and Human Development Explanations of Crime: Conflict and Consensus." *Criminology* 23: 711–41.

Durkheim, E. 1895. *Les Règles de la Méthode Sociologique.* Paris: Alcan (1960, Nouvelle Édition, Presses Universitaries de France).

Durkheim, E. 1897. *Le Suicide, Étude Sociologique.* Paris: Alcan (1960, Nouvelle Édition, Presses Universitaries de France).

Durkheim, E. (1934). *De L'éducation Morale.* Paris: Alcan (1963, Nouvelle Édition, Presses Universitaires de France).

Elliott, D. S., D. Huizinga, and S. S. Ageton. 1985. *Explaining Delinquency and Drug Use.* Beverly Hills: Sage Publications.

Elliott, D. S., D. Huizinga, and S. Menard. 1989. *Multiple Problem Youth: Delinquency, Substance Abuse, and Mental Health Problems.* New York: Springer-Verlag.

Empey, L. T. 1978. *American Delinquency*. Homewood: Dorsey Press.

Empey, L. T. and S. G. Lubeck. *Explaining Delinquency: Construction, Test and Reformulation of a Sociological Theory*. Lexington: Heath Lexington Books.

Erickson, E. H. 1972. *Adolescence et Crise., la Quête de L'identité*. Paris: Flammarion.

Eysenck, H. J. 1977. *Crime and Personality*. London: Granada.

Fararo, T. J. 1989. *The Meaning of General Theoretical Sociology, Tradition and Formalization*. New York: Cambridge University Press.

Farrington, D. P. 1986. Stepping-stones to Adult Crime Careers. In *Development of Antisocial and Prosocial Behavior*, ed. D. Olweus, J. Block, and M. R. Yarrow. New York: Academic Press.

Feldman, M. P. 1978. *Criminal Behavior: A Psychological Analysis*. New York: John Wiley & Sons.

Felson, M. 1986. "Linking Criminal Choice, Routine Activities, Informal Control and Criminal Outcomes." In *The Reasoning Criminal: Rational Choice Perspectives on Offending*, ed. D. B. Cornish and R. V. Clarke, 119–28. New York: Springer-Verlag.

Felson, M., and M. Gottfredson. 1984. "Social Indicators of Adolescent Activities Near Peers and Parents." *Journal of Marriage and the Family* 46: 709–14.

Figueira-McDonough, J. 1991. "Community Structure and Delinquency: A Typology." *Social Service Review* 65(1): 68–91.

Flavell, J. H. 1971. "Stage Related Properties of Cognitive Development." *Cognitive Psychology* 2: 421–453.

Fréchette, M., and M. Le Blanc. 1987. *Délinquances et Délinquants*. Montréal: Gaétan Morin.

Freud, S. 1905. *Trois Essais sur la Théorie de la Sexualité*. Paris: Gallimard (1964).

Freud, S. 1963. *An Outline of Psychoanalysis*. New York: Norton.

Gibbs, J. P. 1985. "The Methodology of Theory Construction in Criminology." In *Theoretical Methods in Criminology*, ed. R. F. Meier, 23–50. Beverly Hills: Sage Publications.

Gibbs, J. P. 1989. *Control Sociology's Central Notion*. Chicago: University of Illinois Press.

Gleick, J. 1987. *Chaos, Making of a New Science*. New York: Viking Penguin.

Gottfredson, D. C., R. J. McNeil, and G. D. Gottfredson. 1991. "Social Areas Influences on Delinquency: A Multilevel Analysis." *Journal of Research in Crime and Delinquency* 28: 197–226.

Gottfredson, G. D., and D. C. Gottfredson. 1985. *Victimization in Schools*. New York: Plenum Press.

Gottfredson, M. R. and T. Hirschi. 1990. *A General Theory of Crime*. Stanford: Stanford University Press.

Hagan, J. 1994. *Crime and Disrepute*. Thousand Oaks: Pine Forge.

Hagan, J. 1988. *Structural Criminology*. New Brunswick: Rutgers University Press.

Hanneman, R. A. 1988. *Computer Assisted Theory Building, Modelling Dynamic Social Systems*. Beverley Hills: Sage Publications.

Hawkins, J. D., D. M. Lisher, R. F. Catalano, and M. O. Howard. 1986 "Childhood Predictors of Adolescent Substance Abuse: Toward an Empirically Grounded Theory." *Journal of Children in Contemporary Society* 8: 11–40.

Hindelang, M. J. M. R. Gottfredson, and J. Garofalo. 1978. *Victims of Personal Crimes*. Cambridge: Ballinger.

Hirschi, T. 1969. *Causes of Delinquency*. Berkley: University of California Press.

Hirschi, T. 1979. "Separate and Unequal is Better." *Journal of Research in Crime and Delinquency* 16(12): 34–38.

Hirschi, T. 1986. "On the Compatibility of Rational Choice and Social Control Theories of Crime." In *The Reasoning Criminal, Rational Choice Perspectives and Offending,* ed. D. B. Cornish and R. V. Clarke. New York" Springer-Verlag.

Hirschi, T. 1989. "Exploring Alternatives to Integrated Theory." In *Theoretical Integration in the Study of Deviance and Crime: Problems and Prospects,* ed. S. F. Messner, M. D. Krohn, and A. E. Liska. Albany: State University of New York Press.

Hodgins, S. 1985. "Biological Factors Implicated in the Development of Criminal Behaviors." In *Criminology, a Canadian Perspective,* ed. R. Linden. Toronto: Holt, Rinehart, Winston.

Horowitz, F. D. 1987. *Exploring Developmental Theories: Toward a Structural/Behavioral Model of Development.* Hillsdale: Lawrence Erlbaum.

Hunter, A. J. 1985. "Private, Parochial and Public School Order: The Problem of Crime and Incivility in Urban Community." In *The Challenge of Social Control: Citizenship and Institution Building in Modern Society,* ed. G. H. Suttles and M. N. Zald. Norwood: Ablex Publishing.

Jessor, R., J. E. Donovan, and F. M. Costa. 1991. *Beyond Adolescence, Problem Behavior and Young Adult Development.* New York: Cambridge University Press.

Johnson, R. E. 1979. *Juvenile Delinquency and its Origins: An Integrated Approach.* Cambridge: Cambridge University Press.

Kagan, J., and H. Moss. 1962. *Birth to Maturity.* New York: Wiley.

Kempf, K. 1993. "Hirschi's Theory of Social Control: Is it Fecund but not Yet Fertile?" *Advances in Theoretical Criminology 4:* 143–86.

Knoblich, G., and R. King. 1992. "Biological Correlates of Criminal Behavior." *Advances in Theoretical Criminology 3:* 1–23.

Kohlberg, L. 1976. "Moral Stages and Moralization: The Cognitive-Developmental Approach." In *Moral Development and Behavior,* ed. T. Lickong. New York: Holt, Rinehart and Winston.

Kornhauser, R. R. 1978. *Social Sources of Delinquency: An Appraisal of Analytic Models.* Chicago: University of Chicago Press.

Krohn, M. D. 1986. "The Web of Conformity: A Social Network Approach to the Explanation of Delinquent Behavior." *Social Problems* 33: 601–13.

Laub, J. H., and R. Sampson. 1988. "Unraveling Families and Delinquency: A Reanalysis of the Gluecks' Data." *Criminology* 26: 355–80.

Le Blanc, M. 1992. "Family Dynamics, Adolescent Delinquency and Adult Criminality." *Psychiatry* 55: 236–53.

Le Blanc, M. 1993a. "Prevention of Adolescent Delinquency, an Integrative Multilayered Theoretically Based Perspective." In *Linking Community and Individual Levels Explanations of Crime,* eds. D. P. Farrington, R. Sampson, & P-O. Wikström. Stockholm: National Council on Crime Prevention.

Le Blanc, M. 1993b. "Measures of Escalation and Their Personal and Social Predictors." In *Longitudinal Research on Human Development and Criminal Behavior,* ed. H. J. Kerner and E. Weitekamp. Amsterdam: Kluwer Academic Publishers.

Le Blanc, M. 1995. "The Relative Importance of Internal and External Constraints in the Explanation of Late Adolescence Delinquency and Adult Criminality." In *Coercion and Punishment in Long-Term Perspectives,* ed. J. McCord. London: Cambridge University Press.

Le Blanc, M. 1994. "Family, School, Delinquency and Criminality, the Predictive Power of an Elaborated Social Control Theory for Male." *Mental Health and Criminal Behavior* 4, 2:101–17.

Le Blanc, M., and L. Biron. 1980. *Vers une Théorie Intégrative de la Régulation de la Conduite Délinquante des Garçons.* Montréal, Groupe de rechercle sur l'inadaptation juvénile, Université de Montréal.

Le Blanc, M., and A. Caplan. "Theoretical Formalization, a Necessity: The Example of Hirschi's Bonding theory. "Advances in Theoretical Criminology 4: 239–343.

Le Blanc, M., and M. Fréchette. 1989. *Male Criminal Activity, From Childhood through Youth: Multilevel and Developmental Perspectives.* New York: Springer-Verlag.

Le Blanc, M., and M. Fréchette. 1993. The Montreal 1960 Generation, a Two Samples Longitudinal Study. From Egocentrism in Mid-Adolescence to Allocentrism in Early Thirties, Developmental trajectorties of Self-Control.

Le Blanc, M., P. McDuff, and M. Fréchette. 1990. *MASPAQ: Mesures de L'Adaptation Social et Personnelle pour les Adolescentrs Québécois.* Montréal, Groupe de Recherche sur L'inadaptation Psychosociale Chez L'enfant, Université de Montréal.

Le Blanc, M., M. Ouimet, and R. E. Tremblay. 1988. "An Integrative Control Theory of Delinquent Behavior: A Validation 1976–1985." *Psychiatry* 51: 164–76.

Le Blanc, M., E. Vallières, and P. McDuff. 1992. "Adolescents' School Experience and Self-Reported Offending: A Longitudinal Test of a Social Control Theory." *International Journal of Youth and Adolescence* 8: 197–247.

Le Blanc, M., E. Vallières, and P. McDuff, 1993. "School Experience, Self-Reported Delinquency, and Adult Criminality, the Predictive Power of a Social Control Theory for Male Adolescent." *Canadian Journal of Criminology* 35(4): 459–78.

Lemert, E. M. 1951. *Social Pathology.* New York: McGraw-Hill.

Lenski, G. 1988. "Rethinking Macrosociological Theory." *American Sociological Review* 53: 163–71.

Lerner, R. M. 1986. *Concepts and Theories of Human Development.* New York: Random House.

Liska, A. E., M. D. Krohn, and S. F. Messner. 1989. "Strategies and Requisites for Theoretical integration in the Study of Crime and Delinquency." In *Theoretical Integration in the Study of Deviance and Crime: Problems and Prospects,* ed. S. F. Messner, M. D. Krohn, and A. E. Liska. Albany: State University of New York Press.

Lizotte, A. J., T. P. Thornberry, M. D. Krohn, and D. Chard-Weirscheim. 1993. "Neighborhood Context and Delinquency: A Longitudinal Analysis." In *Cross-National Longitudinal Research on Human Development and Criminal Behavior,* ed. H. J. Kerner and E. Weitekamp. Dordretch: Kluwer Academic Publishers.

Loeber, R., and M. Le Blanc. 1990. Toward a Developmental Criminology. In *Crime and Justice: An Annual Review* ed. M. Tonry and N. Norris, 373–473. Chicago: The University of Chicago Press.

Lytton, H. 1990. "Child and Parent Effects in Boys' Conduct Disorder: A Reinterpretation." *Developmental Psychology* 26: 683–97.

Mannheim, H. 1965. *Comparative Criminology,* vol. II. London: Routledge and Kegan Paul Ltd.

Matsueda, R. L. 1988. "The Current Status of Differential Association Theory." *Crime and Delinquency* 34: 277–306.

Matza, D. 1957. *Delinquency and Drift.* New York: Wiley.

Meier, R. F. 1985. *Theoretical Methods in Criminology.* Beverly Hills: Sage.

Merton, R. K. 1957. *Social Theory and Social Structure.* New York: Free Press.

Messner, S. F. M. D. Krohn, and A. E. Liska. 1989. *Theoretical Integration in the Study of Deviance and Crime: Problems and Prospects.* Albany: State University of New York Press.

Moffit, T. E. 1990. The Neuropsychology of Juvenile Delinquency: A Critical Review. In *Crime and Justice: An Annual Review.* ed. M. Tonry and N. Morris. Chicago: The University of Chicago Press.

Nagin, D. S. and D. P. Farrington. 1992a. "The Stability of Criminal Potential from Childhood to Adulthood." *Criminology* 30: 235–60.

Nagin, D. S. and D. P. Farrington. 1992b. "The Onset and Persistence f Offending." *Criminology* 30 (4): 501–23.

Nye, F. I. 1958. *Family Relationships and Delinquent Behavior.* New York: Wiley.

Oden, S. 1988. Alternative Perspectives on Children's Peer Relationships. In *Integrative Process and Socialization: Early to Middle Childhood.* ed. T. D. Yawkey and J. E. Johnson. Hillsdale: Erlbaum.

Ouiment, M., and M. Le Blanc. 1993. Événements de Vie et Poursuite de la Carrière Criminelle au Cours de L'âge Adulte. *Revue Internationale de Criminologie et de Police Technique* 93 (3): 321–44.

Paternoster, R. 1987. "The Deterrent Effect of the Perceived Certainty and severity of Punishment: A Review of the Evidence and issues." *Justice Quarterly* 4: 173.

Patterson, G. R., J. B. Reid, and T. J. Dishion. 1992. *Antisocial Boys.* Eugene: Castalia.

Pearson, F. S., and N. A. Weiner. 1985. "Toward an Integration of Criminological Theories." *The Journal of Criminal Law and Criminology* 76: 116–150.

Piaget, J. 1967. *La psychologie de L'intelligence.* Paris: Armand Colin.

Pinatel, J. 1963. *Traité de Criminologie.* Paris: Dalloz.

Quetelet, A. 1835. *Sur L'homme et le Développement de ses Facultés, ou Essai de Physique Sociale.* Paris: Bachelier.

Reckless, W. C. 1961. "A New Theory of Delinquency and Crime." *Federal Probation* 25 (December): 42–46.

Reid, L. D. 1989. "A Path Analytic Examination of Differential Social Control Theory." *Journal of Drug Education* 19: 139–56.

Reiss, A. J. 1951. Delinquency as the Failure of Personal and Social Controls. *American Sociological Review* 16(2): 196–207.

Sampson, R. 1988. Local Friendship Ties and Community Attachment in Mass Society. *American Sociological Review* 53: 766–79.

Sampson, R. 1991. "Linking Micro and Macrolevel Dimensions of Community Social Organization." *Social Forces* 70: 43–64.

Sampson, R. J. 1992. "Family Management and Child Development: Insights from Social Disorganization Theory." *Advance in Theoretical Criminology* 3: 63–95.

Sampson, R. J. 1993. "Family and Community Level Influences on Crime: A Contextual Theory and Strategies for Research Testing.," In *Linking Community and Individual Levels Explanations of Crime,* ed. D. P. Farrington, R. Sampson, and P-O. Wikström. Stockholm: National Council on Crime Prevention.

Sampson, R. J., and J. H. Laub. 1993. *Crime in the Making, Pathways and Turning Points through Life.* Cambridge: Harvard University Press.

Schuerman, L. A., and S. Kobrin. 1986. "Community Careers in Crime." In *Crime and Justice: An Annual Review. Communities and Crime,* ed. A. J. Reiss and M. Tonry, 67–100. Chicago: University of Chicago Press.

Schwartz, P., and J. Ogilvy, 1979. *The Emergent Paradign: Changing Patterns of Thought and Belief.* Menlo Park, California: SRI International.

Sellin, T. 1938. *Culture Conflict and Crime.* New York: Social Science Research Council.

Shaw, C. R., and H. D. McKay. 1969. *Juvenile Delinquency and Urban Areas.* 2d ed. Chicago: University of Chicago Press.

Shoemaker, D. J. 1990. *Theories of Delinquency: An Examination of Explanations of Delinquent Behavior.* New York: Oxford University Press.

Short, J. F. 1985. "The Level of Explanation Problem in Criminology." In *Theoretical Methods in Criminology,* ed. R. F. Meier. Beverley Hills: Sage Publications.

Short, J. F. 1989. "Exploring Integration of the Theoretical Levels of explanation: Notes on Juvenile Delinquency." In *Theoretical Integration in the Study of Deviance and Crime: Problems and Prospects,* ed. S. F. Messner, M. D. Krohn, and A. E. Liska. Albany: State University of New York Press.

Simcha-Fagan, O., and J. E. Schwartz. 1986. "Neighborhood and Delinquency: An Assessment of Contextual Effects." *Criminology* 24: 667–703.

Spergel, I. A. 1990. "Youth Gangs: Continuity and Change." *Crime and Justice: An Annual Review* 12: 171–276.

Sutherland, E. H., and D. R. Cressey. 1960. *Principles of Criminology.* 6th ed. Chicago: Lippincott Co.

Szabo, D., M. Le Blanc, L. Deslauriers, and D. Gagné. 1968. "Interprétations Psycho-Culturelles de L'inadaptation Juvénile dans la Société de Masse Contemporaine." *Acta Criminologica* 1: 9–134.

Tarde, G. 1924. *La Criminalité Comparée.* Paris: Alcan.

Thornberry, T. P. 1987. "Toward an Interactional Theory of Delinquency." *Criminology* 25(4): 963–892.

Thornberry, T. P. 1989. Reflections on the Advantages and Disadvantages of Theoretical Integration. In *Theoretical Integration in the Study of Deviance and Crime: Problems and Prospects,* ed. S. F. Messner, M. D. Krohn, and A. E. Liska. Albany: State University of New York Press.

Thornberry, T. P., A. J. Lizotte, M. D. Krohn, and M. Farnworth. 1994. "Delinquent Peers, Beliefs, and Delinquent Behavior: A Longitudinal Test of Interactional Theory." *Criminology* 32(1): 47–84.

Thornberry, T. P., A. J. Lizotte, M. D. Krohn, M. Farnworth, and S. J. Jang. 1991. "Testing Interactional Theory: An Examination of Reciprocal Causal Relationship Among Family, School and Delinquency." *Journal of Criminal Law and Criminology* 82 (12): 3–33.

Thrasher, F. M. 1927. *The Gang.* Chicago: University of Chicago Press.

Udry, J. R. 1988. "Biological Predisposition and Social Control in Adolescent Sexual Behavior." *American Sociological Review* 53: 709–22.

Van Dijk, J. J. M. 1989. Sanctions Pénales et Processus de Civilisation. *Revnue Internationale de Criminologie et de Police Scientifique* 89(3): 249–61.

Wagner, D. G., and J. Berger. 1985. "Do Sociological Theories Grow?" *American Journal of Sociology* 90: 697–728.

Walgrave, L. 1992. *Délinquance Systématisée des Jeunes et Vulnérabiliteé Sociétale, Essai de Construction d'une Théorie Intégrative.* Genève: Éditions Médecine et Hygiène.

Werner, H. 1957. "The concept of Development from a Comparative and Organismic Point of View." In *The Concept of Development,* ed. D. B. Harris. Minneapolis: University of Minnesota Press.

West, D. J. 1982. *Delinquency, its Roots, Careers and Prospects.* London: Heineman.

Wikström, P-O. H. 1990. "Delinquency and the Urban Structure." In *Crime and Measures against Crime in the City,* ed. P-O. H. Wikström. Stockholm: National Council for Crime Prevention, Sweden.

Wilson, J. Q., and R. J. Herrnstein. 1985. *Crime and Human Nature.* New York: Simon & Schuster.

Wohlwill, J. F. 1973. *The Study of Behavioral Development.* New York: Academic Press.

Wolfgang, M. E., and F. Ferracuti. 1967. *The Subculture of Violence.* London: Tavistock Publications.

Zarro, R. 1979. *L'attachement.* Paris: Delachaut et Niestlé.

7

Crime and Capitalization: Toward a Developmental Theory of Street Crime in America

John Hagan

In one sense, most of the classical sociological theories of crime are developmental. That is, most of these theories focus on delinquency, which is considered important not only because it involves a peak period of illegal behavior in the lives of individuals, but also because it is a formative period that is predictive of later life chances, including involvement in adult crime and related socioeconomic outcomes. Yet the renewal of longitudinal research in criminology is stimulating a more searching appraisal of the developmental implications of the classical theories of delinquency and crime. This appraisal reveals that while these theories are a rich source of ideas for the developmental study of crime, they may also leave much to be desired as orienting frameworks for future research.

To begin, these theories are outpaced by recent social and economic developments in American life. These developments include shifts in capital investment and labor demands connected to movements in the world economy, substantial losses in American manufacturing jobs, alterations and disruptions in family relations, and changes in tax and welfare policies linked to tax revolts and reductions in public spending. These developments are in turn associated with increased levels of minority street crime in America. The classical sociological theories of delinquency and crime predate these changes and remain largely unaltered.

As well, the classical theories of sociological criminology have not provided a conceptual language that effectively joins the interests of researchers from qualitative as well as quantitative research traditions, the wellsprings for much of our knowledge about delinquency and crime. More specifically, important new ethnographies of poverty and crime (Sullivan 1989; Anderson 1980; Moore 1991; Hagedorn 1988; Sanchez-Jankowski 1992; Padilla 1992) make little or no use of the classical theories of sociological criminology, and more quantitatively oriented sociological criminologists may for this reason, as well as others, often return the favor by ignoring the new ethnographies of crime.

The classical sociological theories also have not proven useful in bridging the division between macro- and micro-level research on crime. Studies of neighborhoods, cities, states and nations often are done by different researchers than those who focus on individuals, and while there is theoretical overlap, researchers often have chosen disconnected conceptual languages to address their chosen levels of analysis, with little progress in establishing a theoretical discourse that bridges this gap. To illustrate, while one set of macro-level researchers focuses on differential opportunities or social disorganization, their micro-level counterparts are more likely to speak of strain or control. The absence of a common language impedes the stimulation and integration of new sources of knowledge about delinquency and crime.

The classical sociological theories of crime also have encouraged an artificial division in the study of criminal behavior and responses to it. This division is reified in the separation of labelling theory from other classical theories of crime, a separation that inhibits researchers from engaging in the study of effects of responses by official control agents and agencies to criminal behavior along with other etiological influences. For many years sociological criminologists were trained in theoretical camps that discouraged overlap in their research, for example, in attending to family socialization and police processing as coexisting causes of criminal behavior. As these barriers recede, there is a need for a theoretical language that accommodates the broader research agenda.

This paper seeks to articulate a new and more synthetic sociological framework for the developmental study of street crime in America. This framework incorporates historical as well as contemporary currents that involve closely connected social and economic processes in the study of American society. The more specific focus of this perspective is on processes of capitalization. This theoretical approach is built around such concepts as capital disinvestment and recapitalization, social and cultural capital, criminal capital and embeddedness, and deviance service centers and ethnic vice industries. The adoption of these concepts is intended as a synthesizing strategy that can be useful in blending qualitative as well as quantitative research interests, while bridging macro- and micro-level studies focused on official reactions as well as other community and family socio-environmental causes of crime. The latter influences notably include dramatic macro- and micro-level changes in the social and economic contexts of crime, which no developmental theory of crime should today ignore, and which we therefore consider first.

Crime and Capital in Context

The last half century has brought extraordinary social and economic change that sets the macro-level context for a developmental theory of crime in the advanced capitalist countries generally, and the United States more specifically. With the most extreme periods of economic expansion and recession of the past four or five decades smoothed over, the last fifty years can be divided more generally into a "golden age" that roughly covers the third quarter of this century, and a period of economic slowdown that has followed (Glynn and Miliband 1994).

Lasting from about 1954 to 1974, the golden age was a post- World War II boom that produced economic growth of about five percent a year in the advanced capitalist countries (Margolin and Schor 1990). From this period on, with peaks and troughs removed, economic growth decreased by almost half, to levels of about two and one half percent per year.

The economic slowdown that marks the last quarter of this century is characterized by increased unemployment and income inequality, led by the loss and only partial replacement of core sector manufacturing jobs with less stable and poorer paying service sector jobs. In general, the poorest minority men and women in the United States lost most in this process, with actual declines in real incomes during the 1980s.

Individual fortunes were also made by some Americans during this period, as some of the very wealthy became moreso. However, this was most often accomplished through liquidation of assets, leveraged debt, downsizing of industries, and the relocation of higher wage employment into lower wage domestic and foreign labor markets where existing production levels were maintained with fewer and/or more poorly paid employees. Secure high wage manufacturing jobs were lost permanently from the core sector of the American economy (Revenga 1992; Averitt 1992).

The golden age of economic growth in the third quarter of this century was a period that included some reductions in social and economic inequality in American life, while the economic slowdown brought a reversal of this trend and increasing inequality. This was reflected in national policies that reallocated resources across the social and economic landscape of American life. Most notably for our purposes, the economic slowdown was part of a period in which national policies and processes of "capital disinvestment" increased residential segregation, racial inequality, and the concentration of poverty in America's poorest neighborhoods and communities. These processes of capital disinvestment have altered and intensified the contexts in which much American street crime occurs in low- income minority communities. The three processes of capital disinvestment overlap one another, but each is also distinct and requires its own introduction.

Residential Segregation

Massey (1990; 1993) calls the national process of capital disinvestment involved in residential segregation "American Apartheid." This process occurs through housing market discrimination against African and Puerto Rican Americans who share a black racial identity. This discrimination involves policies and decisions that range from the location of freeway networks (Skogan 1986) and public housing (Bursik 1989) by governments, to the "redlining" practices of banks and the "blockbusting" tactics of real estate agents. The effects of segregation began to hit black American communities especially hard during the economic slowdown that took hold in the mid- 1970s, when the loss of core sector manufacturing jobs began.

The loss of manufacturing jobs drove poverty rates up most sharply in those cities and parts of cities where blacks were most segregated residentially. Massey observes that, "segregation creates the structural niche within which a self-perpetuating cycle of minority poverty and deprivation can survive and flourish" (1990: 350). Practices of racial segregation are processes of capital disinvestment that make affected communities extremely vulnerable to economic downturns and to crime problems associated with the concentrated poverty that follows. Peterson and Krivo (1993) demonstrate that apart from the relative socioeconomic inequality and absolute concentrations of poverty that we introduce next, residential segregation by race has led to higher rates of several forms of homicide victimization among African Americans.

Racial Inequality

African Americans experienced some labor market gains relative to whites during the golden age of the third quarter of this century in the United States. National policies including the implementation of the 1964 Civil Rights Act, affirmative action programs, and court-enforcement of anti-discrimination laws were instrumental parts of a period during which the demand for black workers increased and the racial gap in earnings among younger adults with similar schooling may even have nearly disappeared (Bound and Freeman 1992).

However, during the economic slowdown that followed, African American economic conditions worsened and wage inequality and unemployment grew, with black college and high school graduates as well as dropouts losing ground relative to whites. This was a period of opposition through the courts to affirmative action laws and regulations, as well as reductions in the real minimum wage. These are policies of capital disinvestment and they impacted most heavily on young African Americans with low levels of education.

Blau and Blau (1982) argue that when social and economic inequalities are associated with an ascriptive characteristic such as race they produce "a situation characterized by much social disorganization and prevalent latent animosities" (119), including subjective feelings of resentment, frustration, hopelessness, and alienation. These feelings lead in turn to "diffuse aggression," which often takes the form of violent crime. Race-linked economic inequalities are a reflection of capital disinvestment in particular groups that in this case most prominently includes black Americans, with consequences that often are unplanned and violent (Messner and Rosenfeld 1993). Recent macro-level American studies support this thesis by establishing associations between race-linked inequality and homicide (e.g., Messner and Golden 1992; Balkwell 1990; Crutchfield 1989; Land et al. 1990).

Concentration of Poverty

The economic slowdown that began in the last quarter of this century also involved a capital disinvestment process that is captured in William Julius Wilson's (1987; 1991) conception of the concentration of poverty. The nature of this process is summarized when Wacquant and Wilson (1989:10) write that,

> the social structure of today's inner city has been radically altered by the mass exodus of jobs and working families and by the rapid deterioration of housing, schools, businesses, recreational facilities, and other community organizations, further exacerbated by government policies of industrial and urban laissez-faire that have channelled a disproportionate share of federal, state, and municipal resources to the more affluent.

Wacquant and Wilson argue that these forces have transformed the "traditional ghetto" of a half century ago into a "hyperghetto."

Weak labor force attachment in these concentrated settings is an increasingly common condition that Wilson connects directly to involvements in crime, observing that "a social context that includes poor schools, inadequate job information networks, and a lack of legitimate employment opportunities not only gives rise to weak labor force attachment, but increases the probability that individuals will be constrained to seek income derived from illegal and deviant activities" (1991: 10). Concentrations of poverty increase these risks because individuals and families confront the effects of not only their own difficult situations but also the compounding effects of the situations that surround them (Sampson and Wilson 1994).

Concentrations of poverty create conditions of absolute deprivation that are associated with crime in much recent research. Recent studies in large U.S. cities reveal high levels of homicide victimization in census tracts with high concentrations of poor families, and low levels of such victimization for both whites and blacks in higher socioeconomic areas (Lowry et al. 1988; Centerwall 1984; Munford et al. 1976). This suggests that absolute differences in experiences of poverty, which are pervasively greater among black Americans, are explanatory factors (Short In Press). There is also a positive and frequently significant relationship observed between unemployment and property crime in macro-level studies (Chiricos 1987), especially when these studies are undertaken with time series data (Cantor and Land 1985; Land et al. 1994) and at levels approaching neighborhoods (Land et al. 1990). Much recent research supports the thesis that absolute concentrations of neighborhood poverty directly effect violent crime (e.g. Sampson, 1985; Curry and Spergel 1988; Taylor and Covington 1988; Williams and Flewelling 1988; Bursik and Grasmick 1993).

However, and despite the conceptual and empirical bases we have established for linkages between capital disinvestment processes and contemporary patterns of crime in America, much remains to be explained. In particular, it is important to explain how processes of disinvestment at the neighborhood and community level influence the lives of individuals. A key part of the perspective we propose extends attention from capital disinvestment at the community level to compensating efforts at "recapitalization" by individuals and in groups. The latter process involves efforts to reorganize what are often diminished, legally deviant and disparaged resources to reach attainable goals. However, before we further articulate this process of recapitalization, we first introduce a more basic conceptualization of capital that is fundamental to the perspective we propose.

Social and Economic Forms of Capital

America would like to imagine itself as a society of unrestricted competition and opportunity. However, the French social theorist, Pierre Bourdieu (1986), uses a gambling metaphor to illustrate what our economic lives would be like if we did not each begin with an accumulation of assets that differentiates our life chances:

> Roulette, which holds out the opportunity of winning a lot of money in a short space of time, and therefore of changing one's social status quasi-instantaneously, and in which the winning of the previous spin of the wheel can be staked and lost at every new spin, gives a fairly accurate image of this imaginary universe of perfect competition or perfect equality of opportunity, a world without inertia, without accumulation, without heredity or acquired properties, in which every moment is perfectly independent of the previous one, every solider has a marshal's baton in his knapsack, and every prize can be achieved, instantaneously, by everyone, so that at each moment anyone can be anything. (241)

Our social lives differ from roulette in that we acquire at birth and accumulate through the life cycle unequal shares of various kinds of capital that incrementally alter and determine our life chances. This process of accumulation is greatly influenced by capital investments made at the national, community, and family levels.

Physical and Human Capital

Tools, machinery and other productive equipment form the *physical capital* that is commonly recognized as the foundation of economic relations. However, modern economists add to this the further idea of *human capital*, which consists of the skills and knowledge that individuals acquire through education and training (Schultz 1961; Becker 1964). Although human capital may be less tangible than physical capital, both include a transformative process involving the creation of resources or power, so that "just as physical capital is created by making changes in materials so as to form tools and facilitate production, human capital is created by changing persons so as to give them skills and capabilities that make them able to act in new ways" (Coleman 1990: 304). Education and training mould and create the skills and capabilities that allow individuals to increase their productive power and resources.

Social and Cultural Capital

Even less tangible but no less important is the role of social capital. Social capital consists of the creation of capabilities through socially structured relations between individuals in groups (Coleman 1988; 1990). For example, parents often use their social capital to help create the skills and capabilities of their children. In this instance, the value added by social capital in the creation of human capital derives from the relationships between family members [e.g., parent(s) and child(ren)] that are necessary to transmit skills and capabilities and to advance cognitive development. Socially structured relationships are a prerequisite to the transfer of such knowledge. Thus, Sampson and Laub (1993:18) observe that effective social capital typically derives from strong social relations, or strong social bonds, that can develop as a child in a family, as an adolescent in school, or as an adult in a job. This is social capitalization. Coleman (1990) refers to the social structure of this transformative process as involving a closure of social networks, and this can more generally refer, for example, not only to the functioning of intact nuclear and extended families, but also to well-integrated neighborhoods, communities and even nation-states.

The concept of social capital therefore bridges community- and individual-level processes and involves investments in individuals as well as larger social units. Of course, this is also true of physical and financial capital, which is accumulated by groups as well as individuals. Social capital refers to the aspects of structured groupings that increase their capacities for action oriented to the achievement of group and individual goals. Capital disinvestment policies and processes often discourage and disrupt the development of social capital.

Groups and individuals must constantly adapt themselves to existing and continuing accumulations of capital that characterize the settings that they inherit and inhabit. Adaptations to these circumstances are expressed through various formations of cultural capital. When social capital is abundant in the community and family, these cultural adaptations may easily include the accumulation of the credentials of higher education and even involvements in high culture, for example, including participation in the arts and their supporting institutions, such as museums, the symphony, and the theatre. In these community and family settings, social capital is used to successfully endow children with forms of cultural capital that significantly enhance their later life chances (see DiMaggio 1982; 1987; DiMaggio and Mohr 1985).

However, in less advantaged community and family settings without such abundant social and cultural capital, and especially in the context of capital disinvestment policies and processes that further diminish access to these resources, parents are less able to endow or transmit opportunities to their children. Survival itself is often a struggle, and children and families must adapt to the reduced circumstances and opportunities they confront. So while many parents who are well-situated within secure and supportive social networks may be destined or driven by their capital positions and connected inclinations to endow their children with forms of social and cultural capital that make success in school and later life quite likely, the children of less advantageously positioned and less driven and controlling parents may more often drift or be driven into and along less promising paths of social and cultural adaptation and capital formation (Hagan 1991).

These latter forms of adaptation and capital formation are sometimes subcultural in the sense that they involve the cultivation of attitudes and actions that diverge from, or are in actual opposition to more routine and conforming societal norms and values. However, they are often also the only or best life choices available, and these adaptations can become powerful influences on later life outcomes (Hogan and Astone 1986; Hagan and Wheaton 1993). When these choices and adaptations are made within groups, they can gain added salience. The closure of networks within these groups is a form of social embeddedness (Granovetter 1985) that we will consider later as leading more specifically to criminal embeddedness. Meanwhile, Coleman (1990) notes the ironic reversal of purpose to which social capital can be put within the context of deviant groups, observing that, "any organization which makes possible such oppositional activities is an especially potent form of social capital for the individuals who are members of the organization" (303). Individuals within such groups or organizations sometimes acquire an added form of criminal capital that is also discussed below.

It is important to again emphasize that disadvantaging social and economic processes of capital disinvestment at the societal and community levels can make divergent and oppositional adaptations and formations of social and cultural capital more common in particular social settings. Processes of capital disinvestment are destructive of conventional forms of social and cultural capital, and they often produce subcultural adaptations, which are in effect forms of recapitalization, consisting of efforts to reorganize what resources are available, even if illicit, to reach attainable goals. This process of recapitalization often is linked to the development of and participation in deviance service industries.

Recapitalization through Deviance Service Industries

Throughout this century, and even as we approach its end, a great deal of law enforcement still is focused around the policing of deviance service centers (Clairmont 1974) that are organized around ethnic vice industries (Light 1977) and that disproportionately involve the urban and minority poor (Boritch and Hagan 1987). This was true in the early part of this century, in areas like New Orlean's Basin Street, San Francisco's Barbary Coast, Denver's Market Street Line, and New York's Bowery and Five Points. And it remains true in relation to urban and ethnic vice industries concentrated in many of today's distressed minority neighborhoods.

The sociological concept of a deviance service center parallels in an ironic way the economic notion of a free enterprise zone, except for the very notable fact that a deviance service center is distinguished by its organization around illegal services and substances, which form the base for vice industries. These centers are social locations in which activities otherwise defined as illegal (e.g., including prostitution, drugs and alcohol) are allowed to develop and serve a clientele from within and outside the community. Such centers have existed throughout this century, but today are centered in Hispanic and African American inner-city ghettoes, which we have otherwise identified as sites of capital disinvestment.

The process of recapitalization involved in the development of deviance service industries is partly indigenous to communities and partly a product of the actions of external authorities. The key to the development of these vice centers is that illegal markets emerge whenever desired substances and services—such as narcotic drugs, prostitution, and gambling—are made illegal. Authorities with responsibility for the enforcement of such laws, whether they wish to or not, have the power to regulate the development and operation of these markets, and members of communities that are without adequate access and involvement in legal labor markets often pursue these illegal opportunities to accumulate criminal forms of social and cultural capital, that is, to develop criminal capital.

The linkage between deviance service industries and social mobility is given an historical grounding in the concept of ethnic succession, which refers to the fact that for lack of alternatives, first the Irish, then the Jews, later Italians, and most recently African and Hispanic Americans have sought to move upward in the American social structure through organized vice (Ianni 1972; 1974). However, while earlier groups did so with some success, America's diminished dominance of the world economy and the dire state of America's cities have made contemporary prospects for upward mobility through organized forms of urban vice less promising and more hazardous.

Part of the hazard derives from the periodic crackdowns of law enforcement agencies on the operations of vice industries. These crackdowns probably reflect not only the ambivalence of public attitudes toward drugs, prostitution and gambling, but also the economic role these behaviors play in the social organization of inner-city American life, and the fact that activities surrounding these vice industries have become more violent. In any case, at the end of this century as at the beginning, and now perhaps in a more concentrated way, illegal sex and drugs are a central part of the capitalization of the social and economic life of America's distressed minority communities.

Lacking other sources of social and cultural capital, youth in low-income minority communities are today drawn to the promise of deviance service industries. Felix Padilla (1992) is explicit in drawing the connection between the concept of an ethnic vice industry and the activities of an Hispanic gang, the Diamonds, he studied in Northwest Chicago. He observes that, "the business operated by the Diamonds parallels an 'ethnic enterprise': a distinctive entrepreneurial strategy historically developed and used by immigrants and their descendants in response to their marginal economic position" (3).

Mercer Sullivan (1989), in his study of juvenile gang activity in three New York City neighborhoods, goes on to articulate the functional implications of this involvement in deviance service industries. In doing so, Sullivan emphasizes the reciprocal and redistributive roles that these activities can play in low-income minority communities, noting that the economic exchanges involved can sometimes function much like the selling of illegal alcohol beverages did during Prohibition:

> Inner-city residents supply criminalized goods and services first to the local population and then to the wider community.... Inner-city entrepreneurs risk violence and stigmatization in their personal careers in return for a flow of money back to them and into their neighborhoods. Respectability flows out and money flows back in. (241)

This passage makes clear that while deviance service centers promise to bring desperately needed additional resources into the inner city, they also play a role in maintaining the inner city on the moral, as well as physical, periphery of the economic system. So for communities, as well as for the individuals who work within them, the ethnic vice industries of today are not the mobility ladders they once promised to be.

This last point, involving the failed role of ethnic vice industries as contemporary mobility ladders, firmly connects the community-level presence of these illegal enterprises to the fates of individuals. This is why a developmental theory of delinquency that is relevant to America's low-income minority crime problems needs to systematically trace how youth in these communities become involved in activities linked to these vice industries, and with what consequences. This can be done by tracing a process of criminal embeddedness that is closely connected to problems of labor market entry and advancement in contexts of communities that experience capital disinvestment.

The Process of Criminal Embeddedness

A combination of qualitative ethnographic community studies, like those previously introduced, and quantitative individual level life course studies, like those that will be introduced, are beginning to fill the spaces in our knowledge of the developmental process of a criminal embeddedness that often involves or is influenced by deviance service industries.

Greenberg (1979) points out that youth in our money and media-driven society are under unique pressures to consume. Many youth are under further pressure to express age-linked notions of masculinity, as well as to accomplish the transition to adulthood, all without adequate access to legitimate labor markets. Inadequate availability of employment is perhaps the biggest obstacle to successfully traversing the gap between a troubled adolescence and the entry into a more stable adulthood. This gap is nowhere bigger than for the one third or more residentially segregated and concentrated inner-city minority youth who are unable to find stable and reasonable paying work in the United States (Allan and Steffensmeier 1989).

A key problem is that while for many youth early and sustained employment contacts enhance the prospects of getting a job and subsequent occupational mobility (Granovetter 1974), connections into crime are likely in a converse way to increase the probability of unemployment. Youthful involvements in delinquency as well as criminal involvements of friends and family, integrate adolescents and young adults into a criminal underworld, and simultaneously distance them from job contacts that initiate and sustain legitimate occupational careers. Criminal embeddedness can be a source of criminal capital, with resulting short-term benefits discussed below, but this embeddedness is a liability in terms of prospects for stable adult employment.

The costs of criminal embeddedness are compounded by the risks of becoming officially labelled and known as a criminal offender, especially in distressed community settings where few core sector jobs are available in any case. This process of separation and stigmatization can in some respects be subtle, operating through the absence rather than the presence of social ties to assist and protect minority youths. Delinquent youth run a high risk of becoming criminally embedded in contexts that isolate them from the closure of more conventional social networks and the accumulation of social capital that can derive from legitimate employment in whatever jobs are available at a particular point in time.

Several long-term studies of delinquency in the life course reveal the lasting effects of these involvements on subsequent behavior as well as reduced occupational achievements (Robins 1966 ; Sampson and Laub 1990), at least for youth from less advantaged family settings (Hagan 1991). The risks of criminal conviction are further revealed in a recent analysis of youth tracked from childhood to adulthood in a London working-class neighborhood (Hagan 1993). This study indicates that intergenerational patterns of criminal conviction make youth especially prone to subsequent delinquency and adult unemployment (Hagan and Palloni 1990; Hagan 1993; see also Ward and Tittle 1993). Other studies similarly show that working-class males with conviction records are uniquely disadvantaged in finding employment (Schwartz and Skolnick 1964), and that a criminal arrest record can have negative effects on employment as much as eight years later (Freeman 1991; Grogger 1991). Sampson and Laub's (1993: 168) long-term study of predominately lower socioeconomic status Boston delinquents indicates that "incarceration appears to cut off opportunities and prospects for stable employment in later life." Criminal sanctions can cause further problems by making offenders who are already disadvantaged more defiant (Sherman 1993). This is one more way in which the social and cultural capital of such youth is further jeopardized.

Recapitalization and the Drug Economy

Much of what we have described in the preceding sections can be illustrated in a more specific way in relation to the underground drug economy, which represents America's currently most active deviance service industry. During the same approximate period beginning in the mid-1970s and intensifying through the 1980s when access to legitimate job networks linked to stable manufacturing sector jobs declined in many distressed minority communities, networks of contact into the world of drugs and drug-related crime proliferated, paving the way for many youth to become embedded in the criminal economy of drugs. Participation in the drug economy is increasingly studied as a specific example of the opportunity that many minority youth take to recapitalize their lives.

Thus Elijah Anderson (1990) observes that "for many young men the drug economy is an employment agency.... Young men who 'grew up' in the gang, but now are without clear opportunities, easily become involved; they fit themselves into its structure, manning its drug houses and selling drugs on street corners" (244). Recent estimates are that one in six African American males born in the late 1960s in Washington D.C. were arrested for drug selling between 1985 and 1987, and actual participation in drug selling is presumably much higher (Reuter et al. 1990:46). Street-level sellers are estimated to have incomes ranging from $15,000 to $100,000 annually (Williams 1989). The profits are large enough that a Boston study concludes disadvantaged youth during the economic boom of the mid-1980s would have had to take sharp reductions in income to move from drug selling to legal jobs (Freeman 1991). This compounds the perhaps more salient problem that youth embedded in drug crime networks are unlikely to have the credentials and contacts that make conventional employment in good paying and stable jobs a realistic possibility.

Meanwhile, even low-level participation in the drug economy is a cultural adaptation with compelling short-term capital attractions. Fagan (1993) finds in field studies with over a thousand participants in the Washington Heights and Central Harlem neighborhoods of New York City that this criminal economy employs large numbers of individuals in collateral roles (e.g., lookouts, prostitutes, etc.) as well as in selling drugs. For many youth, activities connected to drug selling are a primary route to gaining material symbols of wealth and success in the neighborhood. Fagan points out that the drug industry also offers the hope, however illusory, of self-determination and economic independence, as contrasted with the petty humiliations and daily harassment faced in secondary service sector jobs.

The drug economy is a contemporary institutionalized link to the deviance service centers and ethnic vice industries of America's past. As in earlier eras, this underground activity can assume an important role in the neighborhood economy. White collar as well as blue collar customers can bring cash into the community, and at least some of these funds may be redistributed in the community. However, in the longer run this underground economy is more hazardous than it is rewarding, and the accumulation of its criminal capital is costly in terms of the disruption and damage done to more conventional forms of social and cultural capital.

A central problem is that today's drug economy is much more competitive, violent and unstable than in the past. Where drug distribution was once centralized through relatively circumscribed networks of heroin and later cocaine users who retailed drugs on the street, the more recent experience with crack has involved a less regulated market with violent competition for territory and market share (Williams 1989). Fagan (1993) points out that while entry-level roles and the market for drugs more generally have increased, the redistribution of profits has declined. This contrasts with an earlier period, for example, when marijuana sales predominated. Drug income now is less often invested in local businesses, and profits more often are concentrated among individuals elsewhere in the city and outside the country (see also Ianni 1974).

Recent ethnographies of poverty and crime make the point that the material gains associated with embeddedness in the drug economy usually prove to be short term. For example, although Sullivan draws on the classic analysis of Paul Willis (1977) to argue that participation in this underground economy temporarily achieves for minority youth a "penetration of their condition," he also reports that "over time, this penetration becomes a limitation, binding them back into [the social] structure as they age out of youth crime and accept...low wage, unstable jobs...." (1989: 250). Joan Moore, in *Going Down to the Barrio*, suggests a similar conclusion when she observes that, "...the very culture of defiance at best dooms the boys to jobs just like their fathers hold...," serving in the end "...to keep working-class kids in the working class" (1991: 42). Felix Padilla echoes this theme in his ethnography of *The Gang as an American Enterprise*, noting that "instead of functioning as a progressive and liberating agent capable of transforming and correcting the youngsters' economic plight, the gang assisted in reinforcing it" (1992: 163). In each of the above ethnographies, and in related studies, it is embeddedness in crime networks, including the criminal justice system, that seals the economic fate of these youths. For example, Sullivan writes of the New York City youth he studied that, "their participation in regular acts of income-producing crime and the resulting involvement with the criminal justice system in turn kept them out of school and forced them to abandon their earlier occupational goals" (64). Felix Padilla quotes one of his respondents to illustrate the costs of embeddedness in crime and criminal justice networks:

> ...I need a diploma, but I got kicked out of school because I was hanging out in the neighborhood selling drugs. And one thing that sucks about gang-banging is that you get locked up a lot.... You sell drugs, and you get caught for that (166).

However, it is Joan Moore who puts the issue most starkly in her introduction to John Hagedorn's *People and Folks*, an ethnography based on gangs in Milwaukee. She argues that in Milwaukee and Los Angeles, and by implication elsewhere, there is a link between the emergence and growth of an urban underclass and the increased reliance on imprisonment in dealing with ghetto youth who become embedded in the drug economy. Drawing from her own research, Moore observes that, "the more successful East Los Angeles natives continuously migrate out to the suburbs, and the gang members that remain tend to be 'leftovers' from unsuccessful families and/or the children of men and women who return to the barrios after a period of imprisonment" (16). The implication of Moore's analysis is that the underground ethnic drug industry is the source of a growing minority underclass.

Redeveloping the Developmental Theories of Delinquency

The classical theories of delinquency are a rich source of insights into developmental processes that lead to adolescent and adult involvement in crime. However, social and economic events are outpacing the relevance of these theories to the understanding of contemporary problems of street crime in America. A framework organized around processes of capitalization can increase attention to closely connected social and economic processes that are a source of these changes.

This conceptualization begins with the premise that structural changes beyond the control of affected individuals have brought increasing inequality into the American economy and into the lives of individuals who live in its most distressed communities, with rising levels of crime as one of the associated costs. Three theoretically distinct but empirically interconnected processes of macro-level capital disinvestment have intensified the crime problems of these communities: residential segregation, racial inequality and the concentration of poverty. These processes of capital disinvestment are intensified by business practices and government policies that often are premised on unsubstantiated beliefs that efforts to reduce social inequality diminish individual initiative and economic efficiency. Meanwhile, capital disinvestment impairs the formation of social and cultural capital, including the ability to structure socially organized activity toward the achievement of approved goals in distressed communities and families. In this way, capital disinvestment encourages subcultural adaptations by the affected individuals who often organize their efforts within groups and gangs. These individual- and group-based adaptations are often forms of recapitalization; that is, they represent efforts to reorganize available (albeit usually illicit) resources to reach attainable goals.

Often these efforts at recapitalization occur through participation in ethnic vice industries and the formation of deviance service centers in distressed community settings. When these industries and centers are allowed to evolve with little interference by external authorities, they can develop as virtual free enterprise zones of crime. One of the most enduring of these illicit industries involves illegal drugs. This illicit enterprise has sometimes provided as an external source of financial capital that can serve a redistributive function in distressed ethnic communities and that can recapitalize the economic and social lives of individuals involved. Involvement in this illicit enterprise can provide short-term capital gain, in social and economic terms, bolstering self-image and feelings of social competency at the same time as it generates income. However, the more recent American experience with drugs, especially with crack, is more violent, exploitative and disruptive than experiences with alcohol during prohibition and other kinds of illegal drugs during the more recent past (Fagan 1993). Furthermore, as consumption of such drugs has become more concentrated within minority communities, drug sales have redistributed declining amounts of money from outside the affected communities, and have encountered mounting interference from external authorities. The results are increasingly disruptive and dangerous to the communities and individuals involved, as when individuals become so embedded in crime networks that they have few opportunities to leave. The combination of poor education, little or no job experience, and arrest records provide little or no human, social or cultural capital for affected youths to pursue legitimate career paths.

We need to learn more about linkages between the careers of communities and the individuals that live within them. The economic slowdown during the last quarter of this century in the United States has witnessed a withdrawal of capital from distressed minority communities, families and individuals. Employment and crime problems are associated with these changes in contrasting but nonetheless interrelated processes of capitalization that lead to conventional and criminal outcomes. Unfortunately, we have learned a great deal more from demographic, life course and stratification research about conventional processes of acquiring human, social and cultural capital than we have about the related processes that lead to the acquisition of criminal capital and associated problems of criminal embeddedness. Criminology has much to gain by pursuing conceptualizations that place developmental processes that lead to street crime in the forefront of our research agenda.

References

Allan, Emilie and Darrell Steffensmeier. 1989. "Youth, Underemployment, and Property Crime: Differential Effects of Job Availability and Job Quality on Juvenile and Young Adult Arrest Rates." *American Sociological Review* 54: 107–23.

Anderson, Elijah. 1990. *Streetwise: Race, Class and Change in an Urban Community*. Chicago: University of Chicago Press.

Averitt, Robert. 1968. *The Dual Economy*. New York: W.W. Norton.

———. 1992. "The New Structuralism." *Contemporary Sociology* 21: 650–53.

Balkwell, James. 1990. "Ethnic Inequality and the Rate of Homicide." *Social Forces* 69: 53–70.

Becker, Gary. 1964. *Human Capital*. New York: Columbia University Press.

Blau, Judith and Peter Blau. 1982. "The Cost of Inequality: Metropolitan Structure and Violent Crime." *American Sociological Review* 47: 114–28.

Boritch, Helen and John Hagan. 1987. "Crime and the Changing Forms of Class Control: Policing Public Order in 'Toronto the Good,' 1859–1955." *Social Forces* 66: 307–35.

Bound, John and Richard Freeman. 1992. "What Went Wrong? The Erosion of Relative Earnings and Employment among Young Black Men in the 1980s." *Quarterly Journal of Economics* 201–30.

Bourdieu, Pierre. 1986. "The Forms of Capital." In *Handbook of Theory and Research for the Sociology of Education,* ed. J.G. Richardson. New York: Greenwood Press.

Bursik, Robert. 1989. "Political Decisionmaking and Ecological Models of Delinquency: Conflict and Consensus." In *Theoretical Integration in the Study of Deviance and Crime,* ed. S. Messner, M. Krohn and A. Liska. Albany: State University of New York Press.

———. 1993. "Economic Deprivation and Neighborhood Crime Rates, 1960–1980." *Law & Society Review* 27: 263–84.

Bursik, Robert and Harold Grasmick. 1993. "Economic Deprivation and Neighborhood Crime Rates, 1960–1980." *Law and Society Review* 27: 263–84.

Cantor, D. and K. Land. 1985. "Unemployment and Crime Rates in the Post-World War II United States: A Theoretical and Empirical Analysis." *American Sociological Review* 50: 317–23.

Centerwall, B. 1984. "Race, Socioeconomic Status and Domestic Homicide, Atlanta, 1971–2." *American Journal of Public Health* 74: 813–15.

Chiricos, Theodore G. 1987. "Rates of Crime and Unemployment: An Analysis of Aggregate Research Evidence." *Social Problems* 34: 187–212.

Clairmont, Donald. 1974. "The Development of a Deviance Service Center." In *Decency and Deviance*, ed. Jack Haas and Bill Shaffir. Toronto: McClelland and Stewart.

Coleman, James. 1988. "Social Capital in the Creation of Human Capital." *American Journal of Sociology* 94: S95–120.

———. 1990. *Foundations of Social Theory*. Cambridge, MA: Harvard University Press.

Crutchfield, Robert. 1989. "Labor Stratification and Violent Crime." *Social Forces* 68: 589–612.

Curry, G. David and Irving Spergel. 1988. "Gang Homicide, Delinquency and Community." *Criminology* 26: 381.

DiMaggio, Paul. 1982. "Cultural Capital and School Success: The Impact of Status Culture Participation on the Grades of U.S. High School Students." *American Sociological Review* 47: 189–201.

DiMaggio, Paul. 1987. "Classification in Art." *American Sociological Review* 52: 440–55.

DiMaggio, Paul and John Mohr. 1985. "Cultural Capital, Educational Attainment and Marital Selection." *American Journal of Sociology* 90: 1231–61.

Fagan, Jeffrey. 1993. "Drug Selling and Licit Income in Distressed Neighborhoods: The Economic Lives of Street-Level Drug Users and Dealers." In *Drugs, Crime and Social Isolation*, ed. A. Harrell and G. Peterson. Washington, D.C.: Urban Institute Press.

Freeman, Richard. 1991. "Crime and the Economic Status of Disadvantaged Young Men." Paper presented to the Conference on Urban Labor Markets and Labor Mobility, Warrenton, VA.

Glynn, Andrew and David Miliband. 1994. "Equality and Efficiency." Institute for Public Policy Research, London. Paper presented on May 14, 1993 to Conference on Equality and Efficiency.

Granovetter, Mark. 1974. *Getting a Job: A Study of Contacts and Careers*. Cambridge, MA: Harvard University Press.

———. 1985. "Economic Action and Social Structure: The Problem of Embeddedness." *American Journal of Sociology* 91: 481–510.

Greenberg, David. 1979. "Delinquency and the Age Structure of Society." In *Criminology Review Yearbook*, ed. S.I. Messinger and E. Bittner. Beverly Hills, CA: Sage.

Grogger, J. 1991a. "The Effect of Arrest on the Employment Outcomes of Young Men." Unpublished manuscript, University of California, Santa Barbara.

———. 1991b. "Destiny and Drift: Subcultural Preferences, Status Attainments and the Risks and Rewards of Youth." *American Sociological Review* 56: 567–82.

Hagan, John and Alberto Palloni. 1990. "The Social Reproduction of a Criminal Class in Working Class London, Circa 1950–80." *American Journal of Sociology* 96: 265–99.

Hagan, John and Blair Wheaton. 1993. "The Search for Adolescent Role Exits and the Transition to Adulthood." *Social Forces* 71: 955–80.

Hagedorn, John. 1988. *People and Folks: Gangs, Crime and the Underclass in a Rustbelt City.* Chicago: Lake View Press.

Hogan, Dennis and Nan Marie Astone. 1986. "The Transition to Adulthood." *Annual Review of Sociology* 12: 109–30.

Ianni, Francis. 1972. *A Family Business.* New York: Russell Sage.

———. 1974. *Black Mafia.* New York: Simon & Schuster.

Land, Kenneth, P. McCall and Lawrence Cohen. 1990. "Structural Co-variates of Homicide Rates: Are There Any Invariances Across Time and Space?" *American Journal of Sociology* 95: 922–63.

Land, K., D. Cantor and S. Russell. 1994. "Unemployment and Crime Rate Fluctuations in the Post-World War II United States: Statistical Time Series Properties and Alternative Models." In *Crime and Inequality,* ed. John Hagan and Ruth Peterson. Stanford, CA: Stanford University Press.

Light, Ivan. 1977. "The Ethnic Vice Industry, 1880–1944." *American Sociological Review* 42: 464–79.

Lowry, P., S. Hassig, R. Gunn, and J. Mathison. 1988. "Homicide Victims in New Orleans: Recent Trends." *American Journal of Epidemiology* 128: 1130–36.

Margolin, Stephen and Juliet Schor. 1990. *The End of the Golden Age.* Oxford: Clarendon Press.

Massey, Douglas. 1990. "American Apartheid: Segregation and the Making of the Underclass." *American Journal of Sociology* 96: 329–57.

Massey, Douglas and Nancy Denton. 1993. *American Apartheid: Segregation and the Making of the Underclass.* Cambridge, MA: Harvard University Press.

Messner, Steven and Reid Golden. 1992. "Racial Inequality and Racially Disaggregated Homicide Rates: An Assessment of Alternative Theoretical Explanations." *Criminology* 30: 421–47.

Messner, Steven and Richard Rosenfeld. 1993. *Crime and the American Dream.* Belmont, CA: Wadsworth.

Moore, Joan. 1991. *Going Down to the Barrio: Homeboys and Homegirls in Change.* Philadelphia: Temple University Press.

Munford, R. S., R. Kazew, R. Feldman and R. Stivers. 1976. "Homicide Trends in Atlanta." *American Journal of Public Health* 14: 213–21.

Padilla, Felix. 1992. *The Gang as an American Enterprise.* New Brunswick, NJ: Rutgers University Press.

Peterson, Ruth and Lauren Krivo. 1993. "Racial Segregation and Black Urban Homicide." *Social Forces* 71: 1001–28.

Reuter, P., R. MacCoun, P. Murphy. 1990. Money from Crime. Report R-3894. Santa Monica, CA: Rand Corporation.

Revenga, Ana. 1992. "Exporting Jobs? The Impact of Import Competition on Employment and Wages in U.S. Manufacturing." *Quarterly Journal of Economics* 255–82.

Robins, Lee. 1966. *Deviant Children Up.* Baltimore, MD: Williams and Wilkins.

Sampson, Robert. 1985. "Race and Criminal Violence: A Demographically Disaggregated Analysis of Urban Homicide." *Crime and Delinquency* 31: 47–82.

Sampson, Robert and John Laub. 1990. "Stability and Change in Crime and Deviance over the Life Course: The Salience of Adult Social Bonds." *American Sociological Review* 55: 609–27.

————. 1993. *Crime in the Making*. Cambridge, MA: Harvard University Press.

Sampson, Robert and William Wilson. 1994. "Toward a Theory of Race, Crime and Urban Inequality." In *Crime and Inequality*, ed. John Hagan and Ruth Peterson. Stanford, CA: Stanford University Press.

Sanchez-Jankowski, Martin. 1992. *Islands in the Stream*. Los Angeles: University of California Press.

Schwartz, Richard and Jerome Skolnick. 1964. "Two Studies of Legal Stigma." In *The Other Side: Perspectives on Deviance,* ed. Howard Becker. New York: Free Press.

Schultz, Theodore. 1961. "Investment in Human Capital." *American Economic Review* 51: 1–17.

Sherman, Lawrence. 1993. "Defiance, Deterrence and Irrelevance: A Theory of the Criminal Sanction." *Journal of Research in Crime and Delinquency*. 30: 445–73.

Short, James F. In Press. *Poverty, Ethnicity and Violent Crime*. Boulder, Colorado: Westview Press. Forthcoming.

Skogan, Wesley. 1986. "Fear of Crime and Neighborhood Change." In *Communities and Crime,* ed. A. J. Reiss and M. Tonry. Chicago: University of Chicago Press.

Sullivan, Mercer. 1989. *Getting Paid: Youth Crime and Work in the Inner City*. Ithaca, New York: Cornell University Press.

Taylor, Ralph and Jeanette Covington. 1988. "Neighborhood Changes in Ecology and Violence." *Criminology* 26: 553.

Wacquant, L. D. and William J. Wilson. 1989. "The Costs of Racial and Class Exclusion in the Inner City." *Annals of the American Academy of Political and Social Science* 501: 8–25.

Ward, David and Charles Tittle. 1993. "Deterrence or Labelling: The Effects of Informal Sanctions." *Deviant Behavior* 14: 43–64.

Williams, Kirk and Robert Flewelling. 1987. "The Social Production of Criminal Homicide: A Comparative Study of Disaggregated Rates in American Cities." *American Sociological Review* 53: 421–31.

Williams, Terry. 1989. *The Cocaine Kids*. New York: Addison-Wesley.

Willis, Paul. 1977. *Learning to Labour*. London: Gower.

Wilson, William J. 1987. *The Truly Disadvantaged: The Inner City, the Underclass, and Public Policy*. Chicago: University of Chicago Press.

————. 1991. "Studying Inner-City Social Dislocations: The Challenge of Public Agenda Research." *American Sociological Review* 56: 1–14.

8

Developmental Aspects of Adult Crime

Kenneth Adams

Much criminological research concentrates on offending throughout the adolescent years. In comparison, adult criminality has received relatively little attention. This is unfortunate because two issues relating to adult crime stand out as having significant implications for the future progress of criminological theory. The first issue is whether adult criminality and juvenile delinquency require different explanations. The second is whether desistance, or the winding down of criminal activity that takes place in young adulthood, requires an exegesis that stands apart from the onset of delinquent behavior in adolescence. Criminological theories generally fail to address these two issues, in part, because they lack a developmental perspective. That is, they do not focus on changing patterns of criminal involvement with age nor do they fully incorporate the many changes in personality, peer relations, family interactions, and life circumstances that take place throughout adolescence and adulthood. This essay examines theories of adult development and their potential applications to the etiology of adult criminality and processes of desistance.

Regarding the distinctive nature of adult criminality, studies indicate that juveniles and adults commit different types of crimes and that some correlates of juvenile and adult criminality differ (Tonry et al. 1991). Although these findings suggest that separate explanations of juvenile and adult crime are warranted, their implications for theory are less than clear, since many of the etiological factors highlighted in delinquency research are not especially pertinent to adult criminality. Delinquency research concentrates on questions of why juveniles become involved in crime and other deviant acts, placing considerable emphasis on the influences of schools, family, and peers. By early adulthood, however, most people have left school, have moved out of their parent's home, have started an occupational career, and have established a family life of their own. Given the many differences in life situations between juveniles and adults, it is still an open question as to which theories and concepts are most useful for explaining adult criminality.

On the topic of desistance from crime, one of the most reliable findings in criminology is that rates of criminal behavior in the aggregate decline markedly in adulthood. Yet, another equally reliable finding is that prior criminal behavior is among the best predictors of subsequent criminal activity. The research on age and crime thus points to changes in behavior, possibly as the result of some common, age-related process, while studies on recidivism emphasize the stability of criminal propensity across the life span. An explanation for this seeming paradox is that two groups—a large group of occasional, sporadic offenders and a small group of persisting, chronic offenders—combine to generate the aggregate age-crime curve. Thus, rapidly changing prevalence rates driven by occasional offenders account for the overall shape of the age-crime curve, while reliably high incidence rates among persistent offenders account for findings in the recidivism studies (Blumstein et al. 1988).

While distinctions between incidence and prevalence rates and between occasional and chronic offenders may help account for observed changes in crime rates with age, these concepts do little by way of explaining the etiological processes that support behavioral stability and change among offenders. A developmental perspective, however, with its central focus on how people remain the same or become different over the life course (Kagan 1980) could bring criminologists to a better understanding of changes in criminal careers across the life span.

Before discussing specific theories of adult development, it may be useful to illustrate how a developmental perspective can facilitate new thinking about adult criminality. Criminologists have struggled with the challenge of interpreting the relation between age and crime, and, while age is among the most familiar variables in criminological investigations, it is among the least understood concepts. Developmental researchers also share a strong interest in documenting the changes that come with age. This task assumes special significance in research on adult development because while everyday experience suggests that continuity is the norm for many aspects of adult behavior, instances of dramatic change can be found (Brim 1973). In studying adult development, researchers have concluded that chronological age is not very useful for understanding behavior because age becomes increasingly less dependable across the life span as an indicator of physical, psychological, and social development. Some developmentalists have argued that an excessive concern with chronological age may have had an invidious influence on adult research (Havighurst 1973). A similar argument could be made for criminological research in which the relation of omnibus variables, such as age and race, to criminality are often difficult to interpret because of the multiple concepts for which they stand as surrogates. If chronological age cannot be used as a convenient and easy to interpret marker variable, as developmental researchers have concluded, then criminologists need to measure key theoretical concepts more directly.

Another general area in which developmental research may prove useful involves the form of causal explanations. Most criminological theories are predicated on relatively straightforward cause-effect relations. For example, if strain resulting from economic deprivation causes crime, then the greater the strain, the more crime, and, the removal of strain leads to the cessation of criminal activity. Although such explanations benefit from simplicity and parsimony, they involve assumptions that may be unwarranted. For example, many criminological theories assume that the same concepts are equally significant at all ages. Furthermore, many theories assume that the absence of factors that led to adolescent involvement in delinquency subsequently results in desistance from crime in adulthood. Developmental theories, likewise, may embrace relatively straightforward relations. For example, developmental growth is a plausible explanation for widespread changes in behavior (e.g., maturing out from crime), while thwarted development may account for unexpected stability (e.g., chronic offending). Developmental theories, however, are sensitive to the possibility that causal factors may carry differential importance at various ages. They also emphasize the possibility that new factors, ones that might transform, outweigh, neutralize, or perhaps, even belatedly create an individual's antisocial propensities, come into play over the life course.

In examining the potential contributions of developmental theories to adult criminality, the discussion begins with a consideration of the biological changes with age. It then moves to consider life span changes in cognitive development, moral development, intellectual development and personality development. Finally, normative life events are discussed with an emphasis on influences that can be traced to changes in social roles.

Biological Development

Currently, there is a renewed interest in the biological elements of crime. This interest has been fueled in part by research that points to the strong influence of heredity on behavior. Additionally, the discovery of links between biology and crime promises to illuminate the difficult to ignore yet hard to explain fact that criminality is largely a phenomenon of young males.

An obvious connection between biology and adult crime lies in the area of strength and physical ability. Some crimes (e.g., assault), if they are to be carried out successfully, require physical strength, while speed, agility, and quickness can be key elements of proficiency for other types of crimes (e.g., burglary, auto theft). Physical strength may also be a factor in how a person responds to institutional settings, such as jails and prisons, where the incidence of predatory behavior tends to be high.

Physiological studies indicate that somewhere around thirty years of age, muscle mass and strength reach their peak and then decline across the life span (Rossman 1982). Also, it has been demonstrated that these physiological changes coincide with performance levels for activities that depend on strength and agility. In 1953, Lehman studied the peak ages of productivity for a variety of occupations (as reported in Hayflick 1982). This research showed that the peak ages of performance for physically demanding sports (e.g., football, prize fighting, baseball, tennis, auto racing) range from twenty-two to thirty years. In contrast, performance in occupations that rely less heavily on strength, endurance, and agility often peak later in life.

Changes in physical ability with age also appear to be reflected in levels of involvement in predatory criminal activity. Using 1977 UCR arrest data, Cline (1980) observes that property crime is most characteristic of adolescents (under 20 years), that violent crimes peak in young adulthood (ages 20 to 29 years), and that gambling and alcohol offenses (drunkenness, drunk driving) are disproportionately characteristics of the middle-aged (30 years and older). Cline (1980) further notes that studies by Glueck and Glueck (1940), McCord and McCord (1959), and Robins (1966) support the hypothesis that increased involvement with violent crime coincides with increased levels of physiological development. More recent analyses conducted by Wilson and Herrnstein (1985) with 1980 UCR data show a similar pattern of results. Finally, Shover (1985) reports that middle-aged offenders will cite feelings of physical tiredness, weariness, and exhaustion as reasons for abandoning criminal activity.

Psychological mechanisms may mediate the impact of physiological development on criminal activity. Age brings a slowing of the body's ability to heal from injury, and criminal offenders, if sensitive to this downturn, may become more conscious of their mortality. As feelings of vulnerability become more salient, increasing anxiety over possible future threats may produce a shift in the offender's risk calculus such that a criminal lifestyle becomes increasingly less attractive.

Some scholars argue that the key feature of the age-crime curve that needs to be explained is its steep rise and swift decent. Gove (1985:138), for example, argues that "while social roles, psychological well-being, and psychological maturation are all compatible with the notion that deviance should peak at an early age and then decline, by themselves they cannot account for the rapidity of both the rise and fall of deviant behavior as one ages. To explain the rapidity of the decline in deviant behavior by age, we need to look at physical strength, energy, psychological drive, and the reinforcement of an adrenaline high." As Farrington (1986) points out, however, the curve describing the relation between age and testosterone levels does not peak at the same point as the age-crime curve.

These observations by Gove and by Farrington raise issues about the interpretation of aggregate curves at the level of individual behavior and about the possible causal relation that can be inferred from aggregate curves that describe two different phenomena. The aggregate age-crime curve is the product of many different individual curves, which means that the aggregate curve may not accurately reflect behavior patterns at the individual level. Some scholars, as previously noted, argue that the rise and fall in criminal activity with age reflects mostly changes in participation rates (i.e., the number of persons engaging in crime) rather than incidence rates (Blumstein et al. 1988). This argument, if correct, has important implications for the types of explanations we should seek. If the overall shape of the age-crime curve is determined largely by participation rates, then we need to explain why large numbers of persons become involved in crime for a short time and then promptly bring their criminal careers to an end. Contrary to Gove's argument, this situation is amenable to a variety of non-biological explanations that focus on changes in social roles, responsibilities, and lifestyles that typically accompany the transition to adulthood. If, on the other hand, incidence rates are primarily at issue, explanations need to be compatible with the notion of a winding down process, one that occurs relatively quickly but that nonetheless spans at least a decade of life.

Cognitive Development

Although there are many theories of cognitive and intellectual development, only a few deal explicitly with development in adulthood. Some theories that address postchildhood development are difficult to operationalize (e.g., Freud's theory of psychosexual development) and therefore have not gained favor with researchers. One theory that has been researched extensively is Piaget's theory of cognitive development.

Piaget's is a stage theory in the sense that it postulates an invariant, irreversible sequence of cognitive development. The developmental stage most relevant to adulthood is formal operations, which typically is reached in early adolescence and which represents the final stage of development in Piaget's scheme. Originally, it was assumed that everyone reached this stage and that development was completed at this point. Recent investigations, however, suggest that development can stop short of formal operations. For example, studies of older adolescents and adults as reviewed by Neimark (1975, 1979) indicate that not all persons reach the stage of formal operations (Lerner 1986: 258). In fact, two studies (Elkind 1962; Towler and Wheatley 1971) reviewed by Neimark (1975) found that more than one-third of college students failed to complete a task indicative of formal operational thought (Lerner 1986:259). Other studies suggest that development beyond the formal operations stage may take place, although most of the speculation in this regard is focused on creativity and divergent thinking (Rebok 1987: 382–83) and so may not be relevant to street crime. The important point, however, is that there is evidence to suggest that changes in cognitive structures occur in adulthood.

What are the characteristics of formal operations and of the preceding stage of concrete operations? In concrete operations, individuals can only think in terms of real and tangible objects and cannot think hypothetically or counterfactually. As a result, they show an inability to solve problems by means of general theories or by systematic examination of all possible solutions (Lerner 1986). Individuals in the concrete operations stage also have difficulty distinguishing between actual experiences of reality and thoughts about reality. Furthermore, when their ideas of reality are challenged, they will reinterpret the evidence to fit an already formed ideational scheme (Lerner 1986).

In comparison, persons in the formal operations stage can think hypothetically and are therefore capable of dealing with all potentially relevant aspects of a problem. This capability is achieved by transforming, altering or rearranging a problem so as to identify all its possible forms (Lerner 1986: 257). According to Piaget, adolescents, upon entering formal operations, show a distinct type of egocentrism that is revealed in a preoccupation with their own perspectives. This egocentrism gradually diminishes over time through a decentering process that is brought about by interactions with peers and adults and, most importantly, by the assumption of adult roles and responsibilities. A major catalyst in the decentering process is entry into the occupational world, an experience that forces adolescents to become adults (Lerner 1986: 260–61).

Given the differences between formal operations and concrete operations, what applications might Piaget's theory find in relation to criminal behavior? A general hypothesis is that offenders are more likely to be at the stage of concrete operations rather than formal operations. In terms of adult criminality, it could be argued that arrested or blocked cognitive development may account for chronic offending, while the normal developmental process may account for desistance. Indeed, some prison psychologists have characterized career criminals as suffering from cognitive immaturity and as being stuck at an adolescent stage of development (Walters 1990).

If concrete operational thought is characteristic of offenders, this relation may help to explain several aspects of delinquency and criminality. Researchers, as well as practitioners, often observe that delinquents justify their illegal behavior quite spiritedly and convincingly, arguing that they had no real choice in the matter, that there were special circumstances justifying the delinquent act, or that the victim was deserving of the crime. A somewhat cynical interpretation of these statements is that delinquents are very adept at rationalizing illegal behavior. When delinquents are viewed as having mastered the art of such manipulation, they often are labeled as psychopathic. Other observers describe such statements by delinquents as techniques of "neutralization," or methods whereby offenders construe situations in ways that free them psychologically from the moral obligations of the criminal law (Matza 1964). In either case, the implication is that the offender knows at some level that his or her delinquent conduct is wrong.

If, however, the "manipulative" offender is operating at the level of concrete operations, he or she would have a highly egocentric perspective, believing that the world is as he or she presents it. The offender would not necessarily share the view that delinquent behavior is wrong and may be unable to recognize the legitimacy of another person's claim to fair and just treatment. In this regard, the delinquent might be characterized as being at a less advanced stage of moral development, and, as we shall see in a later section, research indicates that cognitive and moral development are related and that delinquents operate at a lower level of moral development than do nondelinquents.

Another way of viewing the relation between cognitive development and criminal propensity is in terms of the abilities that a person fails to develop by not advancing to the formal operations stage. A key feature of formal operations is hypothetical thought, which brings the ability to identify and analyze all aspects of a problem or situation. The capacity to think hypothetically, or to think in "what if" terms, can be an important factor in a person's decision-making processes, including decisions to engage in criminal behavior. This ability becomes more consequential if, lacking hypothetical thought, the person cannot identify novel solutions to problems and must rely on experiential knowledge, especially when experience teaches that antisocial behavior is a viable option.

Another key feature of Piaget's theory for the study of adult criminality is the decentering process, which is the diminishing of egocentric perspectives that occurs when the adolescent assumes adult roles and responsibilities. According to Piaget, the transition to adulthood brings specific alterations in cognitive abilities because new role demands cannot be addressed fully by the cognitive structures that exist in adolescence. If the adolescent fails to complete this stage of cognitive development, a variety of problems in adult role performance will appear. With regard to criminal behavior, we might expect that delinquents who successfully complete the decentering process will be less likely to continue in their criminal careers, and, conversely, we might expect that delinquents who are unsuccessful in this developmental transition are more likely to become chronic offenders. We can also expect that these chronic offenders will show associated problems in other areas of adult role performance.

Although there are few criminological studies directly germane to Piaget's theory, there is research indicating that delinquents differ from nondelinquents in cognitive and intellectual skills. Redl and Wineman (1951) have documented in considerable detail the ego deficits of chronic delinquents, and many of these deficits resemble limitations on cognitive processes. Also, appreciable differences in IQ test scores between delinquents and nondelinquents are reliably observed (Hirschi and Hindelang 1977), and cognitive development is substantially correlated (at about .5) with intelligence. The link between cognitive development and delinquency could be made stronger, however, by demonstrating how specific cognitive processes are associated with criminality across the life course. Piaget's theory predicts that cognitive development is affected by social experiences and adult role demands, that cognitive development is linked to adult role performance, and that cognitive and moral development are interconnected. Thus, the theory offers a psychological link between common adult experiences, such as employment and involvement in criminal behavior. Studies of work experience that highlight these connections may provide new insights into the nature of adult criminal behavior.

There are, however, potential methodological problems in studying adult cognitive development, particularly with Piaget's stage theory. Many tests of cognitive abilities, such as those of formal operational thought, involve skills that are practiced in school (Kuhn et al. 1983). Given that some tests of cognitive development build on school-related tasks, the appropriateness of these measurement techniques for adult subjects can be questioned, since the tasks will lack relevance for persons who have been out of school for some time. These problems of relevancy and familiarity may be compounded for delinquents who, as a group, show a greater propensity for truancy.

Noting the questionable appropriateness of traditional measurement techniques for assessing adult cognitive development, some scholars have set about to develop new methods. These methods are built around tasks that are more familiar and relevant to life situations of adults. Although the reliability and validity of these methods have not been established definitively, the expectation is that the subject's motivation for completing the task will be increased and that the new test protocols will yield more accurate results (Kuhn et al. 1983). Nonetheless, the development of these new techniques has proved to be very challenging.

Moral Development

Given that the criminal law represents a set of injunctions against harmful behaviors as backed by the moral authority of the legal system, the ability to distinguish between morally acceptable and unacceptable behaviors is clearly relevant to questions of why some people are criminal. Among the few developmental theories that speak directly to the learning of morality is Kohlberg's theory of moral development. The theory, which represents an extension of Piaget's work on cognitive structures, views moral development as progressing through a series of hierarchical stages, each reflecting a different thought process used to arrive at moral judgments.

Recent statements of the theory (Kohlberg 1986) describe moral development as progressing through three levels comprising a total of six stages.

Level 1—Preconventional
  Stage 1—Heteronomous morality—Laws are obeyed to avoid punishment.
  Stage 2—Individualism, instrumental purpose and exchange—Laws are obeyed to serve one's own needs or interests.
Level 2—Conventional
  Stage 3—Mutual interpersonal expectations, relationships and interpersonal conformity—Belief in the Golden Rule.
  Stage 4—Social system and conscience—Laws are obeyed to avoid a breakdown of the system.
Level 3—Post-conventional or principled
  Stage 5—Social contract or utility and individual rights—Laws are obeyed out of obligation to a social contract that promotes the welfare of all people.
  Stage 6—Universal ethical principles—Belief in the validity of universal moral principles.

As individuals progress across levels of moral development, they move in the direction of increasingly greater scope and greater abstraction, or from a highly egocentric, individualistic perspective (level 1), to a perspective that incorporates social expectations and obligations (level 2), to a broader, more universal, perspective based on principles regarding the rights of individuals and the values of society (level 3).

Kohlberg's theory is relevant to issues of adult criminality because moral development has been linked to age. In particular, several studies demonstrate that moral reasoning moves to a higher level in late adolescence and early adulthood (Eisenberg and Fabes 1988; Eisenberg 1986; Rest 1983). Furthermore, it is reasonable to assume that delinquents are more likely to be at the level of preconventional moral thinking, with its emphasis on egocentricity, than nondelinquents, and there are studies to support this view (Raine 1993: 237). Conversely, the link between prosocial behavior and higher levels of moral thinking, which emphasize social approval, conscience, and principled conduct, is easy to see.

Thus, as with Piaget's theory, we can postulate that the normal course of moral development may help account for desistance, which often is characterized as maturing out of crime, while thwarted development may help account for protracted criminality into adulthood. However, a straightforward inverse relation between moral development and illegal behavior can be too simplistic. Kohlberg's theory focuses on reasoning processes, not behaviors, and the decision to act in a given moral (or immoral) way can be arrived at by very different reasoning paths. Disjunctures can occur when persons at higher stages violate the law for moral reasons (e.g., civil disobedience), or when persons at the lower end of the developmental spectrum obey the law for less than virtuous motives.

Kohlberg's theory is also significant because it shows how moral reasoning interacts with social, cognitive, and personality development, and, in this regard, the theory can contribute to an integrated developmental view of criminality. For example, Harris et al. (1976) found that children with higher levels of moral reasoning showed greater resistance to temptation and were more likely to be perceived by peers as prosocial (Lerner 1986: 286). These findings indicate that the types of social interactions experienced by young people are related to levels of moral reasoning.

There is also evidence to suggest that advances to higher levels of moral reasoning hinge on changes in social and cognitive processes (i.e., the achievement of formal operation) associated with adolescence and adulthood (Tomlinson-Keasey and Keasey 1974). For example, college students show more advanced moral reasoning than noncollege students (Rest 1983). Noting that Kohlberg (1973) emphasizes the effect of social role-taking on learning of principles of morality, Rest suggests that the difference can be attributed to the fact that college settings involve more intense experiences of perspective-taking (Rest et al. 1974). On the other hand, Lerner (1986) argues that a relation between IQ, formal relations, and moral development may explain this difference.

Kohlberg's theory highlights the relation between cognitive and moral development. In discussing the nature of this connection, Kohlberg notes that moral development does not depend heavily on direct personal experiences in making moral choices, and given that the stages of moral development represent generalized forms of thinking, the capacity for operating at higher stages will develop more readily in cognitively enriched environments. Thus, the theory predicts that moral development will proceed at a slower pace or perhaps even be curtailed in cognitively deprived environments, and this relation may help to explain the association between social class and crime.

Finally, moral development processes are connected to the achievement of identity and thereby become relevant to personality development. Podd (1972), for example, reports that principled moral thought, formal operational reasoning, and identity achievement are positively related. In addition, adolescents with a diffuse identity status tend to operate at the level of preconventional moral reasoning (Lerner 1986: 324).

Intellectual Development

For the purposes of this essay, there are two important sets of research findings on intelligence. The first set indicates that intelligence is a multidimensional construct and that scientists have yet to agree completely on the full set of mental abilities that are subsumed by the concept of intelligence. As a corollary, global intelligence tests obscure important differences in specific types of mental abilities. Another important set involves systematic differences in findings between cross-sectional and longitudinal designs regarding changes in intelligence with age. For the most part, cross-sectional research shows that intelligence remains constant or declines with age. In contrast, longitudinal studies indicate that intelligence increases with age when measurements are taken on the same group of subjects at different points in time. Thus, in contrast to other researchers, developmental and life span researchers argue that intelligence shows considerable plasticity over time.

Global indicators of intelligence can obscure variations in primary mental abilities. An example of this phenomenon pertinent to adult criminality can be found in Cattell's research. Cattell classified primary mental abilities into two higher-order or latent factors referred to as fluid and crystallized intelligence. Fluid intelligence involves abilities to reason about novel and unfamiliar material, and the development of these abilities is thought to occur by processes of casual and incidental learning (Featherman 1983). In contrast, crystallized intelligence is strongly influenced by acculturation experiences and is largely the product of interactions with parents, teachers, and others (Horn and Donaldson 1980). More particularly, "[c]rystallized intelligence refers to the universe of abilities embodied in the symbolic culture of a society; it is knowledge and mental skills that a community deems valuable and essential for its maintenance and that are instilled through child rearing practices and adult socialization in social roles.... it underlies the capacity to cope with social situations according the conventional mores of a community" (Featherman 1983: 26).

Given that crystallized intelligence reflects a person's ability to learn from socialization experiences and that this ability relates directly to the person's capacity to behave in a prosocial or conventional manner, we can hypothesize that offenders will have below-average levels of crystallized intelligence. This hypothesis goes beyond the general finding that delinquents score lower on IQ tests than nondelinquents because it makes reference to a more limited set of mental abilities and because it identifies a mechanism through which intelligence relates to delinquency.

Another important aspect of Cattell's research is that crystallized and fluid intelligence have different developmental paths. While fluid intelligence increases to about age twenty-five or thirty, and then declines, crystallized intelligence tends to increase across the life span. When global measures of intelligence are used, test scores appear to be stable or to decline gradually with age owing to a cancellation of two diverging developmental paths. Some researchers conclude that the decline in fluid intelligence reflects a neurological deterioration that can be traced to an accumulation of insults to the brain as a normal part of the aging process (Horn and Donaldson 1980). In contrast, the sequence of adult roles typically experienced in adult life provides opportunities to practice and sharpen the mental abilities that constitute crystallized intelligence (Horn and Donaldson 1980).

The concept of crystallized intelligence suggests that an increased propensity for crime is associated with deficits in specific mental abilities that hinder learning of the norms of socially acceptable behavior, as these norms are communicated through adult roles and socialization experiences. Furthermore, increases in crystallized intelligence, which are linked to greater degrees of acculturation as a result of greater exposure to adult social situations, may provide a partial explanation for the fact that criminal involvement declines substantially in the adult years. Given that most persons show a slow and steady increase in crystallized intelligence throughout adulthood, the cumulative effects of this process are amenable to explanations of a long-term winding down of adult criminal activity, with the possibility that a specific threshold must be reached before effects become noticeable in relation to chronic offending. As in Piaget's theory, the possible relations of adult roles, adult socialization experiences, and the development of mental processes to adult crime and desistance are highlighted.

Finally, developmental researchers point to the need for studying changes in specific types of mental abilities. Since most of the research on intelligence and delinquency is based on general IQ scores, it remains to be determined how the mental abilities of delinquents and nondelinquents differ in more particular terms. Research showing that the developmental paths of various mental abilities differ across adulthood suggests that disaggregating the measure of intelligence may be critical in the study of adult criminal careers.

Personality Development

Issues of stability and change are core concerns for developmental researchers, and these issues are strikingly evident in the study of personality development. On the one hand, there is impressive evidence to suggest that personality traits are stable and enduring features of an adult's psychological makeup. Yet, other research indicates that changes in dispositions do occur, and the consequences of these changes may be highly significant for understanding changes in levels of criminal involvement. The task of summarizing and evaluating the research on personality development is a difficult one because issues of research design (e.g., cross-sectional vs. longitudinal vs. cohort sequential analyses; ipsative vs. stage vs. differential approaches) are often raised to challenge the generalizability and validity of a particular set of findings. Rather than attempt to summarize all existing studies, the discussion concentrates on a handful of investigations that illuminate issues of personality development relevant to adult criminal behavior.

With regard to the constancy of personality traits, the Oakland Growth Study (Tuddenham 1954, as reported in Moss and Sussman 1980) found aggression to be remarkably stable with age. The sample involved seventy-two subjects who were tested first in early adolescence, at around fourteen years old, and then nineteen years later at about thirty-three years old. Tuddenham reported that while the average correlation for personality dimensions between adolescence and adulthood for men was .27, the correlation for aggression was more than twice the mean (.68) and was the highest correlation observed in the sample. In further support of this finding, Skolnick (1966), analyzing the results of the Thematic Apperception Test (TAT) administered to the sample at age seventeen and at age thirty-seven, observed significant stability coefficients for measures of power and aggression. These findings indicate that aggression is among the most stable personality trait for males, a position that has been advanced by some criminologists (Olweus 1979).

Another noteworthy study of personality is that by Kagan and Moss (1962). The sample consisted of eighty-nine children, with an almost equal number of males and females, who were enrolled in Fels Research Institute from 1929 to 1939. Given that the children were predominately white, upper to middle-class midwesterners, the generalizability of the results can be questioned. All children were assessed on multiple occasions from birth through early adolescence (age fourteen), and seventy-one children participated in a second phase of data collection that took place when they were between nineteen and twenty-nine years old.

Among the more significant findings reported by Kagan and Moss was that some behaviors in the preschool years (ages 3 to 6 years) and many behaviors in the early school years (ages 6 to 10) were good predictors of conceptually similar behaviors in young adulthood. For example, aggression towards mother, behavioral disorganization, and dominance during ages six to fourteen predicted aggressive retaliation for adult males (Kagan and Moss 1962: 94). Continuity was dependent on whether behaviors were consistent with traditional sex role expectations. Aggressive and angry behaviors showed continuity for males, whereas passive and dependent behaviors showed continuity for females. Although Kagan and Moss invoked the concept of sex roles to explain their findings, they did not rule out the possibility that biological or constitutional factors may be implicated in the causal picture.

Another important aspect of this research is that persons showed genotypic continuity across phenotypically different behaviors. This finding in the context of male aggression suggests that the processes that sustain chronic offending may be manifested in different ways across the life span. In studying the causes of adult criminality, then, it is important to examine a variety of genotypic behavioral precursors, while, in understanding desistance, it is important to consider noncriminal behaviors that are conceptually related to criminality.

The research on personality and age points to both stability and change, depending, in part, on which dimensions of personality are examined and on how the data are analyzed. These divergent findings can be observed in a study of personality development by Block (1971). In this project, Block utilized data from the Berkeley Guidance Study and the Oakland Growth Study to study the period from junior high school through adulthood. Owing to data limitations, only 171 subjects, almost equally divided between males and females, were studied from a total of 460 subjects. In both of the original samples there was a tendency to overrepresent families of high socioeconomic standing, so that sample selection criteria, as well as sample attrition due to noncomparability of data, raise questions of generalizability.

Block's initial analyses showed substantial correlations across time for personality attributes, although the evidence for personality stability became weaker as the time period under consideration lengthened. From junior to senior high school, the average correlation for males was .77, while from senior high school to early adulthood the average correlation was .56. The average correlations for females were almost identical, being .75 and .54, respectively.

Block reported that the set of correlations (corrected for attenuation) ranged from -.01 to 1.00 for the period from junior to senior high school and from -.40 to .99 for the senior high school to early adulthood period (Block 1971: 92). Recognizing that mean correlations can disguise substantial variation at the individual level, he next investigated individual-level patterns of change and stability to determine whether some persons could be categorized as "changers" and others as "non-changers."

Using factor analysis, Block identified five distinct patterns of male personality development. Two of these types—belated adjusters (13% of sample) and unsettled undercontrollers (12% of sample)—appear relevant to criminological research. In particular, the "belated adjusters" appear to resemble the maturing out pattern that is typical of many delinquents, while the "unsettled undercontrollers" include persons who show chronic difficulties in relating to authority figures and in adhering to limits on behavior.

The "belated adjusters" showed considerable change in their personality profile as they moved from adolescence into adulthood. In junior high school, these individuals, described as "nasty adolescents" of "limited talents," were hostile, self-indulgent, self-defeating, extrapunitive and negativistic. Although still negativistic in senior high school, they had become by this time less hostile, less irritable, more warm and more aware of impressions made on others. As adults, however, these individuals were described as dependable, sympathetic, giving, caring, likable, warm, calm and cheerful.

These findings demonstrate that changes from adolescence to adulthood can be dramatic and that a common developmental pattern involves movement from negativistic, hostile attitudes towards more conforming and prosocial dispositions. This pattern coincides with the maturational reform from crime evidenced by most delinquents. In speculating about the reasons for this change, Block, in a manner reminiscent of Erikson's discussion of the adolescent identity crisis, hypothesized that the "belated-adjusters" successfully resolved the threats of change precipitated by adolescence by finding a niche in society that provided for a circumscribed and predictable life.

In contrast, the "unsettled undercontrollers" showed a consistent pattern of undesirable personality attributes. From junior high school through senior high through early adulthood, these individuals were reliably described as rebellious, hostile, extrapunitive, irritable, undercontrolled, moody and negativistic. This pattern, on the face of it, is consistent with a picture of chronic offending from adolescence into adulthood. In attempting to explain the source of this personality pattern, Block notes that the "unsettled undercontrollers" were reared in conflicted families in which the father was often absent and the mother was lacking in maternal values, thus highlighting the importance of childrearing experiences.

Some features of personality appear to decline reliably with age, as indicated by research on changes in MMPI scores (Costa et al. 1983; Gynther 1980). In particular, there is a decline in rebelliousness to authority, suspiciousness, autistic thinking, and impulsivity with entry into young adulthood (Costa et al. 1983: 235). Studies by Eysenck and by Sealy and Cattell also report lower neuroticism, lower extroversion and higher socialization scores with age (Costa et al. 1983). Self-restraint appears to increase with age, being the second most consistent finding reported in the handbook for the Guillford Zimmerman Temperament Survey (Costa et al. 1983). Studies of personality assessment, then, suggest that people become less rebellious and impulsive and more socialized and restrained as they age, and it is easy to see how these changes may be linked to declining involvement in crime throughout adulthood.

Similarly, there are studies to suggest that persons generally become more risk-aversive with age. Glenn (1980), using the Strong Interest Inventory, found an age-related decline in items related to physical activity and risk-taking. The decline, which continues to around forty years of age, is sharpest between fifteen and twenty. Similarly, Kogan and Wallace (1961), in comparing the attitudes of college-aged youth to those of middle-aged adults, found evidence that persons become more cautious with age. In discussing the sources of these changes, Kuhlen (1968) noted that an individual's responsibilities and commitments increase with age, as do experiences of social and physical loss. He argued that these experiences lead to increased feelings of vulnerability and greater levels of anxiety. As a result, individuals undergo a transformation of motivations and interests, and they develop defensive mechanisms, such as risk-aversiveness, that further restrict behavior.

Research linking perceptions of threat and anxiety to systematic patterns of life experiences and behaviors is important to criminologists on several counts. To begin with, Shover (1985) reports that adult criminal offenders cite perceptions of threat and related anxiety as critical factors in desistance from crime, and these observations find support in the developmental literature. More significantly, Loeber and Le Blanc (1990) find that a high level of neuroticism is among the few factors that inhibit crime. This observation, which supports Kuhlen's aging hypothesis in the context of criminal propensity, may help to explain not only why people avoid crime, but also why they become less involved with crime as they age.

Research on changing perceptions of threat has considerable practical implications, given that the criminal justice system makes age-based distinctions in terms of the nature, duration, and type of punishments meted out to offenders. These differences are seen most readily in the change in jurisdiction from the juvenile to the adult justice system during the teenage years, around which time the developmental literature indicates that persons start to become more cautious and circumspect in their outlook. While this confluence of events may be fortuitous, there may be an increase in the deterrent effectiveness of criminal sanctions and a decrease in criminal activity as persons move from one system to the other. However, the extent to which the transition to the adult justice system is related to changing levels of criminal activity over the life course has yet to be investigated.

Studies of changes in personality reveal that, given longitudinal data, conclusions as to stability or change are influenced partly by the choice of analytic strategies and methods. Block's research suggests that between-group comparisons, which often involve a comparison of central tendencies, are more likely to show stability, whereas ipsative analyses, or within-individual analyses whereby a person's behavior is compared at different points in time, are more likely to reveal change. This research also highlights the importance of subgroup analyses in the study of developmental processes and the need to identify key moderator variables that lead to differences in outcomes.

Some longitudinal studies of personality change find that abrupt and significant turnabouts do occur. In particular, the move from hostile, rebellious attitudes in adolescence to more pleasant, socially conforming dispositions in adulthood, is directly relevant to the decline in criminal involvement in early adulthood. While other relevant personality changes may take place in later adulthood, these changes probably are slower paced so that cumulative changes over extended periods of time may be critical elements in later development. Glenn concludes that there is evidence to support the hypotheses of greater change proneness during early adolescence and of subsequently increasing stability throughout the adult years. He also concludes that a greater degree of receptivity to change among older adults can be linked to motivations of self-interest. However, issues of what types of change, how much change, and at what rate change occurs during adulthood need further investigation.

Kagan and Moss (1962) also highlight the central position of social roles in adult personality development. More particularly, their research suggests that sex roles may be an important factor in maintaining aggressive behaviors in males and in restraining those behaviors in females. The finding is important because it indicates that social role expectations have a major influence on adult behavior.

A general tendency for cautious attitudes to increase with age implies that criminological studies of the aging process might profitably focus on changing perceptions of threat and experiences of generalized anxiety as mechanisms of desistance. Lastly, the findings of personality research suggest that aggressive behavior may show much more stability and continuity than criminal behavior over the life course (Olweus 1979).

Normative Life Events

Developmental researchers distinguish between normative life events, which refer to events that are predictably experienced by most people at a particular time of life (e.g., marriage), and nonnormative life events, which refer to less regular and less predictable life experiences (e.g., illnesses, accidents). Among the many normative events that are experienced in the transition from adolescence to adulthood, several can be distinguished in terms of their significance—marriage, parenthood, and employment. Each of these events brings a change in role status that alters the general pattern and character of a person's social relationships, creates a distinctive set of role expectations, and requires persons to undergo experiences of role socialization. While other changes in personal affiliations, such as those stemming from social and geographic mobility, can lead to changes in role status, marriage, parenthood, and employment have been characterized as "critical periods" in development owing to the predictable and substantial changes in social relationships that take place (Brim 1973). Consequently, we will focus on these normative socialization experiences in terms of the implications for developmental studies of persistence in and desistance from criminality.

Marriage

Brim (1973) characterizes marriage as the most influential relationship of adult life, involving intense and demanding interpersonal contact over a substantial period of time. As a partnership, marriage works against egocentric perspectives by creating pressures for less selfish outlooks in ways that range from demands for simple courtesies to expectations of more altruistic behaviors. Emotionally, marriage creates pressures for intimacy that are best met through sensitive and caring styles of communication, while, in terms of social skills, there are pressures to demonstrate principles of negotiation, compromise, and fairness in personal relationships.

Marriage is often viewed as a discrete event occurring at a specific point in time, but, as Ahammer (1973) points out, marriages are usually preceded by courtship and dating experiences. Also, cohabitation may precede marriage or serve as its functional equivalent. For this reason, it may be misleading to use marital status as an indicator of change, and it therefore becomes important for researchers to measure theoretically relevant dimensions of interpersonal relationships and lifestyles before, during and after wedlock.

Given the intimate and intense character of marital relationships, changes in individual dispositions of the marriage partners can be expected to take place over time. In discussing this possibility, Brim (1966: 23–24) highlights a study by Vincent (1964), which documents changes in scores on the California Personality Inventory in connection with marriage. An interesting aspect of this finding is that the amount of change appears to be greater for persons who marry earlier in life, suggesting that flexibility in personality is negatively related to age.

It has been hypothesized that couples will tend to become more similar over time if the marital relationship is reinforcing, or, put more colloquially, if the marriage is a happy one (Ahammer 1973: 264–65). An implication of this hypothesis is that it is important to measure the characteristics of both partners and of the relationship itself if the effects of the marriage relationships are to be fully understood. As a broad framework, Brim (1973) has suggested that research should focus on interpersonal and social aspects of the marital relationships as related to the initial personality attributes of the marriage partners and to the degree and character of personality changes over the course of the marriage relationship (Brim 1973).

Criminological research has found that under the right circumstances, marriage can have a restraining or corrective effect on an offender's career. Sampson and Laub (1990) found that marital attachment, as reflected in cohesiveness rather than marriage per se, is an important predictor of criminal activity in later adulthood. West (1982) found that the propensity for criminal offending among males decreases subsequent to marriage provided that the wife lacks a criminal record. On the other hand, he also found evidence for assortative mating in that delinquents are inclined to marry women with a criminal record. Under these circumstances, marriage can increase the propensity for offending. West's research, therefore, not only supports the homogamy principle but also supports arguments for the increasing similarity of marital partners over time.

Parenthood

Many writers have observed that adults experience little formal training and preparation for parenthood, and, on the basis of this observation, the birth of the first child is often characterized as a crisis, albeit a normative one, owing to the considerable demands that are made on parents. The perceived severity of the crisis, however, is a matter of debate among researchers (Dion 1985).

The experience of raising children can bring about changes in attitudes, values, and lifestyles in a number of ways. During infancy, children depend entirely on their parents or other caretakers to attend to their basic needs. Since infants are unable to communicate, except in primitive fashion, and since they lack substantial capacities for deferring gratification and for regulating their behavior, part of the challenge of parenthood is to learn how to discern an infant's specific needs and to attend to those needs promptly and reliably.

As children grow older they become increasingly independent, but the responsibilities of parenting do not necessarily become lighter. Throughout childhood, the demands that offspring make on parents are considerable, and the requirements of effective parenting dictate that these exigencies be handled in a mature, nurturing, and loving manner. The process of learning to be a parent has been described as follows: "What is to be learned is not aspects of culture different from the adult's, as might be the case in marital adjustment, but attitudes and motives pertaining to the satisfaction of another's wishes, which on the whole require of the adult unselfishness, control of aggression, mature handling of numerous mild frustrations, and adaptation to an interrupted work schedule and interrupted leisure" (Brim 1973: 210).

Just as marriage needs to be seen as a dynamic social process, the experience of parenthood continuously refashions itself with the aging of the parents and the growing of the child (Ahammer 1973). As the child develops, parents must continually adjust and respond to changing situations by learning new strategies of childrearing and by developing new attitudes, values, and beliefs. Moreover, it is a simplification to think of the parent-child relationship as a one-way affair. Children can affect the behavior and attitudes of parents as much as parents can affect their children, although the influence of children on parents is rarely studied by social science researchers (Brim 1973).

A principal way in which parenthood, as well as marriage, is thought to influence behavior is by facilitating a person's emotional development, especially in terms of empathic capacity, which is the ability to put one's self psychologically in another's place and to experience vicariously another's feelings, thoughts, emotions and desires. Among the key features of empathic ability are cognitive and affective role-taking skills. Research indicates that well- developed role-taking skills can influence empathic ability by altering personal goals and values and by advancing levels of moral reasoning (Eisenberg and Fabes 1988). Persons with limited role-taking skills, in contrast, are less capable of discerning another person's emotional and mental states and are less likely to react emotionally when someone is distressed (Eisenberg and Fabes 1988). Empathic abilities, as they increase from childhood to adolescence, may partly explain an increase in prosocial behavior during this phase of the life cycle.

A theoretical link between empathy and prosocial behavior has been postulated by many psychologists, and from this it might be inferred that a lack of empathic abilities is associated with antisocial behavior. Empathy and role-taking skills are important considerations in understanding behavior when inferences about another person's emotional state are likely to enhance (diminish) prosocial (antisocial) responding (Eisenberg and Fabes 1988). For some behaviors, empathic capacity is not a highly relevant consideration. In the case of criminal behavior, empathy is not a pertinent factor in "victimless" crimes or perhaps in property crimes where the victim and offender remain relatively anonymous. However, empathy may be an important factor in violent crimes, where the physical and emotional anguish of the victim becomes plainly obvious to the offender in a face-to-face encounter.

Regarding the possible role of empathy in desistance from crime, Lerner (1986) cites research that suggests that improvements in role-taking and perspective-taking abilities are related to advances in moral reasoning (Eisenberg-Berg and Mussen 1978; Yussen 1976; Costanzo et al. 1973). In particular, it appears that adult role experiences promote advances in moral reasoning by facilitating the decentering of adolescent egocentrism (Lerner 1986; Arbuthnot 1975). The evidence in support of age-related increases in empathic abilities beyond early adolescence is not conclusive, and some scholars argue that nonnormative influences are the most likely catalyst of enduring changes in empathic capacities in later periods of development (Eisenberg and Fabes 1988). However, given the lack of research, it is premature to rule out the possibility that normative socialization experiences such as marriage and parenthood, bring about an increase in empathic capacity that inhibits crime.

Employment

The process of developing commitment to an occupation is viewed as a critical developmental task by many life span theorists (Havighurst 1972), and some will argue that occupational adjustment is the primary developmental activity in early adulthood for men. Developing occupational commitment involves several different aspects of socialization and learning. There are the technical aspects of work, which vary in nature and degree of complexity across occupations, that must be mastered, and there are attitudes, values, and behaviors, such as those pertaining to sources of motivation and reward, that are shaped and cultivated by work experiences. Furthermore, most people must learn as employees to accommodate the demands of a supervisor or employer in the context of an unbalanced power relationship. Since one's occupational role helps to define who one is and where one fits into the larger fabric of society, issues of social status, self-concept, and life satisfaction are connected to work experiences.

In her review of the occupational development literature, Dion (1985) concludes that work experiences can influence an individual's values and attitudes. In particular, Dion cites research by Kohn and Schooler (1969) showing that men of low socioeconomic standing tend to be concerned with rule conformity in work situations and to emphasize the extrinsic aspects of work (e.g., salary, job-related security), whereas men of higher socioeconomic status emphasize self-direction. This finding suggests that occupational experiences may contribute to class-related differences in attitudes, values, and beliefs. Dion (1985) also points to research that supports the hypothesis that occupational experiences are linked to changes in a person's self-image during specific phases of the life span, as reflected, for example, in a mid-life career crisis. The connection of these changes, if any, to antisocial behavior remains to be explored. In one study, however, Sampson and Laub (1990) conclude that job stability is negatively related to excessive alcohol use, general deviance, and criminality in later adult life, taking into account the effects of prior criminal involvement.

Normative Life Events and Role Socialization

Brim (1966) contrasts child and adult socialization by suggesting that childhood socialization is characterized by the acquisition of fundamental values, whereas adult socialization is focused primarily on role-related behaviors. In discussing the contrast, Brim is not especially sanguine about the potential of adult socialization experiences for changing or instilling basic values. He notes that, unlike childhood socialization, adult socialization typically involves little power differentiation among actors and that social interactions tend to be affectively neutral. As he sees it, only within the context of relationships resembling those in childhood (i.e., relationships characterized by high affectivity and high power) can fundamental change in personality and values take place. This type of relationship is uncommon in adulthood, although religious conversion experiences are a good example, and, in a criminal justice context, prison incarceration may be a relevant example. Other researchers share similar opinions on the impact of adult socialization experiences, arguing that influences are likely to be limited to particular role contexts (Dion 1985).

With regard to these issues, Brim (1966) identifies two limitations on the potential of adult socialization experiences for changing personality. These limitations relate to the person's biological capacities for learning and to prior learning or the lack thereof. He suggests that there may be critical periods in development such that subsequent learning is restricted if earlier learning has not taken place. Also, the degree of congruence between prior and subsequent learning can facilitate or hinder subsequent learning. In this regard, it may be relatively difficult to replace antisocial values learned in childhood and adolescence with prosocial values learned in adulthood. On the other hand, criminal propensity that surfaces first in adulthood should be easier to neutralize.

Another interesting observation made by Brim (1973) pertains to the sources of motivation for change. He argues that self-initiated socialization is often a greater source of adult personality change than demands for change from others. Brim (1973) states "[l]ittle attention has been given to the quite obvious self-initiated attempts by a person to change and improve his performance of certain roles in life. As far as we have been able to find out, no major investigation has ever been made of the kinds of changes adults may be seeking to make in their personalities; that is, evidently no one has systematically asked adults about this, even though adults, clearly more than children, are able to, and surely do, initiate their own socialization" (Brim 1973: 189).

Regarding the possible application of Brim's observations to criminality, the criminal justice system stands as an institutionalized effort to change individual behavior. Such changes are often predicated on a reorientation of basic values, and offenders who are subjected to the various ministrations of the justice system typically are seen as lacking prosocial values and as having overdeveloped antisocial values. An offender's experiences with the criminal justice system clearly involve a power differential between actors, and the affect that attaches to these experiences may be highly charged, although quite possibly negative in character if, for example, the offender views himself as having been treated unfairly or unjustly. This framework for change is relevant to issues of how the actions of the justice system influence an adult offender's behavior, although the possible impacts of such actions have yet to be explored fully.

Questions regarding the nature and extent of self-initiated socialization in adulthood are provocative, and these questions take on added dimensions in the context of criminal behavior. Many offenders experience pressures to change their behavior, and these pressures come from intimate companions, such as family members and friends, and from social institutions, most notably, the criminal justice system. However, thinking of criminal reform as self-initiated socialization highlights a side of the equation often ignored by researchers. Substantial and lasting changes in criminal behavior rarely come about only as a result of passive experience, and such changes are best conceptualized as the outcome of a process that involves significant participation by the offender, who, in many respects, acts as his or her own change agent. Brim's notion of self-initiated socialization sensitizes us to the fact that the motivations for change involve a dynamic interplay of forces, some of which are external to the individual and others that reside within the person. Thus, offenders can be viewed as active participants in the process of desistance, acting in ways that can facilitate or impede pressures for reform from outside sources.

Conclusion

Among the issues that stand out in the study of adult criminality is the need to take a long-term perspective of development. It may be tempting to infer from the aggregate age-crime curve that researchers need not be concerned much with offenders beyond thirty years of age, since the vast majority of offenders are younger. However, if the focus is on criminal careers or on developmental issues, then a research strategy in which only experiences in adolescence and young adulthood are investigated is too circumscribed.

There are at least four interrelated reasons why a broader time perspective should be taken. First, adulthood covers a substantial portion of the life cycle. If we are to chart the connections between human development and crime, then research needs to describe the variety of experiences over the broad expanse of adult life. Second, it appears that developmental change proceeds slowly in adulthood, as compared to childhood, and consequently researchers need more time to observe developmental processes at work. Third, the timing of many important experiences and life events in adulthood varies significantly, and some of these events and experiences are repeated in nonidentical ways. If these events are to be captured in criminological research, the data need to cover an extended time frame. Fourth, to the extent that there is an interest in studying desistance from and chronicity in offending, it becomes important to investigate patterns of behavior into middle adulthood and preferably beyond. The available studies of older offenders indicate that the influences of many of the processes thought to discourage the continuation of offending in adulthood are not realized fully until about the fifth decade of life (Shover 1985).

Another point to be made in research on adult criminality is that measurement strategies and techniques should be appropriate for adults and relevant to their life situations and experiences. Researchers studying adulthood face the problem that many of the instruments in developmental research have been constructed for use mostly on child subjects. The difficulty can be seen with some measures of cognitive development that involve tasks familiar to school children and practiced in the classroom. Adults are clearly at a disadvantage when asked to perform such tasks. In some cases, instruments can be easily modified for use with adults, but in other situations the conversion process is more complex and raises serious questions of reliability and validity. Non-comparability of measurement is a particularly thorny issue for researchers interested in development across stages of the life cycle, although the notion of genotypic similarity becomes useful when dealing with age-graded measures of the same concept.

Finally, in terms of analytic strategies, ipsative analysis, or analysis of within-individual change, can be a useful tool for studying developmental processes. The strategy of investigating development by comparing an individual to himself or herself across time becomes even more powerful if, through such comparisons, individuals can be classified into subgroups with shared regularities in behavior or other aspects of development. Block's research, which found personality attributes to be very stable over time in group level comparisons, also found at the individual level that many adolescents showed changes in personality and that these changes are patterned and can be organized into a meaningful typology.

The available research suggests that changes in intelligence, personality, cognitive functioning, moral judgment, and role socialization are related to criminal behavior throughout adolescence and adulthood. There are significant relations among these various aspects of development, and these relations are important because they help to explain how adult socialization experiences bring about consequential psychological changes. For example, Erikson argues that the continuation of personality development into adulthood depends upon the successful resolution of the adolescent identity crisis, generally meaning that the adolescent must become committed to a social role. In a related manner, Piaget argues that the adolescent becomes an adult in cognitive terms upon finding a role to play in society, given that this experience facilitates the emergence of formal operational thought. Additionally, Kohlberg argues that achievement of an identity is a prerequisite for advancing to the stage of principled moral thought.

Research also indicates that adult socialization experiences can influence behavior by means of socioemotional and sociocognitive skills. In particular, new social roles create opportunities to practice and increase certain mental skills, such as those under the heading of crystallized intelligence. Role socialization experiences also present novel problems and situations to the individual, and the process of resolving these challenges may lead to the emergence of new cognitive structures. There is a need to identify and study these sociocognitive changes if we are to better understand adult development in relation to criminal behavior. Future criminological research might build upon recent work that deals with information processing as related to decision making, problem solving, coping strategies, and interpersonal skills.

With regard to socioemotional development, changes in empathic capacity and in moral reasoning as influenced by adult role socialization are important areas for future criminological investigation. Better role-taking skills, which are practiced and refined through social experience, can increase a person's ability to empathize with others and to reason along more principled lines of morality. Given solid grounds for linking empathy and moral development to criminal behavior, developmental researchers interested in criminality should invest more effort in the measurement and operationalization of these concepts.

The adoption of new social roles in the transition from adolescence to adulthood is a critical aspect of development. In this regard, there is a need for research that measures key elements of adult roles in greater detail in order to understand the developmental process. Experiences of marriage, parenthood, and employment vary considerably across individuals. For some persons, marriage is an intense, intimate relationship bringing new demands and challenges that lead to change, while, for other people, marriage is viewed as a set of nonreciprocal, self-serving obligations or as a legal technicality to be disregarded when convenient. Understanding the effects of critical life events, such as marriage, on adult development and on criminal behavior, requires that we investigate the conditions under which different effects or outcomes are observed. Criminologists need to plan their studies around hypotheses of underlying causal processes and then directly measure key concepts in the causal process in order for the conclusions of the research to be less speculative and more convincing. In addition to describing the external attributes of life experiences (e.g., presence of a marriage partner, number of children, number of jobs, etc.), commitment to social and occupational roles—a concept that is emphasized as critical by researchers from a variety of perspectives—needs to be measured.

Likewise, there is a need for measuring other aspects of development with greater specificity. Many studies show a negative relation between IQ test scores and delinquency, although most of these studies have used global measures of intelligence. The measurement of distinct mental skills needs to be emphasized because mental skills show different developmental paths and because dimensions of intelligence, particularly with regard to mental skills that increase capacity to act in congruence with the norms of society, may relate differently to delinquent behavior. A variety of schemes have been developed for identifying and organizing the mental abilities that constitute intelligence, and these schemes need to be incorporated into the study of criminal behavior.

We have also seen how the course of biological development intersects with aspects of psychological development. In particular, the normal biological processes of aging have been linked to changes in time perspectives that bring a greater focus on time remaining in life, an increased awareness of physical vulnerability and mortality, and higher levels of generalized anxiety, all of which may make crime less attractive and may lead offenders to adopt a more risk-aversive perspective. Other aspects of the biological process of aging may be relevant to criminal behavior, and these possibilities should be explored if the goal is to develop a broad-based interdisciplinary theory of human development and crime.

With regard to theories of personality, there are only a handful of fully articulated theories that deal explicitly with adulthood, and, most of the major longitudinal studies on adult personality development have been somewhat eclectic in their theoretical perspective. Erikson's psychosocial theory of personality is a potentially useful framework for informing research questions. In particular, Erikson's theory builds on concepts such as commitment, identity, intimacy, isolation, generativity, and stagnation that may be useful to researchers who are interested in constructing a more integrated picture of social and psychological development in adulthood. Another potentially useful framework is Loevinger's theory of ego development, given that scholars (Lerner 1985: 285) have identified connections between this theory (Loevinger 1976, 1966; Loevinger and Wessler 1970) and Kohlberg's (1973) theory of moral development.

Much of the work on adult development is compatible with existing criminological theories. The rational choice perspective, for example, highlights the shifting calculus of advantage and disadvantage that accrues to criminal activity over the life course. Gartner and Piliavin (1988) argue that this paradigm is consistent with many of the known facts about adult criminal involvement and is potentially the most useful framework for studying issues of adult criminality. Developmental research on adulthood allows us to expand and elaborate on the rational choice perspective in important ways. Changes in cognitive structures, moral reasoning, primary mental abilities, empathic capacity, and values and beliefs are all relevant aspects of decision-making processes that can be used to interpret how changes in life situations can influence levels of criminal involvement with age.

Finally, late bloomers or persons who begin their criminal careers in adulthood, have not been discussed at any great length in the criminological literature. This group may provide important contrasts with offenders who show the conventional aging-out pattern or a model of chronic criminal involvement. Developmental researchers interested in criminality should examine how theories and research on adulthood may be used to explain why some adults who have led a conventional lifestyle belatedly enter into careers of crime.

References

Ahammer, I. M. 1973. "Social Learning Theory as a Framework for the Study of Adult Personality Development." In *Life-span Developmental Psychology: Personality and Socialization*, ed. Paul Baltes and K. Warner Schaie. NY: Academic Press.

Arbuthnot, J. 1975. "Modification of Moral Judgment through Role Play." *Developmental Psychology* 11: 319–24.

Becker, H. S. 1968. "Personal Change in Adult Life." In *Middle Age and Aging*, ed. Bernice Neugarten. Chicago: University of Chicago Press.

Block, J. 1971. *Lives through Time*. Berkeley, CA: Bancroft.

Blumstein, A., J. Cohen, and D. Farrington. 1988. "Criminal Career Research: Its Value for Criminology." *Criminology* 26(1): 1–35.

Brim, O. Jr. 1973. "Adult Socialization." In *Socialization and Society*, ed. John Clausen. NY: Wiley.

———. 1966. "Socialization through the Life Cycle." In *Socialization after Childhood: Two Essays*, ed. O. Brim Jr. and S. Wheeler. NY: Wiley.

Cline, H. F. 1980. "Criminal Behavior and the Life-span." In *Constancy and Change in Human Development*, ed. Orville Brim Jr. and Jerome Kagan. Cambridge, MA: Harvard University Press.

Costa, P., R. McKrae, and D. Arenberg. 1983. "Recent Longitudinal Research on Personality and Aging." In *Longitudinal Studies of Adult Psychological Development,* ed. K. Warner Schaie. NY: Guilford Press.

Costanzo, P. R., J. D. Coie, J. F. Grumlet, and D. Farnill. 1973. "A Re-examination of the Effect of Intent and Consequences on Children's Moral Development." *Child Development* 44: 154–61.

Dion, K. 1985. "Socialization in Adulthood." In *Handbook of Social Psychology,* vol. 2, 3d ed., ed. Gardner Lindzey and Elliott Aronson. NY: Random House.

Eisenberg, N. and R. Fabes. 1988. "The Development of Prosocial Behavior from a Life-span Perspective." In *Life-span Development and Behavior,* ed. Paul Baltes, David Featherman, and Richard Lerner. NY: Academic Press.

Eisenberg, N. 1986. *Altruistic Cognition, Emotion, and Behavior.* Hillsdale, NJ: Lawrence Earlbaum and Associates.

Eisenberg-Berg, N., and P. Mussen. 1978. "Empathy and Moral Development in Adolescence." *Developmental Psychology* 14: 185–86.

Elkind, D. 1962. "Quantity Conceptions in College Students." *Journal of Social Psychology* 57: 459–65.

Farrington, D. 1986. "Age and Crime." In *Crime and Justice: An Annual Review of Research,* ed. Michael Tonry and Norval Morris. Chicago: University of Chicago Press.

Featherman, D. L. 1983. "Life-span Perspectives in Social Science." In *Life-span Development and Behavior,* vol. 5, ed. Paul Baltes and Orville Brim Jr. NY: Academic Press.

Frenkel-Brunswick, E. 1968. "Adjustments and Reorientation in the Course of the Life-span." In *Middle Age and Aging,* ed. Bernice Neugarten. Chicago: University of Chicago Press.

Gartner, R., and I. Piliavin. 1988. "The Aging Offender and the Aged Offender." In *Life-span Development and Behavior,* ed. Paul Baltes, David Featherman, and Richard Lerner. Hillsdale, NJ: Lawrence Earlbaum and Associates.

Glenn, N. 1980. "Values and Beliefs." In *Constancy and Change in Human Development,* ed. Orville Brim Jr. and Jerome Kagan. Cambridge, MA: Harvard University Press.

Glueck, S., and E. Glueck. 1940. *Juvenile Delinquents Grown Up.* New York: Commonwealth Fund.

Gove, W. R. 1985. "The Effect of Age and Gender on Deviant Behavior: A Biopsychosocial Perspective." In *Gender and the Life-course,* ed. Alice S. Rossi. NY: Aldine.

Gynther, M. D. 1980. "Aging and Personality." In *New Directions in MMPI Research,* ed. J. N. Butcher. Minneapolis: University of Minnesota Press.

Haan, N., M. Smith, and J. Block. 1968. "Moral Reasoning of Young Adults: Political-social Behavior, Family Background, and Personality Correlates." *Journal of Personality and Social Psychology* 10: 183–201.

Harris, S., P. Mussen, and E. Rutherford. 1976. "Some Cognitive, Behavioral, and Personality Correlates of Maturity of Moral Judgment." *Journal of Genetic Psychology* 128: 123–35.

Havighurst, R. J. 1972. *Developmental Tasks and Education.* NY: David McKay.

———. 1973. "History of Developmental Psychology: Socialization and Personality Development through the Life-span." In *Life-span Developmental Psychology: Personality and Socialization,* ed. Paul Baltes and K. Warner Schaie. NY: Academic Press.

Hayflick, L. 1982. "Why Grow Old?" In *Adult Development and Aging*, ed. K. Warner Schaie. Boston: Little Brown.

Hirschi, T., and M. Gottfredson. 1983. "Age and the Explanation of Crime." *American Journal of Sociology* 89: 571–87.

Hirschi, T., and M. Hindelang. 1977. "Intelligence and Delinquency: A Revisionist View." *American Sociological Review* 42: 552–84.

Horn, J., and G. Donaldson. 1980. "Cognitive Developments in Adulthood." In *Constancy and Change in Human Development,* ed. Orville Brim Jr. and Jerome Kagan. Cambridge, MA: Harvard University Press.

Kagan, J. 1980. "Perspectives on Continuity." In *Constancy and Change in Human Behavior,* ed. Orville Brim Jr. and Jerome Kagan. Cambridge, MA: Harvard University Press.

Kagan, J., and H. Moss. 1962. *Birth to Maturity: A Study in Psychological Development.* NY: John Wiley and Sons.

Kogan, N., and M. Wallace.1961. "Age Changes in Values and Attitudes." *Journal of Gerontology* 16: 272–80.

Kohlberg, L. 1986. "A Current Statement on Some Theoretical Issues." In *Lawrence Kohlberg: Consensus and Controversy,* ed. J. Modgil and C. Modgil. Philadelphia: Falmer Press.

———. 1978. "Revisions in the Theory and Practice of Moral Development." *New Directions for Child Development* 2: 83–88.

———. 1973. "Continuities in Childhood and Adult Moral Development Revisited." In *Life-span Developmental Psychology: Personality and Socialization*, ed. Paul Baltes and K. Warner Schaie. NY: Academic Press.

Kohn, M., and C. Schooler. 1969. "Class, Occupation, and Orientation." *American Sociological Review* 34: 659–78.

Kuhlen, R. G. 1968. "Changes in Motivation." In *Middle Age and Aging*, ed. Bernice Neugarten. Chicago: University of Chicago Press.

Kuhn, D., N. Pennington, and B. Leadbeater. 1983. "Adult Thinking in Developmental Perspective." In *Life-span Development and Behavior*, vol. 5, ed. Paul Baltes and Orville Brim Jr. NY: Academic Press.

Kurtines, W., and E. Greif. 1974. "The Development of Moral Thought: Review and Evaluation of Kohlberg's Approach." *Psychological Bulletin* 81: 453–69.

Lerner, R. *Concepts and Theories of Human Development*. 1986. 2d ed. NY: Random House.

Loeber, R., and M. Le Blanc. 1990. "Toward a Developmental Criminology." In *Crime and Justice: An Annual Review of Research*, vol. 12, ed. M. Tonry and N. Morris. Chicago: University of Chicago Press.

Loevinger, J. 1976. *Ego Development*. San Francisco: Jossey-Bass.

———. 1966. "The Meaning and Measurement of Ego Development." *American Psychologist* 21: 195–206.

Loevinger, J., and R. Wessler. 1970. *Measuring Ego Development*, vol. 1. San Francisco: Jossey-Bass.

Matza, D. *Delinquency and Drift*. 1964. New York: John Wiley and Sons.

McCord, W., and J. McCord. 1959. *Origins of Crime: A New Evaluation of the Cambridge-Somerville Youth Study*. New York: Columbia University Press.

Miller, S., and S. Dinitz. 1973. "Measuring Institutional Impact: A Follow-up." *Criminology* 11: 417–26.

Moss, H., and E. Sussman. 1980. "Longitudinal Study of Personality Development." In *Constancy and Change in Human Development*, ed. Orville Brim Jr. and Jerome Kagan. Cambridge, MA: Harvard University Press.

Neimark, E. D. 1975. "Intellectual Development During Adolescence." In *Review of Child Development Research*, vol. 4, ed. F. D. Horowitz. Chicago: University of Chicago Press.

———. 1979. "Current Status of Formal Operations Research." *Human Development* 22: 60–67.

Olweus, D. 1979. "Stability of Aggressive Reaction Patterns in Males: A Review." *Psychological Bulletin* 86: 852–75.

Podd, M. H. 1972. "Ego-identity Status and Morality: The Relationship between Two Developmental Concepts." *Developmental Psychology* 6: 497–507.

Raine, A. 1993. *The Psychopathology of Crime: Criminal Behavior as a Clinical Disorder*. San Diego: Academic Press.

Rebok, G. 1987. *Life-span Cognitive Development*. NY: Holt, Rinehart, and Winston.

Redl, F., and D. Wineman. 1951. *Children Who Hate: The Disorganization and Breakdown of Behavior Controls*. NY: Free Press.

Rest, J. R. 1983. "Morality." In *Handbook of Child Psychology*, vol. 3, ed. P. Mussen. NY: Wiley.

Rest, J. R., D. Cooper, R. Coder, J. Masanz, and D. Anderson. 1974. "Judging the Important Issues in Moral Dilemmas - An Objective Measure of Moral Development." *Developmental Psychology* 10: 491–501.

Robins, L. 1966. *Deviant Children Grown Up: A Sociological and Psychiatric Study of Sociopathic Personality*. Baltimore, MD: Williams and Wilkins.

Rossman, I. 1982. "Bodily Changes with Aging." In *Adult Development and Aging*, ed. K. Warner Schaie. Boston: Little Brown.

Sampson, R. J. and J. H. Laub. 1990. "Crime and Deviance over the Life Course: The Salience of Adult Social Bonds." *American Sociological Review* 55: 609–27.

Shover, N. 1985. *Aging Criminals*. Beverly Hills: Sage.

Skolnick, A. 1966. "Stability and Interrelationships of Thematic Test Imagery over Twenty Years." *Child Development* 37: 389–96.

Tomlinson-Keasey, C., and C. B. Keasey. 1974. "The Mediating Role of Cognitive Development in Moral Judgment." *Child Development* 45: 291–98.

Tonry, M., L. Ohlin, and D. Farrington. 1991. *Human Development and Criminal Behavior*. New York: Springer-Verlag.

Towler, J. O., and G. Wheatley. 1971. "Conservation Concepts in College Students: A Replication and Critique." *Journal of Genetic Psychology* 118: 265–70.

Tuddenham, R. D. 1954. "The Consistency of Personality Ratings over Two Decades." *Genetic Psychology Monographs* 60: 3–29.

Vincent, C. E. 1964. "Socialization Data in Research on Young Marriers." *Acta Sociologica* 8: 118–27.

Walters, G. D. 1990. *The Criminal Lifestyle: Patterns of Serious Criminal Conduct*. Newbury Park, CA: Sage.

West, D. 1982. *Delinquency: Its Roots, Careers, and Prospects*. Cambridge, MA: Harvard University Press.

Wilson, J. Q., and R. Herrnstein. 1985. *Crime and Human Nature*. NY: Simon and Schuster.

Yussen, S. R. 1976. "Moral Reasoning from the Perspective of Others." *Child Development* 47: 551–55.

Comment
"Setting the Record Straight":
A Response to Hagan, Gillis and Simpson

Gary F. Jensen

In 1976 Raymond Eve and I published an analysis of gender differences in self-reported delinquency, observing that the survey data provided considerable support for sociological explanations of differences between males and females. In addition to variations in gender differences by offense, over time and among subgroups, we reported greater similarity by gender when measures of social relationships, activities and beliefs were controlled. We concluded that article with the following statement:

> The nature of relationships with other people, institutions, and belief systems dwarfs the importance of sex as a variable in the explanation of delinquency and accounts for a goodly proportion of its contribution to delinquency. Coupled with the gradual decline in differences over time as well as cultural and subcultural variations there does appear to be adequate reason for accepting sociological interpretations as 'infinitely more persuasive' than most nonsociological ones. (Jensen and Eve 1976: 446)

While there have been numerous studies of the gender difference since that early work, it was not until the late 1980s that the gender difference was approached based on what was presented as a new sociological view, combining the study of class and gender. Drawing on the work of Bonger (1916) and other neo-Marxist ideas stressing the importance of power in understanding class and gender differences in behavior, John Hagan, A. R. Gillis and John Simpson proposed a "power-control" theory of common delinquency (1985, 1987; Hagan 1989). In contrast to other theories it predicted a positive relationship between class and delinquency but, consistent with other theories, it predicted greater delinquency for

males than females. It also predicted a certain pattern of interaction between class and gender.

In two articles (1990, 1993), including one in Volume 4 of this series,
I criticized several features of the theory and the power control theorists
have responded with countercritiques. When my first critique (1990)
concentrated on class differences, I was chastised for ignoring the gender
difference (Hagan, Gillis and Simpson 1990). My response (1993) was
that my critique involved class differences because that was their most
controversial claim. But, I also argued that were the focus shifted to
gender differences, power-control theory had not been shown to explain
gender differences better than theories such as social learning or social
control theory.

In volume 4 of this series, Hagan, Gillis and Simpson (1993: 382)
responded to that comparative critique of power-control theory with the
following charge:

> By arguing that the 1976 analysis fully accounts for the gender-delinquency rela-
> tionship, and then providing no scope conditions or specifications for this argu-
> ment, Jensen assumes that this analytic framework can anywhere and everywhere
> account for the gender-delinquency relationship, which he assumes further to be
> always and in all places to be the same. This argues that the effect of gender on
> delinquency is invariant across social conditions, and that this relationship is in-
> dependent of historical, cultural or structural context. (1993: 382)

They go on to argue that such arguments are an extreme form of
Gottfredson and Hirschi's (1991) "self-control" theory of criminality and
that "Jensen's assumption of an unconditional constancy or invariance
in the gender-delinquency relationship across time and place associates
gender with such differences in propensities for self-control (1993: 383)."

Given the summary of the 1976 article quoted at the beginning of the
paper, I was quite surprised by their critique. The 1976 analysis *challenged* nonsociological theories, which predict constancy in the gender
difference. We focused on variation in the gender difference and sought
to explain that difference in terms of variables much like those used by
power-control theorists. The only hint of "invariance" was the fact that
we could not totally eliminate an independent effect of gender. Thus, the
final sentence in the paper acknowledged that "the persistence of 'unex-
plained' group differences can be given a sufficient number of alternative interpretations to stimulate further inquiry and a degree of humility
(1976: 446)." We were not able to fully account for the gender-delin-

quency relationship. The charge that our 1976 analysis assumed invariance is easily countered by simply reading the article.

The charge that we assume constancy in the factors that explain the gender difference is wrong as well. The critique in Volume 4 of Advances argued that power control theory had not been shown to explain the gender difference better than earlier theories. Hagan, Gillis and Simpson take a statement about "comparative" explanatory power and translate it into a claim that the gender difference has been fully explained for all time and places. After summarizing the 1976 analysis, I stated that "At present, there is no reason to accept power-control theory as a superior explanation of gender differences when compared to social control, social learning, or a variety of other theories (1993: 374)." I am at a loss to discern how such a statement can be translated into either (1) a claim of invariance in the gender difference; (2) a claim that the gender difference is fully explained; or (3) a claim that the gender difference has been fully explained for all time. Even a casual reading of the 1976 article and the 1993 critique shows such charges to be false.

The jump from my comparative statement about control theories to the view that my critique advocates an extreme version of Gottfredson and Hirschi's theory of "self-control" (1990) is equally perplexing. They contend that a focus on self-control "involves reconceptualizing the social bond, which is given primacy in Hirschi's social control theory, as the 'product' rather than the cause of self-control (1993: 382)" and that I propose a "kinds of people" argument emphasizing inner propensities towards criminality.

I will leave it to Gottfredson and Hirschi to take issue with that criticism as it applies to their work but it has nothing to do with the arguments in my 1993 critique or the 1976 analysis. The focus on the nature of relationships with people, institutions and belief systems is clear and unambiguous throughout the 1976 analysis. The conclusion to the 1976 article (cited above) clearly emphasizes the primacy of social bonds and social relationships. There is no mention of the concept of "self-control" or any thing remotely close to inner propensities in either the 1976 article or any of my subsequent critiques. Indeed, the power control theorists introduction of "tastes for risk" as an internalized motivation for delinquency is more amenable to such criticisms than any of the variables used in the 1976 research.

While there are no grounds for the assumptions attributed to my work in the countercritiques of power-control theorists or for the claim that my arguments are a version of self-control theory, the power-control theorists are correct in their claim that my critiques stressed the lack of main effects of class in my initial challenge to power-control theory. In the 1985 article they did state that the main effects of class represent "only a small part of their theoretical interests (1985: 1165)." However, they also state that their "core assumption" is that power is a positive correlate of delinquency. The hypotheses that can be derived from that statement are of equal theoretical importance. It is the fit of data with the full range of derivative hypotheses that determines the validity of a theory, not a post hoc weighting of importance. Their core assumption has implications for variations in delinquency by class, race, gender and a variety of other correlates of delinquency. Given that core assumption, there is no theoretical basis for according main effects lesser theoretical importance than gender or class-gender interactions. Indeed, the most iconoclastic claim in the original article and the first issue to be dealt with empirically was the positive class-delinquency relationship.

My critique in Advances also noted that their argument about gender differences in power-balanced and imbalanced households was on shaky ground when their own data were reexamined (Jensen and Thompson 1990) and that attempts at replication using measures identical to their research reported the exact opposite findings concerning gender and power-balance interactions (Singer and Levine 1988). Thus, whether the focus is on main effects or interaction effects power control theory has not fared well as a means of salvaging structural variables.

The "paramount" implications and scope conditions of the theory are somewhat illusive because the theory has never been stated as a set of hypotheses, which would allow a summation of positive and negative results. Even its subject matter shifts from study to study. For example, a "scope" condition specified for the theory in view of its obvious conflict with traditional class-based theories (including Bonger and other neo-Marxists such as Colvin and Pauley 1983) is that it "is a theory of common delinquency, not serious delinquency or adult crime (1993: 394)." Indeed, in their countercritiques they have focused on gender differences in smoking (1993) or shoplifting (1990).

The limitation to nonserious offenses has been reiterated several times, allowing findings of negative class-delinquency relationships to be attributed to the seriousness of the offenses examined. This limitation has been deceptive for the simple reason that the items they used to measure common delinquency included offenses ranging from shoplifting to grand theft and from vandalism to potential assault. Not only were there no variations in their class-delinquency relationships for offenses varying in seriousness in their own reported results but, as summarized in the table below, all but one of the items used to measure common delinquency are included in subsequent work by Hagan as measures of a "subculture of delinquency." The items included under the rubric of a subculture are presented as a measure of a type of delinquency that is supposed to be inversely related to measures of SES. Yet, five of the six items used to measure common delinquency in tests of power control theory correspond with items identified as measuring a serious "subculture" of delinquency elsewhere (together with gang fighting and running from the police).

Items Used to Measure Common and Subcultural Delinquency

Delinquency and Drift Hagan, ASR, 1991	Power-Control Hagan et al. AJS 1985, 1987
Subculture of Delinquency (Negatively Related to SES) Offenses Included:	**Common Delinquency** (Positively Related to Class) Offenses Included:
Stealing little things (e.g. shoplifting)	How often in the last year have you taken things of little value (worth less than $2) that did not belong to you?
	How often in the last year have you taken things of some value (between $2 and $50) that did not belong to you?
Stealing expensive things (e.g., worth over $50)	How often in the last year have you taken things of large value (worth more than $50) that did not belong to you?
Breaking into schools, breaking up school property Breaking streetlights, windows, etc.	How often in the last year have you intentionally banged up something that did not belong to you?
Fighting (in gangs) Fighting (between individuals)	Excluding fights with a brother or sister, how often in the last year have you intentionally beaten up or hurt someone?
Running from police	How often in the last year have you taken a car for a ride without the owner's permission?

It is not unreasonable to challenge a theory when the scope conditions and its relevance to the revival of a structural criminology are so elusive. If a positive class-delinquency relationship is found, then it is explained by a power-control theory of common delinquency. If a negative relationship is found, then it is explained by a cultural theory relevant to a "subculture" of delinquency. Never mind that the items used to measure the two are nearly the same.

I do not want to further elaborate my critique of power-control theory here. The purpose of the comparison of power control theory with other theories in the 1993 Advances article was to encourage comparative theoretical and empirical analyses of theories. The response took the form of allegations about hidden assumptions underlying the critique. The main purpose of this comment is to set the record straight concerning the "assumptions" attributed to my earlier work. Even a casual reading of my actual comments will support the contention that the power-control theorists' countercritique misrepresents the 1976 paper, distorts the 1993 critique and alleges assumptions that are directly contrary to the actual statements in those papers. In the process, they deflect attention from the reasonable issues raised about the comparative explanatory power of their theory in relation to earlier theories, the illusive and shifting meaning of the mysterious concept of "common" delinquency and the implications of their actual findings for a theory that was proposed as a cornerstone for resurrecting a structural criminology.

References

Bonger, W. 1916. *Criminality and Economic Conditions*. Boston: Little, Brown and Company.

Colvin, M. and J. Pauley. 1983. "A Critique of Criminology: Toward an Integrated Structural-Marxist Theory of Delinquency Production." *American Journal of Sociology* 89: 513–51.

Gottfredson, M. R. and T. Hirschi. 1990. *A General Theory of Crime*. Stanford, CA: Stanford University Press.

Hagan, J. 1989. *Structural Criminology*. New Brunswick, NJ: Rutgers University Press.

———. 1991. "The Poverty of a Classless Criminology." *Criminology* 30: 1–19.

———. 1992. "Destiny and Drift: The Risks and Rewards of Youth." *American Sociological Review* 56: 567–82.

Hagan, J., A. R. Gillis and J. Simpson. 1985. "The Class Structure of Gender and Delinquency: Toward a Power-Control Theory of Common Delinquent Behavior." *American Journal of Sociology* 90: 1151–78.

———. 1987. "Class in the Household: A Power-Control Theory of Gender and Delinquency." *American Journal of Sociology* 92: 788–816.

————. 1990. "Clarifying and Extending Power-Control Theory." *American Journal of Sociology* 95: 1024–37.

————. 1993. "The Power of Control in Sociological Theories of Delinquency." In *Advances in Criminological Theory*, vol. 5, ed. F. Adler and W. S. Laufer, 381–98. New Brunswick: Transaction Publishers.

Hirschi, T. 1969. *Causes of Delinquency*. Berkeley: University of California Press.

Jensen, G. F. 1993. "Power Control versus Social Control Theories of Juvenile Crime." In *Advances in Criminological Theory*, vol. 5, ed. F. Adler and W. S. Laufer, 365–81. New Brunswick: Transaction Publishers.

———— and R. Eve. 1976. "Sex Differences in Delinquency: A Test of Popular Sociological Explanations." *Criminology* 3: 427–48.

———— and K. Thompson. 1990. "What's Class Got to Do With It? A Further Examination of Power-Control Theory." *American Journal of Sociology*. 95: 1009–23.

Singer, S. I. and M. Levine. 1988. "Power-Control Theory, Gender and Delinquency: A Partial Replication with Additional Evidence on the Effect of Peers." *Criminology* 26: 627–47.

Name Index

Subject Index

Adolescents
  actions symbolizizng independence and maturity, 31–32
  antisocial behavior, 13–17
  communities and families in development of, 90–92
  crime and strain theory, 101–32
  developmental differences, 88–90
  deviant friends and antisocial behavior, 59
  emotional distress, 121–25
  environment viewed as adversive, 119–21
  etiological theory of behavior, 17–39
  goal blockage, 116–19
  independence from adults, 117
  inexperience leading to delinquency, 122
  learning and the Matching Law, 60–70
  life-course contingencies in behavior, the Matching Law approach, 55–99
  Matching Law and antisocial behavior, 55–99
  meeting adversity through delinquency, 121–23
  noncompliance and antisocial behavior, 58
  options for change, 36–37
  popularity with peers, 117–19
  school environment, 59–60
  self-esteem and aspirations, 118
  social mimicry as way of life, 25–31
  strain and hostility blocking goals, 116–19
  teenagers avoiding delinquency, 32–35

  tobacco use, 59
  transition from elementary to secondary school, 113–19
Adult crime
  biological development, 312–14
  cognitive development, 314–18
  developmental aspects of, 309–42
  employment, 332–33
  intellectual development, 320–22
  marriage, 328–30
  moral development, 318–20
  normative life events, 328–33, and role socialization, 333–38
  parenthood, 330–32
  personality development, 322–28
Adulthood
  adult crime, developmental aspects of, 309–42
  family responsibility and interationism of the adult, 196–200
  role models amd crime, 196–205
  youngsters continuing antisocial behavior, 21–23
  see also Adult Crime,
Aggressiveness
  concept of, 107–99
  impact on crime, 109–11
  retaliatory response to, 144–45
  and strain theory, 107–9
Alcohol use and adolescent behavior, 57
Antisocial and delinquent behavior
  as a development progression, 76–77
  family influencs, 82–84
  individual differences in development, 94–95
  the Matching Law, 70–76
  school and community relationships, 86–87

355

DATE DUE